Eighth Edition

Anatomy of a Business Plan

**The Step-by-Step Guide
to Building Your Business
and Securing Your
Company's Future**

Linda Pinson

published by

OM..IM

**Out of Your Mind...
and Into the Marketplace™**

This publication is designed to provide accurate and authoritative information in regard to the subject matter covered. It is sold with the understanding that the publisher is not engaged in rendering legal, accounting, or other professional service. If legal advice or other expert assistance is required, the services of a competent professional person should be sought.

Author: Linda J. Pinson

Assistant Publisher: Ndaba Mdhlongwa

Editor: Nancy Sampson

Interior and cover design: Linda Pinson

Cover Photo: The cover photo is used by permission and copyrighted by the photographer, Andres Rodriguez. (© Andres Rodriguez. Image from BigStockPhotos.com)

Published by **OUT OF YOUR MIND...AND INTO THE MARKETPLACE**™
13381 White Sand Drive
Tustin, CA 92780-4565

714-544-0248 (Information)
800-419-1513 (Orders)
www.business-plan.com

Printed in the United States of America

Pinson, Linda.
    Anatomy of a business plan: the step-by-step guide to building a business and securing your company's future/Linda Pinson—8th ed.
        p.   cm.
    Includes index.
    ISBN-13: 978-0944205-55-6
    ISBN-10: 0-944205-55-0
    1. Business planning. 2. New business enterprises—Planning. I. Title
HD30.28.PS 2008
658.4'012—dc22

Out of Your Mind...and Into the Marketplace™ business books and software are available at quantity discounts to use in educational institutions, as premiums and sales promotions, or for use in corporate training programs. For more information or to place an order, please call our toll free number (800-419-1413), email LPinson@business-plan.com, or write to Out of Your Mind...and Into the Marketplace, 13381 White Sand Drive, Tustin, CA 92780-4565.

PRAISE FOR PREVIOUS EDITIONS

Anatomy of a Business Plan
and
Automate Your Business Plan

"*Anatomy of a Business Plan* and *Automate Your Business Plan* have served as excellent business planning and financial analysis tools for Dale Carnegie© Training Centers Worldwide."

Marc K. Johnston
Senior Vice President, Franchise Development
Dale Carnegie© Training Centers Worldwide

"*Anatomy of a Business Plan* is one of the best books on the basics of putting together a thoughtful, thorough, and professional business plan."

Jeffrey L. Seglin
Inc. Magazine

"Simply put, *Anatomy of a Business Plan* with its companion software, *Automate Your business Plan*, is the best step-by-step guide to starting, building, and raising capital for your business. We have raised over $20 million for our clients by using it, and we have an additional $15 million pending. Use it; it works!"

Thomas Jay Wacker
Centaur Holdings Corporation

"I recently reviewed two loan applications that included business plans. The most noteworthy item in both of these applications was the business plan. After reading each one, my confidence was greatly boosted. Each applicant stated that Linda Pinson's software and book were easy to use. By the way, both loans were approved."

Nancy Russell
Comerica Bank

"Most business plan books need updating to account for new tax laws and other changes. This 6th edition (of *Anatomy of a Business Plan*) is one of the newest — and best — on the topic."

Mark Henricks
Crain's Chicago Business

About the **A**uthor

Linda **P**inson is an award-winning author, business planning expert, speaker, consultant, and nationally recognized business educator with a specialty in financial management and small business curriculum development. The author of nine popular entrepreneurial books, she has also developed and published the best selling business plan software program, Automate Your Business Plan™. Linda's books are widely used as curriculum in colleges and universities. They have been translated into several foreign languages including Spanish, Chinese, and Italian. *Anatomy of a Business Plan* has also been localized for Australia and the UK. Automate Your Business Plan™ has been customized for corporations and associations including Dale Carnegie® Training Centers Worldwide and The American Bar Association. Linda has been widely recognized and utilized as a business planning and financial expert, contracting with the U.S. Government Accountability Office, Visa, MSN, and others.

For seven years, Linda was on the Executive Board of Directors of the Small Business Financial Development Corporation (CA state lending program). She also served for several years on the Tri County SBDC Advisory Board and as a member of the Entrepreneurial Advisory Committee at California State University at Fullerton. Her dedication to the small business community has been recognized through awards from the U.S. Small Business Administration, the National Association of Women Business Owners, and the State of California. Linda served as a delegate and tax issue chair at the White House Conference on Small Business.

Linda resides in Tustin, California with her husband Ray. She is an avid golfer (one hole-in-one) and bowler, paints watercolors, and loves to fish. Linda and Ray have two sons, two daughter-in-laws, two grandsons, and one granddaughter (all great, of course).

Dedication

It is with a great deal of pleasure that I dedicate this book to Tom Drewes, former President and founder of Quality Books, Inc., my mentor and friend. His kindness and encouragement was my inspiration in 1986. Because of his belief in me, my books are now being used in libraries across the nation. Thank you, Tom for your many years of tireless dedication to independent publishers and for your willingness to share yourself with so many—and ask for nothing in return.

Acknowledgments

During the writing and revising of seven editions of *Anatomy of a Business Plan*, it has been my good fortune (and the readers') to have input from many business associates whose expertise in certain areas admittedly exceeds my own. I would like to acknowledge four of those individuals here.

- **Bernadette Tiernan**, owner of Tiernan & Associates, in Ridgewood, NJ, was instrumental in helping me with the development "Chapter 5, The Marketing Plan". Bernadette was the Assistant Dean of the School of Business at Rutgers University and the author of *E-Tailing* and the great marketing book, *The Hybrid Company*.

- **Dr. Donald R. McCrea,** President of Bus-Ed Partners, Inc., Irvine California (www.bus-edpartners.com) wrote the "Product-Market Analysis" section on pages 64-67. This is a very valuable tool for narrowing your target market to realistic customers. Don was also the developer of my interactive marketing research web page for AUTOMATE YOUR BUSINESS PLAN. He has 35 years of experience and was formerly Director of Executive Education in the Graduate School of Management at University of California, Irvine. Prior to that he directed the Executive Degree Program at the Peter Drucker Graduate School of Management at Claremont Graduate University.

- **John Neal, CPA,** of Paulin Neal Associates (www.paulinneal.com) helped me with "Developing an Exit Strategy" on pages 7-11. His company provides interim management and special projects. Their services include strategic planning and business plan development, business modeling, capital formation, financial management, and others. John serves on several for profit and not-for-profit boards and was chairman of the Small Business Committee of the California Chamber of Commerce.

- **Jan Norman,** now living in McKinney, Texas, wrote the great article on Social Media on pages 71-74. Jan was the "It's Your Business" columnist for 25 years (1988-2013) for The Orange County Register. Her columns were syndicated throughout the United States.

- **Ndaba Mdhlongwa,** the owner of Business Plan Solutions in Addison, Texas (www.businessplanprofessionals.com) was the writer of the *Wholesale Mobile Homes.com* business plan in Appendix III and worked with the owner to write the Karma Jazz Café business plan in Appendix IV. He also wrote the new Appendix V nonprofit business plan for Road Runners, Inc. Ndaba has worked with me as my assistant publisher for fifteen years on various other book and software projects, including the development of a great Instructor's Manual for *Anatomy of a Business Plan*.

Thank you, Bernadette, Don, John, Jan, and Ndaba. *Anatomy of a Business Plan* is a better book because of you. I thank you—and I know that my readers would also thank you personally if they had the chance.

Table of Contents

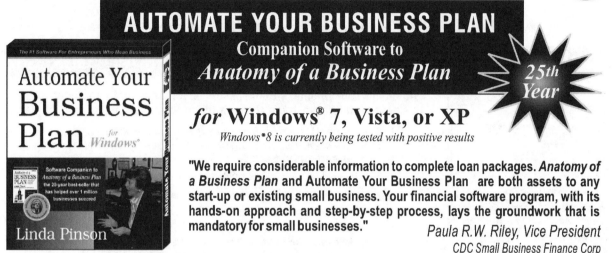

Preface

Thank you for choosing *Anatomy of a Business Plan* as the tool to help you write your business plan. I think you will be pleased with this new edition.

It has often been said that, *"You can run your business by the seat of your pants—but you will probably end up with torn pants."* One of the principal reasons for business failure is the lack of an adequate business plan. In today's world, both small and large businesses have come to understand that they need to take the time to evaluate their business potential and map a plan for the future. It is also understood that lenders and investors no longer risk their money on a business unless they have good reason to think that it will be successful (i.e., profitable).

It is the goal of this book to give you a clear, concise, and easy-to-understand process to follow as you develop your business plan. I have been working with business owners for many years and most of them have the same problem—they are experts in their industries, but are novices when it comes to business planning. In fact, many times, the prospect of writing a business plan is so formidable that business owners avoid it until it becomes a requirement for one reason or another.

I, on the other hand, am not an expert in your industry. My job is to guide you step-by-step through the business planning process. If I am successful, you can follow that process, apply your industry expertise, and write a winning business plan for your company.

Who is this book for?

I frequently get asked if *Anatomy of a Business Plan* is appropriate for a big business or a tiny business—a start-up business or an existing business—high tech or low tech—a business seeking funding or a business looking for an internal planning tool—a product business or a service business—a restaurant or a technology business—a sole proprietorship or a corporation—or a nonprofit organization—or a division within a company. The answer is that it is the right book for all of the above. No matter what you are, the business planning process is the same.

It is your focus that differs. If you are a smaller business and your business plan is intended only for internal use, your plan may be shorter and you may choose to address only certain issues. On the other hand, if your business is larger and more complex, you will probably need to put key people to work on the development of a more critical business plan that will be in keeping with your company vision.

If you need funding, you will have to consider the goals of the lender or investor and address those issues. If you are a new business, you will only have projections. If you are an existing business, you will also have historical information. If you are a nonprofit, you have to target both your funding sources and your program beneficiaries. If you are a pure service business, you have no cost of goods. If you are a product business, you do. If you are high tech or low tech, the process is still the same. The variable is how you focus on your specific business and industry.

The simplification of your business planning task has always been the primary goal of *Anatomy of a Business Plan*. In order to get the most out of the book and to make your job easier, I would suggest that the first thing you do is read the book to give you a general overview of the format and content. After reading, you will be ready to begin working your way through the actual business planning process.

Example Business Plans

In the back of the book (Appendix I, II, III, IV, and V) you will find five full-length business plan examples that are for five different kinds of business. All five were written by the business owners and/or consultants they worked with. The common tools that they used were *Anatomy of a Business Plan* and its companion software, *Automate Your Business Plan*.

- **Marine Art of California** is a start-up product business. The plan is for a sole proprietorship dealing in fine art pieces. The owner is seeking short-time limited partners and plans to recapture 100% ownership within about four years.

- **Dayne Landscaping, Inc.** is a one-year-old landscaping and snow removal (service) business. It is a small corporation, seeking to expand into new territories. Dayne Landscaping, Inc. is planning to seek funding from a traditional lending institution (bank).

- *Wholesale Mobile Homes.com, Inc.* is a dot.com bricks and clicks start-up corporation planning to go after $10 million in venture capital. Because the business is more complex and is seeking venture capital, the executive summary, and the organizational and marketing plans are researched more heavily and written in more detail.

- **Karma Jazz Café** is an upscale restaurant that is scheduled to open in Fort Worth, Texas. This is the owner's second location of the same restaurant. The first Karma Jazz Café is in Atlanta, GA and is successfully up and running. The newest restaurant is considered to be a start-up business, but is patterned on and utilizes projected and historical financial information and other knowledge gained from the Atlanta location.

- **Road Runners, Inc.** is a nonprofit organization serving disadvantaged youth in the New Orleans area. The organization has been in existence for more than a year, but has been operating on a very small scale. Their plan was written to serve as a guide to future growth.

The interesting thing about the five plans is that they were researched and written by various people. As you read them, you will find that each of the writers brings something new and different into the planning process that will prove valuable to you in your own efforts.

Thank you again for choosing *Anatomy of a Business Plan* to help you accomplish your goal. I appreciate your confidence in *Anatomy of a Business P*lan and wish you success in the writing of your business plan!

Linda Pinson

Business Plan Considerations

A well-written business plan will provide a pathway to profit for any new or existing business. Your business plan will also provide the documentation that a lender or investor requires if you find it necessary to seek outside funding sources for your business.

This chapter is designed to give you some background information and guidelines to consider prior to writing your business plan.

Why do you need a business plan? If you need access to additional capital, what does the lender or investor want to know? What are the key words that make your plan more effective? How do you develop an Exit Strategy? Where do the numbers come from in your financial plan? What is different about a business plan for a nonprofit organization? These questions will be addressed on the following pages.

✓ *Why Do You Need a Business Plan?*

✓ *What Do Lenders and/or Investors Look For?*

✓ *The "Key" to Effective Writing*

✓ *Developing an Exit Strategy*

✓ *Developing Financial Assumptions*

✓ *Guide to Using this Book for a Nonprofit Plan*

✓ <u>*Bonus:*</u> *Steps to E-tailing*

Why Do You Need a Business Plan?

Every business will benefit from the preparation of a carefully written business plan. There are two main benefits and an additional one if you do business internationally.

1. To serve as a guide for your business

The most important reason for writing a business plan is to develop a guide that you will follow throughout the lifetime of your business. The business plan is a blueprint of your business and will provide you with the tools to analyze your business and implement changes that will make your business more profitable. It will provide detailed information on all aspects of your company's past and current operations, as well as its projections for the next few years. Of course, new business owners have no history and will base the information in their plans on projections developed through current research of the industry. To be of value, your plan must be kept up-to-date. While plans presented to lenders must be bound, you may choose to keep your working copy of the plan in a loose-leaf binder. Then you may add current financial statements, updated rate sheets, recent marketing information, and other data as they become available.

2. As documentation for financing

A business plan is a requirement if you are planning to seek financing. If you are seeking capital, the business plan details how the desired investment or loan will further the company's goals and increase its profits. Every lender wants to know how you will maintain your cash flow and repay the loan (with interest) on a timely basis. Every investor also wants to know how his investment will improve the overall net worth of the company and help him to achieve his desired return on investment. You will have to detail how the money will be used and back up your figures with solid information such as market research, timing, estimates, etc. Lenders and investors have access to statistics that are considered normal for various industries, so be sure that your projections are reasonable.

3. To work in foreign markets

If you do business internationally, a business plan provides a standard means of evaluating your business potential in a foreign marketplace. More than ever before, world trade is essential to the health of the American economy and to the growth of most U.S. companies. No business today can afford to overlook the potential of international commerce brought about by changes in communications, technology, and transportation. The development of a business plan will demonstrate ways in which your business can compete in this global economy.

Take the time to write a clear, concise and winning business plan. The success of your business depends on it! One of the principal reasons for business failure is lack of planning. I firmly believe in the often repeated quotation:

"The business that fails to plan, plans to fail."

What Do Lenders and Investors Look For?

If you are looking for lenders or investors to provide debt or equity capital for your company, it is to your advantage to understand the elements that each would most want to see in a well-written business plan. If you are seeking debt capital from a traditional lender (banker), you will have to prove that you can repay the loan with interest. You will present your business plan to the loan officer who will in turn prepare the loan package and present it to the bank's loan committee for approval. Investors (or venture capitalists) become equity (ownership) partners in your company and have different expectations. They want to know that the money they are investing in your company will result in a specified return on the investment. You can increase your chances of success with lenders and investors by considering the following:

1. **What is your credit history?**

   Whether it's a credit card, a car loan, a personal loan or a mortgage – lenders will want to know your credit risk level and will look at your credit score. The most widely used credit scores are FICO scores developed by Fair, Isaac based solely on information in consumer credit reports maintained at the credit reporting agencies. A FICO score considers payment history (tradelines and derogatory references), amounts owed, length of credit history, new credit and types of credit in use. Your credit influences the credit that's available to you, and the terms (interest rate, etc.) that lenders offer you. FICO scores are utilized by lenders to make millions of credit decisions every year. More information on credit scoring can be found online at www.myfico.com

   In short, you will need to provide a credit history that demonstrates that you are a good risk. A past bankruptcy or a history of late payments will serve as a "red flag" and send out a warning signal that you may be a bad risk. Existing businesses will submit business financial history statements, copies of profit & loss statements, balance sheets and tax returns for previous years. If you are a new business, your personal financial history will be examined. The owners of your company will probably be required to submit personal balance sheets listing their assets. Copies of personal tax returns may also be requested. Lenders and investors frequently determine character based on prior business and/or personal financial performance.

2. **What collateral do you have?**

   What assets do you have—and what are you willing to risk for the success of your business? You may be asked to use your home and other liquid assets such as CDs or other investments that qualify as collateral. Evaluation of collateral is generally at liquidation rate and the lender will establish the order of his right to claim and sell the collateral and the personal assets of guarantors or borrowers. The amount and type of collateral you provide shows your commitment to your company and removes risk on the part of the investor (your new equity partner) or the lender (the bank, etc. that is granting your loan request).

3. **Can you meet the lender's or investor's financial goals?**

   Lenders and investors want to know that you appreciate their needs and that you have given consideration to your company's ability to fulfill their financial goals.

   a. **If you are seeking a lender**

      Your lender (banker) wants to know that your company can repay the loan plus interest and, for the period of the loan, maintain a positive cash flow that will allow you to continue to operate your business.

If the loan is to increase assets, any asset that you want to finance must last at least as long as the loan period. For example, you cannot get a five-year, $25,000 loan on a piece of electronic equipment that is expected to become obsolete within two years of the date of purchase. The asset should generate the repayment of funds. Show in your financial projections that the object of the loan will increase sales, increase efficiency, or cut costs and will, in turn, generate added revenue for repayment of the loan plus interest. If the loan is for working capital, show how the loan plus interest can be repaid through cash (liquidity), generally during the next year's full operating cycle.

b. If you are seeking an investor

Venture capitalists and other equity investors will frequently require that you provide them with an exit strategy. They will want to know where the business is ultimately heading. The venture capitalist firm is most concerned that the company has a high profit potential, that it is competitive, sustainable, and that it is something that they understand. They will want to see a financial plan that shows how the company will move toward its goals and produce the desired profit to be distributed to them under a predetermined agreement. As equity partners, investors have a say in how the company is operated. They will want to see a strong management team and will be the hardest to satisfy because they are putting their own funds at risk.

4. Is there a demand for your product or service?

Be prepared to show evidence that your product or service is well-received by your target market (your customers) and that the demand will be sustainable. You can demonstrate demand through a favorable sales history, accounts receivable information, or purchase orders. If you are a new service company or a business with a new product, show customer acceptance through test market results, questionnaire and survey data, and testimonials. To be valid, the responses must come from your target market and not from friends and family. Test market your product and get some evaluations. Ask people who have tried your products or utilized your services to write testimonial letters.

5. Do you have an experienced management team?

Business failure is, more often than not, due to management problems. It is a well-known fact that, in the 1990s, many technology companies went under – in spite of their state-of-the-art development skills – because they were sorely lacking when it came to management. Lenders and investors will undoubtedly take a close look at qualifications of the people who are running the business. Industry expertise is a definite plus, but management experience may be the defining factor for achieving profitability.

6. Have you established a proprietary position?

This means that you have secured your position in the market in some manner. It is important that there is something unique about your business and that you have protected this uniqueness in some way. This may be through copyright, trademark or patent. If you are located in a mall or shopping center, proprietary position might be established by working with the management to limit direct competition within a given radius of your store.

7. Are your projections realistic?

Lenders and investors will measure your projections against current industry standards available to them through various sources. Base your figures on your current market share. Explain your opportunities for growth and demonstrate how you plan to make use of these opportunities. Each industry has its range of accepted financial results and market approaches. The most common error is overstating revenues and understating expenses. Projections that are outside of industry standards will quickly kill the perceived credibility of your business plan. Examine the annual reports of public companies in your field. Read trade journals, business publications, and government and industry reports to determine trends in your business area. Work out a realistic timetable for achieving your goals. *Remember that lenders and investors judge your plan and goals in terms of your industry's practices and trends.*

8. Do you have a strong marketing plan?

When a lender or an investor is reviewing your business plan, one of the primary areas of focus will be your marketing plan. As you write your marketing plan, you will learn that much of the emphasis is placed on the development of a highly targeted market that can be effectively served by your business—customers who need what you have to offer and who will choose you over your competitors and pay you to solve their problems and fill their needs.

The lender will make an assessment regarding the logic of your marketing plan and will decide whether or not it is probable that, during the term of your loan, you will be able to sell to those customers in a volume that is sufficient to repay your loan plus interest.

An investor (or venture capitalist) will not be looking at your marketing plan solely in terms of your current plans. As a potential equity partner, he or she will also focus on your long-term marketing goals, making a determination as to whether or not it is likely that the company can continue to increase its market share accordingly and generate the desired return on investment.

The Key to Effective Writing

The text of the business plan must be concise and yet must contain as much information as possible. This sounds like a contradiction, but you can solve this dilemma by using the *key word* approach. Write the following key words on a card and keep it in front of you while you are writing:

Who?	**When?**	**How Much?**
What?	**Why?**	**Unique?**
Where?	**How?**	**Benefit to the Customer?**

Answer all of the questions asked by the key words in one paragraph at the beginning of each section of your business plan. Then expand on that thesis statement by telling more about each item in the text that follows. Stress any uniqueness and benefit to the customer that may pertain to the section in which you are writing. Examples will be given in the following chapters to give you guidance. Keep in mind, if you are seeking financing, that the lender's or investor's time is limited and that your plan is not the only one being reviewed. Often the first paragraph following a heading will be the only area read, so it is important to include as much pertinent and concise information as possible.

Effective Use of Your Time

There is no set length to a business plan. The average length seems to be 30 to 40 pages. Break the plan down into sections. Set up blocks of time for work with target dates for completion. You may find it effective to spend some time at the library where you will not be interrupted by telephones or other distractions. An added bonus is that the reference material you need is close at hand either on the shelves or via the Internet. It takes discipline, time, and privacy to write an effective business plan.

Supporting Documents

You will find it time-saving to compile your list of Supporting Documents while writing the text. For example, while writing about the legal structure of your business, you will realize the need to include a copy of your partnership agreement. Write "partnership agreement" on your list of Supporting Documents. When it comes time to compile that section of your plan, you will already have a listing of necessary documents. As you go along, request any information you do not have, such as credit reports. If you gather the necessary documents in this manner, the materials you need for the Supporting Documents Section will be available when you are ready to assemble it. Remember that you do not need to include copies of all supporting documents in every copy of your business plan. If a potential lender or investor needs additional information, you can provide copies on demand.

Business Plan Outline

With the previous considerations in mind, you will be ready to begin formulating your plan. The pieces of a business plan presented in this book are as follows:

Cover Sheet	Organizational Plan
Table of Contents	Marketing Plan
Executive Summary	Financial Documents

Each of the areas of the business planning process is covered in a separate chapter of the book. *Anatomy of a Business Plan* is designed to help you write a complete, concise, and well-organized plan that will guide you and your company toward a profitable future.

****

The remainder of this chapter addresses four subjects that will help you to focus on your goals and write your business plan more effectively.

- ✓ **Developing Your Exit Strategy**
- ✓ **Developing Financial Assumptions**
- ✓ **Business Planning Instructions for Nonprofits**
- ✓ **Steps for E-tailers**

Develop an Exit Strategy:
START THE RACE WITH THE FINISH LINE IN SIGHT

Before you begin the business planning process, I would like to introduce you to the concept of planning your exit strategy. An exit strategy is not a plan for failure. It is a plan for success. Developing an exit strategy before you write your business plan will enable you to make the best decisions for your business. When you have read the following pages, you should understand what an exit strategy is and how you can apply it to the business planning process.

It is always good to utilize the talents of experts who specialize in areas that are beyond your specific expertise. With that in mind, I asked John P. Neal, CPA to work with me to develop a section on planning an Exit Strategy. John is a Managing Principal of Paulin Neal (www.paulinneal.com), providing interim executive and consulting services to improve the profitability and enterprise value of client companies. He has founded several companies and serves on the Boards of a variety of companies and organizations, including the California Chamber of Commerce.

Where is the Finish Line?

Have you ever seen runners line up for a race not knowing where the Finish Line is? This would never happen, right? Whether you are starting a new business or expanding a current business, the implication is the same. *Before you begin the race you need to know where you expect to finish.*

Businesses are started for many reasons. Some of the more common reasons include:

- To build a business for yourself instead of for someone else
- To pursue a passion (e.g. "I've always wanted to own a restaurant.")
- To be your own boss and the master of your own time
- To earn money doing what you really like to do (woodworking, quilting, photography, writing, etc.)
- To capitalize on an invention
- To replace income from the loss of a job
- To create net worth (long-term capital appreciation)

It is also inherent in the makeup of entrepreneurs to think early on about future expansion of their enterprises. What new products or services can be added? Can new markets be reached? Should additional locations be added? What kind of resources will be needed to reach my goal? The list of reasons for start up and expansion could go on and on. What's really important, though, is to understand that, in all cases, it is critical to develop an *exit (liquidity) strategy*.

Developing an Exit Strategy Is the Secret

It is a given that most investors (i.e., Angels, Private Equity, and Venture Capitalists), will require a well thought out exit strategy as part of the business plan for any venture in which they plan to invest. However, most entrepreneurs, intent on creating an immediate source of income or just caught up in the excitement of launching or expanding their businesses, have a habit of overlooking the "finish line". Consequently, they are unprepared for this certain-as-death and taxes event.

So, what should your strategy be? Understand that there are no right or wrong strategies, only different ones. *Your* strategy should fit *your* goals. The logical place to start is with your long-term goals. The most obvious and often cited goal is retirement. Some entrepreneurs like to develop one business and then sell it to start another venture. You may have other reasons that you foresee will eventually cause you to exit your own business. Whatever your goals may be there are three things that you need to know before you begin to build a better business plan:

1. **Where you are headed**

2. **When you want to get there**

3. **What your business will look like when you arrive**

What are Some of the Forms of Exit?

Some of the potential forms of exit include:

- **Selling all or a portion of the business.** It may be possible to sell the business outright to an independent buyer. In that case, you will want to maximize the net income of the business and avoid having assets tied up in the business, which you would intend to later keep in your personal possession (e.g. real estate).

- **Passing the business to a family member.** This can be a good way to transfer value to your heirs in a way that minimizes estate taxes. Proper structuring is important, as well as determining who will be in charge of running the business. Heirs are frequently unprepared for the latter.

- **Selling to an Employee Stock Ownership Plan (ESOP).** This can be a valuable vehicle when the new owner group is comprised of key employees in the business. There are certain tax advantages to ESOPs. Existence of the ESOP can also add to the value of the enterprise by giving employees a sense of ownership in the business.

- **Taking the company public.** For those interested in gaining liquidity quickly while having the option to share in future stock appreciation, this might be a good option. The complexities of this form of exit are substantial, as is the demand on management's time leading up to and continuing on after the "event". This option is not for the faint of heart and requires a good deal of guidance from CPAs and attorneys!

- **Liquidation.** In some cases, the best option to gain liquidity may be to simply discontinue conducting business, sell off the business assets, pay off creditors, and keep the proceeds (after taxes, of course). While this is, in some respects, the simplest option, it often yields the least return to the owners because there is no value given for the "going concern" or goodwill of the business. This is often the method used when the business value is closely tied to real estate or other productive assets. It is also common for sole proprietor service businesses where income production is dependent solely on the owner practicing his or her skills.

Each of the above involves a variety of considerations. For instance, if you plan to sell the business, what kind of market can you expect for your type of business? How big might it need to be to achieve optimal value? Will you be expected to stay on for a period of time? If you plan to pass it on to a family member, who will that be? How will you train them to run the business? Will whomever you have in mind to succeed you be interested in taking over when you are ready to get out? When will you need to begin the transition? Many of these questions are difficult to answer, but ultimately your successful exit will depend on it.

Make Decisions Based on Your Exit Strategy

If you will take the time to think about and answer some of these questions, a clear picture of your business will begin to take form. Three of the major decisions you will be better prepared to make will be: 1. selecting the source, type, and amount of capital you will need for your business, 2. deciding on the current form of organization, or legal structure, (sole proprietorship, partnership, or corporation) that will best serve your needs, and 3. considering tax issues that will impact your business.

Financing Your Business

Your choice of financing (source of capital) is important and will directly influence your choice of exit. Keep in mind, when considering financing options, not only the ease with which you can raise the funds you require to reach your goals, but the costs of each type of financing in terms of both money and relationships. In the simplest sense, capital is available from four sources: 1. yourself, 2. friends and family, 3. financial institutions, and 4. the public at large (including Venture Capital and Private Equity). The monetary cost of each of these options is generally inversely proportional to its personal or "relationship" cost.

- **Yourself (owner financing).** The first question you should ask yourself is, "Do I really need additional financing to meet my goals, or do I just need to manage my cash flow effectively?" The second is, "Am I willing to risk what I already have to pursue the new venture?"

- **Friends and Family.** Friends and family can be the easiest, quickest, and least expensive form of financing. However, the emotional or relationship cost can be very high. What if your business fails and you are unable to repay your friends and family? Receiving funds from a traditional lender or a venture capital firm will take far longer, but failure to repay them isn't likely to affect your family gatherings.

- **Financial Institutions (debt capital).** In the middle is the traditional bank or finance company. Like the venture capitalist (below), they want to see a completed business plan before loaning any money to you. However, they don't tend to focus on *your* exit. Instead they focus on *their* exit, which is repayment of the loan when it is due along with interest and other applicable fees. These lenders want to see that management will be able to generate sufficient income and manage cash flow in such a way as to ensure timely repayment. They typically require personal guarantees of the owners and often will require additional collateral, such as a lien on your house or other property, to further ensure repayment.

- **Venture Capital and Private Equity (equity capital).** Venture capitalists and private equity firms typically invest in opportunities in which they expect to earn a high compound rate of return and that will provide an exit (return of their capital along with a return, or profit, on that capital) within five to seven years. They require a complete business plan with a strong exit strategy. Exit in this case, is usually via an Initial Public Offering (IPO) or acquisition by a larger, often public, company. In either case, such an exit typically results in a change of management and loss of control of the entity by the founders. While the venture capital option can be attractive, obviously it is not appropriate under many circumstances.

Dealing with Legal and Tax Issues

It is always a good idea to seek the advice of an experienced corporate attorney and a business accounting professional. Since laws vary from state to state, it is best to choose advisors familiar with the state in which you will operate and live.

The determination of financing needs has a direct bearing on the form of legal structure you will need for your business. Thinking about your exit strategy will provide the basis for determining the form or organization that will best serve your needs as you pursue your goals. If you are a new business and the choice is not clear-cut, your attorney and tax advisor can help you make the best decision. Alternatively, if you are a current business that is planning to expand through the use of debt or equity capital, you may be advised that you need to change to a legal structure that will enable you to protect your personal assets and to ensure your ability to deal with your lender or investor.

1. **Some legal issues that you and your advisors need to consider:**

    - Liability of owners, directors, and officers: Owners, directors, and officers may become liable for the actions and debts of the company in certain events. Reasonable protection from such liability can be achieved by a combination of effective use of elections and structuring alternatives and supplemented with Directors and Officers (D&O) insurance.

    - Applicability of state and federal securities laws: Rules regarding solicitation of investors are complex and require close compliance to avoid civil and criminal penalties.

    - Rights of minority owners: Access to books and records and minimum disclosure requirements create obligations requiring strict compliance.

    - Ease and cost of transfer of ownership: Depending on your time frame for exit, some legal structures are easier to deal with than others.

- Buy-sell agreements among partners or shareholders: Terms and conditions for buying out a partner/shareholder or their heirs should be spelled out clearly up front to avoid later disputes.

2. Some of the tax issues to be considered:

- Treatment of capital gains upon the sale/transfer of the business: Tax events need to be planned far in advance. This includes available tax elections to minimize taxes incurred when all or a portion of your interest in a business is sold.

- Corporate and personal taxes: Proper structuring can strike an optimal balance between corporate and personal taxes and avoids double taxation.

- Title to any real property owned: Certain property may be best owned by partners/shareholders individually and leased to the business in order to achieve the lowest overall tax bill.

- Reasonable compensation limits: The IRS and state taxing authorities can set limits on the level of salaries to owner employees. Payments in excess of these limits become dividends that are taxable to the owner and not allowed to be deducted by the corporation.

- Retirement plans: A strong retirement plan can be a key tool for attracting high quality employees as well as providing for the owners' retirement. A wide variety of plans exist ranging from simple IRA's to complicated 401K plans. Each has advantages and limitations.

- Unrelated Business Income: If you are planning to start a "not-for-profit" corporation, which is not subject to normal income taxes, you will need to follow specific guidelines restricting the types of revenue you can generate. Sales of products unrelated to your not-for-profit business purpose may subject the organization to taxation.

Exit Planning Just Makes Good Sense!

By now you can see that thinking in terms of your future exit strategy will help you with your financing decisions and with your legal and tax considerations as you write your business plan. Obviously, the less complex your business is, the fewer decisions you will have to make.

It does not matter whether you are writing a business plan for a new business or for an existing business that is moving in a new direction. Business planning is an ongoing process. As you continue to operate, your goals may change radically. The current and future goals and their impact on your exit strategy need to be continually reflected in your business plan.

With your vision established and sound financial, legal, and tax strategies decided upon, you can confidently build your business plan and ....

Start the race with the finish line in sight!

Developing
Financial Assumptions

What are Financial Assumptions?

Financial assumptions are the rationale upon which you base the numbers that you enter in your financial statements. A simplified example would be explaining that a marketing expense projection of $28,000 is based on sending out four mailings during the year (January, April, August, and October) at a cost of $10,000 for the initial mailing and $6,000 for each subsequent mailing.

Adding Financial Assumption Explanations to Your Business Plan

When you are writing the text portion of your business plan, each part of the plan should be developed not only as a conceptual idea, but in terms of how it will generate revenues and/or incur expenses. For example, when you decide which legal structure suits your purpose, go one step further and find out what costs you will incur during the process. When you make decisions as to who your management team will be and what their jobs will entail, plan also what their compensation and your costs will be in terms of salary, taxes, and benefits. When you consider a marketing campaign, determine its costs, probable response, and projected revenues.

In essence, every financial statement could have a sheet appended to it that explains how you arrived at your numbers. There are several scenarios you can choose to follow.

- You can develop a full sheet of assumptions for your pro forma cash flow statement and append it to the back of the cash flow statement. On the other statements you can clarify only items that need explanation.

- On all financial statements you can add explanations at the bottom to clarify any items that would be confusing to the reader. In this instance, you would make no reference at the bottom to numbers that you feel need no clarification.

- You can include a page labeled "Financial Assumptions" either before or after your financial documents (or at some other location that is documented in your table of contents). On this page(s), you can list your financial assumptions. It is best in this instance to divide them into categories: revenues, inventory expenses, fixed and variable expenses, loans received, loan repayments, fixed asset purchases, etc. Also have a start-up cost category if you are a new business.

My choice is number 1. After a certain amount of time, even the most astute business planner tends to get confused about where some of the numbers came from. This method puts the clarification in close proximity to the number it describes.

Having the pro forma cash flow statement fully explained has an additional advantage if you are approaching a lender or investor. The pro forma cash flow statement is of the highest priority in determining the validity of your request for funding. If you take the time to develop a full assumptions sheet for your cash flow statement, it saves the lender or investor valuable time in trying to determine the premises upon which your numbers are based.

What Is the Process for Developing Your Assumptions?

There is a logical process for creating financial assumptions. The steps are as follows:

1. As you develop each piece of your business plan, remember to develop it in terms of revenues you expect to generate and expenses you expect to incur (as in the examples above).

2. Keep notations. As you determine the revenue and expense dollars related to the task you are working on, jot down the assumptions that you have developed. Be sure to include explanations of *when* revenues will be realized and *when* expenses will be incurred.

3. When you are ready to develop your financial plan, gather your assumptions together in one place and use them as the basis for the dollar amounts you input. Finally, append your assumptions to your financial statements where they are needed for clarification.

Oh, No! Another Job to Do!

Every time I revise this book or its companion software and think of something more to add to the business planning process, I also think the reader will cringe because there is one more job to do. Let me assure you that the benefit of going through the Financial Assumption process will be extremely valuable to you.

One of the most frequent errors made by people writing a business plan is that what they say in the text portion of the plan does not correlate with the numbers they use in their financial documents. In fact, some people try to develop their financial plans first and then develop their organizational and marketing plans. *This is a fatal error.* You must develop the qualitative information and then quantify it in your financial plan. If the numbers do not work out, then you go back to the drawing board and make new decisions that will give you better financial results.

By utilizing the financial assumption process, you will be developing your plan the right way—write the text, thinking in terms of revenues and expenses; list the assumptions on a sheet of paper; transfer the numbers into your financial documents; append any assumptions that are needed for clarification of numbers to your financial documents.

The financial assumption process will do two things for you. It will save you time because you will have all of your numbers at your finger tips when you are ready to develop your financial plan. The most important benefit, however, will be that your business plan will have absolute continuity between what you say in words in the text portion of your plan and what you say in numbers in the financial plan. In other words, *the qualitative part of your plan will say the same thing as the quantitative part of your plan and the plan will be both credible and defensible.*

Qualitative = Quantitative = Credibility + Defensibility

On page 26 of the Dayne Landscaping, Inc. sample business plan (Appendix II), you will find an example of one way of documenting a list of financial assumptions. The writer in this example chose to include it at the end of the Financial Documents. You can also see an example of a clarification of a single line item in the pro forma cash flow statement at the bottom of page 20 of the Marine Art of California plan.

Nonprofit Organizations

For nonprofits in the 8th edition of
Anatomy of a Business Plan

In the past twenty plus years, I have been asked many times by start-up and existing social entrepreneurs if *Anatomy of a Business Plan* could be used to write a business plan for their nonprofit organizations.

My answer has always been,

> *"Yes, it can. The process for business planning is the same for a nonprofit organization as for a for-profit business. However, there are some topics in the text part of the plan that should be approached in a slightly different manner to reflect the mission and goals of a nonprofit. One example would be how you deal with target marketing. A for-profit company targets its customers. A nonprofit's target market is referred to as it's target audience and is divided into two categories – program recipients and funding sources.*
>
> *Also, there are some differences in the financials. For example, the chart of accounts is built around the nonprofit's program services. In place of the product and/or service income categories used by for-profits, a nonprofit will have income categories based on its revenue sources, such as corporate and foundation support, grants and public funds, individual contributions, etc. Its expense categories differ in that variable expenses will be program-related. Terminology also differs. For a nonprofit, a profit and loss (income statement) is known as a statement of activities and a balance sheet is called a statement of financial position."*

Chapter 9
Business Planning for Your Nonprofit

Although, we always answered your questions, it took us until the last edition to include a chapter devoted to guiding you through the specific differences that need to be incorporated in the business planning process for a nonprofit.

 New in this edition—Plan for a Nonprofit Organization. You will also be happy to see a complete real-world business plan example for a nonprofit (Appendix V: Road Runners, Inc., a nonprofit serving disadvantaged youth).

How to Use the Nonprofit Chapter

Business planning for the most part is the same process for a nonprofit organization as it is for a for-profit company. For that reason, you need to follow the book through each of the sections of your business plan, but you also need to know two things:

- **When you are addressing a topic that is different for nonprofits**
- **What it is that you need to do that will be appropriate to a nonprofit**

Follow The Process Below

- **Spend some time reading the book.** My first suggestion would be for you to spend a couple of hours going through *Anatomy of a Business Plan* to acquaint yourself with the business planning process and to look at the example business plans in the appendices.

- **Read Chapter 9.** Next, I would strongly urge you to read the nonprofit chapter to gain a general understanding about business planning for nonprofits and to see an overview of the differences that will need to be addressed during the planning process.

- **Follow the book.** Now you are ready to start working on your business plan. Follow the book just the same as you would if your organization were not a nonprofit. Most tasks will be the same for a nonprofit organization and a for-profit company.

- **Use our icon.** As you go through the next several chapters and develop your business plan, you will see an icon in line with the headings of those sections that will need special attention if you are planning for a nonprofit organization. The icon will look like the one below.

NPO is short for nonprofit organization. The page number below the letters will tell you the page to go to in Chapter 9, Business Planning for a Nonprofit, that will address the differences for the current topic that you are dealing with in your business plan.

- **Refer to the referenced page.** Go to the page shown in the icon. Read the instructions under the same heading. They will guide you as you develop that section of your business plan so that it will now be appropriate for your nonprofit.

- **Return to the main part of the book to address the next topic.** If there is no NPO icon by the topic, you will follow the same instructions as a for-profit company.

By following the above process and referring to the example plan for Road Runners, Inc. in Appendix V, you should find it fairly easy to develop a credible business plan for your nonprofit organization. It should have all of the needed elements that are appropriate to all businesses, but still have that special focus that is so necessary for developing and expanding a successful nonprofit.

I hope you are pleased with the nonprofit chapter and with the example business plan. Hopefully, the question I have been asked for many years is at last answered in this edition of *Anatomy of a Business Plan*. Best wishes to you as you develop a business plan for your nonprofit organization.

Summary of Steps to E-tailing

Are You Planning to Be an E-tailer?

If you are planning to sell via the Internet, the following are steps to follow as you plan, design, and set up your web site. As you write your business plan, incorporate the steps into the appropriate sections of your plan—organization, marketing, and financial.

Step 1: *Set Your Goals.*
- ❑ Be consistent with your Business Plan.
- ❑ Address potential problems from the start.
- ❑ Reinforce your marketing strategy.

Step 2: *Access the Internet.*
- ❑ Determine which connection components should be upgraded.
- ❑ Implement changes (ISP, transmission speed, etc.) as needed.
- ❑ Will your current methods work to support your e-commerce goals?

Step 3: *Promote Your Web Site.*
- ❑ Establish your presence on the Internet (domain name registration, SEO).
- ❑ Link to and from other sites that serve your target market.

Step 4: *Design Your Web Site.*
- ❑ Project a professional image.
- ❑ Be sure your web site is easy to navigate.

Step 5: *Create an Electronic Catalog.*
- ❑ Achieve the best balance of graphics and text.
- ❑ Consider online venues for your catalog.

Step 6: *Identify Your Distribution Channel.*
- ❑ Determine other sellers (Amazon, eBay, Craig's List, etc.).
- ❑ Create appropriate links.

Step 7: *Develop a Method of Order Processing.*
- ❑ Have electronic funds transfer capability.
- ❑ Offer real-time payment solutions (credit cards, debit cards, PayPal, etc.).
- ❑ Choose a shopping cart that meets your needs.

Step 8: *Select Security Systems.*
- ❑ Safeguard your customers' privacy through PCI compliance.
- ❑ Protect your confidential company records/data.

Step 9: *Develop Inventory Tracking Procedures.*
- ❑ Cut your costs by tracking and controlling.
- ❑ Link to suppliers and/or customers as needed.

Step 10: *Refine Your Customer Interface.*
- ❑ Encourage feedback from your customers.
- ❑ Track customer purchase patterns.
- ❑ Communicate with your customers.

Modified and reprinted by permission: © Bernadette Tiernan (from her book, "E-Tailing")

The Cover Sheet
and Table of Contents

The Cover Sheet of your business plan is like the cover of a book. It provides the first impression to the reader of your business plan. It should be neat and attractive and should contain information that will grab the reader's attention.

The Table of Contents is also an important element of every good business plan. It enables the reader of your plan to quickly find information on the various aspects of your business.

The next three pages cover the following:

✓ *What to Include on a Cover Sheet*

✓ *Sample Cover Sheet*

✓ *Table of Contents Help*

The Cover Sheet

What to Include on a Cover Sheet

The first page of your business plan will be the cover sheet. It serves as the title page and should contain the following information:

- **Company name**
- **Company address**
- **Company phone number (including area code)**
- **Web address, if you have a web site**
- **Logo, if you have one**
- **Names, titles, addresses, and phone numbers of the owners or corporate officers**
- **Month and year in which plan is issued**
- **Name of the preparer**
- **Number of the copy**
- **Confidentiality statement (optional)**

The company name, address, phone number, and web site address should appear in the top one-third of the page. If you have a logo it will be an added enhancement to the page, especially if it is printed in color.

Information regarding the owners or corporate officers of the business will appear in the center of the page.

The bottom third of the page will contain the remaining information. The month and year in which the plan was written lets the lender know if it is up-to-date. For instance, if your plan is five months old, a lender or investor might request an update on certain financial information. Many lenders and investors prefer that the plan be written by one or more of the business owners or officers. This signifies a hands-on approach to the running of the company. Numbering your copies helps you keep track of them. Lastly, you may choose to add a confidentiality statement. See the example cover sheet in Appendix III, *Wholesale Mobile Homes.com, Inc.* cover sheet.

Keep a log with the following information: number of copy, name of person reviewing the copy, reviewer's phone number and date submitted. This way you can keep up with the reviewing process and can make follow-up calls to the lender if necessary.

A sample cover sheet follows. As you can see, this one page contains a lot of information. It provides the name, location, and phone number of your business. By listing the sole proprietor, partners, or corporate officers, a lender or investor will know the legal structure of the business and how to contact key people directly for additional information. Keep in mind that lenders and investors must review many business plans in a limited amount of time. It is to your advantage to help them by making your plan thorough and concise.

Sample Cover Sheet

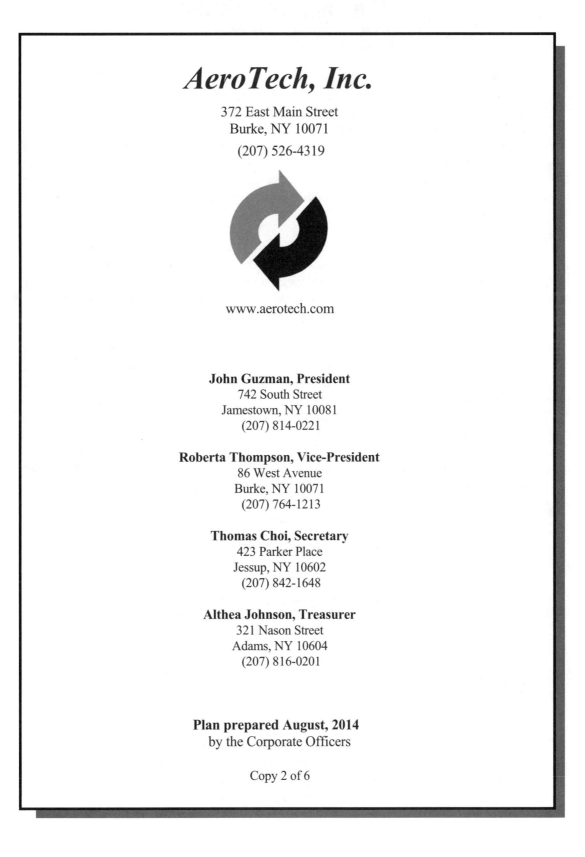

AeroTech, Inc.

372 East Main Street
Burke, NY 10071

(207) 526-4319

www.aerotech.com

John Guzman, President
742 South Street
Jamestown, NY 10081
(207) 814-0221

Roberta Thompson, Vice-President
86 West Avenue
Burke, NY 10071
(207) 764-1213

Thomas Choi, Secretary
423 Parker Place
Jessup, NY 10602
(207) 842-1648

Althea Johnson, Treasurer
321 Nason Street
Adams, NY 10604
(207) 816-0201

Plan prepared August, 2014
by the Corporate Officers

Copy 2 of 6

The Table of Contents

The Table of Contents is an important part of your finished business plan. It needs to be well-organized so that the reader can quickly find information on any aspect of your business. For example, if your executive summary gives an overview of the managers of your company, the reader should be able to look in the table of contents and find the page number in your organizational plan where you address the management. By the same token, the page in which the resumes can be found in the supporting documents section should also be listed. In the same way, marketing results can be traced through the marketing plan and backed up with copies of demographic studies, etc. in the supporting documents.

Obviously, the Table of Contents cannot be finished until your plan is complete. You can use the headings in your business plan to develop the table of contents. Once you have finished your plan you can insert the page numbers. If, at some time, you alternately choose to print and bind only portions of your plan, the table of contents can be scaled down to match that version.

The length of the Table of Contents will be dependent on the complexity of your plan. Most small start-up businesses will need only one page. Existing companies will have historical information and financial statements as well as projections. Larger, more complex companies will most likely have more detailed headings, especially if the company is going after venture capital.

In all cases, your business plan will have the following major divisions in the table of contents. The subheadings will depend on your decision as to what you include in your plan.

- **Executive Summary**
- **Part I: Organizational Plan**
- **Part II: Marketing Plan**
- **Part III: Financial Documents**
- **Supporting Documents**

 The Tables of Contents in the example business plans at the back of the book should help you to see how your own can be organized.

Chapters 3 through 7 of this book will cover the above subjects in order and will guide you through the content and development of each one. As you think through each section, you can make your own decisions as to what you will address in your own plan and as to how the headings for those topics will fit within the table of contents.

Executive Summary

The Executive Summary is the abstract of your business plan. It summarizes who you are, what your company does, where your company is going, why it is going where it is going, and how it will get there. If you are seeking funding, it specifies the purpose of the funding you seek and justifies the financial feasibility of your plan for the lender or investor.

Although the executive summary appears near the front of the plan, it is most effectively written after the rest of your business plan is complete. At that time, your concepts will be well-developed and all of the important information and financial data will be available.

Use the *Key Word* approach mentioned earlier in the book. In a concise, but powerful statement you will sum up the essence of your business plan by including answers to the following questions:

> ✓ *Who?*
>
> ✓ *What?*
>
> ✓ *Where?*
>
> ✓ *When?*
>
> ✓ *Why?*
>
> ✓ *How?*

What is an Executive Summary?

As stated in the introduction, the Executive Summary is the abstract of your business plan. It summarizes the content and purpose of your finished business plan, covering all of the key points. It specifies who you are, what your company does, where your company is going, why it is going where it is going, and how it will get there. The Executive Summary can be approached from either of the two following perspectives.

If your plan is for internal use only and you are not seeking funds

The executive summary would summarize your business. It would be a brief overview of the company's goals and statement of how it will focus to meet its projections.

If you are seeking funding

The Executive Summary specifies the purpose of the funding you seek and justifies the financial feasibility of your plan for the lender or investor. A lender or investor reading only the executive summary should quickly see the name, age, legal structure, location, nature, and uniqueness of your business including strengths and risks. The Executive Summary should provide a quick overview of your business' past performance and of its future goals and how you plan to reach them. Information on the management team is imperative if you are seeking venture capital. Finally, the executive summary would include the amount and purpose of the loan or investment request, timing needs, justification for financing, and a repayment statement (lender) or statement of potential return on investment (venture capitalist).

> **For a lender.** Address the question of loan repayment. The lender needs to see your company's ability to meet interest expense as well as principal repayments. The lender will want to know when the loan is needed and what you will use as collateral. Your credit rating will also be an important factor.

> **For angels.** The angel investor, jokingly referred to as the "Bank of Mom and Dad," is generally a wealthy individual who becomes personally involved with a start-up company—loaning expertise, experience, and money. It is best to have a solid business plan to justify the funding. However, depending on the level of familiarity, you may be able to get by with a less than perfect plan.

> **For a venture capitalist.** The days of the easy flow of venture capital are long gone. Since the April 2000 public market correction, companies can't depend on prospective future funding. They need to show evidence of progress and strong relationships. Remember that an investor will be an equity partner in your company and you will have to address how you will meet his/her goals for growth and profitability. After funding, the venture capitalist will very likely sit on your board of directors and serve as an advisor to your management. Increasingly, investors have been looking for an annual return of 45% to 60% over three to five years.

Your executive summary should generate excitement and give the reader an awareness of the uniqueness of your business and the qualifications of your management team. Do not exaggerate your potential. Rather, stick to projections that you can back up with facts. One of the greatest errors of business plan writers is the overstatement of projected market share and potential revenues.

Finish Your Business Plan Before You Write the Executive Summary

As you write your business plan and refine your ideas, you will probably discover new ideas and information that you will want to incorporate into your business plan to make your business more effective and profitable. For this reason, the Executive Summary is most effectively written after your plan has been completed. At that time, all the information and financial data will be available and you can draw it from the written text and financial spreadsheets.

In addition, periodic updates of your business plan may require that you revise your Executive Summary to reflect the changes that will constantly be taking place in your business.

Use the Keyword Approach

Use the keyword approach. The Executive Summary is generally contained on one page if it is for internal use. If you are trying to approach a lender or investor, it should not exceed two or three pages. In a concise and clear one- or two-page statement you will sum up the essence of your business plan by including answers to the following questions: *Who? What? Where? When? Why? How?*

---

*The following pages will guide you
as you write your Executive Summary*

Introductory Overview

Begin your Executive Summary with a brief but concise overview of your business: who you are, where you are located, what you do, when the company was (or will be) established, and what makes your company unique.

Example. The following paragraph is a *simplified* overview for *AeroTech, Inc.* To see a fully developed example, take some time to study that executive summary in the ***Wmhinc.com*** example business plan in *Anatomy of a Business Plan*, Appendix III.

"AeroTech, Inc. was established in 2005 to meet the demand for specialized parts in the aerospace industry. This industry experienced moderate growth with an increase in contracts beginning in 2010. Industry projections indicate a growing demand for the type of products the company manufactures. AeroTech, Inc. maintains a competitive edge

with prompt order fulfillment, excellent customer relationships, and custom design capabilities .The company is adequately housed in a 10,000 square-foot facility and desires to meet the growing demand for its products through the purchase of new and more modern equipment, which will provide the opportunity for broader scope bidding, increased custom design capabilities, lower per unit costs, and faster turnaround time. In the next three to five years, AeroTech, Inc. plans to increase its current 20% market share to 35%."

Market Opportunity

Clearly define the opportunities in the marketplace that you are positioned to take advantage of. This information will come from your market research and SWOT analysis.

Capital Requirements

If your company is seeking funding, state how much capital you need. If your company is not seeking funding, delete this section from your own executive summary.

Breakdown of Use of Funds

Provide a breakdown of how and when your company is planning to utilize loan or investment funds. (See example table below). If your company is not seeking a loan or investment, delete this section from your own executive summary.

Breakdown of Use of Funds	
Construction of New Facility	**Amount**
1. Payment upon signing contract (4-01-14)	$ 200,000 (from owners)
2. Completion of framing (6-01-14)	$ 250,000 (from loan)
3. Completion of project (8-15-14)	$ 250,000 (from loan)
Total from Owners **Total from Loan Funds**	**$ 200,000** **$ 500,000**

Loan Repayment

State your plans to repay the loan. What type of loan are you seeking? How many years/months will you have to repay the loan? What will be the amount and frequency of your loan payments? When do your payments begin and end?

If you have figured out how much you will need, you can use an amortization application (such as the one in our Automate Your Business Plan software) to auto-calculate your principal and interest payment for any number of years. If your company is not seeking a loan, delete this section from your own executive summary.

Mission

State the mission of your company. The mission statement is a concise description of how you want your company to be viewed by its customers. It also states your company's vision as to future directions toward which it intends to move.

> **Example.** The following is a mission statement for *Wmhinc.com*.

> *"At Wmhinc.com, our mission is to provide the most innovative and practical web based housing solutions. Wmhinc.com plans are to become a dominant player in the online marketplace, providing new, factory over-run, and bank-owned homes direct to the consumer."*

Management

Provide a brief profile on each owner. If you have key staff members who participate or will participate in the management of your company, also include a brief profile on each one. List their experience in industry specific areas. Include a brief experience statement as well as honors, awards, and recognition received.

Competitors

Provide a brief profile on each of your direct competitors. Limit this section to major competitors. Also include brief profiles of your indirect competitors. List each competitor and give an overview of what services they offer. List the strengths and weaknesses of each.

Competitor's Strengths and Weaknesses

Outline the strengths and weaknesses of your competitors.

Your Company's Competitive Advantages

Describe the factors within your company that give you a competitive advantage. This information can come from the Strengths section of the SWOT analysis you developed in the Organizational Plan.

Financial Projections

Provide a summary of your income statement projections for the next three years. Include expected revenue, expense, and net profit projections for the three-year period.

> **Example.** The following is a *simplified* example for *AeroTech, Inc.*

> *"Forecasts for identified revenue growth resulting from a devoted and loyal client-base and aggressive marketing initiatives indicate that AeroTech, Inc will exceed $11 million by the end of year 3. Net profit for the three years is forecast to be in excess of $4 million."*

In Summary

The Executive Summary is just that—a summary of your business plan. If you are writing your plan to serve as a guide for your firm, and not planning to seek a lender or investor, writing an executive summary will help you to formulate a good overall picture of where you are planning to go in your business. If you are seeking a lender or investor, the Executive Summary will be the first introduction to your business and should answer key questions regarding your company and its potential for growth and profitability.

Remember that the rest of the plan must back up what you say in the Executive Summary. For example, if you are sponsoring an event at a trade show in order to increase revenue, you must not only show figures on its cost, but must also demonstrate a ready market for the event in the marketing and financial sections. In supporting documents, you can back up the amount requested with information, such as event attendance, historic benefits of sponsorship, and the company's personal experience.

When you have finished with the formulation of your business plan and answered the key word questions, you will be ready to write your Executive Summary.

> **Note.** To help you, there are examples on the next four pages — one for a company whose business plan is for internal purposes only and one for a company that is seeking loan funds.

Two Example Executive Summaries

1. If you are not planning to seek a lender or investor

The following is an example Executive Summary for a company whose goal does not involve seeking financing from a lender or investor. It is different from the second example in that it does not involve justification of financing or a schedule for receipt of funds, repayment of a loan, or plans for return on investment to a venture capitalist (equity partner).

BestCARE Company
Executive Summary

BestCARE Company is a partnership established in 2009, whose purpose is to provide quality full-time care to the elderly through licensed residential board and care homes.

The company is administratively located at 1234 Hillside Drive in the city of Laguna Hills, California, the home of Jennifer Lopez, R.N., one of two partners. In addition to attending to the administration and accounting duties, Ms. Lopez also oversees medical services for the elderly residents. Her partner, Henry Johnson, oversees maintenance of the homes and does all of the shopping for food, furniture, patient supplies, etc.

BestCARE Company owns and operates three five-bedroom homes within Orange County, California. Each home provides 24-hour per day, full-care services for up to six residents. Two fully-trained caregivers have been hired for each home and live on the premises. Contract-service caregivers work on the live-ins' days off.

The three current homes have now been running profitably for the last three years. Current research shows that there are twice as many families seeking board and care homes as the preferred lifestyle for their elderly parents than was the case in 2007. This has created a high demand where the supply is short.

BestCARE Company is now planning to expand by purchasing two more homes over the next five years. The two new homes will be mortgage-free. They will be purchased with cash from previous profits from the company that have been retained and invested by the partners.

This business plan will serve as a five-year plan that will guide the company through the administrative, marketing, and financial issues that are inherent in reaching a growth goal that will double the size of the company.

2. If you are planning to seek a lender or investor

The following is an example Executive Summary for a company whose goal is to seek financing from a lender or investor. Unlike the previous example, this executive summary will have to address the financing needs of the company in terms of how much money is needed, when it is needed, how the company plans to use the funds, how the use of those funds will achieve a desired outcome, and how and when repayment will take place to the lender. In the case of venture capital, you will project the investor's return on investment. The lender or investor will also look for information regarding the management of the company.

See: *Anatomy of a Business Plan*, Appendix III, Wholesale Mobile Homes.com, Inc. business plan for the most comprehensive example of an Executive Summary (page 247).

AeroTech, Inc.
Executive Summary

Formed in 2005, *AeroTech, Inc.* was established with the objective of custom designing and manufacturing specialized parts for the aerospace industry. *AeroTech, Inc.* is an S corporation operating from a 10,000 square-foot manufacturing and warehousing space in Aerospace Tech Park, a light industrial park, located at 372 E Main Street, Burke, New York. In the past two years, the Economic Development Corporation (EDC) of Burke has been successful in encouraging large aerospace and technology corporations to relocate to the Tech Park. *AeroTech, Inc.* has developed excellent working relationships with the relocated companies. The company currently serves 20% of the total market with gross revenues of $3,650,000.

Market Opportunity

Burke EDC projections through the year 2017 indicate a 30% increase in tenancy in the Tech Park by aerospace companies. Federal government statistics project a 25% increase in the United States in aerospace development through the year 2030. Information from engineering and aerospace trade associations indicates that automation is needed to allow the company to remain competitive. By building on past working relationships with current companies and by actively marketing to new residents of the Tech Park, *AeroTech, Inc.* will be able to capture an additional 15% of the market; the Corporation's share will be 35% of the total market.

cont. next page

Capital Requirements

The company is seeking growth capital in the amount of $250,000 for the purpose of purchasing automated equipment and for training existing personnel in the use of that equipment. Modernization of equipment will result in a 35% increase in production and will decrease the unit costs by 25%.

Funding is needed in time for the equipment to be delivered and in place by May 23, 2014. There is a two-month period between order placement and delivery date. Training of employees on the new equipment is projected to cover a two-week period following equipment placement.

Breakdown of Use of Funds

Provided below is a breakdown of the use of funds.

Activity	Amount
Automated Equipment	$ 230,000
Personnel Training	20,000
Total	**$250,000**

Loan Repayment

Repayment of the loan and interest can begin promptly within 30 days of receipt of funds. The loan can be secured by company-owned real estate that has a 2013 assessed valuation of $800,000.

Mission

The mission of *AeroTech, Inc.* is to serve the aerospace industry, providing premium quality parts, value added services, and quality workmanship. The company's experience and proven service to the aircraft industry have demonstrated its capability to meet current and future aerospace requirements.

Management

AeroTech, Inc. has a very strong management team as well as a board of directors comprised of several industry and community leaders. Brief profiles of the management team are provided below (See resumes in Supporting Documents).

John Guzman, President and Chief Executive Officer

John Guzman was previously CEO for Omni Aerospace and was the force behind its well-documented growth between 1996 and 2004.

cont. next page

Management, *cont.*

Roberta Thompson, VP Marketing Director
Roberta Thompson previously served as marketing head of the products division of ABC Corporation.

Thomas Choi, Corporation Secretary
Thomas Choi heads up Administration, capitalizing on his twelve years as an administrative executive with USAmerica Air.

Althea Johnson, CFO
Althea Johnson was a senior partner with JFG Accounting and successfully achieved turnarounds for several multi-million dollar corporations

Donald Smith, Production
Donald Smith came to *AeroTech, Inc.* following 20 years as an R&D and production engineer with Bordman Electronics.

Competitors

Competitive threats come from Aerospace Manufacturing and Technology, AeroDesigns, Inc., Aero Parts & More, and Space Technology, Inc. While Aerospace Manufacturing and Technology and AeroDesigns, Inc. have longer operating histories, their technology is obsolete and subject to several inherent disadvantages. These disadvantages include longer installation time, more complex components and assembly, and excessive weight issues. Aero Parts & More and Space Technology, Inc. have technology that meets the unique demands of the marketplace. However, both companies have a short operating history and lack the credibility demanded by customers.

AeroTech, Inc.'s Competitive Advantages

AeroTech, Inc. boasts a world-class management team with extensive experience in the aerospace industry and a successful record of running multi-million dollar corporations. *AeroTech, Inc.* benefits from first-mover initiatives as the company introduces groundbreaking parts designed specifically for the latest technology in the aerospace industry. Additional competitive advantages include: patented technology, state-of-the-art equipment, and long-term contracts with key clients including the United States military.

Financial Projections

The company is expected to break even 24 months after completion of the employee training period. Forecasts for identified revenue growth resulting from a devoted and loyal customer-base and aggressive marketing initiatives indicate that *AeroTech, Inc.* will exceed $13 million by the end of year 3. Net profit for the three years is forecast to be in excess of $1.3 million.

CHAPTER 4

Part I
The Organizational Plan

The first major section of your business plan addresses the organizational details of your business. It begins with a description of your business and its products and/or services. The remainder of the organizational plan is devoted to administrative setup—or how your business is put together in order to function in an efficient and cost-effective manner.

Using short, but descriptive statements, address the following areas. Feel free to include other organizational topics that you think are key to your particular industry.

✓ *Summary of the Business*
(Mission, Business Model, Strategy, Strategic Relationships, SWOT Analysis)

✓ *Products and/or Services*

✓ *Administrative Plan*
(Location, Legal Structure, Management and Personnel, Accounting and Legal, Insurance, Security, Intellectual Property)

Summary of the Business
(Organizational Plan: Section I)

Establish the Foundation Upon Which You Will Build Your Business.

Describing your business in this section will help you to think about it in conceptual terms. You need to understand your own vision of the business – what you want to accomplish and how you want your business to be viewed by others. Based on that vision, you will determine the strategy you will use and the strategic relationships that you will develop to help you reach your goals and objectives.

Begin with a broad overview of the nature of your business.

Using the key word approach, begin by telling when and why the company was formed. Describe the nature and uniqueness of the products and/or services provided and briefly review the general history and future goals of the company. After the company has been introduced in a paragraph or two, the summary of the business can be completed by addressing each of the following topics:

NPO
Page 140

Mission

State your company's *mission*, projecting a sense of what your goals are regarding its future place within your industry and within the community. A mission statement is a brief (one or two sentences) description of the company's fundamental purpose including, nature, values, and its work. It should clearly explain why the company exists and what it plans to achieve in the future.

Business Model

Describe your company's *business model* and why it is unique to your industry. A business model is the method of doing business by which a company can generate revenue and sustain itself.

Strategy

Give an overview of the company's *strategy*—its short-term and long-term objectives and how you plan to realize those objectives. A strategy is a plan of action designed to achieve a particular goal that has been established.

Strategic Relationships

If you have *strategic relationships*, tell who they are with and how they will benefit your company. A strategic relationship is a mutually beneficial formal contractual alliance established between two or more organizations.

SWOT Analysis

Finally, conduct an analysis on your business, examining key factors that are internal and external to your business. See *"What is a SWOT Analysis?"* and *"How to Conduct a SWOT Analysis"* – next two pages)

 Note. We have two worksheets (*Summary of the Business* and *SWOT Analysis*) that will help you develop the above topics. See pages 340 and 341 in Appendix VI.

What is a SWOT Analysis?

SWOT stands for Strengths, Weaknesses, Opportunities, and Threats. A SWOT analysis is an in-depth examination of key factors that are internal (strengths and weaknesses) and external (opportunities and threats) to a business.

- **Internal Factors.** The examination of internal factors takes a close look at the organization, laying out core competencies and areas in which a business has a competitive advantage. It also looks at areas in which a business has a lack of certain strengths.

- **External Factors.** An examination of external factors takes a look at the marketplace in which a business operates and helps to identify new areas in which the business can grow and niche markets that can be pursued, all which will ultimately lead to greater profits for the business. It also looks at changes and trends in the marketplace that may affect a company's business operations.

Benefits of a SWOT analysis

Conducting a SWOT analysis will enable a business to channel its focus into those areas that present the greatest opportunities and those competencies in which it is strongest. Concurrently, the business will look into ways to mitigate its weaknesses and develop plans and strategies to overcome any threats that present themselves. When conducting a SWOT analysis, you should be realistic about the strengths and weaknesses of your business.

How to Conduct a SWOT Analysis

To conduct a SWOT analysis, answer the following questions in each section:

Strengths

- Do you have a proprietary product/technology?
- Do you have a superior location?
- Do you have a unique business model?
- Do you have any value added services?
- What advantage(s) do you have over your competitors?
- What specialized areas do you have expertise in?
- What recognition have you received?

Weaknesses

- What aspects of the operations of the business can be improved upon?
- What aspects of the product(s) and/or service(s) can be improved upon?
- Is there a lack of expertise in any area?
- Is the location of your business a problem?
- Have you received any negative press?

Opportunities

- Are there any markets that are not being served with your product(s) and/or service(s)?
- Are there any emerging niche segments within your industry?
- Are there any target market and/or industry trends that are of interest to you?
- Are there any changes in technology that could be beneficial to you?
- Is there an emerging/developing market within your industry?
- Have some of your competitors left the marketplace?
- Are there any companies that can be taken over?
- Are there any companies with whom strategic alliances can be formed?
- Are there any opportunities in international markets?

Threats

- Are there any new competitors emerging?
- Are existing competitors gaining strength?
- Are the prices of your competitors going up or down?
- Are competitors introducing new products and/or services to the marketplace?
- Are there any challenges that are emerging within the industry?
- Are there any new government regulations being enforced?

 Example Summary of the Business. To see a fully developed example addressing all of the elements discussed in the Summary of the Business, take some time to study that section in the ***Wmhinc.com*** example business plan in Appendix III.

Products or Services
(Organizational Plan: Section II)

NPO
Page 141

In this section of your plan you will describe your products and services. What are you selling? In the Marketing Plan (Chapter 5) you will analyze whether or not there is a real need for *all* your products and services or if your repertoire should be limited to those items that are truly in demand.

If you are the manufacturer and/or distributor of a product

- **Manufacturers.** Describe your products and give a general description of their development from raw materials to finished item. The development of a flow chart or time line can help you to identify the various stages of research and development (R&D) and production.

A time line can also be used to demonstrate when raw materials must be ordered, how much time is needed in the production process, and how much time is involved in inventory storage and in shipping and handling. Discuss the raw materials that are used and how much they will cost. Who are your suppliers, where are they located, and why did you choose them? Although you may order from one main supplier, include information on alternate suppliers.

Address how you could handle a sudden increase in orders or a loss of a major supplier. How will the work get done and at what cost? Project peak production times and determine when money will be needed for key purchases. Include cost breakdowns in the Supporting Documents section to back up your statements.

Describe your production equipment and other product assets in terms of what you already own, what you plan to purchase, and how much it will cost. Again think in terms of dollars. When you are projecting cash flow, this information will provide the source for your financial assumptions regarding production equipment.

- **Distributors.** Describe the products that your company will be distributing and the manufacturers that will be your source for those products. Do you have alternate manufacturers that you can use or are you dependent on certain manufacturers. As a distributor, will you purchase your products prior to selling them – or – will you purchase at a discount as the sales are made? What are your terms? You might find it helpful to use a table with columns listing the products, manufacturers, terms, and alternate sources.

- **Manufacturers and Distributors.** If you are anticipating importing raw materials or finished products for distribution in this country and/or abroad, expand your business plan to include global information.

  Be sure that you can identify the steps involved in bringing goods into this country or in shipping them overseas along with the time and costs involved. You may be working with foreign manufacturers and agents. You will deal with freight forwarders and custom brokers. The cost of their services and the time and method of payment will also affect your cash flow.

If you are a retailer

Describe the main types (or categories) of products that you sell. Describe your product selection process and why specific suppliers or vendors were chosen. If you are the retailer of a small number of products, you can list them individually followed by information on the source, purchase price (discount), and selling price (markup).

If timing is of significance, you can use a flow chart to demonstrate the distribution process. How do the products you sell in your shop get from the manufacturer through your industry's normal distribution channels, into your store, onto your shelves, and into your customers' hands?

What is your system for managing and tracking inventory? How do you determine the volume of goods you need to stock in inventory and see that it is maintained?

"Bricks" and/or "Clicks" Retailers

Who are you? Do you have a straight brick and mortar business or are you strictly an online retailer (e-tailer) — or are you a combination of both? In many ways the retailing process is much the same whether you do your selling online or from a physical location. You still need to deal with wholesalers, product mix, promotion, etc.

However, the way you deal with inventory may be significantly different. Although brick and mortar businesses often sell their goods via the Internet, they traditionally stock their full line of products and offer immediate fulfillment of orders. Retailers who sell solely via the Internet, however, frequently stock only high volume items and consignment goods. It is not uncommon for e-tailers to stock no inventory and to depend on the wholesaler for fulfillment of their orders.

 E-Tailers. *If you are planning your website, you will find it very useful to check out the Summary Steps for E-Tailers on page 16.*

If you provide a service

Tell what your service is, why you are able to provide it, how it is provided, who will be doing the work, and where the service will be performed. Tell why your business is unique and what you have that is special to offer to your customers. If you have both a product and a service that work together to benefit your customer (such as warranty service for the products you sell), be sure to mention this in your plan.

Consider equipment and supplies needed to perform your service together with associated costs. Think about other related overhead. Will you be providing service at the customer's location or will you work from an office or shop?

Of primary concern to a service provider is the relationship between the amount of time spent in providing the service and the amount of time that can actually be billed to the customer. Even if the service is billed by the job, rather than by the hour, it will be necessary to plan carefully to see that compensation is adequate to cover the time spent providing the service. Remember that time involved and billable hours are a key to success for a service provider.

In all cases

You will need to know if you will be selling the same products and/or services online as you do offline or if you will limit your website sales to specific items? You will also need to consider future services or products that you plan to add to your business.

Try to think about potential problem areas and work out a plan of action.

Administrative Plan
(Organizational Plan: Section III)

This section of the Organizational Plan will show how your business is put together administratively. It will help you to setup your business so that it will function in an efficient and cost-effective manner.

Keep in mind, as you write about each of the following areas, that you will need to approach them in terms of revenues and expenses that will be related to each of your decisions. That way, when you are working on the Financial Plan, you will have the dollar figures to carry over into your financial statements.

Examples

- *If you plan to have employees, project how many hours they will work and at what rate. Also project increased revenue you might expect because you have those employees.*

- *If you have decided to incorporate, address associated costs (attorney, incorporation fee, etc.).*

- *If you are leasing a building, find out about associated costs, such as utilities, insurance, improvements, etc. If the building is larger than a previous facility, what effect will the added space have on revenues you generate or costs you incur?*

- *If you develop a website, how much will you spend on the initial development? How often and at what cost will it be updated? Will you have an in-house web specialist? What are your web hosting costs?*

Location

If location *is not* a marketing decision, you will include it in this section. Two examples of businesses of this type might be a web seller or a manufacturer that ships by common carrier such as United Parcel Service. Their locations would not be directly tied to their target markets. However, if location *is* a marketing consideration, you may prefer to address it in your marketing plan. For example, if you are opening a retail shop that needs to be directly accessible to customers, your choice of location will be determined by your target market and might, therefore, be more aptly addressed in your Marketing Plan. You might begin writing about your location as follows:

> *AeroTech, Inc.* is housed in 10,000 square feet of warehouse space located at 372 E. Main Street, Burke, NY. This space was chosen because of accessibility to shipping facilities, good security provisions, low square footage costs, and proximity to sources of supply.

Now expand on each reason and back up your statements with a physical description of the site and a copy of the lease agreement.

Your lease or rental agreement will contain the financial information needed for monthly cost projections for the Cash Flow statement. The value of property owned will be transferred to a balance sheet in the Financial Documents section. If you are a new business, you should plan for associated costs such as utilities, improvements, office furniture, and equipment.

Give background information on your site choice. List other possible locations and tell why you chose your location. You may want to include copies of pictures, layouts, or drawings of the location in the Supporting Documents section.

A **Location Analysis Worksheet** is included at on page 343 of this book. This worksheet is intended as a guideline for writing a location (site) analysis.

Legal Structure

Describe the legal structure you have chosen and explain why it is the most advantageous for your business. Name the owners or corporate officers, highlight their strengths and weaknesses, and include resumes of each one in the Supporting Documents section of your business plan.

If you anticipate changing your legal structure in the future, make projections regarding why you would change, when the change would take place, who would be involved, and how the change will benefit the company (for example, if your exit strategy is to form an IPO).

If you are a sole proprietor. Give a brief overview of your experience and abilities. As a sole proprietor, you assume 100% of the risk. Evaluate your strengths and weaknesses and state your plans for getting help in needed areas. Do you have current relationships with associates who will serve as advisors in various capacities?

If you have formed a partnership. Explain why the partners were chosen, what they bring to the company, and how their abilities complement each other. Show their experience and qualifications by including copies of their resumes. Include a copy of your partnership agreement in the Supporting Documents section. Your agreement should include provisions for partners to exit and for the dissolution of the company. Spell out distribution of the profits and financial responsibility for any losses. Explain the reasoning behind the terms of your agreement.

If you have formed an LLC or a corporation. Outline the company's legal structure (limited liability company, S corporation, nonprofit corporation, professional corporation, etc.) and give highlighted information on the owners or corporate officers. Who are they, what are their skills, why were they chosen, and what will they bring to the organization? Include a copy of the charter and articles in the Supporting Documents. If you have a Board of Directors or Advisory Board, tell who they are and what they bring to the table that will further your company's goals.

Management and Personnel

Your management and personnel needs will be determined by the capabilities of the business owners, by the amount of time they will be able to commit to the business, and by the demands of the marketplace. Small businesses usually start up with the owners doing most of the work. As the business becomes larger and sales increase, your management and personnel needs will also change. Project your company's goals for growth and plan for the changes that will be necessitated in management and personnel.

Management

The most critical issue to be addressed in your business may well be that of management. Many potentially profitable operations have failed due to inability to effectively manage the company's overall operation. One of the first questions that a potential lender or investor will ask is, "Why should your management team be entrusted with our money?" Several years ago investment capital was flowing heavily into high tech start-ups based on great ideas, but little experience. Most of them failed. There is still available capital, but the rules have changed. The new investment business model is the company with the proper mix of entrepreneurial vision and an experienced management team.

As the decision maker in your business, two of the questions you will need to ask yourself are, "What are the key areas of management in my business?" and "What outside help will I require?"

Managerial hiring policies, job descriptions, and employee contracts are all part of making the right choices. Decide how your managers will be compensated: salaries, benefits, bonuses, vacation time, stock purchase plans.

An organizational chart (see example below) can visually show areas of responsibility and the personnel in charge of each section along with the number of employees they will manage. For example, you may need key people in charge of administration, operations, marketing, and finance. Each of these individuals may have middle managers that they will supervise. In turn, the vice president of marketing might be directly responsible for middle managers whose responsibilities are divided into website marketing, media advertising, and public relations. If you are involved in global trade, you may need a manager for international marketing.

Partial Organizational Chart
AeroTech, Inc.

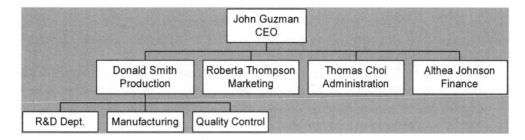

Personnel

How many employees will be needed for the company to operate efficiently? What jobs will you need them for? At what stage in the business will they be hired? What qualifications/experience will they need to have? What hours will they work? What salaries and benefits will they be paid?

Some businesses fail because they hire too many people too soon, anticipating more than their market share of business. Other businesses fail because they become too successful too soon and they are not organizationally ready. Your business plan is the key to responding promptly to the unexpected in order to keep your business progressing smoothly.

If you are seeking a lender or an investor, you will frequently hear them refer to what is known as the "Best- and Worst-Case Scenarios." They want to know that you will be able to identify potential problems and to work out solutions before these difficulties occur. It is to your advantage to prepare for the unexpected so your business can continue to run smoothly. In the "best-case," do you have enough people to handle an unexpected influx in sales? In the "worst-case," if sales projections are not achieved, are there other ways in which you can generate revenue? Will you be required to reduce staff or will they be able to fill other positions? For example, if sales drop off at your sporting goods store, could personnel increase revenues by teaching in-store classes or by holding sports clinics?

I like to use this section to list the current employees on the company payroll and follow with a hiring plan for the future. For each, list the type of employee, desired qualifications, salary and benefits, and when you expect the hiring to take place. This will provide the financial assumptions to plan your cash flow.

 Example. To see a good example, see Appendix I, Marine Art of California. Mr. Garcia did an excellent job of addressing this topic in his plan.

Accounting and Legal

Accounting

Describe your accounting department. Tell what accounting system will be used and why it was chosen. What portion of your accounting/recordkeeping will be done internally? Who will be responsible for the reliability and efficiency and those records? Will you be using an outside accountant to maximize your profits? If so, who within your company will be skilled at working with the accountant—and who will be responsible for reading and analyzing the financial statements provided by the accountant?

It is important to show not only that your accounting will be taken care of, but that you will have some means of using your financial statements to implement changes to make your company more profitable. After reading this section, a lender or investor should have confidence in your company's ability to keep and interpret a complete set of financial records. Information regarding your accounting and the auditing of your books is often requested on the Business Financial Statement provided by potential lenders and investors. If you plan to hire someone to do internal accounting, the salaries should be covered under management or personnel. If you will be utilizing outside accounting professionals, be sure to incorporate their fees into your financial projections.

Legal

Murphy's Law will prevail in this area for sure. Just when you think you don't need legal help, you do. Before your company suddenly finds itself in a position that requires the immediate services of a good attorney (contracts, proprietary issues, disputes, etc.), you should practice due diligence and align yourself with a legal firm that specializes in working with your type of business.

Larger firms often have an in-house legal department. Be sure to budget for in-house staff in your personnel plan. If you plan to keep an attorney on retainer, be include the amount in your financial assumptions.

Insurance

Insurance is an important consideration for every business. The goal is to protect your company against common claims and against serious risks for your particular industry. Talk with a reputable insurance agent. Consider the types of coverage appropriate to your business. Plan to adopt aggressive policies to reduce the likelihood of insurance claims.

Product liability is a major consideration, especially in certain industries. Service businesses are concerned with personal liability, insuring customers' goods while on the premises or during the transporting of those goods. If a vehicle is used for business purposes, your insurance must reflect that use. If you own your business location, you will need property insurance. If you lease, you may need insurance relating to content or inventory. Some types of businesses require bonding. Partners may want life insurance naming each other as the beneficiary. Decisions will need to be made about major medical insurance that you intend to provide for management and/or employees.

Exporters may reduce risks by purchasing export credit insurance from the Export-Import Bank of the U.S. agent, the Foreign Credit Insurance Association. Policies for exporters include insurance for financing or operating leases, medium term insurance, the new-to-export policy insurance for the service industry, and the umbrella policy.

 Keep your insurance information current. An **Insurance Update Form** is provided for you in the Blank Forms section of the book on page 342. Use it to maintain information on alternate insurance companies. If your premiums are suddenly raised or your coverage is canceled, you will be able to refer to the form in order to quickly find another carrier.

Security

As many as a third of small business failures are the result of dishonesty. Security involves not only theft of office supplies, equipment, and inventories by employees and/or customers, but also the theft of information. Address the issue of security as it relates to your business.

Again there will be some important decisions to be made. Product businesses will probably have inventory controls to establish. Service businesses may need to protect client information as well as their own business information.

In this age of advanced technology, major concerns have surfaced regarding Internet, Intranet, and Extranet security. Among the important questions to be answered are those relating to the transfer of information via the Internet. Businesses that accept credit cards online need to protect their customer's vital information through the establishment of a secure website. They also need to protect their own proprietary information from intruders into their systems.

Anticipate problem areas in your business, identify security measures you will put into practice. Tell why you chose them and what you project they will accomplish. Discuss this area with your insurance agent. You may be able to lower certain insurance costs while protecting your business.

Intellectual Property

If you own intellectual property or proprietary rights, you can address it at this point. Your designs, products, inventions, and ideas can be protected under United States and international intellectual property laws, which cover trademarks, patents, and copyrights. Intellectual property is a highly specialized area of the law and it is best to speak with an expert who can go over the unique details of your own design. You will need to back up your statements by including copies of registrations, photos, diagrams of products in development, or any other pertinent information in Supporting Documents.

- **Patents** secure an inventor's exclusive right to make, use or sell an invention for a term of years. Your design for a new product may not be an invention in a technical sense, but the idea is certainly your intellectual property.

- **Trademarks** by definition point distinctly to the origin or ownership of merchandise to which it is applied. A trademark is legally reserved to the exclusive use of the owner as maker or seller. A distinctive logo, insignia, or domain name can also be protected by a trademark. The symbol ™ is used when a trademark application is in progress; the symbol ® is used when the trademark is officially registered.

- **Copyright** protection exists for original works of authorship fixed in any tangible medium of expression, such as literary, musical and dramatic works, pictorial, graphic and sculptural works, sound recordings and architectural works. Copyrights are indicated by the symbol © before the name and year of the copyright holder. Copyright protection does not apply to things such as ideas, procedures, processes or concepts. Website material is usually copyrighted; so are lengthy corporate writings.

Summary

In this chapter, you have covered all of the areas that should be addressed in the Organizational Plan. If you have been thorough, it will help you to anticipate problem areas and to be prepared with solutions.

You are now ready to go to the next chapter to formulate your Marketing Plan.

Part II
The Marketing Plan

The marketing section of your business plan defines all of the components of your marketing strategy. When you write your Marketing Plan, you will address the details of your market analysis, sales, advertising, and public relations campaigns. The Plan should also integrate traditional (offline) programs with new media (online) strategies.

This chapter describes a very comprehensive list of marketing plan components. These components represent a full spectrum of marketing possibilities.

If your business is larger and more complex—and you are financially able, you will address most of these components in order to develop an aggressive marketing plan.

> *Note: You can use the headings and subheadings in the **Marketing Plan Outline** at the end of the chapter as a guide to follow in laying out your own Marketing Plan, omitting those that do not apply to your business.*

If your business is very small, you will not need to include all of the components. You will have to decide which ones fit within the scope of your business. However, your marketing plan should still contain the following major sections:

- ✓ *Market Analysis*
  (Target Market, Competition, Industry Trends)

- ✓ *Sales Strategy (Online and Offline)*

- ✓ *Advertising (Traditional and Web)*

- ✓ *Public Relations*

- ✓ *Customer Service*

Overview and Goals of a Marketing Strategy
(Marketing Plan: Section I)

Your marketing strategy is the comprehensive approach your business will take to achieve your business objectives.

Definition of a Marketing Strategy

Your marketing strategy integrates the activities involved in marketing, sales, advertising, public relations, and networking. Each of these components of your overall marketing strategy serves a unique purpose, offers specific benefits, and complements every other component. All components must work together to enhance your company image, reinforce your brand strength, and ensure that your company is distinct from your competitors. A list of the major components of a successful multi-media (online and offline) marketing strategy is shown in Figure 5.1, pages 68-70.

The traditional (offline) and new media (online) components of your marketing strategy should all fit together precisely. These components include promotion of your range of services and products; determination of your prices or rate structure; creation of an advertising plan, public relations endeavors, promotional campaigns; and a long list of multi-media considerations. It is important to think through your strategy and gather information about your market and your competition *before* you set your fee structure or book ad space. Trial-and-error marketing plans are too expensive.

Marketing is one area in which assistance is offered through a wide variety of local and national sources. At its best, marketing is a specialized field where you can learn a lot quickly by listening to experts. Your local Small Business Development Center (SBDC) offers workshops on marketing, publications and reference materials at little or no cost to you. They will have consultants on staff or readily available to help you out. Self-help business books are also available in abundance on every aspect of your marketing plan.

The purpose of this chapter is to outline marketing fundamentals as they relate to formation of the marketing section of your business plan.

Goals of Your Marketing Strategy

What do you hope to accomplish through your marketing strategy? Your market research, advertising campaigns, sales incentives, public relations efforts, and networking plans should all move your business in the direction of achieving your marketing goals. Many companies hope to expand their customer base, increase sales, achieve profitability, promote new products and services, and other similar idealistic objectives. Not every business owner, however, can articulate precisely what these goals mean for his/her own company.

The best marketing plans are results-oriented; they define specific, realistic, measurable goals within time parameters. All sales, advertising, and public relations efforts are then designed to work together to achieve these goals. If the goals are not accomplished within a planned schedule, individual components of the marketing plan should be reassessed and redesigned.

Goals of your marketing strategy, for example, could include creating a strong brand, building a strong customer base, increasing product/service sales, and developing a social media presence. Each goal should be explained in specific terms, that is, what do these goals mean to your company? As an illustration, let's examine four examples of goals:

- **Create a strong brand.** What is the current level of brand awareness for your company/product/service? Are you starting from scratch or building on a familiar name? What are the characteristics of this brand that you want to reinforce in the minds of consumers? What level of brand awareness do you hope to achieve?

- **Build a strong customer base.** Who are your best customers? What customers are most likely to spend money, and return? What is the profile (demographics, psychographics) of your ideal customer? How can you reach this market, online and offline? What particular characteristics of your company/product/service are most likely to inspire loyalty in your ideal customers?

- **Increase product/service sales.** If this is an existing business, what is your current level of sales? If this is a start-up, or new division of an existing business, how can you predict the future demand for your product/service? What new level of sales growth can your business handle? What quantities of your product can you produce/distribute? What level of service can you support through existing or additional staff?

- **Develop a social media presence.** How will you integrate social media into your marketing strategy? Which social media channels, technologies, and tools do you plan to use? How do you plan to utilize them?

Your marketing activities will comprise a significant portion of your overall business expenses, so investors and bankers will need to understand the importance of the results you are seeking. Make it clear in the statement of your marketing goals that the expenditures you are about to delineate are crucial to the development and growth of your company. By clearly identifying the goals of your marketing plan, you will make a convincing case to support your financial projections.

Basic Marketing Questions

Four fundamental questions should be answered in order to identify your marketing goals—who, what, where, when, and how? Specifically:

- **Who** are your customers? Who are your competitors?

- **What** are you selling? What quantities and prices of your products will you sell?

- **Where** is your target market located? Where can you reach your target market?

- **When** are your customers most likely to buy? When are your busy seasons?

- **How** will you reach your customers (stores, offices, website, catalogs)?

Marketing Musts

Four activities will help you organize your marketing efforts in the most effective direction to achieve your goals.

1. **Sell selectively.** This will help you define your market niche. What will *you* offer that is distinctly different (better, less expensive, faster, higher quality, etc.) from *your competitors*? Why should anyone buy from you? What market share can you seek?

2. **Know your niche.** What type of individuals and/or businesses do you plan to serve? Start by answering in general terms (professionals, service companies, manufacturing, retail, etc.), Then try to be very specific. Spell out the demographics first—age, sex, income, etc.

   Then you can move on to psychographics, or lifestyle considerations. When you clearly define the population you hope to sell to, you'll have a better view of what services they require. Where do they spend their free time? What activities are they involved in? How do they spend their disposable income? This information leads you to details about what they read (therefore, where you'll want publicity and advertising coverage), where they hang out (for promotions and appearances), what they watch and listen to (if television and radio spots are on your mind). Then *go out and ask them what they want. Don't try to guess.* Find out what they really *need.* If your market is local (and where *is* local, anyway?), your small local newspapers probably offer affordable ad packages; chambers of commerce and professional organizations have newsletters that offer insert opportunities. But if you don't know *exactly where your market is*, you can't determine what your market reads.

3. **Create your pitch.** Define precisely what "your product/service attributes" mean so that your product or service comes *alive* for your prospective clients. Make it *so* important that they will no longer want to live or work without it. Appeal to their individual needs.

4. **Price for profits.** The goal of your business is to make a profit. Many start-up businesses fail to make a profit as early as projected because they didn't price properly. Know what your competition charges, and determine if you should be less than, equal to or higher priced. Be sure for product pricing that you have covered your materials, labor and overhead costs. Don't forget shipping, handling or storage in the total price. Service, like consulting, can be difficult to pinpoint. Some products and services will fall into an *hourly* rate structure; others are better-suited to a *service fee*. If you provide a service, you may even be on-call for a monthly service fee. Remember that small businesses often do not have big budgets, so if this is your market, your pricing decisions will have to take into account what your market will bear. Learn what your competition charges.

 Note: Worksheets are available in Appendix VI, pages 347-350 for each of the four *"Marketing Musts"* discussed above.

Market Analysis
(Marketing Plan: Section II)

The Market Analysis section of your Marketing Plan contains information about your target market, competitors, and marketing trends. Market research methods and results are also delineated in this section. Details about each of these components follow.

Identify Target Markets

Who are you selling to? Who are your ideal customers? Your target market should be defined in terms of demographics, psychographics, and special characteristics of niche markets, if applicable. For research information about your target market, we developed a special web page at www.business-plan.com/research/aybp.html. You will be guided through a full listing of marketing research sites with *hot links* to each of the resources.

Demographics refer to the statistical data of a population, including average age, income, and education. Government census data is a common source of demographic information.

Psychographics uses demographics to determine the attitudes and tastes of a particular segment of a population. Psychographics examines lifestyles: where people spend their vacations, where they shop, how they spend their disposable income, what sports they participate in or watch, which clubs/organizations they join, and more. Social media have proved to be of great value in helping businesses to research customer behavior and preferences.

Niche markets are a small segment of the population that shares common characteristics, interests, spending habits, etc. Successful niche marketing focuses on a small segment of a total market. It is the best strategy for a small business to achieve a market leadership position. It is expensive, and bland, to try to be all things to all people.

Examples of niche markets include SOHOs (small office/home office), Generation X or Y, cultural niches, hip hop, to name a few. Niche markets are better informed than the mass market experts in a particular area of special interest. They will demand communication that is content-rich and substantial to match their level of intelligence and depth of understanding.

BONUS. On pages 64-67, you will find a discussion on *"The Product-Market Analysis."* If you take the time to read and study it, you will learn the **Four Rules of Target Marketing** — or how to narrow your target market by making two important decisions: which customer needs you will satisfy and who the specific customers are to whom you wish to sell your products and/or services.

Research Your Competition

Who is competing with you? After you have identified your target market, it is important to discern what other companies are after the same market. What are their strengths and weaknesses relative to your business? If you are not certain who your competitors are, use several search engines to see what company names are presented when you seek your own products and services online. Remember that because it is so easy to check out any company online and obtain far more detail than you could have acquired by a telephone call or brochure, many individuals and businesses will follow this procedure. If you *don't* do it, you'll be working in the dark.

Check trade associations, and manufacturing company listings, and other directories available in your library Reference section if you want to do an offline search. An easier place to start, however, is to hunt for information about your competitors at www.business-plan.com/research/aybp.html (our special website). Click on the link to "Using the Internet for Competitive Intelligence" and you can go directly to an article archived on the CIO.com website.

In researching your competitors, check out the general health of the business, their approach to marketing, and their financial information. In addition, specifically investigate the following in depth:

> **Check out their websites.** Examine their design, format, and content. Is the site professional and complete? What features and benefits do they promote? How do they position their product/services to their target market? What websites do they link to? What is the nature of the content they provide? Do they offer any community-building, message boards, or chat rooms? Do they feature special events?

> **Determine their level of activity on social media.** What sites do they have links to? What are they doing on those sites that will enhance their businesses?

> **Investigate the prices of their products and services.** How do they compare to yours? Do they offer the same products/services? Do they offer discounts? Any other special offers?

☞**Note:** You will find a *Competition Comparison Worksheet* on page 346 in Appendix VI. You can fill out a worksheet for each of your major competitors.

Assess Market Trends

Your marketing plan should reflect your observations and insight about trends in your industry and in your target market. Information about the general direction of the marketplace can help you target *what people want*. Futurist Faith Popcorn identified sixteen market trends in her book, *Clicking* (HarperCollins, 1996) that are still accurate today. She coined the phrase "cocooning" to describe the phenomenon of staying-at-home to relax and unwind. Dramatic increases in the sales of home theatre equipment, rentals of VHS/DVD movies, and take-out food are a testimonial to the longevity of this trend. Another of her trends, called "small indulgences," which describes our desire to reward ourselves for our hard work with affordable luxuries, is evident as Starbucks coffee and Godiva chocolate shops become neighborhood staples and shopping mall anchors. What market trends will have an impact on your business, influencing the demand for your products and services? Are you on-trend?

Industry trends influence almost every business within its segment. These are major trends such as the increase in service businesses in the U.S., the decline of manufacturing, the precarious position of Internet pure-plays, to name a few.

Target market trends, like the events categorized by Faith Popcorn and other marketing gurus, have an impact on the direction of a smaller segment of the population or business community. Trends can be influenced by demographics, such as the aging of our population and huge number of baby-boomers reaching age 50 every minute, or by cultural and social influences outside the realm of demographics. Examples of market trends that evolve from demographic shifts include the increase in the number of assisted-living facilities, and the growth of innovative products and services designed for a more "youthful" retired population.

The shifting demographics of online shoppers will have an important influence on companies that plan to reach their target market via Internet sales. The fastest-growing online demographic group today is 45 to 64 year-old Internet users. This means baby boomers are reaching critical mass online as well as offline. The number of online female shoppers is increasing more rapidly than male shoppers in every age bracket. Your marketing plan should demonstrate that you have analyzed market trends and have considered these trends in the creation of your marketing strategy.

Conduct Market Research

Market research can prevent your company from making erroneous decisions that result in expensive design mistakes in new products, marketing campaigns, and more. Market research has traditionally been conducted through techniques such as questionnaires, polls, surveys, and focus groups. Today your business can take advantage of both online and offline market research techniques.

Methods of Research

Questionnaires can be administered by paper or by online surveys. In either case, questionnaires are more likely to be answered if there is an incentive (reward) for the consumer to respond. Questionnaires are administered to a representative sample of the target market. Online questionnaires that are non-intrusive, optional, and offer a "thanks for your time" incentive can provide the most timely and valuable information. The incentive could be a discount on the respondent's next purchase, for example, or a coupon for a popular business product or service.

Focus Groups offer more insight regarding customer preferences and thought processes than questionnaires. In focus groups, small groups of consumers are brought together under the direction of a moderator while researchers record their observations (usually behind one-way mirrors or on videotape), responses, reactions, and comments. Consumer feedback about new product developments, pricing structures, and branding issues can be analyzed relatively quickly using the focus group technique. Participants are usually paid for their time.

Focus groups can also be conducted online using an Internet chat room. The greatest advantage of online focus groups is the speed with which they can be arranged and the reduced travel costs. Observers can watch from their computers, interject questions to probe an issue in more depth, and no one is inconvenienced.

Surveys—telephone surveys are the terror of many quiet dinners and have become increasingly unpopular (and unreliable). Online surveys, on the other hand, meet with surprising success if presented positively. Websites can include several questions (un-intrusive, simple, quick to answer) in their format to elicit comments and suggestions from website visitors, particularly shoppers.

Because surveys are shorter than questionnaires, a *reward* isn't necessary. With guarantees of privacy and a promise not to re-sell or relay the respondents' information to other sources, it is often possible to acquire constructive information quickly.

Database analysis

What kinds of information will you want to collect and store to help you make better executive decisions about your business? If you store information in a data warehouse for later analysis, your data warehouse systems can help you identify trends within your company in sales, marketing, production, and finance. The sales and marketing data will be particularly useful for managing your marketing plan.

Contents of Your Marketing Strategy
(Marketing Plan: Section III)

In this section of your marketing plan, the contents shift from descriptive to extremely detailed. For example, when you describe your sales strategy, you will also elaborate on the materials you will produce and the campaigns you will organize.

When you define your advertising strategy, you will need to identify how you will spend your money on each medium and in what markets. Web advertising campaigns will be described in terms of specific portals, size of banner ads, frequency of e-mail marketing, and more.

General Description

This section of your marketing plan introduces the sections which follow and provides a brief synopsis. This section should include: (1) the allocation of your efforts (i.e., the percentage of your total budget dedicated to online marketing vs. offline marketing), and (2) the components that are expected to generate the greatest percentage of new business.

Method of Sales and Distribution

How will your company reach your customers? Are your sales primarily handled by bricks (physical stores), clicks (website), catalogs (direct mail), or hybrid (multiple channels)? Do you have plans to expand your methods of sales/distribution as sales increase?

Stores or physical offices should be described by size, location, and physical characteristics in reasonable detail. Kiosks and other additional methods of sales should also be included.

Catalogs should be described in terms of size, frequency of mailings, and approximate number of items offered.

Website information should include design information, description of contents and major features, hosting arrangements, technological considerations, credit card processing, security arrangements, and other details about the creation and maintenance of this website. If your business will operate primarily as an online store or distributor, some of this information will already be covered in other sections of your business plan. If your company will be listed in online malls (zShops at Amazon.com, iMall, shopping@Yahoo!, to name a few) include details about your arrangement and fees in this section of your marketing plan.

Packaging

If you provide a product, your *packaging* will be a crucial early consideration. If you are not a trained or talented designer, seek assistance for this. Packaging has a huge impact on the consumer's decision to buy.

If you provide a service, the "package" is you. Your company *image* should be defined before you begin any other marketing efforts. The image of a professional such as a lawyer or accountant, for example, involves building a private practice that will be distinctly different from an advertising agency seeking clients in the fashion industry. Your message should come across loud and clear. Are you conservative? Trendy? Cost-conscious? Flashy? Keep your message consistent and simple for your market. All your online and offline marketing efforts, your sales pitch, public relations activities, advertising, and promotional campaigns should be supportive of one another and of your image.

Pricing Policy

How much flexibility is there in your pricing strategy? What is your price floor (the lowest price you can charge and still cover your costs) and what is your price ceiling (the highest price the market will bear)? Your marketing plan must address your pricing policy and how prices can be adjusted if necessary to increase demand or cover unanticipated revenue shortfalls.

Price strategy. You may find the range between your price floor and price ceiling offers considerable leeway. Somewhere in this range is the right price point for your product or service. How do you find out what that point is? Your pricing strategy can be tested through focus groups and surveys. What price is the average customer willing to pay? Another way to determine pricing that has become a new trend with entrepreneurs is to test-market through online sales on the auction Website eBay (www.ebay.com). This Website can provide insight to what the market will bear and how hot the product really is perceived to be. EBay has become such a popular resource for small business owners that the website now offers special services for small companies to sell their products directly through eBay.

Competitive position. Should your prices be greater than, less than, or equal to your competitors? Do you need to adjust your prices when your competitors make a change? If you are claiming to offer the highest quality and most personalized service, you may be able to justify charging more than your competitors. If you are appealing to a more "elite" clientele than your competitors, you will also be able to establish your pricing independently. If you hope to beat your competitors on price by going lower, you'll have to be sensitive to your price floor—what you can truly afford to discount and still be a profitable business?

If you want to remain equal to your competitors you'll have to be extremely sensitive to any "value-added" offerings and special promotions they are offering that can work as sales incentives, drawing customers away from your business and toward theirs. Your quick and well-formulated response to your competitors' special offers will be critical.

Branding

What do current and prospective customers think of your brand? Branding defines and focuses a company's image. Strong brands today are reinforced through a mix of advertising online and offline, sales and customer service efforts, sales incentives that combine online and offline offerings, and public relations strategies that incorporate all sales channels. Consumer reaction defines the brand in the long run. Branding emphasizes the need to build an emotional connection between your products and your purchasers.

Database Marketing

Database analysis enables a company to personalize their marketing campaign. With personalization, information is presented to customers based on the study of their previous buying patterns. Personalized, or one-to-one, marketing attempts to anticipate what customers are seeking, predicting future behavior from past choices.

If your business integrates customer information from databases that track their shopping behavior from their catalog purchases to their shopping mall trips to their e-commerce buys, you can maximize personalization. Personalization can be used most effectively in Web sales. For example, you can send personalized e-mail notices about upcoming sales, special promotions, or new product releases that may be of special interest based on the individual's past purchases.

Sales Strategies

This section outlines your use of online and offline sales materials to reach your target market. Traditional sales involve the creation of printed materials to accompany your sales efforts. Online sales involve refinement of your Web strategy in order to present your products and services in the best possible manner.

Direct Sales

If you are a start-up company, you may find yourself working as both CEO and chief salesperson (not to mention, head of office maintenance...).

Your marketing plan should identify how you plan to contact prospects, what materials you will send out or deliver, and what follow-up will occur. Your direct sales approach should combine offline (personal) contact with prospective customers and online sales through your website.

> **Offline sales** require materials that can be sent to prospective customers and brought with a salesperson (or you) to presentations. Do you have to design new sales materials? What is required? Will you have to create a new logo and graphics for your material? Consider the traditional list of printed materials: brochures, pamphlets, flyers, stationery, business cards, catalog, promotional flyers, etc. Identify the specific materials that you will need to design and print for use in your sales campaign.

> **Online sales** require a website and social media that double as marketing tools. In addition to the technological considerations of site design, special attention must be directed to engaging the site visitor and providing incentives to buy. Websites and social media sites that contain creative features that attract new visitors and encourage them to return to the site are called "sticky," which refers to the ability of a site to bring visitors back for additional shopping. Your online "pitch" must be just as engaging and irresistible as your in-person sales appeal.

> Two important early steps of your online sales strategy are search engine registration and website and social media optimization. Search engines direct traffic to your website. They rank sites by such things as frequent updating, popularity, etc. Businesses optimize (SEO) their websites and their social media sites so they will be found by the search engines. Frequent updating of your website, Facebook, blogs, tweets, etc. – plus "likes" and "follows" – improve chances to achieve higher placement.

Direct Mail

The cost of direct mail campaigns has been estimated to be about $1 to $2 per item. As postage and paper costs escalate, direct mail becomes a less attractive sales option. If your business decides to conduct a direct mail campaign, you may find it preferable to create your own mailing list rather than purchase a list, unless you deal with a reputable list supplier that guarantees their list is current and highly accurate. But even with the best mailing list, be prepared for a low rate of return. Direct mail coupled with incentive offerings can be slightly more effective.

E-Mail Marketing

Compared to direct mail, e-mail marketing is a bargain at $.01 to $.25 per item. E-mail marketing has now outpaced direct mail, according to experts. E-mail correspondence is more likely to be read than direct mail. It offers opportunities to send personalized offers, based on your understanding of your customers' preferences. However, your company must avoid spamming, or sending unwanted e-mail (like junk mail) to large lists of recipients. To avoid any perception of spamming, your e-mail marketing strategy should allow for "opt-in" and "opt-out"—the method by which your customers and website visitors elect to receive future e-mail correspondence from you or decline if they are not interested.

Affiliate Marketing

Affiliate marketing engages the services of a virtually limitless sales force through some type of commission structure for sales, leads, or website visits. Affiliates are only paid for the actual sales, and their commission is a small percentage of the total sale. One of the most popular affiliate programs is run by Amazon.com (www.amazon.com). Affiliates of Amazon, who link their website visitors to Amazon's website, earn a five percent commission on completed sales. If they elect to sell Amazon products on their own Website they can earn a larger commission of fifteen percent. Affiliate programs can offer a creative strategy for service-based businesses to sell related products on their website without having to develop the products themselves.

Reciprocal Marketing

Arrangements in which one company offers customers a discount for another company's goods, either in their store or on their website, are examples of reciprocal marketing. Creative opportunities within local communities or online communities can make this a beneficial and inexpensive alternative to promote your company. Chambers of Commerce often extend these offers within their own circle of member businesses. Online opportunities can cross these geographic boundaries to offer virtually limitless possibilities among complementary companies.

Viral Marketing

Viral marketing occurs when a company offers something that people find so intriguing that they spread the word on their own. In order to be effective, your company offering must be simple, entertaining, or engaging in some way. It also must include your company's insignia or the whole point is missed. Viral marketing by word-of-mouth has been highly effective, but viral marketing by the Web has even greater impact. Word can spread more quickly, and to greater numbers of people, by e-mail and forwarded web links than by telephone calls. And when people see an e-mail from someone they know, they are most likely to read it.

Sales Incentives/Promotions

Sales incentives can be offered at physical stores and offices, through direct mail, and by your website. A combination of promotional offers that reach customers through multiple channels is most likely to give you the best return on your investment.

The most important consideration is that your sales incentives should have a direct tie-in to your company so that customers remember your business as well as your promotional offer.

Promotions like *free samples*, *give-aways*, and *incentive items* (pens, pads, gadgets, etc.) are important components of any trade show exhibit—they're expected. *Sweepstakes* have the potential to attract attention both online and offline. *Cash-back coupons* and *discount coupons* also work well in both channels. The combination of discount coupons and an e-mail marketing campaign can be particularly effective.

Advertising Strategies

Advertising is the most potentially expensive investment of your marketing strategy. Because of the high costs involved, the efforts should be researched thoroughly before you begin. This is not an area for amateurs. If you hire no other consultants, and you know you need to advertise your business, hire someone with advertising expertise. The standards today are very high, even in the smallest local papers. Online advertising is a relatively new field and uses different guidelines than print. Graphics, photos, layouts, text, and design have to be completely professional for a positive impact in both the online and offline advertising options.

If you can pinpoint your target market in the finest detail, you can specify precisely where your ad campaign should be located. Size, timing, duration, frequency all come into play. Don't try this by trial and error. Get guidance from an expert.

Traditional Advertising

How will you invest your advertising dollars in traditional media? Traditional media includes television, radio, print, and extreme advertising. Your investment in market research truly pays off when you begin to determine how to allocate your advertising budget. Only the venues that have an impact on your target market are worth your investment. What television shows do they watch? What radio programs do they listen to? What do they read for business and for entertainment? Where are they traveling and by what method of transportation? With accurate market research to guide you, you can avoid costly advertising mistakes.

> **Television (network and cable).** Network television advertising remains the most costly advertising investment. Within this top tier, the highest price for commercial time is still the Super Bowl. Network prime time follows in rank-order, followed by non-prime time network buys. In spite of the recent growth of national cable television, network television advertising still has the power to create brands in a way that few other advertising alternatives can. Major corporations seek prime advertising spots, and are willing to pay exorbitant rates to reach huge audiences and create a major impact.
>
> Cable advertising, which is predicted to assume an increasing share of the total television advertising dollars, works at several levels. National cable advertising can be as costly as network television programming, but local cable television offers rates that may be affordable for even very small businesses.

The additional expenses incurred with advertising—such as creating your commercials and identifying your media plan—must be factored into the total cost of your television advertising. A poorly crafted commercial placed in the wrong time slot may be worse than no commercial, and certainly will be worse for your budget.

Radio. Radio advertising offers small businesses an opportunity to reach a national or local audience with a rate schedule far below television advertising. Radio advertisements can reach your target market during business hours as well as personal time, during commute time, and mid-day programming. Since many businesspeople spend inordinate amounts of time driving from meeting to meeting, and others keep a radio on in the background while they work, radio advertising has become increasingly desirable.

Print. Your marketing research should provide you with information about the newspapers, magazines, periodicals, and professional or trade journals that are of interest to your target market. Print ads are most effective when they have a single focal point, a distinctive picture, and an explicit headline message of nine words or less.

Extreme advertising. Extreme advertising includes billboards, bus wraps, blimp, and any other form of oversize outdoor ads. Extreme advertising is most effective when the message is straightforward and simple, without complex graphics and extended narratives.

Web Advertising/New Media

Your online advertising dollars should be invested with the same care and precision as your investment in traditional media. Web advertising options include banner ads, pay per click advertising, mobile device advertising, advertising on portals, and interactive television. Market research again serves as the foundation from which to build your campaign, directing your strategy to include the online options that are most visible to your target market. What websites do they visit? Where do they shop online? What portals do they use?

Banner ads. Banner ads have been widely criticized, but they are still a popular form of online advertising. New standards for online ads, which include a more advertiser-friendly format that closely resembles a traditional print ad and a new form of sidebar, have breathed new life into banner ads. Even critics agree that banner ads offer a method of headlining a brand name over and over again, building brand awareness, even if the "click through" rate is lower than five percent.

Rich media (or multimedia) banner ads are believed to be three to five times more effective than standard ads, because they can be designed to be more creative and interactive. You need to understand your target market and their before you invest in this option.

Pay per click. Pay per click is a form of web advertising where you pay a certain amount when a visitor clicks on the link to your website. It allows you to control your advertising budget by giving you the ability to specify the maximum amount you are willing to pay for each click through. This click amount also determines how high your ad will place in search results. This service is available through various search engine websites such as Google ("AdWords"), Yahoo, and Bing.

Mobile device advertising. Mobile device advertising meets the unique space and size requirements of specific mobile devices. Advertising is most effective when it is specifically designed for these devices rather than personal computers. Web marketing campaigns need to be restructured to meet restrictions of smaller screen space, lack of color and font choices, graphic restrictions, and slow content delivery due to narrow bandwidth—restrictions that will eventually be eliminated. The best use of this form of advertising is to reach consumers on-the-go for things like travel arrangements, comparison pricing, auction bidding, hotel and entertainment plans, and stock activities.

Portals. Portals guarantee a tremendous number of viewers at an extremely high cost. Advertising on a portal is beyond the scope of most small businesses, but placement in a marketplace on a portal may be a way to build online traffic. Amazon.com's zShops, Shopping@Yahoo.com, iMall, and other similar locations offer the opportunity for broader exposure without the high price tag of a portal ad. Advertising on portals requires an understanding of consumer behavior in your target market to achieve the best results.

Interactive television. Interactive advertising, or advertising on "smart television," has evolved from the need to engage consumers in new and different ways to make an impact. Interactive television units are expected to increase worldwide in the next five years to over 81 million units, accompanied by an increase in interactive advertising. Interactive advertising is most effective when they are completely innovative, entertaining, and provide interesting content in a creative way.

Long-term Sponsorships

Sponsorships can be designed to meet the marketing goals of any company. Long-term sponsorships offer the benefit of helping to strengthen brand awareness in niche markets. In both the online and offline areas, long-term sponsorships help to build strong relationships with a business or organization and it's direct market, offering opportunities to co-brand multiple events, functions, advertisements, and more, providing high visibility for the advertiser. Co-branding can be set up as an exclusive arrangement or as a joint sponsorship among several complementary companies.

Public Relations

The primary difference between advertising and public relations is that you always pay for advertising space, while press coverage from your public relations efforts is "free" (aside from the fact that you may have paid to orchestrate the event that subsequently became newsworthy). Activities that demonstrate your strengths and the terrific qualities of your business in a newsworthy way can be of more value in the long run than the most expensive advertising campaign. Public relations campaigns strive to build credibility in the marketplace through routes that are more discreet than direct advertising.

Building an Online Presence

Your website and social media websites offer vehicles for public relations a company without an online presence can't imitate. Increasingly, customers and potential strategic partners check out a business online, and wonder whether a business that doesn't have a website and email address really exists. Research shows that almost two-thirds of people looking for a product or service in their community are more likely to use a business that displays information on a social media site. Different people may have broader or narrower definitions, but most will agree that social media are online platforms to provide interactive communication using web-based and mobile technologies. They are online content in the form of text, photographs, audio, video or graphics that invite comment, collaboration and exchange among participants.

Events (Online and Offline)

Can you create an event that will attract people to your Website or to your physical store or office location? Grand openings, anniversary celebrations, celebrity visits, and other creative events serve a dual purpose. If they are done well, they will reinforce your relationship with existing customers and attract new business. If they are significant and newsworthy events, you may be fortunate enough to receive press coverage.

Publicizing Your Efforts

Seek opportunities for press coverage of your work and your accomplishments whenever you can. Use your social media page to post events, announcements, news, or other company updates. The impact of public relations is cumulative. You may not see immediate results, so consistency is critical.

Press Releases

A simple press release, preferably one-page, accompanied by a photo, can gain more visibility for you than an advertisement if the newspapers pick it up. *Press releases* should be interesting, *newsworthy*, concise, and sent to the right person. Watch the newspapers carefully to determine who the correct contact for your press release is. The Business Editor generally receives huge numbers of releases. If a specific reporter tends to cover stories about your industry or interests, try addressing the release to that individual instead. The media brings you into the broader public view than your advertising can. It is your way to reach larger numbers in less time. Use it wisely.

Send your press releases to:

1. **Weekly newspapers** – reporters are always looking for great new stories.

2. **Daily newspapers** – usually want only a local twist, so stay close to home, unless it's a national story.

3. **Wire Services** – seek up-to-the-second news items, so move quickly if you have a hot item to report.

4. **Magazines** – offer a chance to look like an expert, but you will need longer lead time. Plan ahead.

5. **Radio** – attracts the attention of the mobile and the sedentary. A guest spot can boost you into a whole new spectrum.

6. **Television** – the most important medium to be prepared for. Take the time to learn how to present yourself on television to make effective use of the incredible power of this medium. With television, you need to be concise and controlled, speaking in sound bites to be sure your point gets across the way you want it to and isn't edited out.

Press kits can also be helpful. You can prepare your own press kit or hire a marketing consultant to help you out. Your press kit should build your credibility as an expert in your field or profession. It should include:

- a biography (short and directed to events that are significant today)
- a photo (headshot, 8x10 or 5x7 black and white)
- your brochure
- copies of articles that have quoted or featured you

Press kits can also be sent *electronically* as PDF files, html files, or in the body of emails. A press kit doesn't accompany every press release. It is used to introduce you as a resource, as an "expert" available when members of the media need a resource for quotes, opinions, inside information, validation, and more.

Networking

Networking can mean the difference between isolation and involvement for any business owner. For home-based businesses networking takes on a particularly significant role. It replaces the water-cooler and coffee-pot contact that occurs daily in every corporate office. Networking is by definition a supportive system of sharing information and services among individuals and groups having a common interest. Networking will keep you in contact with the outside world, help you avoid isolation and stagnation, and build your business contacts for current and future plans.

Networking is a two-way street, an *exchange* of information. Real networking requires that you do *more* than reach out to give and receive business cards. *Give* a little information, and *get* a sincere grasp of what one another's skills are. Then you've *really* reached out.

You will need to become involved in several levels of networks to provide contacts for you within:

- the business community at large
- your peer group of professionals
- your local community
- the world at large.

Involvement in some organization at each of these levels of networks will provide public relations opportunities that will not develop from within your own home. The following are a few ideas to get you started in each of these four areas:

The Business Community

Small business organizations offer the potential for small business owners to pull together for a bigger impact. The impact can be political, as it is in organizations whose mission is to lobby, or economic, as in those organizations that emphasize member benefits and discounts. In larger numbers there is certainly more influence. As a member of these groups, you may qualify for corporate rates on products and services, special discounts, and/or group rate health insurance. Examples include: National Association for the Self-Employed (NASE), National Small Business United (NSBU), and a host of local home-based business support groups.

It is a comfort to know that other business owners share your concerns and interests. The organizations mentioned above are very large national groups. Subsets of the business community may find what they need in other organizations, and often will join more than one as time and finances permit. The National Association of Women Business Owners (NAWBO), for example, is designed for women business owners of any size firm. NAWBO has statewide chapters that independently run monthly meetings and events, as well as a strong nationwide offering of conferences and workshops. New corporate discount packages are made available fairly often as this group draws the attention of major corporate sponsors.

Industry organizations often combine large corporations and small businesses, offering business owners an opportunity to meet with a diverse group of individuals. Statewide chambers of commerce and regional industry associations may be worth exploring.

Your Peer Group of Professionals

Professional associations are your link with other business leaders or owners, prospective customers/clients, sales leads, and sources for general business information. Membership fees vary, and benefits of membership include a wide range of products/services, such as membership directories, newsletters and other publications, discounts, group rates for programs, educational opportunities and more. Membership in these groups serves a different purpose for you. These groups are your resource for new information in your profession, mentors, support resources when your business grows and you need to hire help, virtually or actually. You may find it difficult to sell here, especially if you're among a group all selling the same thing. But you will absolutely need these contacts. And if you achieve a leadership position, you can also achieve public recognition. Not bad for public relations purposes.

Trade associations are available for almost every profession. You'll learn the secret handshake for your peer group, just as in professional associations. Membership rates and offerings vary. Monthly and annual meetings can help to keep you current in your own field, and help you find the best suppliers, vendors, etc. for your work. But the same word of caution applies here as above – you may not be closing sales deals within a group of your peers, but you need these contacts to thrive. As a leader, your opportunity for public recognition in your field will help you grow your business.

The Community

Civic organizations provide an opportunity for you to become active in local community service groups. Your local chamber of commerce is a good start. Local chambers will promote their own members' products and services over anyone else in the community. They will often publish their own directory and run their own schedule of business functions. If the mission of the group doesn't track with your objectives, keep the time you spend to a minimum but don't be a stranger. Let your specialty be well known, and define your area of expertise so that referrals will be passed your way. Lead a workshop. Be a speaker at a meeting.

Volunteer activities at local hospital, schools, libraries, and colleges are almost endless. Fundraising activities are usually a top priority. Volunteer to help with a task that offers you an opportunity to demonstrate your skill and talent. In this way, you'll not only help the organization, but also promote your talent through demonstration of your abilities.

The World At-Large

Don't lose your national and international focus, no matter how regional your business is today. Watch for events and opportunities that can bring you in contact with a wide range of people around the country, even if your business is geared to your own community. You can do a better job of serving *any* market you select if you are in touch with the outside world.

As soon as you realize your business has potential beyond the borders of the United States, start making connections in the global community. Use the contacts of corporations that have already opened doors to gain introductions and entry into this rapidly growing area for opportunity. Seek the international organizations that will give you both support and recognition.

Commitment

Your degree of involvement in any organization should reflect the importance of this organization or association to your business success—unless, of course, you are joining for purely social reasons. The best use of your time, however, will be to find and focus on a few organizations that offer both business and personal satisfaction. Why waste your time? In a position of leadership in any type of organization you will give the most time but will also gain the best contacts. You will get to know the most people. You will have the most opportunity for media exposure.

If you know that one particular organization is a great source of direct leads for your business, work your way into an active role in the leadership of the group. Start by participating on a committee to get a sense of the group and the internal dynamics. Determine how you can volunteer your time in a way that also provides you with an opportunity to showcase your skills. Your talents will be most visible to the group if you share them and help the association accomplish its goals. If you are only a name on a mailing list, you are less likely to be approached personally.

Customer Service
(Marketing Plan: Section IV)

Consumer expectations of high quality service must be met if you want to keep your customers. Consumers expect to be able to contact a customer representative with questions, concerns, problems, complaints, and returns. Business customers expect the same. Your business will need to identify your plans to meet these needs.

Description of Customer Service Activities

Will you offer 24/7 access to customer service representatives? Can your customers reach you by phone, fax, or e-mail at any time? As your business grows, you will probably need to consider the addition of the services of a call center, which offers uninterrupted service for your customers. How will you deal with customer contact in the meantime?

Expected Outcomes of Achieving Excellence

It's an old marketing maxim that it is far less expensive to retain existing customers than to add new ones, so your business gains an immediate benefit from building a loyal customer base.

Implementation of Marketing Strategy
(Marketing Plan: Section V)

As the scope of your marketing plan expands to include complex multimedia campaigns, the resources and skills of professionals may be needed to design the best approach.

In-House Responsibilities

Whether or not you outsource any or all of your marketing work, you and your team remain responsible for keeping your marketing plan on track. Your marketing plan should support your overall business objectives and work within the framework of your total business plan. You are ultimately responsible for ensuring that occurs.

Out-sourced Functions

Advertising, public relations, and marketing firms specialize in each component of your marketing plan identified in the previous pages. You may decide to hire an outside firm for only a portion of your marketing activities, such as advertising, for example. Advertising companies can generally offer as much or little support as you choose, from media planning to creating commercials. As a small business, you may be able to find a small advertising business that will offer a fee schedule that fits your budget. It's worth checking out.

Advertising Networks operate in a manner similar to traditional advertising companies, but they specialize in online advertising. Advertising networks like DoubleClick and 24/7 Media serve as brokers of Internet time and space. These companies collect online advertising inventory and sell spots to advertisers, saving clients the effort of examining advertising sites and negotiating deals. Ad networks can also focus on a specific target market segment and identify pertinent Websites. Their fee is paid as a percentage of ad sales or cost-per-thousand rate.

Assessment of Marketing Effectiveness
(Marketing Plan: Section VI)

Once your marketing plan is implemented, you will need to assess your results. You will need to continuously monitor the effectiveness of each online and offline campaign.

- Are your Website promotions reaching your target market?

- What online advertising methods are the most effective in driving traffic to your Website?

- What is the cross-over from online promotions to offline sales, and from offline promotions to online sales?

- Should certain radio, print, or television advertisements be strengthened?

- Should any be abbreviated or eliminated?

Assessment of the effectiveness of your marketing plan provides the management information you need to direct your future efforts and to make the wisest investment of your marketing dollars.

This completes the presentation of
the components of a winning marketing plan.

To Help You

The remaining pages in this chapter are as follows:

- **"Product-Market Analysis"** target marketing contribution by Don McCrea, previously referenced under the Target Market section. (pages 64-67)

- **Multi-Media Marketing Strategy tables** will make it easier to for you to plan your offline and online marketing strategy (pages 68-70).

- **"Social Media – Join the Revolution"** is a 4-page article contributed by Jan Norman, 25-year "It's Your Business" columnist for *The Orange County Register*. Learn what social media means, how their use has grown, how they supplement your marketing plan, what the different types are, and how to use them for your business. (pages 71-74)

- **Marketing Plan Outline** will provide you with an outline overview of the marketing plan components and will help you with the formatting and development of your own marketing plan (pages 75-76).

The Product-Market Analysis

developed and contributed by

Donald R. McCrea

Ph.D. and president of Bus-Ed Partners, Inc.
www.bus-edpartners.com

Before you write your Marketing Plan. The most important thing you need to do is to analyze your market and make a product-market decision. There are two parts to this decision:

1. The choice of which customer needs you will satisfy as reflected in the specific product or service you will sell to your customers.

2. The choice of the specific customers to whom you wish to sell your product or service (your target market segment).

Once you have made these decisions, you will be ready to write your marketing plan, as described previously in this chapter. If you take the time to do this analysis and carefully choose which customers you will market your product or service to, you will find that almost every prospect you talk to will have a need for what you're selling.

Choosing a group of customers to sell to (i.e., selecting a target market segment) means selecting potential customers according to some criteria you have determined are related to the likelihood these customers will want to buy your product or service. These criteria might include demographic factors such as age, income, or where they live; or lifestyle factors such as interest in sports, antique collecting, reading mystery novels, or seeing foreign movies. Your job as a businessperson is to determine what factors relate to your customers likelihood of buying your product or service.

Follow the Four Rules for Marketing and Sales Success

The following four rules for marketing and sales success are designed to help you analyze your market and choose the customers who are more likely to want to buy your product or service. Focusing your marketing and selling efforts on these customers will make finding and keeping new customers easier for you than if you are less selective about which customers you target.

> **Note.** These rules apply equally whether you are selling to consumers or you are selling to other businesses. The rules also apply to you whether you are a start-up or an existing business.

Rule #1:

Find Potential Customers Who Want Your Product or Service

If your potential customers are consumers, will they recognize that they have a need or want? If your customers are businesses, will they recognize that they have a business problem to solve or an opportunity to exploit?

If the group of customers you have chosen to sell to clearly recognize their need, want, problem, or opportunity, then they are more likely to want to buy your product or service. Note, though, that it's not enough that you recognize that your prospects have a need or problem: you will have to determine if they will recognize this, as well.

If your prospects do not recognize their need or problem, then the first action plan of your marketing and selling activities will be to create or heighten your prospects awareness of their need or problem. This will require specific effort on your part, and is typically done through an integrated marketing communications program.

It's far simpler and less costly, however, if (during your analysis) you can identify that there is a selected group of potential customers who already recognize their need or problem. This group then validates your plan by becoming your target market segment, and your marketing and selling tasks become easier with this group.

The question you must answer: What are the characteristics of your potential customers that are related to their need or desire for your product or service? For example, if you are selling an electric toothbrush, people who visit a dentist regularly are more likely to be interested in your toothbrush than those who don't visit the dentist very often. Customer characteristics that relate to the likelihood of visiting a dentist might include income and education. You might therefore choose to sell your electric toothbrush only to individuals making more than $50,000 a year and with at least a college degree.

Rule #2:

Identify Customers Who Are Ready to Buy

Will the want/need/problem/opportunity cause your prospects enough pain or the prospect of enough pleasure that they will be willing to take action?

If your prospects are ready to act to fill their need or solve their business problem, then they will be more likely to buy your product or service. On the other hand, if your potential customers need or problem is not strong enough to motivate them to take action, then you will be required to expend more sales and marketing effort to convince them that they will benefit from filling the need or solving the problem. Keep in mind that your prospects probably have several needs or problems, so you must show them that the one you can fill or solve is of high enough priority that they should fill it before the others.

This again would require specific effort on your part, and will become another requirement for your integrated marketing communications program. You will be able to save yourself much of this effort, however, if you plan to refine your target market segment to include only those prospects who already recognize their need or problem and who are willing to act on that need or problem.

To continue your analysis, then, the next question you must ask yourself is: Are there additional customer characteristics that will tell me that these customers will be ready to buy? To expand on the example above: Of those who visit the dentist regularly, those with a higher likelihood of gum disease may be more ready to buy your electric toothbrush than those with healthy teeth and gums. One customer characteristic that is related to a higher incidence of gum disease is age. You might therefore choose to sell your electric toothbrush to those individuals who are over 45 years of age.

When you combine this characteristic with the income and education characteristics we selected previously, your analysis has determined that your target market segment would now become those individuals earning $50,000 or more per year, with four or more years of college education, and who are over 45 years of age.

To complete your analysis, there are two more rules to apply once you have identified your target market segment. Both rules will help your business achieve success.

Rule #3:
Let the Customers Know That You Can Fill Their Needs

Will your prospects recognize that you can fulfill their need or want, or solve their business problem? If you are an existing business, do your prospects already recognize your ability to fill their need or want, or solve their business problem?

If you are an existing business, and they so, then your marketing communications program has already done its job or you have already built good relations with these prospects. You can move on to Rule #4.

If your prospects do not yet recognize your ability to meet their need or solve their problem, then you must figure out how to demonstrate to them your ability to do so. This activity will become a part of your marketing communications program, and will form the core of your initial selling activities. Your prospects must recognize that you have a solution to their need or problem before they will commit to spending time or resources with you.

If you have chosen a target market segment satisfying Rules #1 and #2, then the bulk of your marketing and sales activities and expenditures will be dedicated to satisfying Rule #3 and Rule #4, below. Rule #3 will be satisfied by your advertising and promotional activities.

Once you have figured out how to educate your prospects on your ability to satisfy their need or solve their problem, you can move on to Rule #4.

Rule #4:
Find Customers Who Will Pay

Will your prospects <u>pay you</u> to meet their need or solve their business problem?

There are two parts to Rule #4:

1. Will your prospect **pay?**   - and -   2. Will your prospect **pay you?**

Even though your prospects recognize their need or problem, are motivated to take action, and recognize that you have a solution, they may not be ready or able to pay, or to pay you.

You must ensure your prospect will have funds budgeted or available to fill this need or solve this problem. You also must ensure you are dealing with the decision-makers. In the case of a family, the husband and wife may make joint decisions, especially on large purchases. In the case of a business, several individuals may comprise the "buying center," including a purchasing agent, an executive, a financial officer, and possibly others.

Once you have determined your prospects' ability and willingness to pay, you must ensure that they are willing to pay you (i.e., they recognize you can fill their need or solve their problem in a way that no other competitor or substitute product can do). They must clearly see greater value in what you have to offer them, and trust you to stand behind your product or services ability to meet their need or solve their problem. If your prospects can't distinguish you from your competitors, don't trust you, or can't distinguish your product or service from other products or services offered to them, then a portion of your marketing and sales activities will have to be spent on educating them about your uniqueness and trustworthiness. Of course, uniqueness and trustworthiness must have value to your prospects before they will be willing to pay for them.

Conclusion

If you are a new business, analyzing your market, remember that every firm must satisfy these four rules for marketing and sales success. If you are an existing business and you are having difficulty finding customers to purchase your product or service or you are spending a lot of time "convincing" your prospects to buy, consider targeting your market segment to satisfy Rules #1 and #2. Then, you'll find that almost every prospect you talk to has a need for what you're selling. You'll then be able to concentrate your marketing and sales efforts on satisfying Rules #3 and #4, to ensure they easily see how you can fulfill their needs better than any of your competitors.

If the results of your product-market analysis show that there are valid customers for your product or service, you are now ready to write your marketing plan. The benefit of following the four rules will be shorter sales cycles, a higher percentage of prospects converted to customers, and more productive use of your marketing and sales dollars.

Components of a Successful
Multi-Media Marketing Strategy

Marketing - Traditional (Offline)	+ New Media (Online)
Identify target market(s). - Demographics - Psychographics - Niche market specifics Research/assess competition. Assess industry trends. Conduct market research. - questionnaires - focus groups - surveys Create packaging/image. Determine pricing strategy. Create branding/image strategy. - logo - slogan - pitch Develop customer database assessment. Identify co-marketing opportunities. Design reciprocal marketing strategies. Evaluate effectiveness of all components of the marketing plan.	Identify online target market(s). - Online demographics - Online psychographics - Online niche market specifics Research /assess competitors' websites. Assess online industry trends. Conduct market research. - e-mail questionnaires - online focus groups (structured chats) - online (website/social media) surveys Mirror branding/image online. Design online customer database assessment. Merge online/offline database analysis. Identify online co-marketing opportunities. Identify links to/from other websites. Evaluate effectiveness of online marketing.

Sales – Traditional (Offline)	+ New Media (Online)
Refine the sales pitch. Design and print all sales materials. - Brochures - Pamphlets, folders - Stationery, business cards, etc. - Catalog - Promotional flyers, other Create direct mail campaign. Instigate viral marketing.	Determine the online sales pitch. Design/implement the website. - Introduce the company - Define products/services - Identify additional content needs Register with search engines. Optimize to improve rankings (SEO) Create an e-mail marketing campaign. Create affiliate programs. Create viral marketing opportunities online.

Figure 5.1 – page 1

Sales Incentive/Promotions (Offline)	+ New Media (Online)
Create in-store campaigns and mailers: - cash back coupons - discounts/coupons - special introductory offers - free samples Design sweepstakes and contests. Identify giveaways. Identify trade show opportunities. - determine level of involvement (exhibitor vs. attendee)	Create campaigns on the website, social media sites, and via e-mail for: - cash back coupons - discounts/coupons - special offers (ex: free shipping) Design online sweepstakes or points programs - example: points for frequent web shoppers) Identify giveaways (e.g., as a thank you for completing a website survey).

Advertising – Traditional (Offline)	+ New Media (Online)
Determine if an advertising agency should be hired. Determine placement, frequency, and prices for each of the following options. - Television (network, cable) - Radio (national, local) - Print (newspapers, magazines, trade journals, bulletins, yellow pages, newsletters, etc.) - Extreme advertising (billboards, buses, blimps, etc.) - Other (event signage, t-shirts, point-of-purchase signs, etc.) Identify opportunities for sponsorship (of events, programs, materials, etc.).	Determine if an advertising network should be hired. Determine placement, frequency, and prices for each of the following options. - Banner ads (vertical, rectangle, click thru) - Pay per click advertising - Mobile device advertising - Portal advertising - Online newsletters, newspapers - Interactive television - Direct TV - Links to/from - Advertorials on other websites Identify opportunities for online sponsorships (of Web events, of portions of a website, of online newsletters).

Figure 5.1 – page 2

Components of a Successful Multi-Media Marketing Strategy

Public Relations – Traditional (Offline)   +   New Media (Online)

Determine if a public relations agency should be hired. Conduct scheduled events for public/niche: - workshops - open house - seminars - celebrations Arrange for: - participation in other events (special lectures, speeches, workshops) - guest appearances (radio, television, guest columnist) - interviews (print) Identify community and charitable events for personal and financial contributions.	Determine if the public relations function should be outsourced. Arrange for online events: - special guest expert chats - regularly scheduled chat groups - community-building activities - message boards - website simulcast of offline events Arrange for guest appearances on other websites: - webinars - webcasts - podcasts - interviews (in online newsletters, magazines)

Networking – Traditional (Offline)   +   New Media (Online)

Identify groups, associations, organizations and conferences: - your local community - trade associations - business organizations - professional groups Determine level of involvement in each: - join - seek a leadership position - attend meetings/events only	Identify online networking opportunities to actively participate in: - social media threads relevant to your business - tweet and re-tweet Twitter comments - participation in free webcasts - professional association websites - other Establish regular e-mail contact with: - current clients - prospective clients - business and professional associates

Figure 5.1 – page 3

Components of a Successful Multi-Media Marketing Strategy

Using Social Media
to Build Your Business

by Jan Norman

"It's Your Business" Columnist, Orange Co. Register 1989-2013

The rise of the Internet and explosion of the sales of personal computers, laptops, tablets and smartphones have opened huge marketing opportunities for businesses that must not be ignored. The buzz phrase is "social media," which encompasses everything from social networking sites such as Facebook to web logs or blogs including Twitter, to photo-sharing websites such as Pinterest.

These media are more than marketing devices to supplement newspaper advertisements or direct mail flyers. Social media fundamentally change how people get and give information, and therefore change marketing from merely pushing information about your business out to potential customers to engaging them in interactive conversations.

In fact, the use of technology to enable online conversations and collaborations among users is a defining hallmark of the second generation of Internet activity, dubbed Web 2.0, going back to 1999. In many cases, your customers and strategic partners will start those conversations themselves, will keep them going and draw in others who might not otherwise be aware of your company's existence.

Social media are for businesses of every size, in every location, and in every industry. The number of online resources for social media interaction grows daily. The challenge for marketers is choosing the right ones for their type of business and marketing goals.

What Does 'Social Media' Mean?

Different people may have broader or narrower definitions, but most will agree that social media are online platforms to provide interactive communication using web-based and mobile technologies. They are online content in the form of text, photographs, audio, video or graphics that invite comment, collaboration and exchange among participants.

Business owners cannot choose for their firms not to use social media. If they try, their customers, critics and competitors still will express their views and experiences online – positive and negative – about the company and its products or services for everyone to see. So, business owners need to monitor and respond to all of those online conversations, even if they think they can avoid setting up web sites, blogs, Facebook pages, Twitter accounts and YouTube channels. Why would entrepreneurs who intend to succeed avoid social media, given its prevalence and continual growth? It would be like not getting a business telephone or a mailing address. It would be like failing to greet customers when they walk into the office or store.

Increasingly, customers and potential strategic partners check out a business online, and wonder whether a business that doesn't have a web site and email address really exists. Research shows that almost two-thirds of people looking for a product or service in their community are more likely to use a business that displays information on a social media site.

Social Media Use Grows

A major reason for businesses to engage in social media is that their potential, ideal customers are probably on social platforms already. Approximately 2.5 billion people worldwide have access to the Internet and the number is growing rapidly. Approximately 1.1 billion use Facebook; 1 billion use YouTube; and 500 million use Twitter. In the United States alone, people spend a cumulative 121 billion minutes annually on social media on their computers and mobile devices, according to audience measurement company Nielsen Co. That usage has been growing by double-digit percentages each year as individuals and businesses find more ways to incorporate social media in their online presence.

Similarly, research shows that three-fourths of businesses use some form of social media; seven out of ten use Facebook and almost half use Twitter. They report that they do so because social media channels are easy to use and inexpensive, and don't require a lot of time, although the assessment of time usage can be deceiving. Entrepreneurs must budget time as well as money to spend on social media, or find themselves with too little of either left for other necessary tasks. Budgeting time to participate in social media will make these efforts habitual, which is important because continual updating is essential to social media success.

Business owners are finding that social media help them with other parts of their marketing plan. Social media can help businesses research customer behavior and preferences, build their brands, develop relationships, manage customer loyalty programs, correct mistakes quickly and deliver sales promotions and discount coupons.

Most important, businesses use social media because they bring in business: One survey of business owners found that six out of ten respondents had won new customers through LinkedIn; half had brought in new customers through Twitter; and four out of ten had attracted customers using Facebook.

Social Media Supplement (not Replace) Your Marketing Plan

Entrepreneurs who want to succeed in business over the long term don't merely buy an ad here or pass out some business cards. They develop their marketing plans to identify their ideal (and most profitable) customers, establish goals, plan strategies and organize marketing efforts into a comprehensive whole. Similarly, they build social media into those plans; they don't merely set up a Facebook page that never changes, tweet once or twice or fill out a profile on LinkedIn.

Planning is vital to successful marketing. The use of social media is an integral part of your marketing plan. It is not a replacement.

- **Define goals and branding.** First, business owners should define their general business goals and what the company's brand will be. That clarity will help understand how they can integrate social media to achieve those goals and they can avoid having their use of social media work at cross purposes or being ineffective in building the company.

For example, some companies have one look for their on-land office or shop, a different look for the web site and a third for their Facebook page. Instead, all should incorporate similar colors, fonts, keywords, core descriptions and images so visitors understand they are visiting the same business whether on the street or online. All information must be kept up to date. If addresses, key executives, hours or other information change, that should be corrected across all social media.

- **Implementation comes from the top.** Support for social media's role as part of a company's marketing strategy must come from the owner and top managers. Implementation must not be left to a low-level intern who does not have adequate knowledge of the industry, the company or the owners' vision. People who represent the business online should understand and buy into that vision so that the message is consistent.

- **The foundation is the same.** Success in social media is built upon the same foundation as a company's success in general: Everyone involved knows who the company is, how it fits into the marketplace and how to keep its message consistent, whether online or in an office or shop. Generally, even with companies that sell online, there isn't a direct correlation between revenue growth and the number of tweets or Facebook updates. Just because a company attracts a lot of Facebook "likes" or Twitter followers doesn't necessarily show up on next month's balance sheet.

- **Return on investment is difficult to measure.** Still, setting goals for social media participation is important. One goal might be to increase traffic to the company web site a specific amount through social media posts. Another might be an increased number of customer interactions such as web site inquiries. Top social media platforms influence search engine rankings, so another goal might be an improvement in online search results.

Types of Social Media

Social media channels, technologies and tools are multiplying so rapidly that any list of the most popular or most effective is quickly obsolete. Even the platforms themselves evolve and expand to retain their users. As social media sites' capabilities expand, they overlap with others. What Facebook or YouTube do today may bear little resemblance to their functions in the future. MySpace, for example, started as an online data storage site, evolved into a social network and then started specializing in music sharing as Facebook eclipsed its general social networking popularity.

An understanding of the variety of social media available will contribute to your marketing plans to grow your business.

- **Facebook** (for years) has been the most visited social media networking platform.

- **LinkedIn** has been growing in popularity among business people looking for career advancement, customers and other work-related uses.

- **Google,** the most-used Internet search engine, created Google+ as a social networking site to encourage use of Google properties, such as Gmail.

- **Twitter** combines social networking and blogging in 140-character bites and has exploded far beyond that basic explanation.

- **YouTube** established itself as the go-to video sharing site.

- **Pinterest** shares images, and within two years of its launch, retailers were getting more referrals from Pinterest than from Facebook, Twitter or Google Plus+.

- **Instagram**, bought in 2012 by Facebook, shares photos and videos.

- **Yelp** is a customer-written review site that has become essential for many types of retail and services.

- **Wikipedia** is a user-written encyclopedia criticized for its inaccuracies and often abused, but nevertheless widely used.

A novice to social media should start with the better known platforms. Set up a Facebook page, Twitter and Pinterest accounts and a LinkedIn profile. Many business web sites include links to their Facebook, Twitter, LinkedIn and YouTube presence. Conversations online and in person with customers may suggest specialty social media presences that are unique to your industry or geographic location. Ask your best customers and partners where they participate in social media online, what content they respond to and where they get information. Those answers are a good place to start in the search for more customers like them. However, it could be a waste of money and effort to try to be on all social media platforms. Decisions about which sites to use – and how much time and effort to spend on them – should be made based on what the business is trying to achieve.

Different Ways to Use Social Media

Business use of social media should contribute to the overall goals of the company. An executive's tweets should reflect company values and marketing goals, not merely personal preferences. Pinterest photos should relate to products and services the company is ready and willing to sell.

One of the most basic ways businesses can use social media is to answer customer questions or to respond to complaints. This activity requires company representatives to monitor frequently what is being said about the company online and respond quickly. A complaint that goes unanswered can enable a critic with a worldwide megaphone.

Entrepreneurs use social media in many different ways. A business can determine the time when and location where a user comments about its products, store appearance, and more. It can use that information for market research, such as when customers are most likely to shop or their reaction to a specific product or in-store display. To encourage that type of feedback, one restaurant chain gave away $5 gift cards randomly to people who checked in at one of the restaurants. A retail clothing store offered 10 percent to 20 percent discounts to social media commenters based on how often they checked in to the company's Facebook page. Social media users love to be asked their opinion, so a bakery created polls to select new flavors of cupcakes to sell.

Some companies build online-only ad campaigns. Utah-based manufacturer Blendtec attracted millions of viewers to its series of "Will It Blend?" YouTube videos that featured founder Tom Dickson putting iPods, marbles, golf balls and remote controls into the company's product and blending them to bits. An environmental clean-up company posted videos of its work following the 2011 Japanese earthquake and tsunami. A California restaurant conducted its initial staff hiring on Facebook. Applicants had to "like" the company to apply and to find out when in-person interviews were scheduled. The restaurant posted photos of would-be servers and cooks lined up outside the restaurant for interviews and used those users to build its online community.

Businesses that sell their professional expertise (example: attorneys, real estate advisers, etc.) share tips and testimonials through Twitter, electronic newsletters and blogs. Such postings should always include a "call to action" that encourages readers to sign up for the newsletter, send questions or call for an appointment.

Use of social media to build a business
is limited only by the entrepreneur's imagination

Marketing Plan Outline

I.   Overview and Goals of Marketing Strategy

A.   Overview of Marketing Strategy

B.   Goals of Marketing Strategy

1. Creating a Strong Brand
2. Building a Strong Customer Base
3. Increasing Product/Service Sales

II.   Market Analysis

A.   Target Market(s)

1. Demographics
2. Psychographics
3. Niche market specifics

B.   Competition

1. Description of Major Competitors
2. Assessment of Their Strengths/Weaknesses

C.   Market Trends

1. Industry Trends
2. Target Market Trends

D.   Market Research

1. Methods of Research
2. Database Analysis
3. Summary of Results

III.   Marketing Strategy

A.   General Description

1. Allocation of marketing efforts (% of budget dedicated to online v. offline)
2. Expected return on investment from most significant components

B.   Method of Sales and Distribution

1. Stores, offices, kiosks
2. Catalogs, direct mail
3. Website

C.   Packaging

1. Quality Considerations
2. Packaging

D.   Pricing

1. Price strategy
2. Competitive position

E.   Branding

F.   Database Marketing (Personalization)

G. Sales Strategies

1. Direct Sales
2. Direct Mail
3. Email Marketing
4. Affiliate Marketing
5. Reciprocal Marketing
6. Viral Marketing

H. Sales Incentives/Promotions

1. Free Samples
2. Cash Back Coupons
3. Sweepstakes
4. Online Promotions
5. Add-ons
6. Rebates
7. Other

I. Advertising Strategies

1. Traditional Advertising (TV, Radio, Print, Extreme)

2. Web Advertising/New Media (banner ads, pay per click advertising, mobile device advertising, portals, interactive television)

3. Long-term Sponsorships

J. Public Relations

1. Building an Online Presence (social media)

2. Events (online and offline)

3. Press releases (print, radio, television, online)

4. Interviews (online newsletters and websites, print, radio, television, online events)

K. Networking (memberships and leadership positions)

IV. Customer Service

A. Description of Customer Service Activities

B. Expected Outcomes of Achieving Excellence

V. Implementation of Marketing Strategy

A. In-House Responsibilities

B. Out-Sourced Functions

1. Advertising, Public Relations, Marketing Firms
2. Advertising Networks
3. Other

VI. Assessment of Marketing Effectiveness *

Note. The assessment is for existing businesses and is added after periodic evaluations.

Part III
Financial Documents

You learned earlier that the body of a Business Plan is divided into three main sections. Having completed the Organizational and Marketing Plans, you are now ready to develop the third area of your plan.

Financial Documents are those records used to show past, current, and projected finances. In this section I will cover the following major documents that you will want to consider and include in your Business Plan. They will consist of both pro forma (projected) and actual financial statements. Your work will be easier if they are done in order.

- ✓ *Summary of Financial Needs*
- ✓ *Dispersal of Loan Funds Statement*
- ✓ *Cash Flow Statement (Budget)*
- ✓ *Three-Year Income Projection*
- ✓ *Break-Even Analysis*
- ✓ *Balance Sheet*
- ✓ *Profit & Loss Statement*
- ✓ *Loan Application/Financial History*
- ✓ *Financial Statement Analysis*

Before You Begin

You are now beginning the Financial Documents section of your business plan. I would strongly suggest that you prepare these documents in the order that I have presented them because it will simplify the process. In the same way that a house builder must lay the foundation, build the walls and finally put on the roof, you will find that your financial statements will build on each other. Each one will use information from the ones previously done. If you try to jump ahead, you will make your task more difficult.

Before you begin work on your financial statements go back to Chapter 1 and reread the section on "Developing Financial Assumptions". Remember that the numbers in your financial plan are derived through the development of organizational and marketing concepts in terms of revenues that will be generated and expenses that will be incurred.

Purpose of Financial Documents

In the first two sections, you have written about the physical setup of your operation and your plans for finding and reaching your customers. The Financial Documents section is the quantitative interpretation of everything you have stated in the text portion of your plan. Well-executed financial statements will provide you with the means to look realistically at your business in terms of profitability. Financial Documents is often the first section examined by a potential lender or investor.

The financial documents included in your plan are not just for the purpose of satisfying a potential lender or investor. The primary reason for writing a business plan is so that it will serve as a guide during the lifetime of your business. It is extremely important that you keep it updated frequently. This means examining your financial statements on a periodic basis, measuring your actual performance against your projections, and revising your new projections accordingly.

Types of Financial Documents

There are four types of financial documents covered in this chapter under Sections I, II, III, and IV. Before you start to develop your financial plan, it is best to gain a basic understanding of what these documents are and why they are important to your business.

- ### Statements of Sources and Uses of Funds from a Lender or Investor
  The first two documents covered are the "Summary of Financial Needs" and the "Loan Fund Dispersal Statement". These two documents, explained in Section I of the chapter, are the only ones that are written in paragraph form rather than as spreadsheets in rows and columns. They are included only if your business is seeking funds from a lender or investor (or other source).

- ### Pro Forma Statements
  The word "pro forma" in accounting means "projected". These are the statements (cash flow, income projections, etc.) that are used for you to predict the future profitability of your business and will be covered in Section II of this chapter. You will not be performing magic and will never be 100% right. However, your projections should be based on realistic research and reasonable assumptions. *It is dangerous to overstate your revenues and understate your expenses.*

- **Actual Performance Statements**

   These are the historical financial statements reflecting the past performance of your business. If you are planning a new business, you have no history. Therefore, you will not have these statements to include. However, once you have been in business for even one accounting period, you will have a Profit & Loss Statement and a Balance Sheet for those periods. The actual performance statements will be explained and illustrated in Section III of this chapter.

- **Financial Statement Analysis**

   Once you have completed the financial documents described above, it is also important to use them as tools to look at your business and enable you to make future decisions that will make your business more profitable. Financial Statement Analysis utilizes the income statement and the balance sheet and is the study of relationships or comparisons of single components in one statement or in two or more comparative financial statements. In Section IV of this chapter, you will learn how to use your income statement and balance sheet to prepare a financial statement analysis of your business.

How to Proceed

The financial documents will be presented in the order discussed in the paragraphs above. It will be necessary for you to determine your individual situation and decide which documents to include in your own business plan. Below are five descriptions. Decide which one fits your business and proceed accordingly:

1. **If yours is a new business — and — you are going to seek a lender or investor.**

   Include the "Application of Loan Funds" and "Loan Fund Dispersal Statement". You will also include all of the pro forma statements. You have no financial history and cannot include actual performance statements. Financial statement analysis will be based on projections only and will utilize your three-year profit and loss (income) projection.

2. **If yours is a new business — and — you are not going to seek a lender or investor.**

   You will <u>not</u> include the "Application of Loan Funds" and the "Loan Fund Dispersal Statement". You will include all pro forma statements. Again, financial statement analysis will be based only on projections and will utilize your three-year profit & loss (income) projection.

3. **If yours is an existing business — and — you are going to seek a lender or investor.**

   You will need to include all financial documents discussed in this chapter.

4. **If yours is an existing business — and — you are not seeking a lender or investor.**

   You will include all financial documents discussed in this chapter with the exception of the "Application of Loan Funds" and the "Loan Fund Dispersal Statement".

5. **If this business plan is being written for a division within a larger business.**

   Consider your division as being a business within a business and include financial documents as indicated in whichever of the above scenarios fits your situation.

Now You Are Ready To
Prepare Your Financial Documents

The four types of financial documents will be presented in the following order:

- ✓ **Section I: Statements of financial needs and uses of lender/investor funds**
- ✓ **Section II: Pro forma statements**
- ✓ **Section III: Actual financial statements**
- ✓ **Section IV: Financial statement analysis**

Helpful hints:

1. **Work in order.** You should work on financial documents in the order that they are presented in the book. It will make your job easier. Most of your financial documents will use information from the ones you will have already completed.

2. **Add explanations when needed.** When you prepare your financial statements, it is a good idea to append a written explanation of any items that are unusual or that would not be immediately clear to your lender or investor.

   Examples:

   - *If you are a manufacturing business and have shut down operations for a period to put in new equipment, appending an explanation would clear up any queries about the reason for decreased revenues or inventory levels during that time.*

   - *If you have a heavy increase in advertising expenses, but the increased revenues will not materialize until a future financial statement period, you can attach a note of explanation about your projected benefits for future periods.*

Example Financial Spreadsheets
in this chapter have no correlation with each other

Do not try to follow the numbers from one spreadsheet to the next. The Appendices contain four business plans with 100% correlation between spreadsheets. You will be able to see from them how the numbers build on each other throughout the financial plan.

★★★★★★★★★★★★★★★★★★★★★★★★★

Section I:

Statements of Financial Needs and
Uses of Funds from a Lender or Investor

The financial text document and example on the next two pages describes your needs for capital to be infused into your company through borrowed or invested funds. It also outlines your intended use of those funds. **Include these statements only if you are seeking funds from a lender or investor.**

- ✓ *Summary of Financial Needs*
- ✓ *Loan Fund Dispersal Statement*

Summary of Financial Needs

If you are applying for a loan, your lenders and investors will analyze the requirements of your business. They will distinguish among the three types of capital as follows:

Working capital. Fluctuating needs to be repaid through cash (liquidity) during the business's next full operating cycle, generally one year.

Growth capital. Needs to be repaid with profits over a period of a few years. If you are seeking growth capital, you will be expected to show how the capital will be used to increase your business profits enough to be able to repay the loan (+ interest) within several years (usually not more than seven).

Equity capital. Permanent needs. If you seek equity capital, it must be raised from investors who will take the risk for dividend returns or capital gains, or a specific share of the business.

Keeping the above in mind, you must now prepare a Summary of Financial Needs. This document is an *outline* giving the following information:

- *Why* you are applying for a loan or investment funds

- *How much* you need to accomplish your goals

Loan Fund Dispersal Statement

Uses of financing. The potential lender will require a statement of how the money you intend to borrow will be used. It will be necessary for you to tell:

- *How* you intend to utilize the loan funds.

- *Back up your statement* with supporting data. The backup statement will show the lender that you have done your homework properly.

The following are two examples that will help to clarify your understanding of the above.

Example 1: **How Money Will Be Used.** Funds for advertising

Back-up Statement. Refer to the advertising section of your plan. That section must contain a breakdown of how you intend to do your advertising. Include rate sheets in the Supporting Documents.

Example 2: **How Money Will Be Used.** Funds for expansion. Include a concise statement explaining how you intend to expand.

Back-up Statement. Include the following information:

- Projected costs of carrying out plans.

- Projections as to how that expansion will ultimately result in increased profits for your business and thereby enable you to repay your loan.

- References to other sections of your business plan that relate to projected expansion.

Sample Page
Summary of Financial Needs & Loan Fund Dispersal Statement

Summary of Financial Needs

1. Genesis Multimedia is seeking a loan to increase growth capital in the following areas of production:
   a. Equipment (new and more modern)
   b. Training of personnel in operation of above

2. Funds needed to accomplish the above goal will be $250,000.

Loan Fund Dispersal Statement

1. Dispersal of Loan Funds
Genesis Multimedia will utilize anticipated loan funds in the amount of $250,000 to modernize its production equipment. This will necessitate the purchase of two new pieces of equipment and the training of present personnel in the operation of that equipment.

2. Back-Up Statement
a. The equipment needed is as follows:

   (1) High-speed F-34 Atlas Press (purchase price: $123,000)
   (2) S71 Jaworski Ebber (purchase price: $110,000)

b. The training is available from the manufacturer as a three-week intensive program. (cost: 10 employees @ $1,200 = $12,000)

c. The remaining $5,000 of loan funds will be used to make the first monthly installment on loan repayment (a period of low production due to training off the premises).

d. The equipment will result in a 35% increase in production and will decrease unit cost by 25%. The end result will be a net profit increase sufficient to repay the loan and interest within three years with a profit margin of 15%.*

* **Note.** Refer to page 17 for production plan of ABC Corporation. See pages 27 and 28 of the marketing section for market research and projected trends in the industry. (See footnote at bottom of page.)

Page numbers at the bottom of the example above are hypothetical and do not refer to page numbers in *Anatomy of a Business Plan*. The production plan referred to in the example would include a description of the equipment, how the work will be done, by whom, and at what cost. Market research would show projected demand for your product, and thus would show how increased production would result in increased sales and ultimately in your company's capability to repay the loan in a timely fashion.

Be sure that your supporting data can be easily found by the loan officer who is examining your application. If your information is not well-organized and easily retrievable, you risk having your loan turned down simply because information cannot be located. The necessity of having a well-written Table of Contents will be discussed in Chapter 10, Packaging and Updating Your Plan.

Section II:
Pro Forma Statements

The financial statements that follow are pro forma statements. They show your projections for the future profitability of your business.

All business plans must contain the following pro forma statements:

✓ *Cash Flow Statement*

✓ *Three-Year Income Projection*

✓ *Break-Even Analysis*

Blank forms of all three pro forma statements are included in the blank worksheet section in the back of the book (Appendix VI of "*Anatomy of a Business Plan*"). They are ready for you to customize and input your numbers.

Projected Balance Sheet

A potential lender or investor may also require that you include a pro forma (or projected) balance sheet for a specific target date in the life of your business (e.g., "end of year one"). You will find instructions for the development of a balance sheet under "Actual Financial Statements" in the next part of this chapter. There are also examples in our sample business plans in Appendices I, II, III, IV and V.

Also included in this section are:

- **Cash to be Paid Out and Sources of Cash Worksheets**
  These worksheets will help you to develop your cash flow statement and may be included in your business plan.

- **Quarterly Budget Analysis Spreadsheet**
  This is your tool for comparing your company's projections with its actual performance. Your cash flow statement will be effective only if it is revised quarterly reflecting the results of a budget analysis.

If you are a new business

You have no actual performance to measure against projections. Therefore, you will not have a quarterly budget analysis until you have been in business for three months.

If you have been in business for one or more quarters

Do a quarterly budget analysis, revise your cash flow statement accordingly and insert the revised cash flow statement in your business plan.

Pro Forma Cash Flow Statement (Budget)

It is a fact that a third or more of today's businesses fail due to a lack of cash flow. The cash flow statement is usually the first thing a lender or investor examines in your business plan. What is cash flow?

What is a Cash Flow Statement?

The Pro Forma Cash Flow Statement is the financial document that *projects* what your business plan means in terms of dollars. A cash flow statement is the same as a budget. It is a pro forma (or projected) statement used for internal planning and estimates how much money will flow into and out of a business during a designated period of time, usually the coming tax year. Your profit at the end of the year will depend on the proper balance between cash inflow and outflow.

The cash flow statement identifies when cash is expected to be received and when it must be spent to pay bills and debts. It also allows the manager to identify where the necessary cash will come from.

This statement deals only with **actual cash transactions** and not with depreciation and amortization of goodwill or other non-cash expense items. Expenses are paid from cash on hand, sale of assets, revenues from sales and services, interest earned on investments, money borrowed from a lender and influx of capital in exchange for equity in the company. If your business will require $100,000 to pay its expenses and $50,000 to support the owners, you will need at least an equal amount of money flowing into the business just to maintain the status quo. Anything less will eventually lead to an inability to pay your creditors or yourself.

The availability or non-availability of cash *when* it is needed for expenditures gets to the very heart of the matter. By careful planning, you must try to project not only *how much* cash will have to flow into and out of your business, but also *when* it will need to flow in and out. A business may be able to plan for gross receipts that will cover its needs. However, if those sales do not take place in time to pay the expenses, your venture will soon be history unless you plan ahead for other sources of cash to tide the business over until the revenues are realized.

Time Period. The Cash Flow Statement should be prepared on a monthly basis for the next tax year (or more) of your business. To be effective, it must be analyzed and revised quarterly to reflect actual performance in the preceding three months of operations.

Steps for Planning Your Cash Flow Statement

1. Prepare individual budgets

Begin by compiling individual projections and budgets. They might be as follows:

- Revenue projections (product and service)
- Inventory purchases
- Variable (selling) expense budget (with marketing budget)
- Fixed (administrative) expense budget

2. Prepare planning worksheets

Because the cash flow statement deals with cash inflow and cash outflow, the first step in planning can be best accomplished by preparing two worksheets.

a. Cash to be Paid Out

This worksheet documents the cash flowing out of your business. It identifies categories of expenses and obligations and the projected amount of cash needed in each category. Use the information from your individual budgets (inventory purchases, selling expenses, administrative expenses, owner draws, etc.).

These expenditures are not always easy to estimate. If yours is a new business, it will be necessary for you to do lots of market research. If you are an existing business, you will combine information from past financial statements with trends in your particular industry.

b. Sources of Cash

Use this worksheet to document the cash flowing into your business. It will help you to estimate how much cash will be available from what sources. To complete this worksheet, you will have to look at cash on hand, projected revenues, assets that can be liquidated, possible lenders or investors, and owner equity to be contributed. This worksheet will force you to take a look at any existing possibilities for increasing available cash.

3. Check out the examples

On the next four pages, you will see examples of the two worksheets along with accompanying information explaining each of the categories used. The worksheets are filled in for our fictitious company, Genesis Multimedia, to help you understand the process.

Please note that the Cash to be Paid Out Worksheet shows a need for $131,000. It was necessary in projecting Sources of Cash to account for $131,000 without the projected sales because payment is not expected to be received until November and December (too late for cash needs January through October). Next year, those revenues will be reflected in cash on hand or other salable assets.

When you do your own worksheets:

- Try to be as realistic as possible. ***Do not overstate revenues and/or understate expenses***, a deadly error frequently made during the planning process.

- Be sure to figure all of your estimates on both worksheets for the same time period (i.e. annually, quarterly, monthly).

Note. Blank forms of the two worksheets are provided in Appendix VI.

Explanation of Categories

Cash to Be Paid Out Worksheet

1. Start-Up Costs

These are the costs incurred by you to get your business underway. They are generally one-time expenses and are capitalized for tax purposes.

2. Inventory Purchases

Cash to be spent during the period on items intended for resale. If you purchase manufactured products, this includes the cash outlay for those purchases. If you are the manufacturer, include labor and materials on units to be produced.

3. Variable Expenses (Selling Expenses)

These are the costs of all expenses that will relate directly to your product or service (other than manufacturing costs or purchase price of inventory).

4. Fixed Expenses (Administrative Expenses)

Include all expected costs of office overhead. If certain bills must be paid ahead, include total cash outlay even if covered period extends into the next year.

5. Assets (Long-Term Purchases)

These are the capital assets that will be depreciated over a period of years (land, buildings, vehicles, equipment). Determine how you intend to pay for them and include all cash to be paid out in the current period. *Note:* Land is the only asset that does not depreciate and will be listed at cost.

6. Liabilities

What are the payments you expect to have to make to retire any debts or loans? Do you have any Accounts Payable as you begin the new year? You will need to determine the amount of cash outlay that needs to be paid in the current year. If you have a car loan for $20,000 and you pay $500 per month for 12 months, you will have a cash outlay of $6,000 for the coming year.

7. Owner Equity

This item is frequently overlooked in planning cash flow. If you, as the business owner, will need a draw of $5,000 per month to live on, you must plan for $60,000 cash flowing out of your business. Failure to plan for it will result in a cash flow shortage and may cause your business to fail.

Note. Be sure to use the same time period throughout your worksheet.

Variable & Fixed Expense Categories Must Be Determined By You

Every business has expenses that are specific to its industry. You will have to customize your variable and fixed expense categories to match your business. The ones used in the examples will give you some ideas. Type your own headings in the working spreadsheets. As you begin to operate your business, you will be better able to determine your true expenditures. *For your business plan, you will need to set your expense headings beginning with this worksheet and use the same ones throughout your spreadsheets.* You can change later if you find that your current categories do not meet your needs.

Cash to Be Paid Out Worksheet

Business Name: Genesis Multimedia   Time Period Covered: Jan 1 – Dec 31, 2014

1. Start-Up Costs:		$ 1,450
Business License	30	
Corporation Filing	500	
Legal Fees	920	
Other Start-up Costs:	0	
2. Inventory Purchases		32,000
Cash out for goods intended for resale		
3. Variable Expenses (Selling)		
Advertising/Marketing	8,000	
Freight	2,500	
Fulfillment of Orders	800	
Packaging Costs	0	
Sales Salaries/Commissions	14,000	
Travel	1,550	
Miscellaneous Variable Expense	300	
Total Selling Expenses		27,150
4. Fixed Expenses (Administrative)		
Financial Administration	1,800	
Insurance	900	
Licenses/Permits	100	
Office Salaries	16,300	
Rent Expenses	8,600	
Utilities	2,400	
Miscellaneous Fixed Expense	400	
Total Administrative Expenses		30,500
5. Assets (Long-Term Purchases)		6,000
Cash to be paid out in current period		
6. Liabilities		9,900
Cash outlay for retiring debts, loans, and/or accounts payable		
7. Owner Equity		24,000
Cash to be withdrawn by owner		
Total Cash to Be Paid Out		$ 131,000

Explanation of Categories
Sources of Cash Worksheet

1. Cash On Hand

Money that you have on hand in your bank accounts and other resources. Be sure to include petty cash and income that you have not yet deposited.

2. Sales (Revenues)

This includes projected revenues from the sale of your products and/or services. If payment is not expected during the time period covered by this worksheet, do not include that portion of your sales. Think about the projected timing of sales. If receipts will be delayed beyond the time when a large amount of cash is needed, make a notation to that effect and take it into consideration when determining the need for temporary financing. Include deposits you require on expected sales or services. To figure collections on Accounts Receivable, you will have to project the percentage of invoices that will be lost to bad debts and subtract it from your Accounts Receivable total.

3. Miscellaneous Income

Do you, or will you have, any money out on loan or deposited in accounts that will yield interest income during the period in question?

4. Sale of Long-Term Assets

If you are expecting to sell any of your fixed assets such as land, buildings, vehicles, machinery, equipment, etc., be sure to include only the cash you will receive during the current period.

Important.   At this point in your worksheet, add up all sources of cash. If you don't have an amount equal to your projected needs, you will have to plan sources of cash covered under numbers 5 and 6.

5. Liabilities

This figure represents the amount you will be able to borrow from lending institutions such as banks, finance companies, the SBA, etc. Be reasonable about what you think you can borrow. If you have no collateral, don't have a business plan, or if you have a poor financial history, you will find it difficult, if not impossible, to find a lender. This source of cash requires **preplanning.**

6. Equity

Sources of equity come from owner investments, contributed capital, sale of stock, or venture capital. Do you anticipate the availability of personal funds? Does your business have the potential for growth that might interest a venture capitalist? Be sure to be realistic in this area. You cannot sell stock (or equity) to a nonexistent investor.

Sources of Cash Worksheet

Genesis Multimedia

Time Period Covered: From January 1, 2014 to December 31, 2014

1. Cash On Hand | **$ 20,000**

2. Sales (Revenues)

Sales	90,000
Service Income	22,000
Deposits on Sales or Services	0
Collections on Accounts Receivable	3,000

3. Miscellaneous Income

Interest Income	1,000
Payments to be Received on Loans	0

4. Sale of Long-Term Assets | 0

5. Liabilities

Loan Funds (Banks, Lending Inst., SBA, etc.)	40,000

6. Equity

Owner Investments (Sole Prop. or Partnership)	10,000
Contributed Capital (Corporation)	N/A
Sale of Stock (Corporation)	N/A
Venture Capital	35,000

Total Cash Available

A. Without product sales = **$ 131,000**

B. With product sales = **$ 221,000**

Using the Worksheets. Now that you have completed the two worksheets, you are ready to use that information. You have estimated *how much* cash will be needed for the year and you now know what sources are available. In the next phase of cash flow planning you will break the time period of one year into monthly segments and predict *when* the cash will be needed to make the financial year flow smoothly.

Project sales on a monthly basis based on payment of invoices, demand for your particular product or service and ability to fill that demand. Figure the cost of goods, fixed and variable expenses in monthly increments. Most will vary. When do you plan to purchase the most inventory? What months will require the most advertising? Are you expecting a rent or insurance increase? When will commissions be due on expected sales? Determine your depreciable assets needs. How much will the payments be and when will they begin? Fill in as much of the cash flow statement as you can, using those projections and any others that you can comfortably determine.

To clarify the process of filling in a cash flow statement, I will walk you through January and February again using Genesis Multimedia the example.

January Projections

1. Genesis Multimedia projects a beginning cash balance of $20,000.
2. Cash Receipts: Product manufacturing will not be completed until February, so there will be no sales. However, service income of $4,000 is projected.
3. Interest on the $20,000 will amount to about $100 at current rate.
4. There are no long-term assets to sell. Enter a zero.
5. Adding 1, 2, 3, and 4 the Total Cash Available will be $24,100.
6. Cash Payments: Product will be available from the manufacturer in February and payment will not be due until pickup. However, there will be prototype costs of $5,000.
7. Variable (Selling) Expenses: Estimated at $1,140
8. Fixed (Administrative): Estimated at $1215
9. Interest Expense: No outstanding debts or loans. Enter zero.
10. Taxes: No profit for previous quarter. No estimated taxes would be due.
11. Payments on Long-Term Assets: Genesis plans to purchase office equipment to be paid in full at the time of purchase. Enter $1139
12. Loan Repayments: No loans have been received. Enter zero.
13. Owner Draws: Owner will need $2,000 for living expenses.
14. Total Cash Paid Out: Add 6 through 13. Total $10,494
15. Cash Balance: Subtract Cash Paid Out from Total Cash Available ($13,606)
16. Loans to be Received: Being aware of the $30,000 to be paid to the manufacturer in February, a loan of $40,000 is anticipated to increase Cash Available. (This requires advance planning.)
17. Equity Deposit: Owner plans to add $5,000 from personal CD.
18. Ending Cash Balance: Adding 15, 16, and 17 the sum is $58,606.

February Projections

1. February Beginning Cash Balance: January Ending Cash Balance ($58,606)
2. Cash Receipts: Still no sales, but service income is $2,000.
3. Interest Income: Projected at about $120.
4. Sale of Long-Term Assets: None. Enter zero.
5. Total Cash Available: Add 1, 2, 3, and 4. The sum is $60,726.
6. Cash Payments: $30,000 due to manufacturer, $400 due on packaging design.
7. Continue as in January. Don't forget to include payments on your loan.

Genesis Multimedia

Partial Cash Flow Statement

	Jan	Feb
BEGINNING CASH BALANCE	20,000	58,606
CASH RECEIPTS		
A. Sales/Revenues	4,000	2,000
B. Receivables	0	0
C. Interest Income	100	120
D. Sale of Long-Term Assets	0	0
TOTAL CASH AVAILABLE	24,100	60,726
CASH PAYMENTS		
A. Cost of Goods to be Sold		
1. Purchases	0	30,000
2. Material	0	0
3. Labor	5,000	400
Total Cost of Goods	5,000	30,400
B. Variable Expenses (Selling)		
1. Advertising	300	
2. Freight	120	
3. Fulfillment of Orders	0	
4. Packaging Costs	270	
5. Sales/Salaries	0	
6. Travel	285	
7. Miscellaneous Selling Expense	165	
Total Variable Expenses	1,140	
C. Fixed Expenses (Administrative)		
1. Financial Admin	80	**CONTINUE**
2. Insurance	125	**as in**
3. License/Permits	200	
4. Office Salaries	500	**JANUARY**
5. Rent Expenses	110	
6. Utilities	200	
7. Miscellaneous Administrative Expense	0	
Total Fixed Expenses	1,215	
D. Interest Expense	0	
E. Federal Income Tax	0	
F. Other Uses	0	
G. Long-Term Asset Payments	1,139	
H. Loan Payments	0	
I. Owner Draws	2,000	
TOTAL CASH PAID OUT	10,494	
CASH BALANCE/DEFICIENCY	13,606	
LOANS TO BE RECEIVED	40,000	
EQUITY DEPOSITS	5,000	
ENDING CASH BALANCE	58,606	

Instructions for Completing
Your Pro Forma Cash Flow Statement

This page contains instructions for completing the cash flow statement on the next page. A blank form for your own projections can be found in Appendix V.

- **Vertical Columns** are for the 12 months plus 6-month and 12-month period columns.

- **Horizontal Positions** on the statement contain all sources of cash and cash to be paid out (chart of accounts). Figures are retrieved from worksheets and individual budgets.

Assumptions are projected for each month, reflecting the flow of cash in and out of your business for a one-year period. Begin with the first month of your business cycle and proceed as follows:

1. Project the Beginning Cash Balance. Enter under "January."

2. Project the Cash Receipts for January. Apportion your total year's revenues throughout the 12 months. Try to weight revenues as closely as you can to a realistic selling cycle for your industry.

3. Add Beginning Cash Balance and Cash Receipts to determine Total Cash Available.

4. Project cash payments to be made for cost of goods to be sold (inventory that you will purchase or manufacture). Apportion your total inventory budget throughout the year, being sure you are providing for levels of inventory that will fulfill your needs for sales projected.

5. Customize your Variable and Fixed Expense categories to match your business.

6. Project Variable, Fixed and Interest Expenses for January. Fill out any that you can for all 12 months.

7. Project cash to be paid out on Taxes, Long-Term Assets, Loan Repayments and Owner Draws.

8. Calculate Total Cash Paid Out (Total of Cost of Goods to Be Sold, Variable, Fixed, Interest, Taxes, Long-Term Asset Payments, Loan Repayments and Owner Draws).

9. Subtract Total Cash Paid Out from Total Cash Available. The result is entered under "Cash Balance/Deficiency." Be sure to bracket this figure if the result is a negative to avoid errors.

10. Look at Ending Cash Balance in each of the months and project Loans to be Received and Equity Deposits to be made. Add to Cash Balance/Deficiency to arrive at Ending Cash Balance for each month.

11. Ending Cash Balance for January is carried forward and becomes February's Beginning Cash Balance. (Each month's ending balance is the next month's beginning balance.)

12. Go to February and input any numbers that are still needed to complete that month. The process is repeated until December is completed.

To Complete the 6-Month and 12-Month Period Columns

1. The Beginning Cash Balance for January is entered in the first space of the "Total" column.

2. The monthly figures for each category (except Beginning Cash Balance, Total Cash Available, Cash Balance/Deficiency, and Ending Cash Balance) are added horizontally and the result entered in the corresponding Total category.

3. The Total column is then computed in the same manner as each of the individual months. If you have been accurate with your computations, the December Ending Cash Balance will be exactly the same as the Total Ending Cash Balance.

 Note. If your business is new, you will have to base your projections solely on market research and industry trends. If you have an established business, you will also use your financial statements from previous years.

Pro Forma Cash Flow Statement

Genesis Multimedia

Year: 2015

	Jan	Feb	Mar	Apr	May	Jun	6-MONTH TOTALS	Jul	Aug	Sep	Oct	Nov	Dec	12-MONTH TOTALS
BEGINNING CASH BALANCE	10,360	72,840	54,488	60,346	65,125	79,253	10,360	81,341	71,401	68,974	55,974	54,718	59,032	10,360
CASH RECEIPTS														
A. Sales/Revenues	14,000	9,500	9,500	15,000	18,000	12,000	78,000	9,000	8,000	9,500	16,000	28,000	43,000	191,500
B. Receivables	400	400	300	500	450	425	2,475	500	750	650	600	1,250	8,000	14,225
C. Interest Income	234	240	260	158	172	195	1,259	213	303	300	417	406	413	3,311
D. Sale of Long-Term Assets	2,000	0	4,000	0	0	0	6,000	0	0	0	0	0	0	6,000
TOTAL CASH AVAILABLE	26,994	82,980	68,548	76,004	83,747	91,873	98,094	91,054	80,454	79,424	72,991	84,374	110,445	225,396
CASH PAYMENTS														
A. Cost of Goods to be Sold														
1. Purchases	800	16,500	3,700	200	200	300	21,700	9,000	430	540	6,700	14,000	12,000	64,370
2. Material	2,000	1,430	200	300	250	200	4,380	359	750	5,000	400	300	350	11,539
3. Labor	4,000	2,800	400	600	500	450	8,750	600	1,500	8,000	750	500	540	20,640
Total Cost of Goods	6,800	20,730	4,300	1,100	950	950	34,830	9,959	2,680	13,540	7,850	14,800	12,890	96,549
B. Variable (Selling) Expenses														
1. Advertising	900	300	900	250	300	700	3,350	350	300	640	1,300	1,200	1,400	8,540
2. Freight	75	75	75	75	180	70	550	75	75	90	180	300	560	1,830
3. Fulfillment of Orders	300	300	300	400	350	300	1,950	300	280	325	450	600	975	4,880
4. Packaging Costs	2,100	0	0	0	600	0	2,700	0	200	230	0	0	0	3,130
5. Sales/Salaries	1,400	900	1,300	1,400	1,100	900	7,000	1,400	1,400	1,400	1,400	1,400	1,400	15,400
6. Travel	0	500	700	0	0	400	1,600	0	540	25	80	0	0	2,245
7. Misc. Variable Expense	100	100	100	100	100	100	600	100	100	100	100	100	100	1,200
Total Variable Expenses	4,875	2,175	3,375	2,225	2,630	2,470	17,750	2,225	2,895	2,810	3,510	3,600	4,435	37,225
C. Fixed Expenses														
1. Financial Admin	75	75	75	475	75	75	850	75	75	75	75	75	75	1,300
2. Insurance	1,564	0	0	0	0	0	1,564	1,563	0	0	0	0	0	3,127
3. License/Permits	240	0	0	0	0	0	240	0	0	0	0	0	125	365
4. Office Salaries	1,400	1,400	1,400	1,400	1,400	1,400	8,400	1,400	1,400	1,400	1,400	1,400	1,400	16,800
5. Rent Expenses	700	700	700	700	700	700	4,200	700	700	700	700	700	700	8,400
6. Utilities	200	200	140	120	80	80	820	75	75	75	90	120	155	1,410
7. Misc. Fixed Expense	100	100	100	100	100	100	600	100	100	100	100	100	100	1,200
Total Fixed Expenses	4,279	2,475	2,415	2,795	2,355	2,355	16,674	3,913	2,350	2,350	2,365	2,395	2,555	32,602
D. Interest Expense	0	0	0	234	233	232	699	231	230	225	223	222	220	2,050
E. Federal Income Tax	1,200	1	1	1,200	0	1,200	3,603	0	0	1,200	0	0	0	4,803
F. Other Uses	0	0	0	0	0	0	0	0	0	0	0	0	0	0
G. Long-Term Asset Payments	0	0	0	214	214	214	642	214	214	214	214	214	214	1,926
H. Loan Payments	0	1,111	1,111	1,111	1,111	1,111	5,555	1,111	1,111	1,111	1,111	1,111	1,111	12,221
I. Owner Draws	2,000	2,000	2,000	2,000	2,000	2,000	12,000	2,000	2,000	2,000	3,000	3,000	3,000	27,000
TOTAL CASH PAID OUT	19,154	28,492	13,202	10,879	9,494	10,532	91,753	19,653	11,480	23,450	18,273	25,342	24,425	214,376
CASH BALANCE/DEFICIENCY	7,840	54,488	55,346	65,125	74,253	81,341	6,341	71,401	68,974	55,974	54,718	59,032	86,020	11,020
LOANS TO BE RECEIVED	65,000	0	0	0	0	0	65,000	0	0	0	0	0	0	65,000
EQUITY DEPOSITS	0	0	5,000	0	5,000	0	10,000	0	0	0	0	0	0	10,000
ENDING CASH BALANCE	72,840	54,488	60,346	65,125	79,253	81,341	81,341	71,401	68,974	55,974	54,718	59,032	86,020	86,020

Quarterly Budget Analysis

Your Pro Forma Cash Flow Statement (yearly budget) is of no value to you as a business owner unless there is some means to evaluate the actual performance of your company and measure it against your projections.

What is a Quarterly Budget Analysis?

A quarterly budget analysis is the financial analysis tool that is used to compare your projected cash flow statement with your business's actual performance. Its purpose is to let you know whether or not you are operating within your projections and to help you maintain control of all phases of your business operations. When your analysis shows that you are over or under budget in any area, it will be necessary to determine the reason for the deviation and to implement changes for the future that will enable you to get back on track.

> **Example.** If you have budgeted $1,000 in advertising funds for the first quarter and you find that you have actually spent $1,600, the first thing you should do is look at the sales that have occurred as a result of increased advertising. If they are over projections by an amount equal to or more than the $600, your budget will still be in good shape. If not, you will have to find expenses in your budget that can be revised to make up the deficit. You might be able to take a smaller draw for yourself or spend less on travel. You might even be able to increase your profits by adding a new product or service.

It should be clear at this point that the correct process to keep you from running out of operating capital in the middle of the year is to make yearly projections, analyze at the end of each quarter and then to revise your budget based on that analysis and current industry trends.

How to Develop a Quarterly Budget Analysis

The Quarterly Budget Analysis needs the following seven columns:

1. **Budget Item.** The list of budget items is taken from headings on the Pro Forma Cash Flow Statement. All items in your budget should be listed.

2. **Budget This Quarter.** Fill in the amount budgeted for current quarter from your Pro Forma Cash Flow Statement.

3. **Actual This Quarter.** Fill in actual expenditures or receipts for quarter.

4. **Variation This Quarter.** Subtract the amount spent or received from the amount budgeted for the current quarter. This will be the amount spent or received over or under budget.

5. **Year-to-Date Budget.** Amount budgeted from beginning of year through and including current quarter (from cash flow statement).

6. **Actual Year-to-Date.** Actual amount spent or received from beginning of year through current quarter.

7. **Variation Year-to-Date.** Subtract the amount spent or received from the amount budgeted from the start of the year through the current quarter.

 Note. You will not have any information to input into columns 3, 4, 5, 6, and 7 until you have been in business at least one quarter.

All items contained in the Budget are listed on this form. The second column is the amount budgeted for the current quarter. By subtracting the amount actually spent, you will arrive at the variation for the quarter. The last three columns are for year-to-date-figures. If you analyze at the end of the 3rd quarter, figures will represent the first nine months of your tax year.

Making Calculations: When you calculate variations, the amounts are preceded by either a plus (+) or a minus (-), depending on whether the category is a revenue or an expense. If the actual amount is greater than the amount budgeted, (1) Revenue categories will represent the variation as a positive (+). (2) Expense categories will represent the variation as a negative (-).

Quarterly Budget Analysis

Business Name: *Genesis Multimedia*   **For the Quarter Ending: September 30, 2014**

BUDGET ITEM	THIS QUARTER			YEAR-TO-DATE		
	Budget	Actual	Variation	Budget	Actual	Variation
SALES REVENUES	145,000	150,000	5,000	400,000	410,000	10,000
Less Cost of Goods	80,000	82,500	(2,500)	240,000	243,000	(3,000)
GROSS PROFITS	65,000	67,500	2,500	160,000	167,000	7,000
VARIABLE EXPENSES						
1. Advertising/Marketing	3,000	3,400	(400)	6,000	6,200	(200)
2. Freight	6,500	5,750	750	16,500	16,350	150
3. Fulfillment of Orders	1,400	950	450	3,800	4,100	(300)
4. Packaging	750	990	(240)	2,200	2,300	(100)
5. Salaries/Commissions	6,250	6,250	0	18,750	18,750	0
6. Travel	500	160	340	1,500	1,230	270
7. Miscellaneous	0	475	(475)	0	675	(675)
FIXED EXPENSES						
1. Financial/Administrative	1,500	1,500	0	4,500	4,700	(200)
2. Insurance	2,250	2,250	0	6,750	6,750	0
3. Licenses/Permits	1,000	600	400	3,500	3,400	100
4. Office Salaries	1,500	1,500	0	4,500	4,500	0
5. Rent	3,500	3,500	0	10,500	10,500	0
6. Utilities	750	990	(240)	2,250	2,570	(320)
7. Miscellaneous	0	60	(60)	0	80	(80)
NET INCOME FROM OPERATIONS	36,100	39,125	3,025	79,250	84,895	5,645
INTEREST INCOME	1,250	1,125	(125)	3,750	3,700	(50)
INTEREST EXPENSE	1,500	1,425	75	4,500	4,500	0
NET PROFIT (Pretax)	35,850	38,825	2,975	78,500	84,095	5,595
TAXES	8,500	9,500	(1,000)	25,500	28,500	(3,000)
NET PROFIT (After Tax)	27,350	29,325	1,975	53,000	55,595	2,595

NON-INCOME STATEMENT ITEMS

	Budget	Actual	Variation	Budget	Actual	Variation
1. Long-term Asset Repayments	2,400	3,400	(1,000)	7,200	8,200	(1,000)
2. Loan Repayments	3,400	3,400	0	8,800	8,800	0
3. Owner Draws	6,000	6,900	(900)	18,000	18,900	(900)

BUDGET DEVIATIONS

	This Quarter	Year-To-Date
1. Income Statement Items:	$1,975	$2,595
2. Non-Income Statement Items:	($1,900)	($1,900)
3. Total Deviation	$75	$695

Three-Year Income Projection

What is a Three-Year Income Projection?

A three-year income projection is a pro forma income (or profit & loss) statement. This statement differs from a cash flow statement in that it includes only projected income and deductible expenses. This difference is illustrated as follows: Your company will make payments of $9,000 on a vehicle in 2015. Of that amount, $3,000 is interest. The full amount ($9,000) will be recorded on a cash flow statement; only the interest ($3,000) will be recorded on a projected income statement. Principal paid on your loan ($6,000) is not a deductible expense.

Variation in Period Covered

There is some difference of opinion as to the period of time that should be covered and whether or not it should be on an annual or month-by-month basis. If you are seeking funds, talk to the lender about his or her specific requirements. If not, I suggest a three-year projection with annual rather than monthly projections. In a rapidly-changing economy, it is difficult to make accurate detailed projections.

Account for Increases and Decreases

Increases in income and expenses are only realistic and should be reflected in your projections. Industry trends can also cause decreases in both income and expenses. An example of this might be in the computer industry where heavy competition and standardization of components caused a decrease in the cost and the sale price of both hardware and software. The state of the economy will also be a contributing factor in the outlook for your business.

Sources of Information

Information for a three-year income projection can be developed from your pro forma cash flow statement and your business and marketing analysis. The first year's figures can be transferred from the totals of income and expense items. The second and third year's figures are derived by combining these totals with projected trends in your particular industry. Also remember that certain expenses from your first year may not be repeated in future years. You may also have new expenses to take into account. For instance, you may have a new product or service, you may begin importing or exporting internationally and have customs and freight, or you may begin offering merchant credit card services and have associated fees. Again, if you are an established business, you will also be able to use past financial statements to help you determine what you project for the future of your business. Be sure to take into account fluctuations anticipated in costs, efficiency of operation, changes in your market, etc.

At the end of each year, you can compare your company's projections against its actual performance. You may be required by some lenders or investors to extend your projection to five years. The process will be the same.

 Note. A filled-in example of a Three-Year Income Projection form is provided on the next page. A blank form for your use is located in Appendix VI.

Three-Year Income Projection

Business Name: **Updated: September 26, 2014**

Genesis Multimedia

	YEAR 1 2015	YEAR 2 2016	YEAR 3 2017	TOTAL 3 YEARS
INCOME				
1. SALES REVENUES	500,000	540,000	595,000	1,635,000
2. Cost of Goods Sold (c-d)	312,000	330,000	365,000	1,007,000
a. Beginning Inventory	147,000	155,000	175,000	147,000
b. Purchases	320,000	350,000	375,000	1,045,000
c. C.O.G. Avail. Sale (a+b)	467,000	505,000	550,000	1,192,000
d. Less Ending Inventory (12/31)	155,000	175,000	185,000	185,000
3. GROSS PROFIT ON SALES (1-2)	188,000	210,000	230,000	628,000
EXPENSES				
1. VARIABLE (Selling) (a thru h)	67,390	84,300	89,400	241,090
a. Advertising/Marketing	22,000	24,500	26,400	72,900
b. Freight	9,000	12,000	13,000	34,000
c. Fulfillment of Orders	2,000	3,500	4,000	9,500
d. Packaging Costs	3,000	4,000	3,500	10,500
e. Salaries/Wages/Commissions	25,000	34,000	36,000	95,000
f. Travel	1,000	1,300	1,500	3,800
g. Miscellaneous Selling Expense	390	0	0	390
h. Depreciation (Prod/Service Assets)	5,000	5,000	5,000	15,000
2. FIXED (Administrative) (a thru h)	51,610	53,500	55,800	160,910
a. Financial Administration	1,000	1,200	1,200	3,400
b. Insurance	3,800	4,000	4,200	12,000
c. Licenses & Permits	2,710	1,400	1,500	5,610
d. Office Salaries	14,000	17,500	20,000	51,500
e. Rent Expense	22,500	22,500	22,500	67,500
f. Utilities	3,000	3,500	3,600	10,100
g. Miscellaneous Fixed Expense	0	0	0	0
h. Depreciation (Office Equipment)	4,600	3,400	2,800	10,800
TOTAL OPERATING EXPENSES (1+2)	119,000	137,800	145,200	402,000
NET INCOME OPERATIONS (GPr - Exp)	69,000	72,200	84,800	226,000
OTHER INCOME (Interest Income)	5,000	5,000	5,000	15,000
OTHER EXPENSE (Interest Expense)	7,000	5,000	4,000	16,000
NET PROFIT (LOSS) BEFORE TAXES	67,000	72,200	85,800	225,000
TAXES 1. Federal, S-Employment	21,700	24,200	28,500	74,400
2. State	4,300	4,800	5,700	14,800
3. Local	0	0	0	0
NET PROFIT (LOSS) AFTER TAXES	41,000	43,200	51,600	135,800

Break-Even Analysis

What is a Break-Even Point?

This is the point at which a company's costs exactly match the sales volume and at which the business has neither made a profit nor incurred a loss. The break-even point can be determined by mathematical calculation or by development of a graph. It can be expressed in:

1. **Total Dollars of Revenue** (exactly offset by total costs)
2. **Total Units of Production** (cost of which exactly equals the income derived by their sale).

To apply a Break-Even Analysis to an operation, you will need three projections:

1. **Fixed Costs.** Administrative Overhead + Interest. Many of these costs remain constant even during slow periods. *Interest expense* must be added to fixed costs for a break-even analysis.
2. **Variable Costs.** Cost of Goods + Selling Expenses. Usually varies with volume of business. The greater the sales volume, the higher the costs.
3. **Total Sales Volume.** Projected sales for same period.

Source of Information

All of your figures can be derived from your Three-Year Projection. Since break-even is not reached until your total revenues match your total expenses, the calculation of your break-even point will require that you add enough years' revenues and expenses together until you see that the total revenues are greater than the total expenses. Retrieve the figures and plug them into the following mathematical formula. (By now you should be able to see that each financial document in your business plan builds on the ones done previously.)

Mathematically

A firm's sales at break-even point can be computed by using this formula:

B-E Point (Sales) = Fixed Costs + [(Variable Costs/Estimated Revenues) x Sales]

Terms Used: *a. Sales = volume of sales at Break-Even Point*
b. Fixed Costs = administrative expense, depreciation, interest
c. Variable Costs = cost of goods and selling expenses
d. Estimated Revenues = income (from sales of goods/services)

Example: *a. S (Sales at B-E Point) = the unknown*
b. FC (Fixed Costs) = $25,000
c. VC (Variable Costs) = $45,000
d. R (Estimated Revenues) = $90,000

Using the formula, the computation would appear as follows:
S (at B-E Point) = $25,000 + [($45,000/$90,000) x S]
S = $25,000 + (1/2 x S)
S - 1/2 S = $25,000

★ **S = $50,000   (B-E Point in terms of $ of revenue exactly offset by total costs)**

Graphically

Break-even point in graph form for the same business would be plotted as illustrated below. There is a blank form for your use in Appendix VI.

Break-Even Analysis Graph

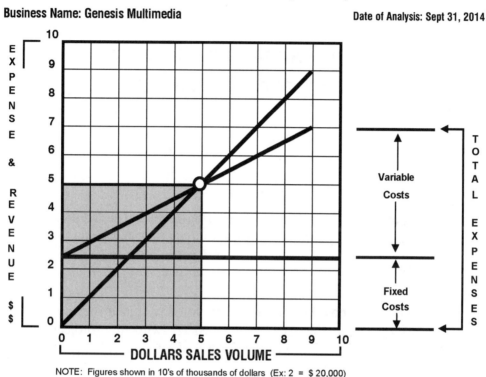

Business Name: Genesis Multimedia

Date of Analysis: Sept 31, 2014

NOTE: Figures shown in 10's of thousands of dollars (Ex: 2 = $ 20,000)

To Complete the Graph. Determine the following projections.

1. **Fixed Costs for Period.** Those costs that usually remain constant and must be met regardless of sales volume (administrative, rent, insurance, depreciation, salaries, etc.). Also add interest expense. (**Ex: $25,000**)

2. **Variable Costs.** Cost associated with the production and selling of your products or services. If you have a product, you will include cost of goods (inventory purchases, labor, materials) with your variable costs (freight, packaging, sales commissions, advertising, etc.) If you wish, these costs may be expressed by multiplying the unit cost by the units to be sold for a product. (**Example: $1.50 per unit x 30,000 units = $45,000**). For a service having no cost of goods, use total of projected selling expenses (variable).

3. **Total Sales Volume.** This figure represents your total projected revenues. You may also calculate revenues by multiplying projected units of product to be sold by sale price per unit. (**Example: 30,000 units @ $3.00 = $90,000**) For a service, you can multiply projected billable hours by your hourly rate. (**Example: 900 hours x $100 = $90,000**)

To Draw Graph Lines

1. **Draw Horizontal Line** at point representing Fixed Costs (25).
2. **Draw Variable Cost Line** from left end of Fixed Cost Line sloping upward to point where Total Costs (Fixed + Variable) on vertical scale (7) meet Total Revenues on the horizontal scale (9).
3. **Draw Total Revenues Line** from zero thru point describing total Revenues on both scales (where 9 meets 9).

Break-Even Point - That point on the graph where the Variable Cost Line intersects the Total Revenue Line. This business estimates that it will break even at the time sales volume reaches $50,000. The triangular area that is below and to the left of that point represents company losses. The triangular area that is above and to the right of the point represents expected company profits.

Section III

Actual Performance (Historical) Financial Statements

The financial statements covered on the following pages are actual performance (or historical) statements. They reflect the *past* activity of your business.

- **If you are a new business owner,** you do not have a business history. Your financial section ended with the projected statements and a Personal Financial History.

- **If you are an established business,** you will include the following actual performance financial documents:

    ✓ *Balance Sheet*

    ✓ *Profit & Loss (Income) Statement*

    ✓ *Business Financial History*
            or
    ✓ *Loan Application*

Balance Sheet

NPO
Page 144

What is a Balance Sheet?

The Balance Sheet is a financial statement that shows the financial position of the business as of a fixed date. It is usually done at the close of an accounting period. The Balance Sheet can be compared to a photograph. It is a picture of what your business owns and owes at a particular given moment and will show you whether your financial position is strong or weak. By regularly preparing this statement, you will be able to identify and analyze trends in the financial strength of your business and thus implement timely modifications.

Assets, Liabilities, and Net Worth

All balance sheets are divided into three categories. The three are related in that, at any given time, a business's assets equal the total contributions by its creditors and owners. They are defined as follows:

> **Assets =** Anything your business owns that has monetary value
>
> **Liabilities =** Debts owed by the business to any of its creditors
>
> **Net Worth (Capital) =** Amount equal to the owner's equity

The relationship between these terms is simply illustrated in the following accounting formula.

Assets - Liabilities = Net Worth

Examined as such, it becomes apparent that if a business possesses more assets than it owes to creditors, its net worth will be a positive. Conversely, if the business owes more money to creditors than it possesses in assets, the net worth will be a negative.

Projected Balance Sheets

If you are seeking financing, your lenders or investors may require that you provide them with projected balance sheets for "day-one" after capital infusion, or "end-of-year one". The financial information for a projected balance sheet as of a fixed date is compiled by using figures from the same-date column of your pro forma cash flow statement and same-date status on inventory, capital assets, long-term loans, and current liabilities. An example of an "end-of-year one" projected balance sheet can be seen in the each of the example business plans in Appendices I-V in the back of the book. The format is the same for projected or actual balance sheets.

Categories and Format

The Balance Sheet must follow an accepted accounting format and contain the previously mentioned categories. By following this format, anyone reading the Balance Sheet can readily interpret it.

 Note. A sample filled-in Balance Sheet and Explanation of Balance Sheet Categories are provided for you on the next two pages. There is also a blank form for your own use in Appendix VI.

Explanation of Categories
Balance Sheet

Assets. Everything owned by or owed to your business that has cash value.

1. ***Current Assets.*** Assets that can be converted into cash within one year of the date on the Balance Sheet.

    - **Cash.** Money you have on hand. Include moneys not yet deposited.
    - **Petty Cash.** Money deposited to Petty Cash & not yet expended.
    - **Accounts Receivable.** Money owed to you for sale of goods and/or services
    - **Inventory.** Raw materials, work in process and goods manufactured or purchased for resale
    - **Short-Term Investments.** Expected to be converted to cash within one year-- stocks, bonds, CDs. List at lesser of cost or market value.
    - **Prepaid Expenses.** Goods or services purchased or rented prior to use (ex: rent, insurance, prepaid inventory purchases, etc.)

2. ***Long-Term Investments.*** Stocks, bonds, and special savings accounts to be kept for at least one year.

3. ***Fixed Assets.*** Resources a business owns and does not intend for resale.

    - **Land.** List at original purchase price.
    - **Buildings.** List at cost less depreciation.
    - **Equipment, Furniture, Autos/Vehicles.** List at cost less depreciation. "Kelley Blue Book" can be used to determine current value of vehicles.

Liabilities. What your business owes; claims by creditors on your assets.

1. ***Current Liabilities.*** Those obligations payable within one operating cycle.

    - **Accounts Payable.** Obligations payable within one operating cycle.
    - **Notes Payable.** Short-term notes; list the balance of principal due. Separately list the current portion of long-term debts.
    - **Interest Payable.** Interest accrued on loans and credit.
    - **Taxes Payable.** Amounts estimated to have been incurred during the accounting period.
    - **Payroll Accrual.** Current Liabilities on salaries and wages.

2. ***Long-Term Liabilities.*** Outstanding balance less the current portion due (business loans, mortgages, vehicle, etc.)

Net Worth. Also called Owner Equity. The claims of the owner or owners on the assets of the business (Document according to the legal structure of your business.)

1. ***Proprietorship or Partnership.*** Each owner's original investment plus earnings after withdrawals.

2. ***Corporation.*** The sum of contributions by owners or stockholders plus earnings retained after paying dividends.

Balance Sheet

Business Name: *Genesis Multimedia*   **Date: September 30, 2014**

ASSETS

Current Assets
Cash	$	8,742
Petty Cash	$	167
Accounts Receivable	$	5,400
Inventory	$	101,800
Short-Term Investments	$	0
Prepaid Expenses	$	1,967

Long-Term Investments $ 0

Fixed Assets
Land (valued at cost)		$	185,000
Buildings		$	143,000
1. Cost	171,600		
2. Less Acc. Depr.	28,600		
Improvements		$	0
1. Cost			
2. Less Acc. Depr.			
Equipment		$	5,760
1. Cost	7,200		
2. Less Acc. Depr.	1,440		
Furniture		$	2,150
1. Cost	2,150		
2. Less Acc. Depr.	0		
Autos/Vehicles		$	16,432
1. Cost	19,700		
2. Less Acc. Depr.	3,268		

Other Assets
1.	$	
2.	$	

TOTAL ASSETS $ 470,418

LIABILITIES

Current Liabilities
Accounts Payable	$	2,893
Notes Payable	$	0
Interest Payable	$	1,842
Taxes Payable		
Federal Income Tax	$	5,200
Self-Employment Tax	$	1,025
State Income Tax	$	800
Sales Tax Accrual	$	2,130
Property Tax	$	0
Payroll Accrual	$	4,700

Long-Term Liabilities
Notes Payable	$	196,700

TOTAL LIABILITIES $ 215,290

NET WORTH (EQUITY)

Proprietorship	$	
or		
Partnership		
John Smith, 60% Equity	$	153,077
Mary Blake, 40% Equity	$	102,051
or		
Corporation		
Capital Stock	$	
Surplus Paid In	$	
Retained Earnings	$	

TOTAL NET WORTH $ 255,128

Assets - Liabilities = Net Worth
and
Liabilities + Equity = Total Assets

Profit & Loss (Income) Statement

What is a Profit & Loss (Income) Statement?

This statement shows your business financial activity over a period of time, usually your tax year. In contrast to the Balance Sheet, which shows a picture of your business at a given moment, the Profit & Loss Statement (P & L) can be likened to a moving picture--showing what has happened in your business over a period of time. It is an excellent tool for assessing your business. You will be able to pick out weaknesses in your operation and plan ways to run your business more effectively, thereby increasing your profits. For example, you may find that some heavy advertising in March did not effectively increase your sales. In following years, you may decide to utilize your advertising funds more effectively by using them at a time when there is increased customer spending taking place. In the same way, you might examine your Profit & Loss Statement to see what months have the heaviest sales volume and plan your inventory accordingly. Comparison of your P & Ls from several years will give you an even better picture of the trends in your business. Don't underestimate the value of this particular tool when planning your tactics.

How to Develop a Profit & Loss Statement

The Profit & Loss Statement (Income Statement) is compiled from actual business transactions, in contrast to pro forma statements, which are projections for future business periods. The P & L shows where your money has come from and where it was spent over a specific period of time. It should be prepared not only at the end of the fiscal year, but at the close of each business month. It is one of the two principal financial statements prepared from the ledgers and the records of a business.

Income and expense account balances are used in The Profit & Loss Statement. The remaining asset, liability and capital information provides the figures for the Balance Sheet covered on the last three pages. At the end of each month, these accounts are balanced and closed. Balances from the revenue accounts and the expense accounts are then transferred to your Profit & Loss Statement.

If you use an accounting professional or have a good in-house software program, either should generate a profit & loss statement and balance sheet for you at the end of every month as well as at the end of your tax year. Many owners of smaller businesses set up their own set of manual books. If your general records are set up properly, the transfer of information should still be fairly simple as long as you understand what information is needed and which general records are to be used as sources.

Format and Sources of Information

The Profit & Loss (or Income) Statement must also follow an accepted accounting format and contain certain categories.

On the next page, you will see the correct format and a brief explanation of the items to be included or computations to be made in each category in order to arrive at *"The Bottom Line"* or owner's share of the profit for the period.

Profit & Loss Statement
Correct Format and Explanation of Categories

Income

1. **Net Sales (Gross Sales less Returns and Allowances).** What were your cash receipts for the period? If accounting is on an accrual basis, what amount did you invoice out during the period? You may wish to have subcategories for different types of sales.

2. **Cost of Goods Sold.** The cost of manufacturing or purchase of products sold for the period. The Cost of Goods is calculated using a, b, and c below. **(a + b - c = C.O.G.)**

    a. **Beginning Inventory.** Product on hand at beginning of accounting period.

    b. **Purchases.** Material, labor, or cost of inventory purchased during accounting period.

    c. **Ending Inventory.** Product on hand at the end of the accounting period.

3. **Gross Profit.** Computed by subtracting Cost of Goods Sold from Net Sales. **(1 minus 2)**

> ➡ If you are in a service business and do not sell any products, you will *not have* any cost of goods to compute. Net sales and gross profit will be the same.

Expenses

1. **Variable Expenses (Selling).** What expenses did you have that were directly related to your product or service? (i.e. - advertising/marketing, freight, fulfillment of orders, sales salaries/commissions, trade shows, travel, vehicles, depreciation (production equip), etc.? These expenses vary and are usually directly proportional to your volume of business. Divide into sub-categories customized to your business.

2. **Fixed Expenses (Administrative).** What expenses did you have during the period on office overhead (accounting/legal, insurance, office supplies, office salaries, rent, utilities, depreciation of office equipment, etc.)? These expenses are often fixed and remain the same regardless of your volume of business. They should also be divided into subcategories customized to your business.

Net Income from Operations. Gross Profit (3.) minus Total Fixed (Selling) Expenses and Variable (Administrative) Expenses (Expenses numbers 1 and 2)

   Other Income. Interest received during the period

   Other Expense. Interest paid out during the period

Net Profit (Loss) Before Income Taxes. The Net Income from Operations plus Interest Income minus Interest Expense. The amount of profit prior to income taxes.

   Income Taxes. List taxes paid out during the period (Federal, State, local, self-employment)

Net Profit (Loss) After Income Taxes. Subtract all income taxes paid out from the net profit (or loss) before income taxes. This is what is known as *"the bottom line."*

Sample Forms. The next two pages contain two Profit & Loss Statement forms. As you will see in the Example 12-Month Profit & Loss Statement, the spreadsheet is divided into columns representing each of the 12 months + 6-month and annual total columns. At the end of your tax year, you will have filled in all monthly columns. After calculating your annual totals, your P&L will be complete. At the end of the year, this form will provide an accurate moving picture of the year's financial activity. The second is a single form to be used for either a monthly, quarterly, or annual profit & loss statement. Blank forms for your own use are provided in Appendix VI.

Profit & Loss (Income) Statement

Genesis Multimedia

For the Year: 2014

	Jan	Feb	Mar	Apr	May	Jun	6-MONTH TOTALS	Jul	Aug	Sep	Oct	Nov	Dec	12-MONTH TOTALS
INCOME														
1. NET SALES (Gross less R&A)	14,400	10,140	10,060	15,658	18,622	12,620	81,500	11,500	9,850	10,150	16,600	29,250	51,000	209,850
2. Cost of Goods to be Sold	2,800	2,900	4,200	7,700	7,350	2,750	27,700	2,959	2,580	2,740	6,250	13,400	23,290	78,919
a. Beginning Inventory	27,000	31,000	48,500	48,600	42,000	35,600	27,000	33,800	40,800	40,900	51,700	53,300	54,700	27,000
b. Purchases	6,800	20,400	4,300	1,100	950	950	34,500	9,959	2,680	13,540	7,850	14,800	12,890	96,219
c. C.O.G. available for sale	33,800	51,400	52,800	49,700	42,950	36,550	61,500	43,759	43,480	54,440	59,550	68,100	67,590	123,219
d. Less ending Inventory	31,000	48,500	48,600	42,000	35,600	33,800	33,800	40,800	40,900	51,700	53,300	54,700	44,300	44,300
3. GROSS PROFIT	11,600	7,240	5,860	7,958	11,272	9,870	53,800	8,541	7,270	7,410	10,350	15,850	27,710	130,931
EXPENSES														
1. Variable (Selling) Expenses														
a. Advertising	900	300	900	250	300	300	2,950	350	300	640	1,300	1,200	1,400	8,140
b. Freight	75	75	75	75	180	70	550	75	75	90	180	300	560	1,830
c. Fulfillment of Orders	300	300	300	400	350	300	1,950	300	280	325	450	600	975	4,880
d. Packaging Costs	2,100	0	0	0	600	0	2,700	0	200	230	0	0	0	3,130
e. Sales Salaries/Commissions	1,400	900	1,300	1,400	1,100	900	7,000	1,400	1,400	1,400	1,400	1,400	1,400	15,400
f. Travel	0	500	700	0	0	400	1,600	0	540	25	80	0	0	2,245
g. Misc. Variable Expense	50	47	73	40	28	62	300	90	73	46	39	74	87	709
h. Depreciation	0	0	0	0	0	0	0	0	0	0	0	0	2,660	2,660
Total Variable Expenses	4,825	2,122	3,348	2,165	2,558	2,032	17,050	2,215	2,868	2,756	3,449	3,574	7,082	38,994
1. Fixed (Admin) Expenses														
a. Financial Administration	75	75	75	475	75	75	850	75	75	75	75	75	75	1,300
b. Insurance	1,564	0	0	0	0	0	1,564	1,563	0	0	0	0	0	3,127
c. Licenses/Permits	240	0	0	0	0	0	240	0	0	0	0	0	125	365
d. Office Salaries	1,400	1,400	1,400	1,400	1,400	1,400	8,400	1,400	1,400	1,400	1,400	1,400	1,400	16,800
e. Rent Expenses	700	700	700	700	700	700	4,200	700	700	700	700	700	700	8,400
f. Utilities	200	200	140	120	80	80	820	75	75	75	90	120	155	1,410
g. Misc. Fixed Expense	54	38	42	57	28	64	283	60	72	31	48	45	89	628
h. Depreciation	0	0	0	0	0	2,660	2,660	0	0	0	0	0	2,660	5,320
Total Fixed Expenses	4,233	2,413	2,357	2,752	2,283	4,979	19,017	3,873	2,322	2,281	2,313	2,340	5,204	37,350
Total Operating Expense	9,058	4,535	5,705	4,917	4,841	7,011	36,067	6,088	5,190	5,037	5,762	5,914	12,286	76,344
Net Income From Operations	2,542	2,705	155	3,041	6,431	2,859	17,733	2,453	2,080	2,373	4,588	9,936	15,424	54,587
Other Income (Interest)	234	240	260	158	172	195	1,259	213	303	300	417	406	413	3,311
Other Expense (Interest)	0	0	0	234	233	232	699	231	230	225	223	222	220	2,050
Net Profit (Loss) Before Tax	2,776	2,945	415	2,965	6,370	2,822	18,293	2,435	2,153	2,448	4,782	10,120	15,617	55,848
Taxes: a. Federal	1,950	0	0	1,950	0	1,950	5,850	0	0	1,950	0	0	0	7,800
b. State	350	0	0	350	0	350	1,050	0	0	350	0	0	0	1,400
c. Local	0	0	0	0	0	0	0	0	0	0	0	0	0	0
NET PROFIT (LOSS) AFTER TAX	476	2,945	415	665	6,370	522	11,393	2,435	2,153	148	4,782	10,120	15,617	46,648

Profit & Loss (Income) Statement

Genesis Multimedia

Beginning: January 1, 2014   **Ending: December 31, 2014**

INCOME		
1. Sales Revenues		$ 209,850
2. Cost of Goods Sold (c-d)		78,919
a. Beginning Inventory (1/01)	27,000	
b. Purchases	96,219	
c. C.O.G. Avail. Sale (a+b)	123,219	
d. Less Ending Inventory (12/31)	44,300	
3. Gross Profit on Sales (1-2)		$ 130,931
EXPENSES		
1. Variable (Selling) (a thru h)		38,994
a. Advertising/Marketing	8,140	
b. Freight	1,830	
c. Fulfillment of Orders	4,880	
d. Packaging Costs	3,130	
e. Salaries/Wages/Commissions	15,400	
f. Travel	2,245	
g. Misc. Variable (Selling) Expense	709	
h. Depreciation (Prod/Serv Assets)	2,660	
2. Fixed (Administrative) (a thru h)		37,350
a. Financial Administration	1,300	
b. Insurance	3,127	
c. Licenses & Permits	365	
d. Office Salaries	16,800	
e. Rent Expense	8,400	
f. Utilities	1,410	
g. Misc. Fixed (Administrative) Expense	628	
h. Depreciation (Office Equipment)	5,320	
Total Operating Expenses (1+2)		76,344
Net Income from Operations (GP-Exp)		$ 54,587
Other Income (Interest Income)		3,311
Other Expense (Interest Expense)		2,050
Net Profit (Loss) Before Taxes		$ 55,848
Taxes		
a. Federal	7,800	
b. State	1,400	9,200
c. Local	0	
NET PROFIT (LOSS) AFTER TAXES		$ 46,648

Business Financial History

The business financial history is the last of the financial statements required in your business plan. It is a summary of financial information about your company from its start to the present.

If Yours is a New Business

You will have only projections for your business. If you are applying for a loan, the lender will require a Personal Financial History. This will be of benefit in that it will show the manner in which you have conducted your personal business, an indicator of the probability of your succeeding in your business.

If Yours is an Established Business

The loan application and your Business Financial History are the same. When you indicate that you are interested in obtaining a business loan, the institution considering the loan will supply you with an application. The format may vary slightly. When you receive your loan application, be sure to review it and think about how you are going to answer each item. Answer all questions and by all means be certain your information is accurate and that it can be easily verified.

Information Needed and Sources

When you fill out your Business Financial History (loan application), it should become immediately apparent why this is the last financial document to be completed. All of the information needed will have been compiled previously in earlier parts of your plan and in the financial statements you have already completed.

To help you with your financial history, the following is a list of information most frequently required. Also listed are the some of the sources you can refer to for that information:

- **Assets, Liabilities, Net Worth.** You should recognize these three as balance sheet terms. You have already completed the Balance Sheet for your company and need only to go back to that record and bring the dollar amounts forward.

- **Contingent Liabilities.** These are debts you may come to owe in the future (for example: default on a co-signed note or settlement of a pending lawsuit).

- **Inventory Details.** Information is derived from your Inventory Record. Also, in the Organizational Plan you should already have a summary of your current policies and methods of evaluation.

- **Profit & Loss Statement.** This is revenue and expense information. You will transfer the information from your Annual Profit & Loss (last statement completed) or from compilation of several if required by the lender.

- **Real Estate Holdings, Stocks and Bonds.** Refer back to your Organizational Plan. You may also have to go through your investment records for more comprehensive information

- **Legal Structure Information (Sole Proprietorship, Partnership or Corporation).** There are generally three separate schedules on the financial history, one for each form of legal structure. You will be required to fill out the one that is appropriate to your business. In the Organizational section, you will have covered two topics that will serve as the sources of needed information—Legal Structure and Management. Supporting Documents may also contain some of the information that you will need.

- **Audit Information.** Refer back to the Accounting & Legal section of your Organizational Plan. You may also be asked questions about other prospective lenders, whether you are seeking credit, who audits your books, and when they were last audited.

- **Insurance Coverage.** You will be asked to provide detailed information on the types of insurance your company has (i.e., liability, earthquake, workers compensation, inventory, machinery and fixtures, buildings, extended coverage, etc.). Your Organizational Plan and Insurance Update worksheet should have all of the information you will need to fill in this section of the financial history.

Business Financial History Form

You will find an example of a Business Financial History that might be required by a potential lender or investor on the next two pages (110-111).

Personal Financial Statement Form

If you are a new business and need your Personal Financial Statement for this section, you will find an example form in *"Anatomy of a Business Plan"*, Chapter 7, "Supporting Documents".

Please Note. Part IV: Financial Statement Analysis will follow after the Business Financial History example. (See pages 112-118)

Analysis of your financial statements will help you to make decisions and implement changes that will make your business more profitable.

Business Financial Statement
INDIVIDUAL, PARTNERSHIP, OR CORPORATION

FINANCIAL STATEMENT OF

Name_____

Address_____

Received At_____ Branch

Business_____

at Close of Business_____ 20____

To

The undersigned, for the purpose of procuring and establishing credit from time to time with you and to induce you to permit the undersigned to become indebted to you on notes, endorsements, guarantees, overdrafts or otherwise, furnishes the following (or in lieu thereof the attached, which is the most recent statement prepared by or for the undersigned) as being a full, true and correct statement of the financial condition of the undersigned on the date indicated, and agrees to notify you immediately of the extent and character of any material changes in said financial condition, and also agrees that if the undersigned or any endorser or guarantor of any of the obligations of the undersigned, at any time fails in business or becomes insolvent, or commits an act of bankruptcy, or if any deposit account of the undersigned with you, or any other property of the undersigned held by you, be attempted to be obtained or held by writ of execution, garnishment, attachment or other legal process, or if any of the representations made below prove to be untrue, or if the undersigned fails to notify you of any material change, as above agreed, or if the business, or any interest therein of the undersigned is sold, then and in such case, at your option, all of the obligations of the undersigned to you, or held by you, shall immediately become due and payable, without demand or notice. This statement shall be construed by you to be a continuing statement of the condition of the undersigned, and a new and original statement of all assets and liabilities upon each and every transaction in and by which the undersigned hereafter becomes indebted to you, until the undersigned advises in writing to the contrary.

ASSETS	DOLLARS	CENTS	LIABILITIES	DOLLARS	CENTS
Cash In_____ (Name of Bank)			Notes Payable to Banks_____		
Cash on Hand			Notes Payable and Trade Acceptances for Merchandise_____		
Notes Receivable and Trade Acceptance (Includes $_____ Past Due)			Notes Payable to Others_____		
Accounts Receivable--$_____ Less Reserves $_____			Accounts Payable (Includes $_____ Past Due)____		
Customer's . . . (Includes $_____ Past Due)			Due to Partners, Employees, Relatives, Officers, Stockholders or Allied Companies____		
Merchandise—Finished—How Valued_____			Chattel Mortgages and Contracts Payable (Describe Monthly Payments) . . . . . $____		
Merchandise—Unfinished—How Valued_____			Federal and State Income Tax_____		
Merchandise—Raw Material—How Valued_____			Accrued Liabilities (Interest, Wages, Taxes, Etc.)_____		
Supplies on Hand_____			Portion of Long Term Debt Due Within One Year____		
Stocks and Bonds—Listed (See Schedule B)_____					
TOTAL CURRENT ASSETS			**TOTAL CURRENT LIABILITIES**		
Real Estate—Less Depreciation of: $_____ Net (See Schedule A)			Liens on Real Estate (See Schedule A) $_____		
Machinery and Fixtures— Less Depreciation of: $_____ Net			Less Current Portion Included Above $_____ Net		
Automobiles and Trucks— Less Depreciation of: $_____ Net			Capital Stock—Preferred_____		
Stocks and Bonds—Unlisted (See Schedule B)_____			Capital Stock—Common_____		
Due from Partners, Employees, Relatives, Officers, Stockholders or Allied Companies____			Surplus—Paid In_____		
Cash Value Life Insurance_____			Surplus—Earned and Undivided Profit_____		
Other Assets (Describe_____			Net Worth (If Not Incorporated)_____		
TOTAL			TOTAL		

PROFIT AND LOSS STATEMENT FOR THE PERIOD FROM_____ TO_____			CONTINGENT LIABILITIES (Not Included Above)		
Net Sales (After Returned Sales and Allowances)_____			As Guarantor or Endorser_____		
Cost of Sales:			Accounts, Notes, or Trade Acceptance Discounted or Pledged____		
Beginning Inventory			Surety On Bonds or Other Continent Liability_____		
Purchases (or cost of goods mfd.)			Letters of Credit_____		
TOTAL			Judgments Unsatisfied or Suits Pending_____		
Less: Closing Inventory			Merchandise Commitments and Unfinished Contracts_____		
Gross Profit on Sales			Merchandise Held On Consignment From Others_____		
			Unsatisfied Tax Liens or Notices From the Federal or State Governments of Intention to Assess Such Liens		
Operating Expenses:			**RECONCILEMENT OF NET WORTH OR EARNED SURPLUS**		
Salaries—Officers or Partners			Net Worth or Earned Surplus at Beginning of Period_____		
Salaries and Wages—Other			Add Net Profit or Deduct Net Loss_____		
Rent			Total		
Depreciation			Other Additions (Describe)_____		
Bad Debts			Total		
Advertising					
Interest			Less: Withdrawals or Dividends		
Taxes—Other Than Income			Other Deductions (Explain)		
Insurance			Total Deductions		
Other Expenses			Net Worth or Capital Funds on This Financial Statement		
Net Profit from Operations			**DETAIL OF INVENTORY**		
Other Income					
Less Other Expenses			Is Inventory Figure Actual or Estimated?_____		
Net Profit Before Income Tax			By whom Taken or Estimated_____ When?_____		
Federal and State Income Tax			Buy Principally From_____		
Net Profit or Loss			Average Terms of Purchase_____ Sale_____		
(Total Net Worth or Earned Surplus)_____			Time of Year Inventory Maximum_____ Minimum_____		

Business Financial Statement
INDIVIDUAL, PARTNERSHIP, OR CORPORATION

FINANCIAL STATEMENT OF   Received At_____Branch

Name_____   Business_____

Address_____   at Close of Business_____20_____

To

The undersigned, for the purpose of procuring and establishing credit from time to time with you and to induce you to permit the undersigned to become indebted to you on notes, endorsements, guarantees, overdrafts or otherwise, furnishes the following (or in lieu thereof the attached, which is the most recent statement prepared by or for the undersigned) as being a full, true and correct statement of the financial condition of the undersigned on the date indicated, and agrees to notify you immediately of the extent and character of any material changes in said financial condition, and also agrees that if the undersigned or any endorser or guarantor of any of the obligations of the undersigned, at any time fails in business or becomes insolvent, or commits an act of bankruptcy, or if any deposit account of the undersigned with you, or any other property of the undersigned held by you, be attempted to be obtained or held by writ of execution, garnishment, attachment or other legal process, or if any of the representations made below prove to be untrue, or if the undersigned fails to notify you of any material change, as above agreed, or if the business, or any interest therein of the undersigned is sold, then and in such case, at your option, all of the obligations of the undersigned to you, or held by you, shall immediately become due and payable, without demand or notice. This statement shall be construed by you to be a continuing statement of the condition of the undersigned, and a new and original statement of all assets and liabilities upon each and every transaction in and by which the undersigned hereafter becomes indebted to you, until the undersigned advises in writing to the contrary.

ASSETS	DOLLARS	CENTS	LIABILITIES	DOLLARS	CENTS
Cash In_____			Notes Payable to Banks_____		
(Name of Bank)					
Cash on Hand_____			Notes Payable and Trade Acceptances for Merchandise_____		
Notes Receivable and					
Trade Acceptance (Includes $_____ Past Due)			Notes Payable to Others_____		
Accounts Receivable--$_____ Less Reserves $_____			Accounts Payable (Includes $_____ Past Due)		
			Due to Partners, Employees		
Customer's . . . . (Includes $_____ Past Due)			Relatives, Officers, Stockholders or Allied Companies____		
			Chattel Mortgages and Contracts Payable (Describe		
Merchandise—Finished—How Valued_____			Monthly Payments) . . . . . $_____		
Merchandise—Unfinished—How Valued_____			Federal and State Income Tax_____		
Merchandise—Raw Material—How Valued_____			Accrued Liabilities (Interest, Wages, Taxes, Etc.)_____		
Supplies on Hand_____			Portion of Long Term Debt Due Within One Year_____		
Stocks and Bonds—Listed (See Schedule B)_____					
TOTAL CURRENT ASSETS			**TOTAL CURRENT LIABILITIES**		
Real Estate—Less Depreciation of: $_____ Net			Liens on Real Estate (See Schedule A) $_____		
(See Schedule A)					
			Less Current Portion Included Above $_____ Net		
Machinery and Fixtures—					
Less Depreciation of: $_____ Net					
Automobiles and Trucks—					
Less Depreciation of: $_____ Net			Capital Stock—Preferred_____		
Stocks and Bonds—Unlisted (See Schedule B)_____			Capital Stock—Common_____		
Due from Partners, Employees,					
Relatives, Officers, Stockholders or Allied Companies____			Surplus—Paid In_____		
Cash Value Life Insurance_____			Surplus—Earned and Undivided Profit_____		
Other Assets (Describe_____			Net Worth (If Not Incorporated)_____		
TOTAL			TOTAL		

PROFIT AND LOSS STATEMENT FOR THE PERIOD FROM_____ TO_____			CONTINGENT LIABILITIES (Not Included Above)		
Net Sales (After Returned Sales and Allowances)_____			As Guarantor or Endorser		
Cost of Sales:			Accounts, Notes, or Trade		
			Acceptance Discounted or Pledged_____		
Beginning Inventory			Surety On Bonds or Other Continent Liability_____		
Purchases (or cost of goods mfd.)			Letters of Credit_____		
TOTAL			Judgments Unsatisfied or Suits Pending_____		
Less: Closing Inventory			Merchandise Commitments and Unfinished Contracts_____		
Gross Profit on Sales			Merchandise Held On Consignment From Others		
			Unsatisfied Tax Liens or Notices From the Federal or		
Operating Expenses:			State Governments of Intention to Assess Such Liens____		
Salaries—Officers or Partners			**RECONCILEMENT OF NET WORTH OR EARNED SURPLUS**		
Salaries and Wages—Other			Net Worth or Earned Surplus at Beginning of Period_____		
Rent			Add Net Profit or Deduct Net Loss_____		
Depreciation			Total_____		
Bad Debts			Other Additions (Describe)_____		
Advertising			Total		
Interest			Less: Withdrawals or Dividends		
Taxes—Other Than Income			Other Deductions (Explain)		
Insurance			Total Deductions_____		
Other Expenses			Net Worth or Capital Funds on This Financial Statement____		
Net Profit from Operations			**DETAIL OF INVENTORY**		
Other Income					
Less Other Expenses			Is Inventory Figure Actual or Estimated?_____		
Net Profit Before Income Tax			By whom Taken or Estimated_____ When?_____		
Federal and State Income Tax			Buy Principally From_____		
Net Profit or Loss			Average Terms of Purchase_____ Sale_____		
(Total Net Worth or Earned Surplus)_____			Time of Year Inventory Maximum_____ Minimum_____		

Section IV

Financial Statement Analysis: The Final Tool

The Financial Documents I have presented will probably be sufficient for both your own use and that of a potential lender or investor. Some of the documents may not be required. You should also note that we may have omitted forms required by some lenders or investors. The important thing for you to be aware of when compiling financial statements is that the information must be accurate, it must reflect the assumptions developed in the Organizational and Marketing Plans, and you must have supportive records that back up your numbers.

By now you will have completed all of the pro forma and historical financial statements required for your business. There is an additional financial tool, however, that will help you as well as your lenders and/or investors to look at your business, analyze it according to industry standards, and to make decisions that will increase profitability. That tool is financial statement analysis. It is accomplished by applying a set of formulas to the information on your profit and loss (income) statements and balance sheets.

How to Analyze Financial Statements

In the last pages of this section, I will explain financial statement analysis and give you examples of how you can use it to look at your business. Doing a financial statement analysis of your business is like all of the other tasks you have already completed. There is a definite process and if you follow it step-by-step, you will have added a valuable component to your business plan.

Read the following pages. When you are finished reading, go to the sample business plans in Appendices I, II, III, IV, and V and see how the analyses were done for Marine Art of California, Dayne Landscaping, Inc., Wholesale Mobile Homes.com, Inc., Karma Jazz Café, and Road Runners, Inc. Note that in one case, there a ratio and a financial statement analysis summary. Apply the formulas on the next few pages to your income statements and balance sheets to figure the ratios for your business. You can also complete a vertical analysis using the income statements and balance sheets. A horizontal analysis can only be completed if you have been in business for two or more years.

Analysis Summary

Once you have figured the ratios and completed your vertical (and horizontal, if you have been in business for two or more years) analyses, be sure to develop a summary sheet for your business plan. The summary sheet allows you and/or your lenders or investors to get a quick overview of your business and how it compares to industry standards. The summary should contain: (1) a list of your projected ratios, (2) a list of historical ratios if you are a current business, and (3) a list of standard ratios for your industry. After you list the ratios, you should finish your summary with your comments regarding what your ratios indicate for the future of the company.

Financial Statement Analysis
Putting Your Financial Statements to Work

To better utilize the financial section of your business plan as a working tool, you will use the financial statements that you have prepared to analyze your business. The following pages are devoted to giving you the basics about financial statement analysis. After you have read the material and understand how to apply the formulas to develop ratios, you can do an analysis of your own business and append it to the end of your financial section.

> **Note.** *If you are a new business, your analysis will be based on projections only. If you are a current business, you will use your historical profit and loss (income) statements and your balance sheets.*

Your financial statements contain the information you need to help make decisions regarding your business. Many small business owners think of their financial statements as requirements for creditors, bankers, or tax preparers only, but they are much more than that. When analyzed, your financial statements can give you key information needed on the financial condition and the operations of your business.

Relationships are expressed as ratios or percentages

Financial statement analysis requires measures to be expressed as ratios or percentages. For example, consider the situation where total assets on your balance sheet are $10,000. Cash is $2,000; Accounts Receivable is $3,000; and Fixed Assets is $5,000. The relationships of each of the three to total assets would be expressed as follows:

	Ratio	Relationship	Percentages
Cash	.2	.2:1	20%
Accounts Receivable	.3	.3:1	30%
Fixed Assets	.5	.5:1	50%

Financial statement analysis involves the studying of relationships and comparisons of:

- Items in a single year's financial statement
- Comparative financial statements for a period of time
- Your statements with those of other businesses

> **Note.** A **Financial Statement Analysis Ratio Table** form has been provided in Appendix VI for your use. The form has all of the formulas for figuring your ratios. Input the appropriate numbers from your income statements and balance sheets and calculate according to the formulas. This will give you the information for your analysis summary page.

Analyzing Your
P&L (Income) Statements & Balance Sheets

Many analytic tools are available, but the focus here will be on the following measures that are of most importance to a small business owner in the business planning process. All utilize your profit and loss (income) statements and balance sheets.

Liquidity Analysis	**Measures of Investment**
Profitability	**Vertical Financial Statement Analysis**
Measures of Debt	**Horizontal Financial Statement Analysis**

Liquidity Analysis

The liquidity of a business is the ability it has to meet financial obligations. The analysis focuses on the **balance sheet** relationships for the current assets and current liabilities. The three main measures of liquidity and their formulas are as follows:

1. **Net Working Capital.** The excess of current assets over current liabilities is net working capital. The more net working capital a business has, the less risky it is, as it has the ability to cover current liabilities as they come due.

$$\text{Formula:} \quad \begin{array}{r} \text{Current Assets} \\ \underline{- \text{ Current Liabilities}} \\ \text{Net Working Capital} \end{array}$$

2. **Current Ratio.** The current ratio is a more dependable indication of liquidity than the net working capital. Current ratio is computed using the following formula:

$$\text{Current Ratio} \quad = \quad \frac{\text{Current Assets}}{\text{Current Liabilities}}$$

There are no set criteria for the **normal** current ratio, as that is dependent on the business you are in. If you have predictable cash flows, you can operate with a lower current ratio.

A higher ratio means a more liquid position. A ratio of 2.0 is considered acceptable for most businesses. This would allow a company to lose 50% of its current assets and still be able to cover current liabilities. For most businesses, this is an adequate margin of safety.

3. **Quick Ratio.** Since inventory is the most difficult current asset to dispose of quickly, it is subtracted from the current assets in the quick ratio to give a tougher list of liquidity. A quick ratio of 1.00 or greater is usually recommended, but that is dependent upon the business you are in. The quick ratio is computed as follows:

$$\text{Quick Ratio} \quad = \quad \frac{\text{Current Assets Inventory}}{\text{Current Liabilities}}$$

What are Liquidity Ratios Good For?

Liquidity ratios can be used to see if your business is in any risk of insolvency. You will also be able to assess your ability to increase or decrease current assets for your business strategy. How would these moves affect your liquidity? Your creditors will use these ratios to determine whether or not to extend credit to you. They will compare the ratios with those of previous periods and with industry standard ratios.

Profitability Analysis

A Profitability Analysis will measure the ability of a business to make a profit. This type of analysis will utilize your *profit and loss (income) statements*. Three of these measures and their formulas are as follows:

1. **Gross Profit Margin.** The gross profit margin indicates the percentage of each sales dollar remaining after a business has paid for its goods.

$$\text{Gross Profit Margin} = \frac{\text{Gross Profit}}{\text{Sales}}$$

   The higher the gross profit margin, the better. The *normal* rate is dependent on the business you are in. The Gross Profit Margin is the actual markup you have on the goods sold.

2. **Operating Profit Margin.** This ratio represents the pure operations profits, ignoring interest and taxes. In other words, this is the percentage of each sales dollar remaining after a business has paid for its goods and paid for its variable and fixed expenses. Naturally, a high operating profit margin is preferred.

$$\text{Operating Profit Margin} = \frac{\text{Income from Operations}}{\text{Sales}}$$

3. **Net Profit Margin.** The net profit margin is clearly the measure of a business success with respect to earnings on sales.

$$\text{Net Profit Margin} = \frac{\text{Net Profit}}{\text{Sales}}$$

   A higher margin means the firm is more profitable. The net profit margin will differ according to your specific type of business. A 1% margin for a grocery store is not unusual due to the large quantity of items handled; while a 10% margin for a jewelry store would be considered low.

   Your creditors will look at these ratios to see just how profitable your business is. Without profits, a business cannot attract outside financing. As a business owner, you can see just how profitable your business is. If the ratios are too low, you will want to analyze why.

   - *Did you mark up your goods sold enough? Check your gross profit margin.*
   - *Are your operating expenses too high? Check your operating profit margin.*
   - *Are your interest expenses too high? Check your net profit margin.*

Debt Measures

The debt position of a business indicates the amount of other people's money being used to generate profits. Many new businesses assume too much debt too soon in an attempt to grow too quickly. The measures of debt use the ***balance sheet*** to tell your business how indebted it is and how able it is to service the debts. The more indebtedness you have, the greater will be your risk of failure.

1. **Debt to Assets Ratio.** This is a key financial ratio used by creditors. It shows what you owe in relationship to what you own. The higher this ratio, the higher the risk of failure.

$$\text{Debt to Assets Ratio} = \frac{\text{Total Liabilities}}{\text{Total Assets}}$$

   The acceptable ratio is dependent upon the policies of your creditors and bankers. If, for instance, you had rates of 79% and 74% for two consecutive years, these would be excessively high and show a very high risk of failure. Clearly 3/4 of the company is being financed by other people's money, and it does not put the business in a good position for acquiring new debt.

2. **Debt to Equity Ratio.** This is a key financial ratio used by creditors. It shows what is owed in relationship to the owner's equity in the company. Again, the higher this ratio, the higher the risk of failure.

$$\text{Debt to Equity Ratio} = \frac{\text{Total Liabilities}}{\text{Total Equity (Net Worth)}}$$

   If your business plan includes the addition of long-term debt at a future point, you will want to monitor your debt ratio. If you are seeking a lender, is it within the limits acceptable to your banker?

Investment Measures

As a small business owner, you have invested money to acquire assets, and you should be getting a return on these assets. Even if the owner is taking a salary from the business, he/she also should be earning an additional amount for the investment in the company.

1. **Return on Investment (ROI).** The Return on Investment uses your ***balance sheet*** and measures the effectiveness of you, as the business owner, to generate profits from the available assets.

$$\text{ROI} = \frac{\text{Net Profits}}{\text{Total Assets}}$$

   The higher the ROI, the better. The business owner should get a target for the ROI. What do you want your investment to earn? Many small business owners have successfully created jobs for themselves, but still don't earn a fair return on their investment. Set your target for ROI, and work towards it.

Vertical Financial Statement Analysis

Percentage analysis is used to show relationship of components in a single financial statement.

- **For a balance sheet.** Each asset on the balance sheet is stated as a percent of the total assets, and each liability and equity item is stated as a percent of the total liabilities and owner equity (or net worth).

- **For an Income Statement.** In vertical analysis of the income statement, each item is stated as a percent of the total net sales.

An evaluation of components on single financial statements from one or more years can show changes that may alert you to investigate current expenditures. For example a high percentage increase in cost of goods sold should be cause for investigation. A decrease in gross profit from one year to the next might trigger the owner to look at the mark-up.

You can also evaluate your percentages against those of competitors or against industry standards for your trade to help you make judgments that can help your business be more profitable in the future. If your competitor is making a gross profit of 47% and yours is only 32%, you will want to know the reason why. Does he have a better source for purchasing product? Is his manufacturing process more efficient?

Horizontal Financial Statement Analysis

Horizontal analysis is a percentage analysis of the increases and decreases in the items on comparative financial statements. The increase or decrease of the item is listed, and the earlier statement is used as the base. The percentage of increase or decrease is listed in the last column.

- **For a balance sheet.** Assets, Liabilities, and Owner's Equity of one year are measured against a second year. The increase or decrease of the item is listed followed by the percentage of increase or decrease.

- **For an Income Statement.** In horizontal analysis of the income statement, Income and Expense items of one year are measured against a second year. The increase or decrease of the item is listed followed by the percentage of increase or decrease.

The horizontal financial statement analysis can also alert you to potential or current problems that can decrease your profitability. As an example, if you have an increase in sales, but a decrease in gross profit, you might look at your mark up. If you have a large increase in advertising expense, you will need to see if the expense was justified by increased sales.

Summary

Now, you can see how financial statement analysis can be a tool to help you manage your business.

- If the analysis produces results that don't meet your expectation—or if the business is in danger of failure, analyze your expenses and use of assets. Your first stop should be to cut expenses and increase productivity of assets.

- If return on investment is too low, examine how you could make your assets (equipment, machinery, fixtures, inventory, etc.) better work to your benefit.

- If your profit is low, be sure that your mark up is adequate, analyze operating expenses to see that they are not too high, and review your interest expenses.

- If your liquidity is low, you could have a risk of becoming insolvent. Examine the level and composition of current assets and current liabilities.

- Vertical and horizontal financial statement analysis will reveal trends and compositions that signify trouble. Using management skills, you can take corrective action.

What is Your Situation?

Your Financial Statement Analysis will need to be set up according to your individual situation. For example, a new business will have projections only and will have no historical statements to analyze. A one-year-old business would have historical statements for the first year and projections for the second year. A business that is several years old may wish to analyze more than one year of their past financial statements and show their projections for future years.

Most plans will follow one of the two following two formats:

1. **New Businesses – Projected Analysis for year one**

   You will prepare a ratio table, filling in column three only with projected ratios for your first year of business. You will not input any information in column four. You will also prepare Projected Vertical Income Statement and Balance Sheets for your first year. After you have completed these three spreadsheets, you will do a Financial Statement Analysis Summary, filling in the *Projected* and *Industry Standard* columns. This will complete your analysis.

   When you update your plan at the end of year one, you can come back and fill in the *Historical* column for year one and the *Projected* column for year two. You can also prepare a Historical Vertical Income Statement and Balance Sheet for year one and a Projected Vertical Income Statement and Balance Sheet for year two.

2. **Current Businesses – Historical Analysis of previous year and Projected Analysis for the coming year**

   You will prepare a Ratio Table, filling in column three with historical ratios for your previous business year. In column four you will input your projections for the coming year. You will prepare a Historical Vertical Income Statement and Balance Sheet for the past year and a Projected Vertical Income Statement and Balance Sheet for the coming year. When you have completed these spreadsheets, you will do a Financial Statement Analysis Summary, filling in *Historical, Projected,* and *Industry Standard* columns.

> **Note.** For a more detailed discussion of Financial Statement Analysis see my basic recordkeeping and accounting small business book, *Keeping the Books.*

Part IV
Supporting Documents

Now that you have completed the main body of your Business Plan, it is time to consider any additional records that pertain to your business and that should be included in your business plan.

Supporting Documents are the records that back up the statements and decisions made in the three main parts of your Business Plan. This chapter covers most of the documents which you will want to include. They will be discussed in the following order:

    ✓ *Personal Résumés*

    ✓ *Owner's Financial Statement*

    ✓ *Credit Reports*

    ✓ *Copies of Leases*

    ✓ *Letters of Reference*

    ✓ *Contracts*

    ✓ *Legal Documents*

    ✓ *Location Studies, Demographics, etc.*

About Supporting Documents

After completing the main body of your Business Plan, you are now ready to consider the Supporting Documents that should be included. These are the records that back up the statements and decisions made in the three main parts of your Business Plan. As you are compiling the first three sections, it is a good idea to keep a separate list of the Supporting Documents that you mention or that come to mind. Many of these documents will actually be needed as you write your plan so that you will have solid financial information to use in your projections. For instance, discussion of your business location might indicate a need for demographic studies, location maps, area studies, leases, etc. The information in the lease agreement will state the financial terms. Once you have the location, you will also know the square footage of your facility and you will be able to project other associated costs, such as utilities, improvements, etc.

If you are considering applying for a loan to purchase equipment, your supporting documents might be existing equipment purchase agreements or lease contracts. If you are planning a major advertising campaign, include advertising rate sheets from your targeted advertiser.

If you are doing business internationally, you may wish to include customs documents, trade agreements, or shipping agreements. If you are exporting a product or providing a service in a foreign country, it might be beneficial to include demographics on your target market, competition evaluations, and anything else that is pertinent to your business.

By listing these items as you think of them and gathering them as you are working on your business plan, you will have a fairly complete set of all of your supporting documents by the time you finish writing your organizational, marketing and financial sections. You can sort them into a logical sequence, add them to your working copy, and be ready to add any new ones that become pertinent during the lifetime of your business.

Note. All supporting documents would not be included in every copy of your business plan. Include only that information you think will be needed by the potential lender or investor. The rest should be kept with your copy of the plan and be easily accessible.

The following pages will cover most of the documents you will normally need to include. The end of the chapter includes examples of some of the types of supporting documents.

Personal Résumés

If you are a sole proprietor, include your own résumé. If your business is a partnership, there should be a résumé for each partner. If you are a corporation, include résumés for all officers of the corporation.

It is also a good idea to include résumés for your management and any other key personnel that will be involved in making decisions and affecting the profitability of the company, showing why they were chosen, what their skills are, and how the company will benefit from their management.

A résumé need not, and should not, be a lengthy document. Preferably, it should be contained on one page for easy reading. Include the following categories and information:

- **Work History.** Name of business with dates of employment. Begin with most recent. Include duties, responsibilities, and related accomplishments.
- **Educational Background.** Schools and dates attended, degrees earned, and fields of concentration.
- **Professional Affiliations and Honors.** List active affiliation with organizations that will add to credibility. Tell about any distinguishing individual or business award received.
- **Special Skills.** (For example: relates well to others, able to organize, not afraid to take risks, etc.)

If you find it difficult to write your own résumé, there are professionals who will do it for you for a nominal fee. A well-written résumé will be a useful tool and should always be kept up-to-date. Once written, it is a simple task to update your information, adding new items and eliminating those that will not benefit you in your current endeavors.

An example of a résumé is located on p. 123.

Owner's Financial Statement

This is a statement of the owner/owners' personal assets and liabilities. Information can be compiled in the same manner as a Balance Sheet (See Chapter 6, Balance Sheet). It is also a statement of annual income and expenditures. If you are a new business owner, your personal financial statement will be included as a part of the Financial Documents section and may be a standard form supplied by the potential lender.

See a personal financial statement form on pp. 124-125.

Credit Reports

Credit ratings are of two types, business and personal. If you are already in business, you may have a Dun & Bradstreet rating. You can also ask your suppliers or wholesalers to supply you with letters of credit. Personal credit ratings can be obtained upon request through credit bureaus, banks and companies with whom you have dealt on a basis other than cash.

Copies of Leases

Include all lease agreements currently in force between your company and a leasing agency. Some examples are the lease agreement for your business premises, equipment, automobiles, etc. These agreements will provide solid backup for the financial information that you have projected regarding the lease of property and assets. It is important to note here that all lease agreements should be carefully entered into. In many instances they will contain clauses (especially in the case of site locations) that can eat heavily into a company's profits.

Letters of Reference

These are letters recommending you as being a reputable and reliable business person worthy of being considered a good risk. There are two types of letters of reference:

- **Business references.** Written by business associates, suppliers, and customers.
- **Personal references.** Written by non-business associates who can assess your business skills; not by friends or relatives.

Contracts

Include all business contracts, both completed and currently in force. Some examples are:

- Current loan contracts
- Papers on prior business loans
- Purchase agreements on large equipment
- Vehicle purchase contracts
- Service contracts
- Maintenance agreements
- Miscellaneous contracts

Legal Documents

Include all legal documents pertaining to your business. Examples are:

- Articles of Incorporation
- Partnership Agreements
- Limited Partnership Agreements
- DBAs
- Business Licenses
- Copyrights, trademarks and patents
- Trade agreements (See *example page 126*)
- Licensing agreements
- Insurance policies, agreements, etc.
- Property and vehicle titles

Miscellaneous Documents

These are all the documents (other than the above) that are referred to, but not included, in the Organizational and Marketing sections of your Business Plan.

A good example of what we mean should be those records related to selecting your location in the Organizational or Marketing Plan. Your location might be finalized as the result of the development of a Location Plan. You can refer to this section in your Table of Contents. The potential lender or investor can then turn to this portion of your plan and examine that Location Plan which might include:

- Demographic Studies
- Map of Selected Location
- Area Studies (Crime Rate, Income, etc.)

> ***To Help You.*** The next four pages contain samples of a résumé, a personal financial statement, and a trade offering. You will also find examples of various types of supporting documents in the example business plans provided for you in Appendices I through V at the back of the book.

Sample Résumé

John Smith
742 South Street
Jamestown, NY 10081
(207) 814-0221
JSmith@ABCCorp.com

WORK EXPERIENCE

2008 - Present   **ABC CORPORATION**

Burke, New York

<u>Corporate President</u>. Overall management responsibility for tool and die manufacture providing specialized parts to the aerospace industry. Specific management of Research and Development Department.

2002 - 2008   **ABC COMPONENTS**

Jamestown, New York

<u>Sole Proprietor and General Manager</u>. Sole responsibility for research and development of specialty aircraft parts. Long-term goal of expanding to incorporate and provide specialty parts to aerospace industry.

1992 - 2002   **JACKSON AIRCRAFT CO.**

Burke, New York

<u>Quality Control Supervisor</u>. Responsibility for the development and implementation of a quality control program for automated aircraft assembly facility. Implemented quality control program resulting in $4.3 million in increased profits to the company.

EDUCATION

University of California, Berkeley - Master of Business Administration, Emphasis on Marketing, 2002

Stanford University, Palo Alto, CA – B.S. Civil Engineering, 1992

PROFESSIONAL AFFILIATIONS

American Society of Professional Engineers
New York City Industrial League
Burke Chamber of Commerce

SPECIAL RECOGNITION

New York Businessman of the Year, 2012
New York Council on Small Business, 2009 - present
Director, Burke Chamber of Commerce

SPECIAL SKILLS

Resourceful and well-organized; Relates well to employees;
Self-motivated and not afraid to take risks.

Personal Financial Statement

(DO NOT USE FOR BUSINESS FINANCIAL STATEMENT)

As of _____ 20_____

FINANCIAL STATEMENT OF

Name_____

Address_____

Received at _____Branch

Employed by_____

Position_____Age_____Name of Spouse_____

If Employed Less Than
1 year, Previous Employer_____

The undersigned, for the purpose of procuring and establishing credit from time to time with you and to induce you to permit the undersigned to become indebted to you on notes, endorsements, guarantees, overdrafts or otherwise, furnishes the following (or in lieu thereof the attached, which is the most recent statement prepared by or for the undersigned) as being a full, true and correct statement of the financial condition of the undersigned on the date indicated, and agrees to notify you immediately of the extent and character of any material changes in said financial condition, and also agrees that if the undersigned or any endorser or guarantor of any of the obligations of the undersigned, at any time fails in business or becomes insolvent, or commits an act of bankruptcy, or dies, or if a writ of attachment, garnishment, execution or other legal process be issued against property of the undersigned or if any assessment for taxes against the undersigned, other than taxes on real property, is made by the federal or state government or any department thereof, or if any of the representations made below prove to be untrue, or if the undersigned fails to notify you of any material change as above agreed, or if such change occurs, or if the business, or any interest therein, of the undersigned is sold, then and in such case, all of the obligations of the undersigned to you or held by you shall immediately be due and payable, without demand or notice. This statement shall be construed by you to be a continuing statement of the condition of the undersigned, and a new and original statement of all assets and liabilities upon each and every transaction in and by which the undersigned hereafter becomes indebted to you, until the undersigned advises in writing to the contrary.

ASSETS	DOLLARS	CENTS	LIABILITIES	DOLLARS	CENTS
Cash in Bank _____ (Branch)			Notes Payable B of _____ (Branch)		
Cash on Hand_____ (Other – give name)			Notes Payable _____ (Other)		
Accounts Receivable-Good _____			Accounts Payable _____		
Stocks and Bonds (Schedule B) ____			Taxes Payable_____		
Notes Receivable-Good _____			Contracts Payable _____ (To Whom)		
Cash Surrender Value Life Insurance____			Contracts Payable _____ (To Whom)		
Autos_____ (Year-Make) (Year-Make)			Real Estate indebtedness (Schedule A)____		
Real Estate (Schedule A) _____			Other Liabilities (describe)		
Other Assets (describe)			1. _____		
1. _____			2. _____		
2. _____			3. _____		
3. _____			4. _____		
4. _____			**TOTAL LIABILITIES**		
5. _____			**LESS TOTAL ASSETS**		
TOTAL ASSETS			**TOTAL NET WORTH**		

ANNUAL INCOME			**and** ANNUAL EXPENDITURES (Excluding Ordinary living expenses)		
Salary_____			Real Estate payment (s)_____		
Salary (wife or husband) _____			Rent_____		
Securities Income_____			Income Taxes _____		
Rentals_____			Insurance Premiums _____		
Other (describe)			Property Taxes _____		
1. _____			Other (describe-include installment payments other than real estate)		
2. _____					
3. _____			1. _____		
4. _____			2. _____		
5. _____			3. _____		
TOTAL INCOME			**TOTAL EXPENDITURES**		

LESS TOTAL EXPENDITURES

NET CASH INCOME
(exclusive of ordinary expenses) _____

Personal Financial Statement

Page 2

What assets in this statement are in joint tenancy? _____ Name of other Party _____

Have you filed homestead? _____

Are you a guarantor on anyone's debt? _____ If so, give details _____

Are any encumbered assets or debts secured except as indicated? _____ If so, please itemize by debt and security _____

_____

Do you have any other business connections? _____ If so, give details _____

Are there any suits or judgments against you? _____

Have you gone through bankruptcy or compromised a debt? _____

Have you made a will? _____ Number of dependents _____

SCHEDULE A — REAL ESTATE

Location and Type of Improvement	Title in Name of	Estimated Value	Amount Owing	To Whom Payable
		$	$	

SCHEDULE B — STOCKS AND BONDS

Number of Shares Amount of Bonds	Description	Current Market on Listed	Estimated Value on Unlisted
.		$	$

If additional space is needed for Schedule A and/or Schedule B, list on separate sheet and attach.

INSURANCE

Life Insurance $_____ Name of Company _____ Beneficiary _____

Automobile Insurance:

Public Liability – yes ☐   no ☐   Property Damage – yes ☐   no ☐

Comprehensive Personal Liability – yes ☐   no ☐

STATEMENT OF BANK OFFICER:
Insofar as our records reveal, this Financial Statement is accurate and true. The foregoing Statement is (a copy of) the original signed by the maker, in the credit files of this Bank

_____ **Assistant Cashier-Manager**

The undersigned solemnly declares and certifies that the above statement (or in lieu thereof, the attached statement, as the case may be) and supporting schedules, both printed and written, give a full, true, and correct statement of the financial condition of the undersigned as of the date indicated.

_____ _____
Date signed   Signature

Trading Offer

Capital, Inc.

Capital, Inc. hereby introduces Genesis Multimedia, Inc. This company has been in operation since 2007 and currently has $7,000,000 in annual sales. The company is currently trading on the OTC Bulletin Board.

Listed below is the Bid and Ask price of Genesis Multimedia, Inc., trading symbol (GMMI), CUSIP no. 274106-12-5:

	BID	ASK
Current	34.25	35.5
Discount	5%	6%

Restricted

Capital, Inc. has purchased these shares under an agreement that shares cannot come back into the United States before one year. As a consequence, the transfer agent will issue instructions that no shares being resold under this purchase can be transferred to any person in the United States before one year. Although, Genesis Multimedia, Inc. is a fully reporting company for over one year, these shares can come back into United States pursuant to an exemption from registration or a filing of a registration before 41 days. After 41 days, any sales of these securities can be sold to any U.S. person or to an account of any U.S. person who is outside the United States.

Investor's Qualifications

The shares may be freely traded outside the United States and can be sold or transferred to any non-U.S. person within 41 days and to any U.S. person after 41 days.

U. S. Tax Information:

An Important Aid to Writing Your Business Plan

A basic understanding of the U.S. tax system is an absolute necessity if you are going to write a Business Plan for a company that will operate within or do business with the U.S. It has long been a premise of the majority of taxpayers that the system is unwieldy, complicated, unfair, and a plague to most Americans. If you will try to put those feelings aside temporarily, I will show you how a basic understanding of the tax system can be an invaluable aid to you during business planning.

In this chapter, I have also included the following visual aids and lists that should help you with your business planning in relation to taxes:

✓ *Calendars of Federal Taxes*

✓ *List of Free IRS Publications*

✓ *IRS Information Resources*

★ If you are doing business internationally

Business planning follows the same format throughout the world. With the spread of global trade, all countries are seeking common ground upon which to do business together and a business plan serves as an important link leading to successful international venturing. If you are in the United States and you participate in foreign trade, you will need to understand the legalities pertaining to the countries with which you are doing business. By the same token, those businesses outside the United States will need to familiarize themselves with the American legal and tax systems.

Notice: *This chapter deals only with cursory tax information pertaining to the United States. The reader of this book should in no way construe it as legal or accounting advice.*

Comparing the U.S. Tax System and Business Accounting

Comparison of the U.S. Tax System and business accounting is like studying the chicken and the egg. They cannot be separated. Many new business owners attempt to set up an accounting system without examining and understanding the IRS's tax forms to be completed at the end of the year. This is a gross error for two reasons. The first is failure to account for financial information required by the IRS at tax time. More important, however, is the failure to utilize information and services that will help you to develop an effective accounting system, which will, in turn, enable you to analyze your business and implement changes to keep it on the track to profitability.

The relationship between business planning and the tax system can be more easily perceived by studying a Schedule C for a sole proprietorship. Below is a discussion of the form, listing the information it utilizes and the benefits to be gained by understanding it.

Schedule C (Form 1040)

This form is entitled *Profit or (Loss) From Business or Profession* (required tax reporting form for all sole proprietors).

    a. **Information required.** Gross receipts or sales, beginning and ending inventories, labor, materials, goods purchased, returns and allowances, deductions, and net profit or loss. The net profit is the figure upon which your income tax liability is based.

    b. **Benefits of understanding.** In order to provide the year-end information required on a Schedule C and to figure income tax liability, it will be necessary for you to set up a chart of accounts in your accounting system. An examination of the entries on a Schedule C will be of some help in determining the breakdown of those accounts. The secret to developing a strong set of financial documents is the initial establishment of the chart of accounts that is customized to your industry and specifically to your particular business. That chart of accounts — asset, equity, income, cost of goods, and expense accounts — will be constant throughout your entire set of business plan financial statements. Running account balances enable you to utilize your accounting software at any given moment to generate profit & loss statements and balance sheets for your business. These two financial statements, in turn, supply you with every piece of information that you will need to update the financial spreadsheets in your business plan. This process is the key to analyzing your business and making decisions that will increase your profitability.

    Note. Form 1065, *U.S. Partnership Return of Income* and Form 1120-A or Form 1120, *U.S. Corporation Income Tax Returns* are used for those legal structures.

Federal Taxes for Which You May be Liable

During the tax year, all businesses must comply with reporting regulations and periodic payments of federal taxes. Familiarize yourself with the federal taxes liabilities. Your legal structure will determine required reporting dates. They are not the same for sole proprietorships and partnerships as they are for S corporations and C corporations. Your cash flow statement must reflect these payments. If you fail to account for tax liabilities, you will find yourself with an unbalanced budget and it is possible that a serious cash deficiency could result.

Calendars of Federal Taxes

The tax calendars developed and provided in this chapter (pages 130-133) will help you to meet those requirements.

The four calendars have been set up to give you a quick read on the dates that reports must be filed and taxes paid. Print out a copy of the tax calendar for your legal structure and tack it on your wall as a visual reminder. Be sure to look ahead as the due dates are firm and a penalty may be imposed for not reporting on time.

Free IRS Publications, Forms, and Information

What most of us don't know is that the United States government has spent a great deal of time and money to provide you with free publications and forms, as well as tax workshops, forums, videos, etc. On page 135, we will provide you with a list of some of the most frequently requested publications.

Make a conscious decision to send for (or download) publications and forms.

At least once a year, you should update your IRS file with new publications and forms and you should make it a priority to study revisions that take place in U.S. tax laws.

Remember that your business plan is an ongoing process requiring the implementation of many changes. You may rest assured that many of those changes will be a direct result of new tax laws.

To Help You Understand Taxes and Set up a File of IRS Publications & Forms

In order to help you with your tax planning as related to business planning, the remainder of this chapter will provide you with the following:

- **Calendars of federal taxes** for which a sole proprietor, partnership, S corporation or corporation may be liable. You will find four calendars. Choose the one that is appropriate to your legal structure (pg. 130-133).

- **How to Access IRS Help and Products** by internet, phone, walk-in, mail, or DVD (pg. 134).

- **A suggested list of free IRS publications** that will be helpful to business owners. These publications are updated every November and can be ordered shortly thereafter (pg. 135).

- **An order form** to use when you want to send for free publications and/or forms by mail. (pg. 136).

Sole Proprietor

Calendar of Federal Taxes for Which You May Be Liable

January	15	Estimated tax	Form 1040ES
	31	Social security (FICA) tax and the withholding of income tax Note: See IRS rulings for deposit - Pub. 334	941, 941E, 942, and 943
	31	Providing information on social security (FICA) tax and the withholding of income tax	W-2 (to employee)
	31	Federal unemployment (FUTA) tax	940-EZ or 940
	31	Federal unemployment (FUTA) tax (only if liability for unpaid taxes exceeds $100)	8109 (to make deposits)
	31	Information returns to non-employees and transactions with other persons	Form 1099 (to recipients)
February	28	Information returns to non-employees and transactions with other persons	Form 1099 (to IRS)
	28	Providing information on social security (FICA) tax and the withholding income tax	W-2 & W-3 (to Social Security Admin.)
April	15	Income tax	Schedule C (Form 1040)
	15	Self-employment tax	Schedule SE (Form 1040)
	15	Estimated tax	Form 1040ES
	30	Social security (FICA) tax and the withholding of income tax Note: See IRS rulings for deposit - Pub. 334	941, 941E, 942, and 943
	30	Federal unemployment (FUTA) tax (only if liability for unpaid taxes exceeds $100)	8109 (to make deposits)
June	15	Estimated tax	Form 1040ES
July	31	Social security (FICA) tax and the withholding of income tax Note: See IRS rulings for deposit - Pub. 334	941, 941E, 942, and 943
	31	Federal unemployment (FUTA) tax (only if liability for unpaid taxes exceeds $100)	8109 (to make deposits)
September	15	Estimated tax	Form 1040ES
October	31	Social security (FICA) tax and the withholding of income tax Note: See IRS rulings for deposit - Pub. 334	941, 941E, 941, and 943
	31	Federal unemployment (FUTA) tax (only if liability for unpaid taxes exceeds $100)	8109 (to make deposits)

If your tax year is not January 1st through December 31st:

- Schedule C (Form 1040) is due the 15th day of the 4th month after end of the tax year. Schedule SE is due same day as Form 1040.

- Estimated tax (1040ES) is due the 15th day of 4th, 6th, and 9th months of tax year, and the 15th day of 1st month after the end of tax year.

Partnership

Calendar of Federal Taxes for Which You May Be Liable

Month	Day	Description	Form
January	15	Estimated tax (individual who is a partner)	Form 1040ES
	31	Social security (FICA) tax and the withholding of income tax Note: See IRS rulings for deposit - Pub. 334	941, 941E, 942, and 943
	31	Providing information on soc. security (FICA) tax and the withholding of income tax	W-2 (to employee)
	31	Federal unemployment (FUTA) tax	940-EZ or 940
	31	Federal unemployment (FUTA) tax (only if liability for unpaid taxes exceeds $100)	8109 (to make deposits)
	31	Information returns to non-employees and transactions with other persons	Form 1099 (to recipients)
February	28	Information returns to non-employees and transactions with other persons	Form 1099 (to IRS)
	28	Providing information on social security (FICA) tax and on withholding income tax	W-2 & W-3 (to Social Security Admin.)
April	15	Income tax (individual who is a partner)	Schedule C (Form 1040)
	15	Annual return of income	Form 1065
	15	Self-employment tax (individual who is partner)	Schedule SE (Form 1040)
	15	Estimated tax (individual who is partner)	Form 1040ES
	30	Social security (FICA) tax and the withholding of income tax Note: See IRS rulings for deposit - Pub. 334	941, 941E, 942, and 943
	30	Federal unemployment (FUTA) tax (only if liability for unpaid taxes exceeds $100)	8109 (to make deposits)
June	15	Estimated tax (individual who is a partner)	Form 1040ES
July	31	Social security (FICA) tax and the withholding of income tax Note: See IRS rulings for deposit - Pub. 334	941, 941E, 942, and 943
	31	Federal unemployment (FUTA) tax (only if liability for unpaid taxes exceeds $100)	8109 (to make deposits)
September	15	Estimated tax (individual who is a partner)	Form 1040ES
October	31	Social security (FICA) tax and the withholding of income tax Note: See IRS rulings for deposit - Pub. 334	941, 941E, 941, and 943
	31	Federal unemployment (FUTA) tax (only if liability for unpaid taxes exceeds $100)	8109 (to make deposits)

If your tax year is not January 1st through December 31st:

- Income tax is due the 15th day of the 4th month after end of tax year.
- Self-employment tax is due the same day as income tax (Form 1040).
- Estimated tax (1040ES) is due the 15th day of the 4th, 6th, and 9th month of the tax year and the 15th day of 1st month after end of the tax year.

S Corporation

Calendar of Federal Taxes for Which You May Be Liable

January	15	Estimated tax (individual S corp. shareholder)	Form 1040ES
	31	Social security (FICA) tax and the withholding of income tax Note: See IRS rulings for deposit - Pub. 334	941, 941E, 942, and 943
	31	Providing information on social security (FICA) tax and the withholding of income tax	W-2 (to employee)
	31	Federal unemployment (FUTA) tax	940-EZ or 940
	31	Federal unemployment (FUTA) tax (only if liability for unpaid taxes exceeds $100)	8109 (to make deposits)
	31	Information returns to non-employees and transactions with other persons	Form 1099 (to recipients)
February	28	Information returns to non-employees and transactions with other persons	Form 1099 (to IRS)
	28	Providing information on social security (FICA) tax and the withholding of income tax	W-2 & W-3 (to Social Security Admin.)
March	15	Income tax	1120S
April	15	Income tax (individual S corp. shareholder)	Form 1040
	15	Estimated tax (individual S corp. shareholder)	Form 1040ES
	30	Social security (FICA) tax and the withholding of income tax Note: See IRS rulings for deposit - Pub. 334	941, 941E, 942, and 943
	30	Federal unemployment (FUTA) tax (only if liability for unpaid taxes exceeds $100)	8109 (to make deposits)
June	15	Estimated tax (individual S corp. shareholder)	Form 1040ES
July	31	Social security (FICA) tax and the withholding of income tax Note: See IRS rulings for deposit - Pub. 334	941, 941E, 942, and 943
	31	Federal unemployment (FUTA) tax (only if liability for unpaid taxes exceeds $100)	8109 (to make deposits)
September	15	Estimated tax (individual S corp. shareholder)	Form 1040ES
October	31	Social security (FICA) tax and the withholding of income tax Note: See IRS rulings for deposit - Pub. 334	941, 941E, 941, and 943
	31	Federal unemployment (FUTA) tax (only if liability for unpaid taxes exceeds $100)	8109 (to make deposits)

If your tax year is not January 1st through December 31st:

- S corporation income tax (1120S) and individual S corporation shareholder income tax (Form 1040) are due the 15th day of the 4th month after end of tax year.

- Estimated tax of individual shareholder (1040ES) is due 15th day of 4th, 6th, and 9th months of tax year and 15th day of 1st month after end of tax year.

Corporation

Calendar of Federal Taxes for Which You May Be Liable

January	31	Social security (FICA) tax and the withholding of income tax Note: See IRS rulings for deposit - Pub. 334	941, 941E, 942, and 943
	31	Providing information on social security (FICA) tax and the withholding of income tax	W-2 (to employee)
	31	Federal unemployment (FUTA) tax	940-EZ or 940
	31	Federal unemployment (FUTA) tax (only if liability for unpaid taxes exceeds $100)	8109 (to make deposits)
	31	Information returns to non-employees and transactions with other persons	Form 1099 (to recipients)
February	28	Information returns to non-employees and transactions with other persons	Form 1099 (to IRS)
	28	Providing information on social security (FICA) tax and the withholding of income tax	W-2 & W-3 (to Social Security Admin.)
March	15	Income tax	1120 or 1120-A
April	15	Estimated tax	1120-W
	30	Social security (FICA) tax and the withholding of income tax Note: See IRS rulings for deposit - Pub. 334	941, 941E, 942, and 943
	30	Federal unemployment (FUTA) tax (only if liability for unpaid taxes exceeds $100)	8109 (to make deposits)
June	15	Estimated tax	1120-W
July	31	Social security (FICA) tax and the withholding of income tax Note: See IRS rulings for deposit - Pub. 334	941, 941E, 942, and 943
	31	Federal unemployment (FUTA) tax (only if liability for unpaid taxes exceeds $100)	8109 (to make deposits)
September	15	Estimated tax	1120-W
October	31	Social security (FICA) tax and the withholding of income tax Note: See IRS rulings for deposit - Pub. 334	941, 941E, 941, and 943
	31	Federal unemployment (FUTA) tax (only if liability for unpaid taxes exceeds $100)	8109 (to make deposits)
December	15	Estimated tax	1120-W

If your tax year is not January 1st through December 31st:

- Income tax (Form 1120 or 1120-A) is due on the 15th day of the 3rd month after the end of the tax year.
- Estimated tax (1120-W) is due the 5th day of the 4th, 6th, 9th, and 12th months of the tax year.

Quick and Easy Access to IRS Tax Help and Tax Products

The IRS has provided us with several ways to access its publications, forms, and tax information. They are as follows:

Internet. Access the IRS website 24 hours a day, 7 days a week, at **www.irs.gov** to:

- Access commercial tax preparation and e-file services available free to eligible taxpayers;
- Download forms, instructions, and publications;
- Order IRS products online;
- Research your tax questions online;
- Search publications online by topic or keyword;
- Use the online Internal Revenue Code, Regulations, or other official guidance;
- View Internal Revenue Bulletins (IRBs) published in the last few years;
- Send us comments or request help by e-mail; and
- Sign up to receive local and national tax news by e-mail.

Phone. Order current year forms, instructions, and publications and prior year forms and instructions by calling **1-800-TAX-FORM (1-800-829-3676)**. You should receive your order within 10 days.

Walk-In. You can pick up some of the most requested forms, instructions, and publications at many IRS offices, post offices, and libraries. Some grocery stores, copy centers, city and county government offices, credit unions, and office supply stores have a collection of reproducible tax forms available to photocopy or print from a CD-ROM.

Mail. Send your order for tax products to: Internal Revenue Service, National Distribution Center, 1201 N. Mitsubishi Motorway, Bloomington, IL 61705–6613. You should receive your products within 10 days after they receive your order. If you wish to order publications or forms by mail, you will find an order form on the last page of this chapter.

DVD For Tax Products. You can order Publication 1796, IRS Tax Products DVD, and obtain:

- Current-year forms, instructions, and publications.
- Prior-year forms, instructions, and publications.
- Tax Map: an electronic research tool and finding aid.
- Tax law frequently asked questions.
- Tax Topics from the IRS telephone response system.
- Internal Revenue Code – Title 26
- Fill-in, print, and save features for most tax forms.
- Internal Revenue Bulletins.
- Toll-free and email technical support.

The DVD is released twice during the year. Purchase the DVD from the National Technical Information Service at www.irs.gov/cdorders for $30 (no handling fee) or call 1-877-CDFORMS (1-877-233-6767) toll-free to buy the DVD for $30 (plus a $6 handling fee). The price is subject to change.

A Suggested List of IRS Publications

The following is a list of IRS Publications that may prove helpful to you in the course of your business. Keep a file of tax information. Send for these publications and update your file with new publications at least once a year.

Tax Guide for Small Business
(For Individuals Who Use Schedule C or C-EZ)

Sole proprietors should begin by reading Publication 334, *Tax Guide for Small Business.* It is a general guide to all areas of small business and will give you comprehensive information.

Listing of Publications for Small Business

If you are a business owner, the following IRS publications will provide you with fairly detailed information on specific tax-related topics.

1	*Your Rights as a Taxpayer*
15	*Circular E., Employer's Tax Guide*
15A	*Employers Supplemental Tax Guide*
17	*Your Federal Income Tax*
463	*Travel, Entertainment, Gift and Car Expenses*
505	*Tax Withholding and Estimated Tax*
509	*Tax Calendars*
535	*Business Expenses*
536	*Net Operating Losses*
538	*Accounting Periods & Methods*
541	*Partnerships*
542	*Corporations (S Corporations get instructions for 1120S)*
544	*Sales and Other Dispositions of Assets*
551	*Basis of Assets*
553	*Highlights of Tax Changes*
556	*Examination of Returns, Appeal Rights, and Claims for Refund*
557	*Tax-Exempt Status for Your Organization (SEP, SIMPLE, and Qualified Plans)*
560	*Retirement Plans for the Small Business*
583	*Starting a Business and Keeping Records*
587	*Business Use of Your Home (including Use by Day-Care Providers)*
594	*The IRS Collection Process*
908	*Bankruptcy Tax Guide*
910	*IRS Guide to Free Tax Services*
925	*Passive Activity & At Risk Rules*
946	*How to Depreciate Your Property*
947	*Practice Before the IRS and Power of Attorney*
1066	*Small Business Tax Workshop Workbook*
1544	*Reporting Cash Payments of Over $10,000 (Received in a Trade or Business)*
1546	*The Taxpayer Advocate Service of the IRS*
1779	*Independent Contractor or Employee Brochure*

Order Blank for Forms and Publications

The most frequently ordered forms and publications are listed on the order blank below. You will receive two copies of each form, one copy of the instructions, and one copy of each publication you order. To help reduce waste, please order only the items you need to prepare your return. Please order no more than ten items.

 For faster ways of getting the items you need, go to www.irs.gov and click on the Forms and Pubs folder.

How To Use the Order Blank

Circle the items you need on the order blank below. Use the blank spaces to order items not listed. If you need more space, attach a separate sheet of paper.

Print or type your name and address accurately in the space provided below to ensure delivery of your order. Enclose the order blank in an envelope and mail it to the IRS address shown on this page. You should receive your order within 7 to 10 days after receipt of your request.

Do not send your tax return to the address shown here. Instead, see the back cover.

Mail Your Order Blank To:

Internal Revenue Service
National Distribution Center
1201 N. Mitsubishi Motorway
Bloomington, IL 61705-6613

▲   *Cut here*   ▲

Save Money and Time by Going Online!

Download or order these and other tax products at www.irs.gov

Order Blank

Please print

Name

Postal mailing address   Apt./Suite/Room

City   State   ZIP code

Foreign country   International postal code

Daytime phone number

(   )

Circle the forms and publications you need. The instructions for any form you order will be included.

The items in bold are also available at many IRS offices, U.S. Post Offices, and various libraries.

Use the **blank spaces** to order items not listed.

1040	Schedule H (1040)	1040-ES (2007)	4684	8863	Pub. 505	Pub. 554	
Schedules A&B (1040)	Schedule J (1040)	1040-V	4868	8913	Pub. 523	Pub. 575	
Schedule C (1040)	Schedule R (1040)	1040X	5695	9465	Pub. 525	Pub. 587	
Schedule C-EZ (1040)	Schedule SE (1040)	2106	6251	Pub. 1	Pub. 526	Pub. 590	
Schedule D (1040)	**1040A**	2106-EZ	8283	Pub. 17	Pub. 527	Pub. 596	
Schedule D-1 (1040)	Schedule 1 (1040A)	2441	8606	Pub. 334	Pub. 529	Pub. 910	
Schedule E (1040)	Schedule 2 (1040A)	4506	8812	Pub. 463	Pub. 535	Pub. 915	
Schedule EIC (1040A or 1040)	Schedule 3 (1040A)	4506-T	8822	Pub. 501	Pub. 547	Pub. 970	
Schedule F (1040)	**1040EZ**	4562	8829	Pub. 502	Pub. 550	Pub. 972	

N

Business Planning for a Nonprofit

You may want to start a business based on a societal problem you would like to address. This is called social entrepreneurship. A social entrepreneur recognizes a community problem and uses entrepreneurial skills and traits to start a business that will address the social problem and make a significant change. Your vehicle as a social entrepreneur will most likely be a non-profit organization.

Starting and running a nonprofit organization is much the same as operating a for-profit business. However, there are a few key differences between the two and they must be taken into account when you write your business plan.

What is Different in a Nonprofit Business Plan?

The focus of this chapter is to give you a basic understanding about nonprofits and to highlight the differences that will need to be addressed in each of the major areas of your business plan.

- ✓ *Executive Summary*
- ✓ *Organizational Plan*
- ✓ *Marketing Plan*
- ✓ *Financial Plan*
- ✓ *Supporting Documents*

Understanding Nonprofits

As mentioned above, nonprofit organizations are established with the objective of addressing a social problem. A major difference between nonprofit and for-profit corporations is that the former does not have stockholders. Instead, nonprofits have members who are granted certain rights including the power to vote for the board of directors. Having members however, is not a requirement. Nonprofits must apply and be recognized by the IRS. They may also be required to submit an incorporation form to the state in which they will operate. The state incorporation process gives the organization the rights bestowed to nonprofits under that state's governing laws (also see "Obtaining Legal Nonprofit Status" – next page).

Types of Nonprofit Organizations

There are several different types of nonprofit organizations. Below is a listing of some of the common ones. The number refers to the section of the Internal Revenue Code under which the nonprofit may be organized.

Types of Nonprofit Organizations	
Number	**Description**
501(c)(1)	Corporations Organized Under Act of Congress (including Federal Credit Unions)
501(c)(2)	Title Holding Corporation For Exempt Organization
501(c)(3)	Charitable Organizations - Charitable, religious, educational, scientific, literary, etc. organizations
501(c)(4)	Civic leagues, community organizations, and other social welfare organizations
501(c)(5)	Labor unions, farm bureaus, and other labor and agricultural organizations
501(c)(6)	Trade associations, chambers of commerce, real estate boards, and other business leagues
501(c)(7)	Hobby clubs, country clubs, and other organizations formed for social and recreational purposes
501(c)(8)	Lodges and similar orders and associations

Benefits of Nonprofit Organizations

Forming and operating a nonprofit organization has its benefits. First and foremost, you have an opportunity to make a change in the world. Through your nonprofit, you can accomplish great things that change people's lives. If you have something you are passionate about, you can turn that passion into a business by forming a nonprofit organization. Below are additional benefits of nonprofits:

- Tax exemption (free from paying income taxes on related income)
- Ability to attract donations that are tax deductible to the donor

- Ability to receive grants
- Use of volunteer staff, board members, etc.
- Use of donated facilities and equipment
- Not prohibited on making a profit (just restricted on how they make and spend money)

Qualifications to Become a Nonprofit

To qualify to become a nonprofit, your organization can be any of the following:

- Coalition
- Community organization
- Corporation
- Unincorporated association
- Trust

Nonprofit organizations must serve a scientific, literary, educational, artistic or charitable purpose that benefits the public. A nonprofit does not have to be incorporated. However, to avoid any personal liability for the organization's operations, it is best to incorporate. It is also necessary to be a corporation in order to establish a board and solicit donations.

Obtaining Legal Nonprofit Status

In order to receive the benefits listed above, an organization must formally apply to the Internal Revenue Service to be recognized as a nonprofit organization. This process is accomplished by completing and filing Form 1023 with the IRS. This is a 28 page form that requests much of the information you will be assembling for your business plan. The application process can take several months. It is recommended that you start the process as soon as possible. Many states also require that a similar form be submitted.

Business Planning
For Your Nonprofit Organization

As with any company, the business plan will serve as a roadmap. As your organization grows or as changes take place within it, the plan should be updated to keep you on course. Your business plan will also be used to acquire funding from donors and foundations. In some cases, it is beneficial to establish strategic alliances with other nonprofit organizations. Your business plan will help to layout your vision and the benefits of the potential partnership. Critical to the success of your organization will be the establishment of a board of directors. If you are starting a new organization, potential board members will want to see a detailed business plan so they know what they will be getting involved in.

On the following pages we will look at each of the major sections of a business plan. Note that they are the same for both a for-profit and a nonprofit company. However, there are some things in each of these sections that will need to be specifically addressed if you are a nonprofit. As you are writing your plan, follow the instructions throughout the book, but be sure to incorporate the changes that are explained below.

Executive Summary

In your executive summary, you will concisely and clearly demonstrate the need for the service(s) you will provide and explain the specific problem(s) you will address. It is important to note that, just as in a for-profit business plan, the executive summary will not be written until you have developed the body of your business plan.

Your executive summary will contain all the elements described in Chapter 3. Differences will exist in the management and market opportunity sections.

Market Opportunity
Focus on the problems that you have identified within the community and specify what you will do to address them.

Management
As a nonprofit, your management section will include a profile of the Executive Director, key staff members, and executive board members. In this description, give brief information about their educational background as well as experience.

Part I: Organizational Plan

To develop this section, you will follow the guide in Chapter 4. The only difference will be the tone.

Summary of the Business

As with a for-profit business, begin with a summary of the business. In addition to the information covered in Chapter 4, you will want to give an overview of how the organization came about and the purpose it will serve.

Mission
Remember that nonprofits are mission driven. As such, the mission must be defined clearly. The mission statement for a nonprofit is generally longer than one for a for-profit business. There is no right or wrong way to state your mission. Just be sure that it includes the following elements: services offered, benefits of services, target audience, and the values of the organization.

Business Model
Traditionally, the business model for nonprofits is based on the organization receiving donations or grant funds. Nonprofits also may have income generating opportunities. Describe your organization's business model and explain why it is unique.

Strategy

In the case of a nonprofit, this section will be broader. After discussing your goals and objectives, as explained in chapter 4, you will talk about your organization's planned activities and current resources.

- **Activities.** After laying out your goals and objectives, you will want to outline your organization's planned activities and programs. These are the action items that will be put into play for you to meet each of your desired goals and objectives and help advance the mission of your organization. While this is important for internal purposes, it is equally important that the public know exactly what it is you will do. This will help to get the public involved and to attract contributions.

- **Current Resources.** This section is primarily for start up organizations and should be added after your discussion on activities. Your current resources will be an inventory of what you have to get you going. This includes start up money, people who you have on board to help you get started, your skills and expertise in your service area, and other intangibles. These things should be explained in a brief paragraph.

Strategic Relationships

Nonprofits typically establish strategic alliances in order to facilitate their efforts. Discuss the organizations you plan to partner with. Explain how you will work with them and what the benefits of the partnership will be. You will also want to include public and private community leaders that have expressed support for your organization.

SWOT Analysis

As part of your strategic planning, you will develop a SWOT (strengths, weaknesses, opportunities, threats) analysis. For a nonprofit, the SWOT analysis is commonly called a *Situational Assessment* or an *Environmental Analysis.*

Program Services and Products

For the most part, nonprofits focus on program services that are meant to benefit a specific segment of the population. Some nonprofits also sell products that support their stated cause and (in some cases) provide an additional revenue stream.

Program Services

Provide a description of your program services and why they are unique. In addition, you will want to explain the problems that they address.

You can use a table to illustrate this point. A sample is provided on the next page. If you choose, you can also draw a flowchart that shows the steps in your service fulfillment process.

Canine Program Services	
Description	**Benefit**
1. Training and Providing Service Dogs	1. Assist independent adults with physical disabilities by enhancing the ability to perform daily tasks
2. Training and Providing Facility Dogs	2. Engage patients in activities to stimulate healing and recovery
3. Training and Providing Hearing Dogs	3. Benefit adults who are deaf or hard of hearing by alerting them to important everyday sounds

Products for Sale

Nonprofits often sell products to support their cause. Logo T-shirts and/or hats might be an example. By wearing them, the consumer publicizes the program. Revenue from the sales provides another means of raising funds for the organization. If your organization sells products, tell what they are and how they will contribute to the success of your mission.

Administrative Plan

Most of the sections in the administrative plan for a nonprofit are the same as those found in a for-profit business plan. However, the Management and Personnel section should be expanded to include a segment on the Board of Directors.

Management

A nonprofit business plan will include profiles of the Executive Director and key staff members. Include a write up of how their background and experience will contribute toward the accomplishment of your nonprofit organization's goals and objectives. Be brief in your description and include resumes for each of these individuals in your supporting documents.

Board of Directors

For the board of directors, include a discussion on the composition of the board, the role it will play for your nonprofit, and whether or not its members will be compensated. Give a brief profile of key board members (such as the executive board). Be sure to include resumes of all current board members in your supporting documents.

Part II: The Marketing Plan

Most of the sections in a nonprofit marketing plan will be similar to one of a for-profit business. However, some sections will have significant differences. They are as follows:

Market Analysis
(Marketing Plan: Section II)

Identify Target Markets (Audience)

The target market for a nonprofit is generally referred to as a target audience and can be divided into two categories – program recipients and funding sources. Include details of your research for each target audience in Supporting Documents.

- **Program Recipients.** Begin by identifying and describing the community you plan to serve. Follow that up by segmenting specific groups by demographics and psychographics to clearly define your target audience based on your organization's goals. Create a profile of that audience and show how many people are out there that you will serve.

- **Funding Sources.** Identify the various types of funding sources that you plan to target. Create a profile for each one, describing the benefits it would derive from funding your nonprofit. Estimate the size of each type of funding source.

Research Your Competition

In this section, you will focus on both nonprofit organizations and for-profit entities that pose competitive threats. If there are any gaps that exist in services, describe them and explain why you think they exist. More importantly, show how your organization will close the gaps.

Assess Market Trends

To begin with, you will want to conduct market research to determine if there is a need for the services you plan to offer. In the case of a nonprofit, this is called a *Needs Assessment.* In addition to showing the current conditions, your research should also determine the trends in the needs you want to address. To help you answer some questions, you can conduct a survey or focus group using a sampling of individuals that make up the target audience. You can also interview community leaders who can layout the needs of the community to you directly.

Contents of Your Marketing Strategy
(Marketing Plan: Section III)

Public Relations

A nonprofit organization generally places heavy emphasis on public relations (PR) activities. Your PR plan will be designed to generate as much visibility for your organization as possible, enabling it to gain added support from the community and to attract grant and donor funds.

Part III: Financial Documents

Nonprofits are the same as for-profit companies in that they plan for and analyze their organizations through the use of cash flow and income projections and monthly and annual balance sheets and P&L (income) statements. These pro forma and historical statements are then utilized to perform periodic budget analyses. Based on the results, management and the board of directors can then make decisions and implement changes that will enable the organization to run more effectively.

Develop a Chart of Accounts

The key for a nonprofit is to establish a chart of accounts (asset, liability, net assets, revenue, and expense categories) that will reflect the operations of the organization. These same accounts are used throughout all of your projected and historical financial statements.

The examples below should help you develop your accounts and understand how the financial statements for a nonprofit differ from those of a for-profit company.

Statement of Financial Position (Balance Sheet)

The statement of financial position (aka balance sheet) for a nonprofit organization (NPO) looks much the same as the for-profit balance sheet presented on pages 101-103. However, a nonprofit divides its assets into current assets followed by non-current types of assets, reflecting its liquidity. Net worth is referred to fund balance (or net assets) and is divided according to asset restrictions. It might have accounts similar to the following:

Statement of Financial Position
ABC Nonprofit Corporation

Assets	*Liabilities*
Current Assets	**Current Liabilities**
Cash	Accounts Payable
Accounts (Fees) Receivable	Grants Payable
Pledges Receivable	Notes Payable
Inventory	Mortgage Payable
Prepaid Expenses	Interest Payable
Short-term Investments	Deferred Revenue
	Payroll Accrual
Long-Term Investments	**Non-current (Long-Term) Liabilities**
Fixed Assets	Notes Payable
Land	Mortgage Payable
Buildings	
Equipment	**Total Liabilities**
Furniture	
Vehicles	*Fund Balance (Net Assets)*
Grants Receivable	Unrestricted
Sponsorships Receivable	Temporarily Restricted
Public Funding Receivable	Permanently Restricted
	Revenues in Excess of Expenses
Other Assets	**Total Net Assets**
Total Assets	**Total Liabilities and Net Assets**

Warning! *Nonprofits that sell products will need the Inventory account that is included under Current Assets. The products you sell must be related to the purpose for which the nonprofit was formed. Sales of non-related products are taxable.*

Statement of Activities (P&L or Income Statement)

A profit and loss (income) statement for a nonprofit is alternately referred to as a statement of activities. It follows the same format as a for-profit P&L (page 105), but has categories that reflect its various sources of income and related expenditures. The income and expense in your business plan statement of activities will be divided into general categories, backed up by all of the detail in your organization's books.

Accounts in a statement of activities for your nonprofit might be similar to the example below. *Note:* Nonprofits that do not sell products will not have Cost of Goods Sold.

Statement of Activities Annual for Year 2014	
INCOME	
1. Revenues/Support	
Corporate and Foundation Support	
Grants and Public Funds	
Individual Contributions	
Fees for Services	
Total Revenues/Support	$
2. Cost of Goods Sold	$
3. Gross Profit on Sales (1-2)	$
EXPENSES	
1. Variable (Program Related)	$
Contract Services	
Conferences and Exhibits	
Marketing	
Printing and Publications	
Professional Fundraising	
Programs (specify or group)	
Salaries & Benefits (non administrative)	
Special Events and Meetings	
Travel	
Vehicle	
2. Fixed (Administrative)	$
Accounting & Legal	
Insurance	
Office Supplies	
Rent	
Salaries (Officers) (w-benefits)	
Salaries (Other) (w-benefits)	
Salaries (payroll expense)	
Telephone	
Utilities	
Total Operating Expenses	$
Revenues in Excess of Expenses (Net Income)	$
Beginning Fund Balance (Net Assets)	$
Ending Fund Balance (Net Assets)	$

As you can see in the example on the previous page, there are no categories for taxes. Nonprofits do not report or pay taxes except in the case of earning income that is unrelated to the mission of the organization.

The statement of activities/profit and loss statement for a nonprofit commonly ends by adding the net income increase/decrease to the beginning fund balance (net assets) for the period to arrive at its ending fund balance (net assets).

12-Month Profit & Loss Statement (Statement of Activities)

This is a historical statement of activities documenting the income, expenses and net income by month for a completed one-year period. Follow the instructions and format on pages 104-106 in Chapter 6 (Financial Documents) for this financial statement. Utilize the categories (as in the example above) developed for your nonprofit. The categories will be on the left and there will be fourteen columns to the right – twelve columns for the months, one 6-month total column, and one 12-month total column.

Jan	Feb	Mar	Apr	May	Jun	6-Month Totals	Jul	Aug	Sep	Oct	Nov	Dec	12-Month Totals

Note. *Use same categories (accounts) as developed for Statement of Activities.*

Three-Year Income Projection (Projected Statement of Activities)

This is a pro forma (projected) statement of activities by the year for the next three years. Follow the instructions and format on pages 96 and 97 in Chapter 6 (Financial Documents) for developing this financial statement, but utilize the examples above to develop the categories and headings. Again, they will be the same categories that you used for both the annual and 12-month P&L (Statement of Activities). The categories will be on the left and there will be four columns to the right, one for each of the three projected years and one for totals for the three years.

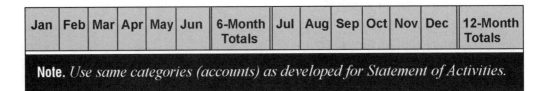

	Year 1	Year 2	Year 3	Total 3 Years
INCOME				
EXPENSES				
REVENUES IN EXCESS OF EXPENSES (Net Income)				
ENDING FUND BALANCE (Net Assets)				

Note. *Use same categories (accounts) as developed for Statement of Activities.*

Pro Forma Cash Flow Statement

One of the major forecasting tools used by all businesses is a Pro Forma Cash Flow Statement or Budget. It deals only with actual cash transactions and not with depreciation, amortization, or other non-cash expense items.

The cash flow projection is used for internal planning and estimates how much money will flow through your nonprofit during a designated period of time, usually the coming fiscal year. Net income at the end of the year will depend on the proper balance between cash inflow and outflow.

There is no magic formula for projecting revenues and expenses, especially for a start-up nonprofit. Estimates will be close at best and will be based on your organization's concept, your research, and standards for your industry. For this reason, it is important to be conservative with your forecasts, taking care not to overstate revenues or understate expenses.

After your nonprofit has been in business for a period of time, your projections will become more accurate because they will be based on a combination of your organization's history and current economic and industry trends.

Steps for Planning Your Cash Flow

As you learned in Chapter 6, Financial Documents, the preparation of your cash flow statement (budget) is most effectively done in three steps:

- Prepare individual income and expense forecasts.

- Use the forecasts to prepare cash to be paid out and sources of cash worksheets covering a one-year period.

- Transfer the worksheet information to the pro forma cash flow statement, breaking the annual information into monthly segments.

Note. *The accounts that were identified during the development of your statement of financial position (balance sheet) and statement of activities (profit and loss) will be used on your worksheets and subsequently in your cash flow projection.*

This is the only financial statement that utilizes income statement (profit and loss) items and non-income statement (balance sheet) items on the same form. This is because it takes into account all cash transactions that cause money to flow into or out of your organization – revenues received, expenses paid, asset purchases, loans infused, loan repayments, and interest paid.

Example Cash Flow for a Nonprofit

Follow the instructions on pages 84-93, Chapter 6, Financial Documents to develop your cash flow statement. Use your chart of accounts for income and expenses and do not list any accounts relating to taxes or owner draws. On the next page, you will see an example of a cash flow statement for a nonprofit.

2015 Cash Flow Projection	Jan	Feb	Mar	etc.
Beginning Cash Balance				
Cash Receipts				
A. Revenues/Support				
1. Corporate and Foundation Support				
2. Grants and Public Funds				
3. Individual Contributions				
4. Fees for Services				
B. Interest Income				
C. Sale of Long-Term Assets				
Total Cash Available				
Cash Payments				
A. Cost of Goods to be Sold				
B. Activity Related (Variable)				
1. Contract Services				
2. Conferences and Exhibits				
3. Marketing				
4. Printing and Publications				
5. Professional Fundraising				
6. Programs (specify or group)				
7. Salaries & Benefits (non admin)				
8. Special Events and Meetings				
9. Travel				
10. Vehicle				
C. Administrative (Fixed)				
1. Accounting & Legal				
2. Insurance				
3. Office Supplies				
4. Rent				
5. Salaries, Officers (w-benefits)				
6. Salaries, Others (w-benefits)				
7. Salaries (payroll expense)				
8. Telephone				
9. Utilities				
D. Interest Expense				
E. Long-Term Asset Payments				
F. Loan Payments				
G. Mortgage Payments				
Total Cash Paid Out				
Cash Balance/Deficiency				
Loans to be Received				
Ending Cash Balance				

Budget Analysis
(also known as Budget Deviation Analysis or BDA)

A budget deviation analysis is the financial tool that is used to compare your projected cash flow statement with your business's actual performance.

A nonprofit's cash flow projection (or budget) is used to estimate the receipt and disbursement of funds and to help guide the organization in its day-to-day operations. In order to maximize the utilization of your budget, it will be necessary to make comparisons between projected cash flow and actual performance for the same period (monthly, quarterly, and/or annually) and take a close look at any deviations that exist.

As with all businesses, when you determine that you are over or under budget in any area, it will be necessary to determine the reason for the deviation and to implement changes for the future that will enable you to get back on track.

How often does a Nonprofit Need to Perform a BDA?

A non-profit should perform a budget deviation analysis on a monthly basis. This will enable the executive director and staff to take immediate steps to correct significant deviations. It is also generally shared with its board of directors to aid in their understanding and decision making in regard to financial matters.

For a monthly analysis, the headings listed on page 95 would change to the following and would not include the year-to-date headings. Also, you will note that we have added a column for percentage of deviation (optional):

Budget Analysis (BDA) For the Month Ending: May 31, 2014				
BUDGET ITEM	**Budget**	**Actual**	**Variation** *Budget - Actual*	**% Deviation** *Variation/Budget x 100*
Example: **Advertising**	**5,500**	**6,472**	**(972)**	**(17.67%)**

For business planning purposes, a quarterly budget analysis may provide the best overview because it tends to eliminate those deviations that average out over a longer period. For example, if you are anticipating a large contribution in February, but it does not materialize until March, your February analysis would indicate the deviation whereas your quarterly analysis would not.

Format and Chart of Accounts for a Quarterly Budget Analysis

The instructions and example in Chapter 6, on pages 94 and 95 should guide you through the development of a quarterly budget analysis form for your nonprofit. The headings will be the same. The categories will be developed from the same chart of accounts (income statement and non-income statement items) that you used in your statement of activities (income statement) and statement of financial position (balance sheet).

Part IV: Supporting Documents

The Supporting Documents will include detailed information referenced in various sections of your business plan. Most of the things you include in your supporting documents will be similar to a for-profit business. The following is a list of additional documents that might be included for a nonprofit organization.

- Bylaws for the organization

- Resumes of the board of directors

- Demographic profiles of the population sector you service with your programs

- Psychographic studies reinforcing the need for your program services

- Agreements with other nonprofit organizations

- Contracts with professional fundraisers

- Grant and/or funding applications

- Support letters from community and industry leaders

Packaging Your Plan
And Keeping It Up-to-Date

Part I: Business Planning Software. Because I often get questions regarding business plan software, I will dedicate some space in the first part of this chapter to addressing what you should look for before making a purchase. *Quick fixes* may be good when it comes to saving time, but they can be the kiss of death when it comes to something as serious as business planning. On the other hand, the right software package (such as our own *Automate Your Business Plan*) can save you many hours of time and frustration.

Part II: Packaging Your Business Plan. This is an important part of the planning process. Putting your plan together the right way will increase its readability and effectiveness for the business itself and for potential lenders and investors. In the first half of this chapter, we will give you some ideas on how to organize and present your business plan for maximum effectiveness.

> ✓ *Business Planning Software*
>
> ✓ *Packaging for Success*

Part III: Keeping Your Business Plan Up-to-Date. Your business plan will serve you well if you revise it often and let it serve as your guide during the lifetime of your business. In order to update it, you as the owner or key decision maker of your company will have the final responsibility to analyze what is happening and implement the changes that will make your business more profitable. The second half of this chapter will address changes to be considered in the following areas.

> ✓ *Changes within the Company*
>
> ✓ *Changes in Customer Needs*
>
> ✓ *Changes in Technology*

Part I: Business Plan Software

There are several software programs on the market today. What the prospective business plan writer hopes for is a quick solution to a difficult problem – a program with questions that can be answered by filling in the blanks after which the software will automatically generate a finished business plan.

Do not Use a Canned Program

There are, in fact, some *"fill in the blanks"* software packages. However, it is not advisable for you to use this type of program. There are at least two good reasons:

- Your business plan serves as the guide for your particular business. Even though you may have the same type of business as someone else, you will have different areas of focus. You will want to fill your own special niche and do things that are unique to your business. These differences should be reflected in your plan. A canned business plan cannot possibly serve you well.

- If you are going to potential lenders or investors, you will find that they will readily recognize and reject business plans that contain the canned statements and generic financial plans that come from certain software applications. These "cookie cutter" business plans are an immediate indicator to that person that you have not put much time and effort into the planning process and that you may not know your business well enough to succeed at it. Since the repayment of your loan depends on your business skills, this may indicate that you will be a poor risk.

Effective Software Programs

The right software package should allow for you to do your own research and write your own executive summary, business description, and organizational and marketing statements. This is the only way that you can create a plan that will make your business unique. Well thought out, individualized business plans will favorably impress your lender or investor by showing them that you have thoroughly researched your business and have the expertise to run it effectively. Thorough planning will also give you the confidence to better run your business.

Integrated (linked) financial statements (or spreadsheets) can be a great help to you in the financial section of your business plan. They should be pre-formatted and pre-formulated and linked together. If so, you will save a great deal of time. You plug in the amounts to the allocated cells and the program should do all of your calculations. Also, any numbers should automatically flow to other related spreadsheets. Your time will be cut considerably, allowing you to make changes or create "what if" situations and see the results immediately.

Even here, a note of caution is called for. Some of the most well known programs claim to have wonderful spreadsheet capabilities but on closer examination, they are full of flaws. Invalid numbers are generated by wizards via guessing games. Quick fix formulation causes unrealistic numbers to flow through your spreadsheets. Meaningless charts and graphs are generated. The upshot is an invalid financial plan that can spell disaster for your business.

A strong financial plan is your best friend. To preserve that strength, it is your responsibility to see that you know what you are getting when you choose your software.

Yes! Our Business Planning Software Will Deliver What It Promises!

In order to further implement the writing of your business plan, we have developed a software program that will guide you neatly through the entire business planning process. **Automate Your Business Plan** *for Windows,* now in its 14th version, is for IBM and compatibles. The software has its own full-powered word processor and an easy-to-use spreadsheet application and *does not* require any additional software. We provide you with instructions and examples and formatted templates for every task. When it comes to your financial plan, we cannot be beat. We have spent years developing and refining a process that will result in a completely customized, integrated (linked), and highly credible set of spreadsheets for your business.

Automate Your Business Plan is *Anatomy of a Business Plan* translated into software. It follows the book step-by-step and will print out a finished business plan. The five business plans in Appendices I, II, III, IV, and V were developed with the software. (See page ix)

Part II: Packaging for Success

When you have finished writing your business plan, there are a few additional considerations that will help in making a favorable impression with a potential lender or investor. Good packaging will also make your plan easier for you to use.

- **Binding and Cover.** For your working business plan, it is best to use a three ring binder. That way information can be easily added, updated or replaced. Your working plan should have a copy of all of your supporting documents. The plan that you take to a potential lender or investor, should be bound in a business type cover.

- **Electronic Copies.** You may very well have requests from potential lenders, investors, or associates asking for copies of all or parts of your plan to be transmitted to them via the Internet. The easiest way to do this is to save a copy of your plan to a pdf file.

- **Length.** Be concise! Generally, you should have no more than 30 - 40 pages in the plan you take to a lender, including Supporting Documents. As you write each section, think of it as being a summary. Include as much information as you can in a brief statement. Potential lenders and investors prefer not to search through volumes of material to get to needed information. You can always have an expanded version of your plan in your own binder, including a complete set of your supporting documents.

- **Presentation.** Make your plan look presentable. However, don't go to the unnecessary expense of paying for professional word processing services unless you cannot do it yourself. Lenders and investors are not interested in seeing expensive looking business plans. What they are looking for is what your business plan says in terms of business concepts and financial numbers.

- **Table of Contents.** Be sure to include a Table of Contents in your business plan. It will follow the Cover Sheet. Make it detailed enough so you or a lender or investor can locate any of the areas addressed in the plan. It must also list any Supporting Documents included, as well as their corresponding page numbers. It might help you to use the Table of Contents in this book as a guide to compiling your own.

- **Number of Copies.** Make copies for yourself and each lender or investor that you wish to approach. Keep track of each copy. Don't try to work with too many potential funding sources at one time. If you are refused, be sure to retrieve your business plan.

Part III: Keeping Your Plan Up-to-Date

Revising Your Business Plan

Revision is an on-going process. Changes are constantly taking place in your business. If your business plan is going to be effective either to the business or to a potential lender or investor, it will be necessary for you to update it on a regular basis. Changes necessitating such revisions can be attributed to three primary sources:

- **Changes within the Company**

  Any number of changes may occur in your organization. You may well choose to expand a brick and mortar company by supplementing it with a strong online presence. Conversely, if you find that your company is not effective as an online business, you may choose to fall back and move your focus to more traditional types of offerings — or you might find your company expanding from B to C (business to consumer) business into the B to B (business to business) arena. Changes from within the company may also necessitate changes in legal structure, the addition of new partners, or changes in management.

- **Changes Originating with the Customer**

  Your product or service may show surges or declines due to your customers' changes in need or taste. This is evident in all the companies who fold because they continue to offer what they like instead of what the customer will buy or use. In the clothing industry, for example, retailers have to pay close attention to current styles, popular materials, and seasonal colors.

  Marketing to a new and expanding customer base will also require careful consideration of both demographic and psychographic factors that may differ from those of current customers. Remember that your customers' buying patterns are also integrally related to the current economy. If money is scarce, you will have to be more innovative in your marketing efforts. You may need to make a strong shift toward increased online marketing and selling to reach more buyers. If you sell your products and services internationally, you need to understand the cultures in order to satisfy the customers.

- **Technological Changes**

  You will have to change your business to stay current with a changing world. As technology changes within your industry, bringing new products and services on the market, you will have to keep up or you will be left behind.

  The computer industry is a perfect example of fast changes in technology. Developers are challenged daily with the problems of keeping their products or losing their niche in the marketplace. The toy industry is another. Little girls and boys are no longer satisfied with storybook dolls and tinkertoys. They want electronic miracles that are programmed to walk and talk and fly and think and feel.

  Technological advances, especially those in the area of communication, have also revolutionized the *ways* in which we do business. The Internet has enabled small business owners to research information, communicate instantly with venders and customers, process credit cards and transfer funds electronically, and to market and sell products and services to their customers via the Internet. Yesterday's typewriters, telephones, and airmail letters have been replaced with computers, cell phones, and e-mail.

Implementing Changes in Your Business Plan

You, as the owner or manager of the company, must be aware of the changes in your industry, your market, and your community. First you must determine what revisions are needed in order for you to accomplish the goals you have set for your company. To make this determination, you will have to look at your current plan and decide what you have to do to modify it in order to reflect the changes discussed above.

If you find that writing the company business plan is an overwhelming task for one person, utilize key employees to keep track of the business trends applicable to their expertise. For example, your buyer can analyze the buying patterns of your customers and report to you. Your research and development person might look at changes in technology and materials for your products. Your webmaster can make suggestions regarding your web site. Your marketing department can develop a plan that will take advantage of new ways that will help you to reach your potential customers. Each department can be responsible for information that pertains to its particular area and report on a periodic basis.

You may also find that it is effective to hire an outside consultant to perform a periodic analysis of your current plan in relation to your company's goals.

Be aware, however, that the final judgment as to the implementation of changes will rest with you, the owner or CEO. You will have to analyze the information and decide on any changes to be effected.

If your decision turns out to be wrong, don't dwell on it. Correct your error and cut your losses as soon as possible. With experience, your percentage of correct decisions will increase and your reward will be higher profits.

Anticipating Your Problems

Try to see ahead and determine what possible problems may arise to plague you. For example, you may have to deal with costs that exceed your projections. At the same time, you may experience a sharp decline in sales. These two factors occurring simultaneously can portend disaster if you are not ready for them.

Also, I might add, a good year can give you a false sense of security. Be cautious when things are too good. The increased profits may be temporary. Also, what sells today may not sell tomorrow. As an example, recreational equipment often sells in cycles that are related to current fads. Today's $100 item will most likely be selling for $29 next year—or it may even be no longer a viable product.

You might think about developing an alternate budget based on possible problems that are likely to be encountered. This may be the time when you will decide that emphasis on a service rather than on a product would be more profitable due to changes in the economy and decreased spending.

For instance, the repair of what is already owned may far outpace the buying of replacement items. Alternately, as the buying of luxury services wanes, the company might plan instead to provide those services that are considered a necessity.

Don't Fall into the Trap!

More often than not, a business owner will spend a lot of time and effort writing a business plan when the pressure is on to borrow funds or to get a business started. The intention is there to always keep that plan up-to-date. Before long, things get hectic and the business plan is put in a drawer, never again to be seen.

When you are tempted to put yours aside, just repeat to yourself, *"the business that operates by the seat of its pants will probably end up with torn pants"*.

Do Remember to Revise Your Plan Often

Awareness of changes within your industry and revision of your business plan reflecting those changes will benefit you greatly. Your business plan can be your best friend. If you nurture your relationship with it, you will have a running start on the path to success!

When you are finished, your business plan should be professional. At the same time, it should be obvious to the lender or investor that it was done by the people who own and run the business. Your business plan will be the best indication the lender will have to judge your potential for success.

Be sure that your business plan is a
representation of your best effort!

It is my hope that you have been able to use this book to help you develop a concise, logical and appropriate plan for your business. When your work is done and your business plan is complete, don't forget to:

Operate within your business plan.
Anticipate changes.
Revise your plan and keep it up-to-date.

Do these things and I will guarantee you that you are well on your way to improving your chances of success and growth as you continue with your business venture. Thank you for utilizing *Anatomy of a Business Plan* to guide you through the planning process.

Linda Pinson

The Next Two Chapters

- **Chapter 11, Financing Your Business** will help you to understand debt and equity financing and provide you with financing resources.

- **Chapter 12, U.S. and International Research Resources** is a comprehensive list of offline and online resources that you can use to obtain marketing and financial information for your business plan.

Financing Your Business

When you are planning to start a new business (or expand your current operation), four very important questions arise relating to finance:

✓ *Will you need to borrow money?*

✓ *If you need outside financing, how much do you need and when will you need it?*

✓ *What are the sources of funding available to meet your needs?*

✓ *How much will it cost?*

In order to make an intelligent decision on a timely basis, you will need to address all four of these questions. If you fail to do so, the lack of sufficient and ready capital can quickly lead to business failure.

Will You Need to Borrow Money?

The first step is to ask yourself some questions that will help you to make the right decision – questions that will help you to realistically understand your financial needs and keep you from making costly errors that may ultimately bankrupt a potentially viable business. To determine whether or not you will need outside financing, some of the questions you might ask yourself are:

1. **Have I written a business plan** that will enable me to make financial decisions based on achieving the desired goals for my business?

2. **Am I willing to risk my own money on my venture?** What are the risks? What are my own sources of available capital? If you are not willing to take a risk, don't expect someone else to.

3. **Do I really need additional financing** or do I just need to manage my present cash flow more effectively?

4. **What do I need the money for?** If I borrow, can I realistically project increased revenues? If so, when will those increased revenues justify the debt?

How Much Do You Need — When Do You Need It?

If you have decided that you will need additional financing, you will then need to carefully assess your needs and determine not only the amount you need, but when you will need it. Many business owners overestimate or underestimate their capital requirements and/or do not time their financing to the best advantage. Either can lead to serious problems.

The first thing you need is a realistic *business plan* and one that you intend to follow as closely as possible. The only way to look at every aspect of your business is through the planning process. It will force you to develop an organizational plan and a marketing plan and to quantify your concepts through the development of projected financial statements whose numbers can then be analyzed and used in the decision making process. Those projections give you an educated estimate of your financial needs and tell you when they will most likely occur. Your business plan will answer such questions as:

- What are my most critical needs?

- If I need the money for immediate operating capital, how much will I need to operate my business until it becomes self-sustaining?

- If I need the money to buy fixed assets for my business, has my research shown that I can reach the target market that will justify the purchase of those assets? If not now, when would be the optimum time to add those assets?

- If I need the money for marketing, what are the most effective ways to reach my target market? How much will it cost to advertise? Will the increased marketing be reflected in even higher increases in revenues? According to my industry trends, what are the best selling periods and when will I need financing in order to have the lead time to advertise for the best results?

What are the Sources Available to You?

I get calls almost every day asking for direction to sources of start-up capital. Sources of financing available to prospective and expanding businesses fall into two broad categories, which we will discuss in this chapter:

- **Debt financing** (dollars borrowed)

- **Equity financing** (ownership dollars injected into the business)

Debt Financing

Debt financing is generally obtained from one of two sources. It can come either from a non-professional source such as a friend, relative, customer or colleague or from a traditional lending institution such as a bank, commercial finance company or, on special occasions, directly from the U.S. Small Business Administration (SBA).

1. Friends or Relatives

Borrowing from a friend or relative is generally the most readily available source, especially when the capital requirements are smaller. This is frequently the least costly in terms of dollars, but may become the most costly in terms of personal relations if your repayment schedule is not timely or your venture does not work out. This avenue should be approached with great caution!

2. Angel Programs

For smaller business owners, women and minorities, there has been a growing trend toward the development of "Angel" programs through business organizations and companies specializing in small business. Individuals and small companies that want to invest smaller amounts in promising businesses are linked with those companies and the two decide whether or not the loan will be made. This avenue is still relatively new, but holds even more promise for the future.

> ## *Research Angel Investors Online*
>
> Several organizations exist that serve as an intermediary between Angel investors and business owners. Business owners can submit their business plans, which will then be matched and submitted to prospective investors with funding interests in specific plans. For a list of intermediary networks and lists of Angel investors, use the following key words in a search on the Internet: "Angel Investors"

3. Traditional Lending Institutions

Banks, savings and loans and commercial finance companies have long been the major sources of business financing, principally as short-term lenders offering demand loans, seasonal lines of credit and single-purpose loans for fixed assets.

You should be aware of the fact that almost all lending institutions are strict about collateral requirements and may reasonably require established businesses to provide one-third of the equity injection and start-ups up to 50% or more. Again, as a borrower, you will be required to have a business plan with adequate documentation demonstrating a projected operating cash flow that will enable you to repay (on time) the loan with interest.

4. SBA Guaranteed Loans

The SBA guaranteed loan program is a secondary source of financing. This option comes into play after private lending options have been denied. The SBA offers a variety of loan programs to eligible small businesses that cannot borrow on reasonable terms from conventional lenders in the amount needed without governmental help. Most of the SBA's business loans are made by private lenders and then guaranteed by the Agency. Though it may not necessarily be easier to be approved for an SBA guaranteed loan, the guaranty will allow you to obtain a loan with a longer maturity at better repayment terms and interest rates, thereby reducing your monthly payments and the initial loan burden.

a. 7(a) Guaranteed Loan Program. This is the SBA's primary loan program. You can use a 7(a) loan to: expand or renovate facilities; purchase machinery, equipment, fixtures and leasehold improvements; finance receivables and augment working capital; refinance existing debt (with compelling reason); finance seasonal lines of credit; construct commercial buildings; and/or purchase land or buildings.

Loan amounts of $150,000 or less receive an SBA guaranty as high as 85%. All other loans receive a 75% SBA guaranty. Currently, the maximum amount for a loan guaranty is $3,750,000 (75% of $5 million). The average size loan is $337,730 with a maximum loan amount of $5 million. The 7(a) loan program is available to businesses that operate for profit and qualify as small under SBA size standard criteria.

You submit a loan application to a lender for initial review. If the lender approves the loan subject to an SBA guaranty, a copy of the application and a credit analysis are forwarded by the lender to the nearest SBA office.

The SBA looks for good character, management expertise, financial resources to operate the business, a feasible business plan, adequate equity or investment in the business, sufficient collateral, and the ability to repay the loan on time from the projected operating cash flow.

After SBA approval, the lending institution closes the loan and disburses the funds; you make monthly loan payments directly to the lender. As with any loan, you are responsible for repaying the full amount of the loan.

Generally, liens will be taken on assets financed by SBA proceeds, and the personal guarantee of the principal owners and/or the CEO are required. The borrower must pledge sufficient assets, to the extent that they are reasonably available, to adequately secure the loan. However, in most cases, a loan will not be declined by SBA where insufficient collateral is the only unfavorable factor. The lender sets the rate of interest: loans under 7 years, maximum prime +2.25%; 7 years or more, maximum 2.75% over prime; under $50,000, rates may be slightly higher. The length of time for repayment depends on the use of proceeds and the ability of the business to repay: usually up to seven years for working capital and up to 25 years for real estate.

b. CAPLines. Eligibility and interest rate rules are the same as for 7(a) guaranteed loans. It is for the financing of assets. The primary collateral will be the short-term assets financed by the loan. SBA will guarantee up to 75% of loans above $150,000 (85% on loans of $150,000 or less). There are four short-term working-capital loan programs for small businesses under CAPLines: (1) The Contract Loan Program, (2) The Seasonal Line of Credit Program, (3) The Builders Line Program, and (4) The Working Capital Line of Credit Program. In addition to financing assets, loan proceeds from the programs can be used for working capital, construction costs, service and supply contracts or purchase orders, or working capital lines of credit.

c. **International Trade Loan Program.** Applicants must establish either that the loan proceeds will significantly expand existing export markets or develop new ones, or that the applicant is adversely affected by import competition. SBA can guarantee 90% of an amount up to $2,000,000 in combined working-capital and fixed-asset loans. The lender must take a first-lien position on items financed. Only collateral located in the United States and its territories and possessions is acceptable as collateral under this program. Additional collateral may be required including personal guaranties, subordinate liens or items that are not financed by the loan proceeds. The proceeds of the loan may not be used for debt repayment. Fees and interest rates are the same as for 7(a)

d. **Export Working Capital Program (EWCP).** This program is for exporters seeking short-term working capital. The SBA will guarantee 90 percent of the principal and interest, up to $1,500,000. When an EWCP loan is combined with an International Trade Loan, the SBA's exposure can go up to $1.75 million. The EWCP uses a one-page application form and streamlined documentation, and turnaround is usually within 10 days. You may also apply for a letter of prequalification from the SBA. Businesses must have operated for the past 12 months, not necessarily in exporting, prior to filing an application. Interest rates are not regulated by the SBA and the lender is not limited to the rates specified for regular 7(a) loans.

Streamlined Applications and Approvals (SBA Loan Guaranty)

There are several options available to lenders that help streamline delivery of the SBA's loan guaranty.

- **SBA Express.** This program makes capital available to businesses seeking loans of up to $350,000 without requiring the lender to use the SBA process. Lenders use their existing documentation and procedures to make and service loans. The SBA guarantees up to 50 percent of an SBA Express loan. Your local SBA office can provide you with a list of SBA Express lenders.

- **Patriot Express Pilot Loan Program.** The Patriot Express Pilot Loan Program is for business start-up or expansion and it adopts many of the SBA Express Loan guidelines including streamlined documentation. To be eligible, the business must be owned and controlled (51% or more) by an eligible veteran and member of the military community. Offered by a wide network of nationwide lenders, the Patriot Express Pilot Program features one of the fastest turnaround times for loan approval. The maximum loan amount is $500,000 with the SBA providing a maximum guarantee of 85% for loans of $150,000 or less and 75% for loans above $150,000. Funds can be used for start-up, expansion, equipment purchases, working capital, and inventory.

- **SBA Export Express.** This is the simplest export loan program available, with an approval time of 36 hours or less. The program, which offers financing up to $500,000, allows lenders to use their own forms and procedures. Loan proceeds are used for business purposes that enhance export development. Export Express can be a term loan or revolving line of credit.

- **Preferred Lenders Program (PLP).** The most active and expert SBA lenders qualify for the SBA's Certified and Preferred Lenders Program. Participants are delegated partial or full authority to approve loans, which results in faster service. Certified lenders are those that have been heavily involved in regular SBA loan-guaranty processing and have met certain other criteria. Preferred lenders are chosen from among the SBA's best lenders and enjoy full delegation of lending authority. A list of participants in the Certified and Preferred Lenders Program may be obtained from your local SBA office.

- **7(M) Microloan Program.** The Microloan Program provides small loans up to $50,000. Under this program, the SBA makes funds available to nonprofit intermediaries; these, in turn, make the loans. The lending and credit requirements are determined by each individual intermediary. The average loan size is $13,000. Completed applications usually are processed by an intermediary in less than one week.

  Micro loans may be used to finance machinery, equipment, fixtures and leasehold improvements. They may also be used to finance receivables and for working capital. They may not be used to pay existing debt or to purchase real estate. Depending on the earnings of your business, you may take up to six years to repay a microloan. Rates will generally be between 8% and 13%. There is no guaranty fee. Each nonprofit lending organization will have its own collateral requirements, but must take as collateral any assets purchased with the microloan. Generally the personal guaranties of the business owners are also required.

- **Small/Rural Lender Advantage (S/RLA).** The Small/Rural Lender Advantage initiative is designed to help lenders in small/rural communities by providing a simpler and streamlined application process as well as procedures. This is all in an effort to help with economic development in local communities that are experiencing population loss, economic dislocation, and high unemployment. The Small/Rural Lender Advantage program allows for loans of up to $350,000 with the SBA providing a guarantee of 85% for loans of $150,000 or less and 75% for loans greater than 150,000. Routine loans are typically processed within a 3 to 5 day window. A one page application (two sided) is used with limited additional information required for loans above $50,000.

- **504 Certified Development Company.** CDCs are nonprofit corporations set up to contribute to the economic development of their communities or regions. They work with the SBA and private-sector lenders to provide financing to small businesses. The program is designed to enable small businesses to create and retain jobs; the CDC's portfolio must create or retain one job for every $65,000 of debenture proceeds provided by the SBA. They provide small businesses with 10 or 20-year financing for the acquisition of land and buildings, machinery and equipment or for constructing, modernizing, renovating or converting existing facilities. To be eligible, the business must operate for profit. Tangible net worth must not exceed $7 million and average net income must not exceed $2.5 million for the past two years.

The maximum loan amount is generally $5,000,000. The amount may go up to $5.5 million if the project meets public policy goals (i.e., business district revitalization, expansion of export, expansion of minority business). Collateral may include a mortgage on the land and the building being financed. Personal guarantees of principals are required. SBA will take business assets as collateral. Interest rates are pegged to an increment above the current market rate for 5- and 10-year U.S. Treasury Bonds and are generally below market rate.

Interest Rates Applicable to SBA Guaranteed Loans

Interest rates are negotiated between the borrower and the lender but are subject to SBA maximums, which are pegged to the Prime Rate. Interest rates may be fixed or variable. Fixed rate loans of $50,000 or more must not exceed Prime Plus 2.25 percent if the maturity is less than 7 years, and Prime Plus 2.75 percent if the maturity is 7 years or more.

Loans between $25,000 and $50.000: Maximum rates must not exceed Prime Plus 3.25 percent if the maturity is less than 7 years, and Prime Plus 3.75 percent if the maturity is 7 years or more.

Loans of $25,000 or less: Maximum interest rate must not exceed Prime Plus 4.25 percent if the maturity is less than 7 years, and Prime Plus 4.75 percent, if the maturity is 7 years or more.

- For current Prime rates, visit *http://www.bankrate.com*

- For more information on SBA programs, visit *http://www.sba.gov/financing*

Equity Financing

If your company has a high percentage of debt to equity (what you owe compared to what you own), you will find it difficult to get debt financing and you will probably need to seek equity investment for additional funds. What this simply means is that you will trade a certain percentage of your company for a specific amount of money to be injected into the company.

Where does equity financing come from?

As with debt capital, this type of capital can come from friends and relatives, from SBA licensed investment companies, or from professional investors known as a *"venture capitalists."*

1. **Friends and Relatives.** Again, be reminded that mixing your friends or relatives and your business may not be a good idea.

2. **SBA licensed investment companies.** The SBA also licenses Small Business Investment Companies (SBICs). They make venture/risk investments by supplying equity capital and extending unsecured loans to small enterprises that meet their criteria. The SBIC Program provides an alternative to bank financing, filling the gap between the availability of venture capital and the needs of small businesses that are either starting or growing. They use their own funds plus funds obtained at favorable rates with SBA guaranties and/or by selling their preferred stock to the SBA. SBICs are for-profit firms whose incentive is to share in the success of a small business. The Program provides funding to all types of manufacturing and service industries.

Internet Info on SBICs

For more information on Small Business Investment Companies visit the following web site: *http://www.sba.gov/category/lender-navigation/sba-loan-programs/sbic-program-0*

---

3. **Professional Investors/Venture Capitalists.** The venture capitalist is a risk taker, usually specializing in related industries and preferring three to five year old companies that have shown high growth potential and will offer higher-than-average profits to their shareholders. These investments are often arranged through venture capital firms that act as "matchmakers".

As risk takers, venture capitalists focus on and have a right to participate in the management of the business. If the company does not perform, they may become active in the decision making process. The most frequent question we get asked is, *"What is the standard amount of equity you have to trade for financing?"* The trade of equity for capital is based on supply and demand. In other words, the deal is made according to who has the best bargaining power.

Venture capitalists also require the inclusion of an *exit strategy* in the company's business plan. The exit strategy lays out the future goals for the company and minimizes risk to the investor by providing a way out if there is a strong indicator that the business will fail to reach its profitability goals.

Which Type of Financing Costs the Most?

The cost of financing is usually related to the degree of risk involved. If the risk is high, so is the cost.

1. **The least expensive money to use is your own.** The cost to you is whatever you would have made on your money by investing it in other sources (savings, money market accounts, bonds, retirement plans, real estate, etc.).

    Note. At this point, I should mention credit cards. Many new business owners borrow heavily on their credit cards only to find themselves up to their ears in debt. Under the right terms, credit cards can provide short-term solutions. However, if they are not used wisely, they can be one of the most expensive sources of cash and may well pave the road to bankruptcy.

2. **Friends and relatives.** The next lowest in cost generally comes from friends and relatives who may charge you a lower interest rate. But don't forget that it may cost you in other ways.

3. **Banks & other traditional lenders.** The third on the cost ladder is probably the traditional lender (banks, SBA, etc.) This lender will want to know what the capital will be used for and will require that it be used for those specific needs. If the risk is too high, most conventional lenders cannot approve your loan because it would be a poor financial decision for the bank's investors. One default out of ten will undermine their whole program.

4. **Outside lenders and venture capitalists.** Traditionally, the most expensive is the outside lender who charges a high interest rate because of the risk involved and the venture capitalist who requires a percentage of your business.

Calculating the Cost

Before you get a loan, take time to understand the terms under which the loan will be made. What is the interest rate? How long do you have to repay the loan? When will payments begin and how much will they be? What are you putting up as collateral? If you have venture capital injected into the business, what will be the overall price to you of the equity and control that you will forfeit?

Any source of financing can and should be calculated as to cost before the financing is finalized. Again back to your business plan. Determine when the financing is needed, plug cash injection, repayment figures, and resulting income projections into your cash flow statement and check out the result.

Will the financing make you more profitable and enable you to repay the lender or distribute profits to the venture capitalist?

In Summary

Securing financing for your company must be planned well in advance. The more immediate your need, the less likely you are to get the best terms. Don't ask your banker to give you a loan yesterday...and don't expect venture capitalists to jump on the bandwagon because you suddenly need their money. Planning ahead for cash flow is one of the best means for determining if and when you will need a lender or investor. It will also help you to determine how much you need.

When you plan for financing, remember that you will not only have to show that your industry has good potential for profit. You will also have to present a strong case for the ability to manage your company through the period of debt. Getting financing is serious business for both you and for the lender/investor.

Take time to plan carefully for your financial needs and your company will prosper and grow accordingly.

U.S. and International
Resources for
Business Plan Research

How Can You Find the Information You Need?

One of the most frequent questions asked by business plan writers is, *"How do I find the information I need to make marketing and financial projections?"*

In this chapter, you will be provided with both online and offline resources that assist you with your marketing and financial research efforts.

Resources in this chapter have been organized in the following sections:

✓ *Internet Research Links*

✓ *Library Resources*

✓ *Publications and Periodicals*

✓ *Indexes to Periodicals and Magazine Articles*

✓ *Books*

✓ *U.S. Government Departments*

✓ *U.S. Small Business Administration*

Internet Resources

Consumer Information

U.S. Demographic Information
http://www.census.gov

Consumer Market Research Information
https://www.npd.com

Values and Lifestyles (VALS)
http://www.strategicbusinessinsights.com/vals/

Foreign Markets

European Demographics Statistics
http://epp.eurostat.ec.europa.eu/portal/page/portal/population/introduction

Foreign Government Data Sources
http://www.lib.umich.edu/browse/International%20Government%20Information

Non Profit

The Society for Nonprofit Organizations
http://www.snpo.org

Establishing a Nonprofit Organization
http://foundationcenter.org/getstarted/tutorials/establish/index.html

Information and services for nonprofits
http://www.usa.gov/Business/Nonprofit.shtml

Company Information

European Business Directory
http://www.europages.com/

Industrial Classifications
http://www.census.gov/

International Company Listing
http://www.trade.gov/

U.S. Small Business Administration
http://www.sbaonline.sba.gov/

Yahoo Industry List of Businesses
http://dir.yahoo.com/Business_and_Economy/Directories/Companies/

Industry Standard Ratios
http://www.bizstats.com

Competitive Analysis

Fortune Magazine
http://money.cnn.com/magazines/fortune/

Hoover's Online
http://www.hoovers.com

International Competitive Analysis
http://www.trade.gov/

U.S. Securities and Exchange Commission
http://www.sec.gov

Country Information

Foreign Government Information
http://dir.yahoo.com/Government/countries

Import and Export
http://www.census.gov/foreign-trade/www/

Middle East
http://arabia.com

Asia
http://www.asia-inc.com

World Trade Search
http://world-trade-search.com

Economic Environment

Economic indicators from the U.S. Census Bureau
http://www.census.gov/econ/www/

Economic Growth Research
http://econ.worldbank.org/programs/macroeconomics/

Entrepreneur Resources

EntreWorld
http://www.entreworld.org/

The Entrepreneurial Edge
http://peerspectives.org

U.S. Small Business Administration
http://www.sbaonline.sba.gov/

Yahoo Business Information
http://dir.yahoo.com/Business_and_Economy/

Wall Street Journal
http://online.wsj.com/public/us

Legal Environment

International Law Dictionary & Directory
http://august1.com/pubs/dict/index.shtml

International Legal Resources
http://www.wcl.american.edu

http://www.lawschool.cornell.edu

http://www.law.indiana.edu

Intellectual Property Law
http://www.patents.com

Law Library of Congress
http://lcweb.loc.gov

Meta-Index for U.S. Legal Research
http://gsulaw.gsu.edu/metaindex

North American Free Trade Agreement
http://www.nafta-sec-alena.org/DefaultSite/index.html

United States Patent and Trademark Office
http://www.uspto.gov

Legislative and Regulatory Environments

Food and Drug Administration
http://www.fda.gov

Federal Trade Commission
http://www.ftc.gov

Federal Communications Commission
http://www.fcc.gov

Thomas Legislative Information on the Internet
http://thomas.loc.gov

Library Resources

The resources listed below can be found in the business section of your local library. The librarian in the business section of your library can help you with locating the materials you need. For your convenience, the resources below have been arranged in alphabetical order.

American Manufacturers Directory (American Business Information). Lists American manufacturers with 25 or more employees.

City and County Data Book (U.S. Dept. of Commerce). This book (updated every three years) contains statistical information on population, education, employment, income, housing, and retail sales.

Directory of Directories (Gale Research Inc.). Describes over 9,000 buyer's guides and directories.

Dun and Bradstreet Directories (Dun and Bradstreet). Lists companies alphabetically, geographically, and by product classification.

Encyclopedia of Associations (Gale Research Inc.). Lists trade and professional associations throughout the United States. Many publish newsletters and provide marketing information. These associations can help business owners keep up with the latest industry developments.

Incubators for Small Business (U.S. Small Business Administration). Lists over 170 state government offices and incubators that offer financial and technical aid to new small businesses.

Industry Norms & Key Business Ratios (Dun & Bradstreet). Provides balance sheet figures for companies in over 800 different lines of business as defined by SIC number.

Lifestyle Market Analyst (Standard Rate & Data Service). Breaks down population geographically and demographically. Includes extensive lifestyle information on the interests, hobbies, and activities popular in each geographic and demographic market.

National Trade and Professional Associations of the U.S. (Columbia Books, Inc.). Trade and Professional Associations are indexed by association, geographic region, subject, and budget.

Reference Book for World Traders (Alfred Croner). This three volume set lists banks, chambers of commerce, customs, marketing organizations, invoicing procedures, and more for 185 foreign markets. Also listed are sections on export planning, financing, shipping, laws, and tariffs are also included, with a directory of helpful government agencies.

RMA Annual Statement Studies (Risk Management Association). Industry norms and ratios are compiled from income statements and balance sheets. For each SIC code three sets of statistics are given with each set representing a specific size range of companies based upon sales.

Sourcebook for Franchise Opportunities (Dow-Jones Irwin). Provides annual directory information for U.S. franchises, and data for investment requirements, royalty and advertising fees, services furnished by the franchiser, projected growth rates, and locations where franchises are licensed to operate.

Standard and Poor's Industry Review. Provides updated information on all industries including current trends, merges and acquisitions, and industry projections.

Statistical Abstract of the U.S. (U.S. Dept. of Commerce). Updated annually, provides demographic, economic, and social information.

Publications and Periodicals

Business Week, McGraw-Hill, Inc., 1221 Avenue of the Americas, New York, NY 10020.

Entrepreneur Magazine, 2392 Morse Avenue, Irvine, CA 92714.

Fast Company, P.O. Box 52760, Boulder, CO 80328.

Inc., 38 Commercial Wharf, Boston, MA 02110.

Small Business Success, Pacific Bell Directory, 101 Spear Street, Rm. 429, San Francisco, CA 94105 (800) 237-4769 in CA - or - (800) 848-8000.

Indexes to Periodicals and Magazine Articles

Also found at the library, periodicals and magazine articles can be researched by subject. Use the index below to find and familiarize yourself with periodicals and articles, which contain information specific to your type of business.

Business Periodicals Index (H.W. Wilson Company). An index to articles published in 300 business-oriented periodicals.

Gale Directory of Publications (Gale Research). Lists periodicals and newsletters.

Magazines for Libraries (R.R. Bowker Company). Directory of publications.

Ulrich's International Periodicals Directory (R.R. Bowker Company). Lists over 100,000 magazines, newsletters, newspapers, journals, and other periodicals in 554 subject areas.

Books

Avdvani, Asheesh. *Investors in Your Backyard: How to Raise Business Capital from the People You Know.* Berkeley, CA: Nolo Press, 2006

Bangs, David. *Non Profits Made Easy.* Irvine, CA: Entrepreneur Media, Inc., 2006.

Clifford, Denis and Ralph Warner. *Form a Partnership.* Berkeley, CA: Nolo Press, 2006.

Gompers, Paul and Lerner, Josh. The Venture Capital Cycle. 2006.

Metrick, Andres, *Venture Capital and the Finance of Innovation.* 2006.

Ogilvy, David. *Ogilvy on Advertising.* New York, NY: Random House.

Pinson, Linda. *Keeping the Books.* Chicago: Kaplan Publishing, 2007.

Pinson, Linda and Jerry Jinnett. *Steps to Small Business Start-up.* New York: Kaplan, 2006.

Scott, David Meerman. *The New Rules of Marketing and PR: How to Use News Releases, Blogs, Podcasting, Viral Marketing and Online Media to Reach Buyers Directly.* 2007.

Steingold, Fred. *The Complete Guide to Buying a Business.* Berkeley, CA: Nolo, 2005.

Vantarakis, Alex and Whitehurst, Bill, *Entrance: A Guide to Buying a Business,* 2005

Wheeler, Alina. *Designing Brand Identity.* 2006.

U.S. Government Departments

Federal agencies are an excellent resource for researching your industry. In addition to the federal agencies provided below, it is recommended that you also gather information from governmental agencies on your state and local level. Please be aware that the phone numbers given for some agencies are for a central office. Upon calling, you can be directed to the department, which can meet your specific needs. To receive appropriate materials and a catalog, be sure to ask to be put on a mailing list.

Consumer Products Safety Commission
Bureau of Compliance
5401 Westbard Avenue
Bethesda, MD 20207

Department of Commerce
14th Street and Constitution Avenue NW
Washington, DC 20230

Department of Education
400 Maryland Avenue SW
Washington, DC 20202

Department of Labor
200 Constitution Avenue NW
Washington, DC 20210

Department of State
2201 C Street NW
Washington, DC 20520

Department of Transportation
400 7th Street SW
Washington, DC 20590

Department of the Treasury
15th Street and Pennsylvania Avenue NW
Washington, DC 20220

Environmental Protection Agency
401 M Street SW
Washington, DC 20460

Federal Communications Commission (FCC)
1919 M Street NW
Washington, DC 20554

Federal Trade Commission
Public Reference Branch
Pennsylvania Avenue and 6th Street NW
Washington, DC 20580

Food and Drug Administration
FDA Center for Food Safety and Applied Nutrition
200 Charles Street, SW
Washington, DC 20402

Internal Revenue Service
1 (800) 829-3676 for tax forms and information.

Library of Congress
Copyright Office
101 Independence Ave. SE
Washington, DC 20540
Public Information Office
(202) 707-2100

Patent and Trademark Office
U.S. Department of Commerce
P.O. Box 9
Washington, DC 20231
Public Information Office
(703) 557-4357

U.S. International Trade Commission
500 E Street SW
Washington, DC 20436

U.S. Small Business Administration

The Small Business Administration is a federal agency, but it is singled out because of its importance to small businesses in America. The SBA offers an extensive selection of information on most business management topics from how to start a business to exporting your products. The SBA has offices throughout the country. Consult the U.S. Government section in your telephone directory for the office nearest you. The SBA offers a number of programs and services, including training and educational programs, counseling services, financial programs and contact assistance. These organizations are available to you through the SBA:

Service Corp of Retired Executives (SCORE). A national organization sponsored by SBA of volunteer business executives who provide free counseling, workshops and seminars to prospective and existing small business people.

Small Business Development Centers (SBDCs). Sponsored by the SBA in partnership with state and local governments, the educational community, and the private sector. SBDCs provide assistance, counseling, and training to prospective and existing business people.

Small Business Institutes (SBIs). Organized through SBA on more than 500 college campuses throughout the nation. The institutes provide counseling by students and faculty to small business clients.

For more information about SBA business development programs and services:

1. Call the SBA Small Business Answer Desk at 1 (800) 827-5722.

2. SBA has a home page on the Internet's World Wide Web, which provides an interactive guide to SBA programs. (http://www.sba.gov)

3. The SBA address is as follows:

U.S. Small Business Administration
1441 L Street NW
Washington, DC 20005

Marine Art of California
Business Plan

The business plan presented in Appendix I is an actual business plan developed by Mr. Robert Garcia for his business, Marine Art of California. Mr. Garcia has generously allowed it to be used in *Anatomy of a Business Plan* and AUTOMATE YOUR BUSINESS PLAN to serve as an illustration that will help you with the writing of your own plan.

Mr. Garcia wrote this plan when he was in the process of organizing his business for startup and looking for investors in the form of limited partnerships. His business has changed direction and he has now been in a related business for a few years and updates his plan regularly to reflect what is actually happening in the operation of his venture.

The plan was written prior to start-up of the original business. For that reason, it included projections only and the financial section ended with a break-even analysis. After one year in business, Mr. Garcia's business plan would also include historical profit & loss statements, a current balance sheet, and financial statement analysis, all of which would be based on the actual transactions of his business.

This plan can help you

As you proceed with the writing of your own plan, it may help you to look at Mr. Garcia's business plan to see how he handled each of the corresponding sections. Some of the research material has been condensed and all of his supporting documents are not included. I have also chosen to omit his personal financial history for privacy reasons.

Regarding the Marketing Plan

In the opening page of Chapter 5, The Marketing Plan, it was stated that smaller start-ups may choose not to address all of the components of a full blown marketing strategy, but should still cover the basic marketing elements.

As you examine the marketing plan section for Marine Art of California, you will see that Mr. Garcia has chosen that path. He does a great job assessing his target market, evaluating his competition, researching his market, and planning his advertising. This is an excellent example of the development of a basic marketing plan. You should especially note how meticulous he has been in the documentation of his resources.

> *Warning!* *The plan is to be examined for Mr. Garcia's handling of content only. It has been used as an example in the book and software because I feel that it is a fine example of a basic business plan. There is no judgement inferred as to appropriateness or financial potential for lenders or investors. Do not use it as a source of research for your own company.*

 Important. *This plan is for illustrative purposes only! I have changed dates, names, contact numbers, and addresses .I have also added to, changed, and/or reorganized some of the information in order to keep the plan up-to-date.* ***Do not try to contact Mr. Garcia or any of the other people mentioned in this business plan. It would not be appropriate.***

I am very pleased that I have the opportunity to include this material in *Anatomy of a Business Plan* and *Automate Your Business Plan* and hope that it will be of benefit to you. I thank Bob Garcia for being so generous and for allowing me to share his interpretation of business planning with so many small business owners.

MARINE ART OF CALIFORNIA
P.O. Box 10059-251
Newport Beach, CA 92658

BUSINESS PLAN

Robert A. Garcia, President

P.O. Box 10059-251
Newport Beach, CA 92658
(714) 997-9100

Plan prepared September 2013

by

Robert A. Garcia

(Private and Confidential)

TABLE OF CONTENTS

MARINE ART OF CALIFORNIA

Executive Summary

Marine Art of California is a Limited Partnership to be established in 2013. The direct mail order and showroom company will be located in Newport Beach, CA. The company is seeking working capital in the amount of $130,000 for the purpose of start-up operations and to cover estimated operating expenses for a six-month period.

Twenty limited partnerships (2.25% each) are being offered in return investments of $6,500 to be treated as loan funds to be repaid over a 15-year period at the rate of 11%. Limited partnerships will have a duration period of four years, at which time the partners' shares will be bought back at the rate of $3,250 for each 2.25% share. At the end of the 15-year loan period, it is projected that the Return on Investment (ROI) for each $6,500 share will amount to $34,084.

The $130,000 in loan funds will enable the company to effectively market its products and services while maintaining proper cash flow. Funding is needed in time for the first catalog issue to be distributed in November 2013 and for a showroom to be operational in the same month for the Christmas buying season. There is a two to three week period between order placement and delivery date.

It is projected that the company will reach its break-even point in the latter part of the second year of operation.

Repayment of the loan and interest can begin promptly within 30 days of receipt of funds and can be secured by the percentage of the business to be held as collateral.

I. ORGANIZATIONAL PLAN
Marine Art of California

Summary Description of Business

Marine Art of California is a start-up company in Newport Beach, marketing the works of California artists through a direct mail-order catalog. The product line is a unique combination of art, gift items and jewelry, all tied together by a marine or nautical theme. This marketing concept is a first! There is no known retailer or catalog company exclusively featuring the works of California artists in either a retail store or by mail-order catalog. I'm targeting a specific genre of the art market that, in terms of marketability, is on the cutting edge.

Having managed Sea Fantasies Art Gallery at Fashion Island Mall in Newport Beach, I was able to discuss my idea personally and collect more than 700 names and addresses of highly interested customers who are marine art lovers. Of these, 90% live in the surrounding communities and the rest are from across the U.S. and other nations.

Currently, I have begun mailings, taking orders and making sales. I have a large number of artists and vendors throughout California with marketing agreements already in place.

I have assets of about $10,000 of miscellaneous items. These include framed and unframed originals, lithographs, posters, bronzes, acrylic boats, jewelry, videos, cassettes, CDs, T-shirts, glass figurines, greeting cards, shells and coral.

Sales will be processed by a four-step marketing plan. First is a direct mail-order catalog published bi-monthly (six times a year). This allows for complete marketing freedom targeting high-income households, interior designers and other businesses located in coastal areas. The second is to generate sales through a retail showroom where merchandise can be purchased on-site and large high-end pieces (exhibited on consignment) can be ordered by catalog and drop shipped from artist/vendor directly to the customer. Third, a comprehensive advertising campaign targeting the surrounding high-income communities shall be conducted (e.g., yellow pages, high-profile magazines, monthly guest artist shows, grand opening mailings and fliers with discount coupons). Fourth is to conduct an ongoing telemarketing program aimed at customers on our mail lists in our local area at minimal cost.

Industry trends have stabilized with the bottoming of the current recession. My plan to counter this situation is to obtain exclusive marketing rights on unique designs and the widest selection in the market of quality items priced affordably under $100.00.

My plan is to secure my ranking as the number two marine art dealer in Southern California, second only to the Wyland Galleries by the end of 2015 and by 2016, through steadily increasing catalog distribution to more than 150,000 copies per mailing, to rank as the #1 dealer in California in gross sales! From 2016 through 2018, projected catalog distribution will increase at a rate of at least 100,000 catalogs per year.

Products and Services

The product line of **MARINE ART OF CALIFORNIA** consists of hand-signed limited editions of bronzes, acrylics, lithographs and posters with certificates. Included are exclusive designs (covered by signed contracts) of (1) originals and prints, (2) glass figurines, and (3) fine jewelry. Rounding out the line are ceramic figures, videos, cassettes, CDs, marine life books, nautical clocks, marine jewelry (14k gold, sterling silver, genuine gemstones) and many more gift items, as well as a specific line for children. The marketing areas covered are both Northern California and Southern California.

The suppliers are artists and vendors from throughout California. They number over 260! I chose them because they best express, artistically, the growing interest in the marine environment. However, due to catalog space, only 30 to 50 artists/vendors can be represented. The retail showroom will be able to accommodate more.

My framing source for art images is a wholesale operation in Fullerton that services many large accounts including Disney Studios.

With an extremely large artist/vendor pool to draw from, I virtually eliminate any supply shortage that cannot be replaced quickly. Also, my shipping policy specifies a maximum of 3 weeks delivery time for custom-made pieces such as limited edition bronzes that need to be poured at foundries. Almost all of my suppliers have been in business for years and understand the yearly marketing trends.

Administrative Plan

Legal Structure

The structure of the company will consist of one (1) General Partner and up to twenty (20) Limited Partners. The amount of funds needed from the Limited Partners is $130,000, which will equal 45% ownership of the business. Each Limited Partner's investment of $6,500 shall equal 2.25% of the business.

The investment will be treated as a loan and will be paid back over 15 years at 11% interest. The loan repayment amount for each 2.25% share will be $79.03 per month. No Limited Partner shall have any right to be active in the conduct of the Partnership's business or have the power to bind the Partnership with any contract, agreement, promise, or undertaking.

Provisions for Exit and Dissolution of the Company

The duration of the Partnership* is 4 years. The General Partner will have the option of buying out the Limited Partners at the end of 4 years for $3,250 for each 2.25% interest. The buyout will not affect the outstanding loan, but the General Partner will provide collateral equal to the loan balance. The value of the business will be used as that collateral.

The distribution of profits shall be made within 75 days of the end of the year. Each Limited Partner will receive 2.25% per share of investment on any profits over and above the following two months' operating expenses (January and February). This amount will be required to maintain operations and generate revenues necessary to keep the company solvent.

In the event of a loss, each Limited Partner will assume a 2.25% liability for tax purposes and no profits will be paid. The General Partner will assume 55% of the loss for tax purposes.

A Key Man Insurance Policy in the amount of $250,000 shall be taken out on the General Partner to be paid to the Limited Partners in the event of the General Partner's death. The policy will be divided among the Limited Partners according to their percentage of interest in the company.

---

* *See copy of Proposal for Limited Partnership in Supporting Documents for remainder of details.*

Management

At present, I, **Robert A. Garcia**, am sole proprietor. I possess a wealth of business environment experience as indicated on my resume. My first long-term job was in the grocery industry with Stater Brothers Markets. I worked from high school through college, rising to the position of second assistant manager. The most valuable experience I came away with was the ability to work cohesively with a variety of personalities in demanding customer situations. It was at this point that I learned the importance and value of the customer in American business. The customers' needs are placed first! They are the most important link in the chain.

With the opportunity for better pay and regular weekday hours, I left Stater Bros. for employment with General Dynamics Pomona Division. For the next eleven years I was employed in Production Control and earned the title of Manufacturing Coordinator, supervising a small number of key individuals. I was responsible for all printed circuit board assemblies fabricated in off-site facilities located in Arizona and Arkansas. My duties included traveling between these facilities as needed. On a daily basis, I interfaced with supporting departments of Engineering, Quality Assurance, Procurement, Shipping and Receiving, Inspection, Stockroom and Inventory Control, Data Control Center, Electronic Fabrication, Machine Shop and Final Assembly areas.

The programs involved were the Standard Missile (Surface to Air Weapon System), Phalanx Close I Weapons System, Stinger System and Sparrow Missile. My group was responsible for all analysis reports for upper management, Naval personnel, and corporate headquarters in St. Louis, Missouri. Duties included: solving material shortages, scheduling work to be released to maintain starts and completions, and driving all support departments to meet final assembly needs for contract delivery. Problem solving was the name of the game. The importance of follow-up was critical. Three key concepts that we used as business guidelines were: (1) production of a *quality product;* (2) at a *competitive price;* and (3) delivered *on schedule.*

I'm currently in contact on a regular basis with eight advisors with backgrounds in marketing, advertising, corporate law, small business start-up, finance, direct mail-order business and catalog production. Two individuals are college professors with active businesses, one is a publisher of my business plan reference book, and two are retired executives with backgrounds in marketing and corporate law involved in the SCORE program through the Small Business Administration (SBA). I meet with these two executives every week.

Pertinent Courses and Seminars Completed

College Course	Supervisory Training	Mt. San Antonio College
College Course	Successful Business Writing	Mt. San Antonio College
Seminar	Producing a Direct Mail Catalog	Coastline Community College
Seminar	Business Taxes and Recordkeeping	SCORE Workshop
Seminar	Business Plan Road Map	SCORE Workshop

Note: See résumé in Supporting Documents.

Manager Salary Plan: Upon the signing of Limited Partnership agreements, I will maintain the status as managing partner and decision maker. For the duration of the Partnership (planned for four years), as the manager, I will draw a monthly salary of $2,000, as per the agreement. In addition, I will retain 55% ownership of the company.

Personnel

The total number of employees to be hired initially will be four. Interviews have been conducted for each position, and all are tentatively filled. I will be on the premises during all business hours for both retail and catalog ordering operations during the first month of business. It will be the owner's duty to hire the following employees:

1. **Store Manager** - part time - $14.00 per hour
2. **1st Asst. Manager** - part time - $10.00 per hour
3. **2nd Asst. Manager** - part time - $10.00 per hour
4. **Sales Consultant** - part time - $15.00 per hour
5. **Administrative Asst.** - part time - $12.00 per hour

TRAINING:

1. All employees will be cross trained in the following areas:

    a. Knowledge of product line and familiarity with key suppliers
    b. Daily Sales Reconciliation Report (DSR)
    c. Catalog order processing
    d. Company policy regarding customer relations
    e. Charges – VISA / MasterCard

PERSONNEL DUTIES:

1. Manager - Reports directly to Owner

    a. Open store (key) - dust and vacuum
    b. Write work schedule
    c. Verify previous day's sales figures
    d. Follow up on any problems of previous day
    e. Head biweekly wall-to-wall inventory
    f. Reconcile any business discrepancies
    g. Responsible for store and catalog operations
    h. Order inventory and process catalog orders
    i. Have access to safe
    j. Conduct telemarketing in spare time
    k. Authorize employee purchase program (EPP)

2. Administrative Assistant - Reports to Manager

    a. Open store (key) and have access to safe
    b. Write work schedule
    c. Perform office functions
        (1) Daily Sales Reconciliation Report   (DSR)
        (2) Accounts Receivable and Payable   (A/R) (A/P)
        (3) Accounts Payable   (A/P)
        (4) Payroll   (P/R)
        (5) General Ledger   (G/L)
        (6) Typing - 60 wpm
        (7) Computer - WP / Lotus / D-Base
        (8) 10-Key Adding Machine
    d. Process catalog orders
    e. Authorize employee purchase program (EPP)

Personnel – cont.

   3. 1st Assistant Manager - Reports to Manager
       a. Close store (Key)
       b. Order inventory
       c. Complete Daily Sales Reconciliation Report (DSR)
       d. Follow up on day's problems not yet solved
       e. Have access to safe
       f. Process catalog orders
       g. Conduct telemarketing in spare time

   4. 2nd Assistant Manager - Reports to 1st Assistant Manager
       a. Is familiar with all 1st Assistant Manager tasks
       b. Process catalog orders
       c. Assist in customer relations follow-up
       d. Dust and vacuum showroom
       e. Conduct telemarketing in spare time

   5. Sales Consultant - Reports to 2nd Assistant Manager
       a. Cover showroom floor
       b. Process catalog orders
       c. Assist in customer relations follow-up
       d. Dust and vacuum showroom
       e. Conduct telemarketing in spare time

EMPLOYEE PROFILE:

    1. Personable, outgoing, reliable, in good health

    2. College background

    3. High integrity and dedication

    4. Neat in appearance

    5. Able to take on responsibilities

    6. Able to follow directives

    7. Demonstrates leadership qualities

    8. Previous retail experience

    9. Basic office skills

   10. Sincere interest in marine art and environment

   11. Likes water sports

   12. Team worker

Legal and Accounting

Legal: Lester Smith of Taylor, Smith, Varges & Whelen, a law corporation will be retained for all legal matters. The firm is located in Orange County, California and specializes in business and copyright law. Mr. Smith is one of the firm's original partners.

Accounting: All bookkeeping activities shall be done by the administrative assistant. John Horist, CPA has been hired to take care of financial reporting and tax accounting. John brings more than 40 years experience in his field. His hourly fee is very reasonable.

Business Software: I would like to point out the key areas of recordkeeping required in the business and explain the software to be used and why. The areas are as follows:

> **Mail Lists** - List & Mail Plus software from Avery. It stores, sorts and prints up to 64,000 addresses with no programming required. It contains pre-defined label formats, or I can create my own. Searching and extracting subsets of the mailing list are possible. It also checks for duplicate entries.

> **Labels** - MacLabel Pro software from Avery. The features include preset layouts for Avery laser labels and dot matrix labels, drawing tools and graphic sizing, built-in clip art and easy mail merge.

> **Accounting** – QuickBooks Pro accounting software. This program automatically updates all accounts, customers, payroll, suppliers, inventory and ledgers in one step. Windows graphics, fonts and integration make it easy to use.

> **Business Planning** - *Automate Your Business Plan* software will be used to analyze and update the company's strategy and financial plan.

The simplicity and power of these reasonably-priced programs make them very attractive.

Insurance

Prospective Carrier:	**State Farm Insurance**	
	2610 Avon, Suite C	
	Newport Beach, CA 92660	
	(714) 645-6000	
Agent:	**Kim Hiller**	
Type of Insurance:	Business/Personal:	$ 150,000.00
	Deductible:	$ 1,000.00
	Liability:	$1,000,000.00
Premium:	Annual Premium:	$ 3,100.00
	Monthly Premium:	**$ 258.00**
	Workers' Comp: 1.43 per/1K of Gross Payroll	

Security

PROBLEM SITUATIONS TO BE CONSIDERED
AND PROTECTIVE MEASURES TO BE USED:

1. **Internal Theft** - Employee Dishonesty

   a. Shoplifting of store merchandise - two closed-circuit monitoring cameras recording showroom activity each business day.

   b. Cash theft - $400 limit of cash on hand. Timely safe drops and daily maintenance of Daily Sales Reconciliation Report will balance cash with receipts.

   c. Falsifying receipts - DSR will detect discrepancies.

   d. Employee Purchase Plan - will reduce inclination to steal. Employee discount is 35% off retail price. Can purchase layaway (20% down - balance over 60 days) or by payroll deduction (deducted from each check over four pay periods). Processed by authorized personnel other than oneself (two signatures required).

   e. Employee Orientation Program - will stress security procedures and employee integrity.

   f. Biweekly wall-to-wall inventory - will reveal any losses.

2. **External Theft** - Customer Shoplifting or Robbery

   a. Walk-in theft - two closed-circuit monitoring cameras recording showroom activity each business day.

   b. Break-in theft or robbery - alarm system plus closed circuit monitoring cameras. All fine jewelry is displayed in locked cases. It is removed and stored in the safe each night.

   c. Wall-to-wall biweekly inventory - will reveal any merchandise loss.

II. MARKETING PLAN
Marine Art of California

Target Market

Who are my customers?

1. **Profile:**

   Economic level - middle to upper class.

   Psychological makeup - art lover, jewelry lover, fashion conscious, ocean lover, eclectic taste, college educated, discriminating buyer, upwardly mobile life-style

   Age - 35 to 55

   Sex - Male/Female

   Income level - $75,000 and above

   Habits - high-expense entertainment, travel, marine-oriented hobbies (shell/dolphin collectors, scuba diver, boat/yacht owner, etc.), patrons of performing arts, concerts and museums

   Work - professional, business owners, business executives, middle management, interior designers

   Shop - middle to high-profile retail establishments

2. **Location:**

   Orange County - coastal areas - home values of $500,000 and above

   San Francisco County, San Diego County, San Bernardino County

3. **Market size:**

   Mail list purchased through wholesale mail list companies. The consumer base will range from 20,000 to 100,000 in the first year of operations.

4. **Competition:**

   Minimal due to unique 2-pronged marketing concept of marketing exclusively California marine art, custom-designed jewelry and giftware by way of (1) direct mail- order catalog and (2) retail showroom. No known operation in either category.

5. **Other factors:**

   As acting distributor for several artists I am able to retain exclusive marketing rights and, in most cases, have contracted to purchase at **10-15% below published wholesale price lists**.

Competition

The two areas of competition to consider will be (1) competitors to the retail showroom and (2) competitors to the direct mail-order operation.

(1) Competition to Retail Showroom

In the Supporting Documents, you will find a Competition Evaluation Worksheet with information on competitors who operate within a radius of 3 miles of proposed store site. Retail Stores to be evaluated have at least 1 of the 4 categories of my product line: *

A. Marine Art - Framed (custom) and framed

B. Marine Sculpting - Cast in bronze and acrylic

C. Marine and Nautical Gift Items

D. Marine and Contemporary Jewelry Designs - Fine and fashion

(2) Competition to Direct Mail-Order Catalog

After investigating scores of catalog companies across the nation for the past year and speaking to artists and vendors across the state of California, we are aware of only one mail-order company with a similar theme but with a very different line and profile than Marine Art of California.

---

* *Supporting documents are not attached to this sample Marketing Plan.*

Market/Industry Trends

Information extracted from: ABI/INFORM DATABASE at UCI Library for Business Research.

Title: *Sharper Image Revamps Product Line. Sells Items Consumers Can Actually Buy.*

Journal: **Marketing News -** Vol. 26, Issue 10, Pg. 2
Summary: Although shoppers will still find upscale items at Sharper Image, the company has doubled the amount of goods that are more affordable. The addition of low-priced items is part of a continuing shift that will last, even if the economy improves.

Title: *What's Selling, and Why*

Journal: **Catalog Age -** Vol. 9, Issue 5, Pg. 5
Summary: Market researcher Judith Langer believes today's mailers must create a value package that combines quality and price. Merchandise is reflecting consumer sentiment about the economy and the desire to buy U.S. goods and services.

Title: *Tripping the Gift Market Fantastic*

Journal: **Catalog Age -** Vol. 9, Issue 6, Pg. 30
Summary: Christmas Fantastic and Celebration Fantastic catalogs feature gifts and decorative accessories and target upscale females age 25 and over. Response has been strong. Average orders of $95 for Christmas Fantastic and $85 for Celebration Fantastic have surpassed company expectations.

Market/Industry Trends – cont.

Title: ***Spring Sales Blossom***

Journal: **Catalog Age -** Vol. 9, Issue 6, Pg. 36
Summary: Spring sales appear to be much stronger than in 2003. Many mailers believe the latest upturn in sales will be long-lasting.

Title: ***Your Catalog's List Is Its Greatest Asset***

Journal: **Target Marketing -** Vol. 15, Issue 2, Pg. 44-45
Summary: There are a number of reasons why greater attention should be paid to the customer mail list rather than prospecting for new customers: 1. It is the primary source of profit for the company. 2. It is the cataloger's most valuable asset. 3. It will outperform a rented list by as much as 10 times in response rate and average order.

Note: *The above articles have been condensed for brevity.*

Market Research Resources

Art Business News (Monthly)
> Monthly trade magazine for art dealers and framers. Foremost business journal in the art industry. It provides readers with a wide range of art industry news, features, sales and marketing trends, and new product information. Reports on trade shows nationally and internationally.

National Jeweler (Monthly)
> Dealer magazine. Provides jewelry industry news, features, sales and marketing trends, fashions, and styles. Lists major manufacturers and wholesalers.

Catalog Age (Monthly)
> Monthly journal featuring articles on mail-order companies. Provides inside information on statistics for mail-order business. Highly informative.

Target Marketing (Monthly) - Monthly trade journal.

Orange County Business Journal (Weekly)

U.S. Small Business Administration
> Free Publications: ***Selling by Mail Order***
> ***Tax & Regulatory Requirements in Orange County***
> ***Partnership Agreements - Planning Checklist***
> ***Understanding Cash Flow***
> ***How to Write a Business Plan***
> ***Insurance Checklist for Small Business***

Anatomy of a Business Plan(8th edition) - Pinson (Out of Your Mind...and Into the Marketplace)

Automate Your Business Plan - Pinson (Out of Your Mind...and Into the Marketplace)

Market Research Resources – cont.

Direct Marketing Handbook - Edward L. Nash (McGraw-Hill)

The Catalog Handbook - James Holland

Direct Marketing Association - Membership organization for catalogers.

Orange County Demographic Overview: Demographic reports, charts and maps provided by the market research department of the Orange County Register.

ABI/INFORM Data Base - University of California, Irvine (see Industry Trends section)
> On-line database located in the library. Contained in this database are abstracts and indexes to business articles that are published in more than 800 different journals. ABI/INFORM is an excellent source of information on:

Companies	Trends	Marketing & Advertising
Products	Corporate Strategies	
Business Conditions	Management Strategies	

Methods of Sales and Distribution

Two-Way Distribution Program

A. Direct Mail-Order Catalog

1. Catalog mailings are distributed through target marketing.

2. Orders are processed via telephone (1-800 #) or by return mail-order forms, accepting checks, VISA/MC, or American Express.

3. Shipping in most cases is done by the artist or vendor directly to the customer per my instructions. All other shipping is done by Marine Art of California.

4. Shipping costs are indicated in the catalog for each item. The customer is charged for shipping costs to reimburse the vendor.

5. UPS shipping is available throughout the United States.

B. Retail Showroom

1. All items shown in the catalog will be available for purchase in the retail store.

2. High-ticket items will be carried on consignment with previous agreements already made with individual artists.

3. General Catalogs will be displayed on an order counter for all products not stocked in the store and that can be shipped on request.

4. All large items will be delivered anywhere in Orange County at no charge.

Methods of Sales and Distribution – cont.

Since I am dealing with more than 260 artists and vendors across the state there should be no problem with the availability of merchandise. I am only able to carry about 55 artists and vendors in the catalog. Most items can be ordered for the store and be in stock within a 2-3 day turnaround.

For more detailed information on shipping arrangements, please see copy of Terms and Conditions for Participants in Supporting Documents section.

Advertising

AT&T:	Yellow/white pages - 1 line	No charge
	Bold - $5.00 extra each	
AT&T:	Sales order # N74717625 (8/21)	
740-5211	Business line installation	$70.45
	Monthly rate	$11.85
	DEADLINE - August 19th - Cannot change without	
	$18.00 per month rate increase	
	Display - 1/4 column listing (per month)	$49.00
	(Yearly cost $588.00)	
	Disconnect w/message (new #) 1 year	No charge
Donnelly:	White pages - 1 line	No charge
1-800-834-8425	Yellow pages - 2 lines	No charge
	3 or more	$10.00
	1/2 add (per month)	$27.00
	DEADLINE - August 21 (30 days to cancel)	
	Change deadline - September 10	
	Deposit due September 11	$183.00
	Monthly rate	$91.50
	(Yearly cost $1098.00)	
Metropolitan Magazine:	Circulation 40,000	
757-1404	Monthly rate	$129.00
Kim Moore		
4940 Campus Drive		
Newport Beach,		
CA 92660		
California Riveria:	1/6 page (per month)	$300.00
494-2659	Art charge - one time	$50.00
Leslie	40% discount - new subscriber	
Box 536	Can hold rate for 6 months (Reg. $575.00)	
Laguna Beach,	Color (per month)	$600.00
CA 92652	Articles	No charge
	Print month end	
	Circulation: 50,000 29K High Traffic	
	21K Direct Mail (92660 - 92625)	

Advertising – cont.

Grand Opening:	4 x 6 Postcard - color	$400.00
	Catering	$200.00
	Artist show	
	Discount coupons	
	Fliers	
	Newspaper ads OC Register - one time cost - $100)	

Orange County News: Will get advertising estimates after 6 months in business.
(714) 565-3881

Orange County Register: Monthly rate $100.00

DONNELLY LISTINGS:

5 Categories:

A. Art Dealer, Galleries

B. Interior Designers and Decorators

a. Framers

b. Jewelers

c. Gift Shops

A. Art Dealers, Galleries:

Original Art, Lithos, Posters, Custom Framing, Bronze & Acrylic Sculptings
Int. Designer Prices, Ask for Catalog

B. Interior Decorators & Designers:

Original Art, Lithos, Posters, Custom Framing, Bronze & Acrylic Sculptings
Dealer Prices, Ask for Catalog

C.   Framers:

Large Selection of California Marine Art, Coastal Scenes, Custom Framing
Matting, Ask for Mail-Order Catalog

D. Jewelers:

Specialty, Marine/Nautical Custom Designs by California Artists, 14K Gold,
Sterling, Gemstones, Ask for Catalog

E.   Gift Shops:

Unique Line of Marine/Nautical Gifts, Glass Figurines, Acrylic Boats, Clocks,
Art, Jewelry, Bronzes, Ask for Catalog

14

Pricing

A. Purchasing

As stipulated in my Terms and Conditions, I request a 10 - 15% discount off published wholesale prices from artists and vendors in lieu of a participation fee. In about 95% of all agreements made, I am receiving this important discount!

B. Catalog Pricing

- Non-Jewelry Items - To recover publication costs, I have "keystoned" (100% markup) all items plus an additional 10-50%. Keystoning is typical in the retail industry. The added margin will cover any additional shipping charges that may not be covered by the indicated shipping fee paid by the customer.

- Jewelry Items - Typical pricing in the industry is "Key" plus 50% (150% markup) to triple "Key" (200% markup). My markup is "Key" plus 10-30% to stay competitive.

C. Store Pricing

All items "Keystone" plus 10 - 20% to allow a good margin for sales on selected items.

D. Wholesale

Mailings and advertising will target Interior Decorators and Designers. To purchase wholesale, one must present a copy of an ASID or ISID license number and order a minimum purchase of $500.00 or more. The discount will be 20% off retail price.

Below is a sample of the computer data base with 16 fields of information on each item in inventory and how the retail price is computed.

File: Price List - Record 1 of 449

Item:	Fisherman's Wharf	Image Pr:	$5.00	Disc:	50% IM
Make:	Poster	Type:	Poster	Adj. Whsl:	$36.50
Vendor:	Chrasta	Frame:	PT4XW	Key+:	10%
Exclusive:	So. California	Frame Price:	$31.50	Retail Price:	$79.50
Size:	21.5 26 Sq.	Whsl. Price:	$36.50	Group:	1
Vendor #:	NAC102WM				

Location

The prime business location targeted for Marine Art of California retail showroom is 1000 square feet at 106 Bayview Circle, Newport Beach, CA 92660. This site was chosen because of large front display windows, excellent visibility and access for the showroom, as well as adequate floor space to house inventory for catalog shipping. Both operations require certain square footage to operate successfully. Demographics and surrounding stores are extremely favorable.

Proposed site: Newport Beach, California

Features: * Retail Shop space of 1000 sq. ft.
* Located in the primary retail and business sector of Newport Beach, Orange County's most affluent and growing community
* Excellent visibility and access
* Median household income in 1 mile radius is $90,000.00

Location – cont.

Demographics [3]	1 Mile	3 Miles	5 Miles
Population:	1,043	111,983	308,906
Income:	$90,000	$61,990	$59,600

Private Sector Employment (Daytime population)

1 Mile	3 Miles	5 miles
43,921	113,061	306,313

Socio-Economic Status Indicator (SESI)

1 Mile	3 Miles	5 Miles
73	79	79

Population by Age

1 Mile		3 Miles	5 Miles
25 - 29		9.2%	8.4%
30 - 34		9.4%	9.9%
35 - 44		16.1%	18.6%
45 - 54		12.3%	12.1%
25 - 54	TOTAL	47.0%	49.0%

Leasing Agent: Chuck Sullivan, CB Commercial, 4040 MacArthur Blvd., Newport Beach, CA 92660

---

[3] Donnelly Marketing Information Service

Gallery Design

After managing Sea Fantasies Gallery at Fashion Island Mall in Newport Beach, I have decided to recreate its basic layout. My goal is to create the most stunning and unique showroom design in Orange County with a product line that appeals to the high-profile customer's taste.

The design theme is to give the customer a feeling of being underwater when they enter. This would be accomplished by the use of glass display stands and live potted tropical plants to simulate lush, green underwater vegetation. Overhead curtains 18 inches wide would cleverly hide the track lighting while reflecting the light on the curtain sides, creating the illusion of an underwater scene with sunlight reflecting on the ocean surface.

A large-screen TV would continuously play videos of colorful underwater scenes with mood music playing on the store's sound system. A loveseat for shoppers to relax in would face the screen. Along with creating a soothing and relaxing atmosphere, the videos, CDs, and cassettes would be available for sale. All fine art pieces (bronzes and framed art) would be accented with overhead track lighting, creating a strong visual effect.

Large coral pieces would be used for display purposes, such as for jewelry. Others would be strewn around the showroom floor area for a natural ocean floor effect. Certain end displays would be constructed of glass with ocean floor scenes set inside consisting of an arrangement of coral, shells, and brightly painted wooden tropical fish on a two-inch bed of sand! All display stands would be available for sale.

This design concept was generally considered to be the most outstanding original store plan in Fashion Island as expressed by Mall customers and the Management Office. By incorporating these tried and proven concepts with my own creative designs, this gallery will have the most outstanding and unique appearance of any gallery from Long Beach to San Clemente. The showroom area will be approximately 800 sq./ft. The rear and stock area is about 200 sq./ft.

Timing of Market Entry

Considering the fact that most of my product line could be viewed as gift items, the upcoming Holiday Season is of **CRITICAL IMPORTANCE!** This is typically the peak sales period in the retail industry. Catalogs from large retailers and mail-order houses are already appearing in the mail for the holidays. These are the dates to consider:

1. OCTOBER 8:   Camera-ready artwork goes to film separator.

                          Turnaround time - 3 days!

2. OCTOBER 11:   All slides and artwork must be ready to be delivered to the printer, Bertco Graphics in Los Angeles.

                          Turnaround time - 11 working days!

3. OCTOBER 22:   Printed catalogs must be delivered to Towne House Marketing in Santa Ana.

                          Turnaround time - 3 days!

4. OCTOBER 29:   Catalogs shipped to Santa Ana Main Post Office.

                          Turnaround time - 2 working days!

5. NOVEMBER 1:   **CUSTOMER RECEIVES CATALOG** - Ordering begins.

6. DECEMBER 4:   Last ordering date to ensure Christmas delivery! Can send via Federal Express all stocked items and all stocked items at vendors.

                          Problem Items:
                                a) High-end cast bronzes
                                b) Hand-made glass figurines
                                c) Original paintings

                          Turnaround time - 3 weeks!

III. FINANCIAL DOCUMENTS
Marine Art of California

Summary of Financial Needs

I. **Marine Art of California**, a limited partnership, is seeking equity capital for start-up purposes.

    A.   Direct Mail-Order Catalog

    B.   Retail/Wholesale Showroom

II. **Funds needed to accomplish above** goal will be $130,000. See "Loan Fund Dispersal Statement" below for distribution of funds and backup statement.

Loan Fund Dispersal Statement

I. Dispersal of Loan Funds

Marine Art of California will utilize funds in the amount of $130,000 for startup of two retail functions: (1) a direct mail-order catalog and (2) a retail showroom to conduct related functions.

II. Backup Statement

Direct mail-order catalog:	a) 24 pages		
	b) 2 editions		
	c) Quantities:	20K	$20,000
		30K	23,300
Startup expense of warehouse – One Time Cost:			25,175
3 Months Operating Expense:			58,364
3 Month Total Loan Repayment Cost @ $1,560:			3,161
		TOTAL	**$130,000**

Pro Forma Cash Flow Statement

Page 1 (Pre-Start-Up & January thru May)

Marine Art of California

For the Year 2014	Start-Up Nov-Dec	Jan	Feb	Mar	Apr	May
BEGINNING CASH BALANCE	0	75,575	65,312	50,837	49,397	37,807
CASH RECEIPTS						
A. Sales/Revenues	41,620	22,065	16,040	42,350	30,300	67,744
B. Receivables (Credit Accts.)	0	0	0	0	0	0
C. Interest Income	0	0	0	0	0	0
D. Sale of Long-Term Assets	0	0	0	0	0	0
TOTAL CASH AVAILABLE	41,620	97,640	81,352	93,187	79,697	105,551
CASH PAYMENTS						
A. Cost of goods to be sold						
Inventory Purchases	29,900	12,213	9,200	22,375	16,375	35,122
B. Variable Expenses						
1. Advertising/Marketing	1,042	221	221	221	521	521
2. Car Delivery/Travel	200	100	100	100	100	100
3. Catalog Expense	27,600	9,600	10,800	10,800	14,600	14,600
4. Gross Wages	5,120	2,560	2,560	2,560	2,560	3,520
5. Payroll Expense	384	192	192	192	192	269
6. Shipping	800	400	400	400	400	400
7. Misc. Var. Exp.	3,000	500	500	500	500	500
Total Variable Expenses	38,146	13,573	14,773	14,773	18,873	19,910
1. Accounting & Legal	820	160	160	160	160	160
2. Insurance + Workers' Comp	904	302	302	302	302	320
3. Rent	3,900	1,300	1,300	1,300	1,300	1,300
4. Repairs & Maintenance	60	30	30	30	30	30
5. Guaranteed Payment (Mgr. Partner)	4,000	2,000	2,000	2,000	2,000	2,000
6. Supplies	600	300	300	300	300	300
7. Telephone	1,050	600	600	700	700	1,000
8. Utilities	630	290	290	290	290	290
9. Misc. (inc. Licenses/Permits)	175	0	0	0	0	0
Total Fixed Expenses	12,139	4,982	4,982	5,082	5,082	5,400
D. Interest Expense	1,192	1,192	1,192	1,192	1,192	1,192
E. Federal/State Income Tax	0	0	0	0	0	0
F. Capital Purchases (Office)	9,000	0	0	0	0	0
G. Capital Purchases (Showroom)	5,300	0	0	0	0	0
H. Loan payments	368	368	368	368	368	368
I. Equity Withdrawals	0	0	0	0	0	0
TOTAL CASH PAID OUT	96,045	32,328	30,515	43,790	41,890	61,992
CASH BALANCE/DEFICIENCY	(54,425)	65,312	50,837	49,397	37,807	43,559
LOANS TO BE RECEIVED	130,000	0	0	0	0	0
EQUITY DEPOSITS	0	0	0	0	0	0
ENDING CASH BALANCE	75,575	65,312	50,837	49,397	37,807	43,559

1. $130,000 15-year loan. 20 limited partners @ $6,500 in exchange for 2.5% equity (each) in company (see proposal in Supporting Docs)

2. Cash business: Prepaid orders and paid on-site purchases only; no open accounts or receivables.

20

Pro Forma Cash Flow Statement
Page 2 (May thru December 2013 + 6 and 12-month Totals)
Marine Art of California

Jun	6-MONTH TOTALS	Jul	Aug	Sep	Oct	Nov	Dec	12-MONTH TOTALS
43,559	75,575	37,462	48,996	46,287	47,992	37,772	80,527	75,575
47,696	226,195	83,508	58,672	67,950	47,700	154,200	105,700	743,925
0	0	0	0	0	0	0	0	0
0	0	0	0	0	0	0	0	0
0	0	0	0	0	0	0	0	0
91,255	301,770	120,970	107,668	114,237	95,692	191,972	186,227	819,500
25,123	120,408	43,054	30,661	35,275	25,150	78,375	54,125	387,048
521	2,226	521	521	521	521	521	521	5,352
100	600	100	100	100	100	100	100	1,200
16,400	76,800	16,400	18,200	18,200	20,000	20,000	20,000	189,600
3,520	17,280	3,520	3,520	3,520	3,520	3,520	3,520	38,400
269	1,306	269	269	269	269	269	269	2,920
400	2,400	400	400	400	400	400	400	4,800
500	3,000	500	500	500	500	500	500	6,000
21,710	103,612	21,710	23,510	23,510	25,310	25,310	25,310	248,272
160	960	160	160	160	160	160	160	1,920
320	1,848	320	320	320	320	320	320	3,768
1,300	7,800	1,300	1,300	1,300	1,300	1,300	1,300	15,600
30	180	30	30	30	30	30	30	360
2,000	12,000	2,000	2,000	2,000	2,000	2,000	2,000	24,000
300	1,800	300	300	300	300	300	300	3,600
1,000	4,600	1,250	1,250	1,500	1,500	1,800	1,800	13,700
290	1,740	290	290	290	290	290	290	3,480
0	0	0	0	0	0	0	0	0
5,400	30,928	5,650	5,650	5,900	5,900	6,200	6,200	66,428
1,192	7,152	1,192	1,192	1,192	1,192	1,190	1,190	14,300
0	0	0	0	0	0	0	0	0
0	0	0	0	0	0	0	0	0
0	0	0	0	0	0	0	0	0
368	2,208	368	368	368	368	370	370	4,420
0	0	0	0	0	0	0	0	0
53,793	264,308	71,974	61,381	66,245	57,920	111,445	87,195	720,468
37,462	37,462	48,996	46,287	47,992	37,772	80,527	99,032	99,032
0	0	0	0	0	0	0	0	0
0	0	0	0	0	0	0	0	0
37,462	37,462	48,996	46,287	47,992	37,772	80,527	99,032	99,032

Three Year Income Projection

Marine Art of California

Updated: September 26, 2013	Nov-Dec 2013 Pre-Start-Up	YEAR 1 2014	YEAR 2 2015	YEAR 3 2016	TOTAL 3 YEARS
INCOME					
1. SALES/REVENUES	**41,620**	**743,930**	**2,651,856**	**4,515,406**	**7,952,812**
Catalog Sales	33,820	672,925	2,570,200	4,421,500	7,698,445
Showroom Sales	4,600	46,325	53,274	61,266	165,465
Wholesale Sales	3,200	24,680	28,382	32,640	88,902
2. Cost of Goods Sold (c-d)	**23,900**	**375,048**	**1,329,476**	**2,261,783**	**3,990,207**
a. Beginning Inventory	6,000	6,000	18,000	25,000	6,000
b. Purchases	23,900	387,048	1,336,476	2,268,783	4,016,207
Catalog	19,600	336,460	1,285,100	2,210,750	3,851,910
Showroom (Walk-in)	2,300	35,163	33,637	37,633	108,733
Wholesale	2,000	15,425	17,739	20,400	55,564
c. C.O.G. Avail. Sale (a+b)	29,900	393,048	1,354,476	2,293,783	4,022,207
d. Less Ending Inventory (12/31)	6,000	18,000	25,000	32,000	32,000
3. GROSS PROFIT ON SALES (1-2)	**17,720**	**368,882**	**1,322,380**	**2,253,623**	**3,962,605**
EXPENSES					
1. VARIABLE (Selling) (a thru h)	**38,146**	**249,332**	**734,263**	**1,316,291**	**2,338,032**
a. Advertising/Marketing	1,042	5,352	5,727	6,127	18,248
b. Car Delivery/Travel	200	1,200	1,284	1,374	4,058
c. Catalog Expense	27,600	189,600	670,400	1,248,000	2,135,600
d. Gross Wages	5,120	38,400	41,088	43,964	128,572
e. Payroll Expenses	384	2,920	3,124	3,343	9,771
f. Shipping	800	4,800	5,280	5,808	16,688
g. Miscellaneous Selling Expenses	3,000	6,000	6,300	6,615	21,915
h. Depreciation (Showroom Assets)	0	1,060	1,060	1,060	3,180
2. FIXED (Administrative) (a thru h)	**12,139**	**68,228**	**71,609**	**75,268**	**227,244**
a. Accounting & Legal	820	1,920	2,054	2,198	6,992
b. Insurance + Workers' Comp	904	3,768	4,032	4,314	13,018
c. Rent	3,900	15,600	16,692	17,860	54,052
d. Repairs & Maintenance	60	360	385	412	1,217
e. Guaranteed Pay't (Mgr. Partner)	4,000	24,000	24,000	24,000	76,000
f. Supplies	600	3,600	3,852	4,123	12,175
g. Telephone	1,050	13,700	15,070	16,577	46,397
h. Utilities	630	3,480	3,724	3,984	11,818
i. Miscellaneous Fixed Expense	175	0	0	0	175
j. Depreciation (Office Assets)	0	1,800	1,800	1,800	5,400
TOTAL OPERATING EXPENSES (1+2)	**50,285**	**317,560**	**805,872**	**1,391,559**	**2,565,276**
NET INCOME OPERATIONS (GPr - Exp)	**(32,565)**	**51,322**	**516,508**	**862,064**	**1,397,329**
OTHER INCOME (Interest Income)	0	0	0	0	0
OTHER EXPENSE (Interest Expense)	1,192	14,300	13,814	13,274	42,580
NET PROFIT (LOSS) FOR PARTNERSHIP	**(33,757)**	**37,022**	**502,694**	**848,790**	**1,354,749**
TAXES: (Partnership)*	0	0	0	0	0
(partners taxed individually according to	0	0	0	0	0
distributive shares of profit or loss)	0	0	0	0	0
PARTNERSHIP: NET PROFIT (LOSS)	**(33,757)**	**37,022**	**502,694**	**848,790**	**1,354,749**

22

Projected Balance Sheet

Business Name:
Marine Art of California

Date of Projection: September 30, 2013
Date Projected for: December 31, 2014

ASSETS

			% of Assets
Current Assets			
Cash	$	98,032	73.96%
Petty Cash	$	1,000	0.75%
Sales Tax Holding Account	$	4,067	3.07%
Accounts Receivable	$	0	0.00%
Inventory	$	18,000	13.58%
Short-Term Investments	$	0	0.00%
	$	0	0.00%
Fixed Assets			
Land (valued at cost)	$	0	0.00%
Buildings	$	0	0.00%
1. Cost	0		
2. Less Acc. Depr.	0		
Showroom Improvements	$	4,240	3.20%
1. Cost	5,300		
2. Less Acc. Depr.	1,060		
Office Improvements	$	4,160	3.14%
1. Cost	5,200		
2. Less Acc. Depr.	1,040		
Office Equipment	$	3,040	2.29%
1. Cost	3,800		
2. Less Acc. Depr.	760		
Autos/Vehicles	$	0	0.00%
1. Cost	0		
2. Less Acc. Depr.	0		
Other Assets			
1.	$	0	0.00%
2.	$	0	0.00%

TOTAL ASSETS	**$ 132,539**	**100.00%**

LIABILITIES

			% of Liabilities
Current Liabilities			
Accounts Payable	$	0	0.00%
Notes Payable	$	4,906	3.79%
Interest Payable	$	0	0.00%
Taxes Payable (Partnership)			
Federal Income Tax	$	0	0.00%
Self-Employment Tax	$	0	0.00%
State Income Tax	$	0	0.00%
Sales Tax Accrual	$	4,067	3.15%
Property Tax	$	0	0.00%
Payroll Accrual	$	0	0.00%
Long-Term Liabilities			
Notes Payable to Investors	$	120,306	93.06%
Notes Payable Others	$	0	0.00%

TOTAL LIABILITIES	**$ 129,279**	**100.00%**

NET WORTH (EQUITY)

			% of N. Worth
Proprietorship	$	0	0.00%
or			
Partnership			
1. Bob Garcia, 55% Equity	$	1,793	55.00%
2. Ltd. Partners., 45% Equity	$	1,467	45.00%
or			
Corporation			
Capital Stock	$	0	0.00%
Surplus Paid In	$	0	0.00%
Retained Earnings	$	0	0.00%

TOTAL NET WORTH	**$ 3,260**	**100.00%**

Assets - Liabilities = Net Worth
and
Liabilities + Equity = Total Assets

1. See Financial Statement Analysis for ratios and notations.

Break-Even Analysis
Marine Art of California

Date of Analysis: September 29, 2013

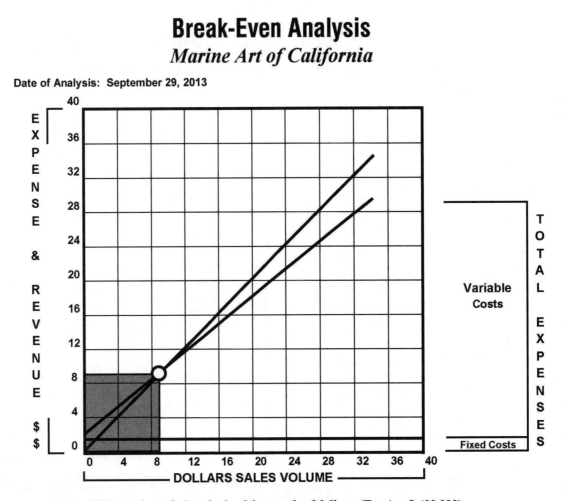

NOTE: *Figures shown in hundreds of thousands of dollars (Ex: 4 = $ 400,000)*

Marine Art of California
Break-Even Point Calculation

B-E POINT (SALES) = Fixed costs + [(Variable Costs/Est. Revenues) X Sales]

B-E Point (Sales) = $ 181,282.00 + [($ 2,750,165.00 / $ 3,437,406.00) X Sales]

B-E Point (Sales) = $ 181,282.00 + [.8001 X Sales]

S - .8001S = $181,282.00   S - .8001S = $181,282.00   .19992S = $181,282.00

S = $181,282.00/.1999

Break-Even Point
S = $906,800
rounded figure

FC **(Fixed Costs)**	= (Administrative Expenses + Interest)	$	181,282
VC **(Variable Costs)**	= (Cost of Goods + Selling Expenses)	$	2,750,165
R **(Est. Revenues)**	= (Income from sale of products and services)	$	3,437,406
Break-Even Point =		$	906,727

Financial Statement Analysis Summary

The following is a summary of 2014 financial statement analysis information extracted from the ratio table calculations on the next page and compared to current industry standards.

Author Note: Writer must research industry standards.

	2014 PROJECTED	INDUSTRY* STANDARD
1. Net Working Capital	$112,126	$100,000 +
2. Current Ratio	13.5	2.0 +
3. Quick Ratio	11.5	1.0 +
4. Gross Profit Margin	49.60%	45.0%
5. Operating Profit Margin	6.9%	6.8%
6. Net Profit Margin	5.0%	12.4%
7. Debt to Assets	97.5%	33.0%
8. Debt to Equity	39.7:1	1.0:1 +
9. ROI (Return on Investment	28.0%	11% +
10. Vertical Income Statement Analysis **		
Sales/Revenues	100.0%	
Cost of Goods	50.4%	50.0% -
Gross Profit	49.6%	40.0% +
Operating Expense	42.7%	35.0% +
Net Income Operations	6.9%	15.0% +
Interest Income	0/0%	N/A
Interest Expense	1.9%	Variable
Net Profit (Pre-Tax)	5.0%	10.0% +

*** All items stated as % of Total Revenues*

11. Vertical Balance Sheet Analysis ***		
Current Assets	91.2%	85.0%
Inventory	13.6%	28.0%
Total Assets	3.7%	
Current Liabilities	3.7%	20.0% -
Total Liabilities	97.5%	
Net Worth	2.5%	50.0% +
Total Liabilities + Net Worth	100.0%	

*** All Asset items stated as % of Total Assets;
Liability & Net Worth items stated as % of Total Liabilities + Net Worth

Notes:

Marine Art of California has an excessively high debt ratio (96.7%). However, it is projected that in its first year of business, the company will maintain its cash flow ($100,000+) and still return a higher amount than originally promised to its investors. Good management of the company by Mr. Garcia plus a timely product with a solid niche would seem to be good indicators that this company's profits will continue to increase rapidly and that the company will be more than able to fulfill its obligations to its limited partners/investors.

Financial Statement Analysis Ratio Table
Marine Art of California

Type of Analysis	Formula	Projected: 2014
1. Liquidity Analysis a. Net Working Capital	**Balance Sheet** Current Assets − Current Liabilities	Current Assets 121,099 Current Liabilities 8,973 **Net Working Capital** **$112,126**
b. Current Ratio	**Balance Sheet** Current Assets Current Liabilities	Current Assets 121,099 Current Liabilities 8,973 **Current Ratio** **13.50**
c. Quick Ratio	**Balance Sheet** Current Assets minus Inventory Current Liabilities	Current Assets 121,099 Inventory 18,000 Current Liabilities 8,973 **Quick Ratio** **11.49**
2. Profitability Analysis a. Gross Profit Margin	**Income Statement** Gross Profits Sales	Gross Profits 368,882 Sales 743,930 **Gross Profit Margin** **49.59%**
b. Operating Profit Margin	Income From Operations Sales	Income From Ops. 51,322 Sales 743,930 **Op. Profit Margin** **6.90%**
c. Net Profit Margin	Net Profits Sales	Net Profits 37,022 Sales 743,930 **Net Profit** **4.98%**
4. Debt Ratios a. Debt to Assets	**Balance Sheet** Total Liabilities Total Assets	Total Liabilities 129,279 Total Assets 132,539 **Debt to Assets Ratio** **97.54%**
b. Debt to Equity	Total Liabilities Total Owners' Equity	Total Liabilities 129,279 Total Owners' Equity 3,260 **Debt to Equity Ratio** **3965.61**

4. Investment Measures
 	
   a. ROI
   (Return on Investment)
	Balance Sheet
	Net Profits
	Total Assets
		Net Profits 37,022
		Total Assets 132,539
		ROI (Ret. on Invest.) **27.93%**

5. Vertical Financial Statement Analysis	**Balance Sheet** 1. Each asset % of Total Assets 2. Liability & Equity % Total L&E **Income Statement** 3. All items % of Total Revenues	**NOTE:** *See FSA Summary* **Balance Sheet and Income Statement**
6. Horizontal Financial Statement Analysis	**Balance Sheet** 1. Assets, Liab & Equity measured against 2nd year. Increases and decreases stated as amount & % **Income Statement** 2. Revenues & Expenses measured against 2nd year. Increases and decreases stated as amount & %	**NOTE:** **Horizontal Analysis Not Applicable** **Only one year in business**

26

IV. SUPPORTING DOCUMENTS
Marine Art of California

Catalog Cost Analysis

Competition Comparison Analysis

Proposal for Limited Partnership

Catalog Cost Analysis

PRINTING QUANTITY	20,000	30,000	40,000	50,000	60,000
CATALOG ITEMS					
24-Page: Price per 1000	521.37	413.92	360.07	336.11	306.49
WEIGHT - 2.208 OZ.					
Extended Cost	10,427.40	12,417.60	14,402.80	16,305.50	18,389.40
Prep & Delivery	756.00	970.00	1,235.00	1,500.00	1,765.00
Mail List Costs - $50.00 per/1000	1,000.00	1,500.00	2,000.00	2,500.00	3,000.00
Postage - $170 per/1000	3,200.00	4,800.00	6,400.00	8,000.00	9,600.00
Film Separations - $64 per/page	3,600.00	2,500.00	2,500.00	2,500.00	2,500.00
Art Work	1,000.00	1,000.00	1,000.00	1,000.00	1,000.00
TOTAL COSTS	**19,983.40**	**23,187.60**	**27,537.80**	**31,805.50**	**36,254.40**
Rounded Numbers	20,000.00	23,200.00	27,600.00	32,000.00	36,500.00
UNIT COSTS	1.00	0.77	0.69	0.64	0.61
COSTS PER PAGE	0.04	0.03	0.03	0.03	0.03
COSTS PER/1000	999.17	772.92	688.44	636.11	604.24

PRINTING QUANTITY	70,000	80,000	90,000	100,000	
CATALOG ITEMS					
24-Page: Price per 1000	291.72	280.29	268.85	261.00	
WEIGHT - 2.208 OZ.					
Extended Cost	20,420.40	22,423.20	24,196.50	26,100.00	
Prep & Delivery	2,030.00	2,295.00	2,560.00	2,825.00	
Mail List Costs - $50.00 per/1000	3,500.00	4,000.00	4,500.00	5,000.00	
Postage - $170 per/1000	11,900.00	13,600.00	15,300.00	17,000.00	
Film Separations - $64 per/page	2,500.00	2,500.00	2,500.00	2,500.00	
Art Work	1,000.00	1,000.00	1,000.00	1,000.00	
TOTAL COSTS	**41,350.40**	**45,818.20**	**50,056.50**	**54,425.00**	
Rounded Numbers	41,500.00	46,000.00	50,500.00	55,000.00	
UNIT COSTS	0.59	0.57	0.56	0.54	
COSTS PER PAGE	0.02	0.02	0.02	0.02	
COSTS PER/1000	590.72	572.73	556.18	544.25	

FOREIGN PRINTING QUANTITY	40,000	50,000	60,000	70,000	
NOTE: 20% will be deducted for foreign printing. Prices are reflected in Profit	27,600.00	32,000.00	36,500.00	41,500.00	
	0.80	0.80	0.80	0.80	
FOREIGN PRINTING COSTS	**22,080.00**	**25,600.00**	**29,200.00**	**33,200.00**	

FOREIGN PRINTING QUANTITY	80,000	90,000	100,000		
	46,000.00	50,500.00	55,000.00		
	0.80	0.80	0.80		
FOREIGN PRINTING COSTS	**36,800.00**	**40,400.00**	**44,000.00**		

Competition Comparison Analysis

	Price Range	Total Retail Prices	% of Total Prices	# of Items	Item RNG %		
COMPANY NAME							
Wild Wings	-50.00	2,092.35	3%	68	19%		
Spring	-100.00	5,269.50	7%	68	19%	-100.00	38%
32 Pages	-200.00	11,302.00	15%	78	22%		
	-500.00	39,905.00	54%	124	35%		
	-999.00	11,045.00	15%	19	5%		
	$1,000.00	4,745.00	6%	2	1%		
		$74,358.85	100%	359	100%		
						Avg Item Price	**$207.13**
			(Based on keystone pricing)			Avg Item Profit	**$103.56**
Sharper Image	-50.00	1,580.65	9%	47	39%		
Jul/Aug	-100.00	2,418.45	14%	31	26%	-100.00	64%
24 of 60 Pages	-200.00	3,898.75	23%	25	21%		
	-500.00	4,879.45	29%	13	11%		
	-999.00	2,797.85	17%	4	3%		
	$1,000.00	1,195.00	7%	1	1%		
		$16,770.15	100%	121	100%		
						Avg Item Price	**$138.60**
			(Based on keystone pricing)			Avg Item Profit	**$69.30**
Sharper Image	-50.00	2,223.60	10%	73	42%		
Jul/Aug	-100.00	3,227.95	15%	41	24%	-100.00	66%
32 of 60 Pages	-200.00	5,088.35	23%	33	19%		
	-500.00	7,129.10	33%	20	12%		
	-999.00	4,047.75	19%	6	3%		
	$1,000.00	0.00	0%	0	0%		
		$21,716.75	100%	173	100%		
						Avg Item Price	**$125.53**
			(Based on keystone pricing)			Avg Item Profit	**$62.77**
Marine Art of California	-50.00	2,826.95	13%	108	54%		
Nov/Dec	-100.00	3,587.65	17%	46	23%	**-100.00**	77%
40 Pages	-200.00	3,461.85	16%	23	12%		
	-500.00	4,528.25	21%	15	8%		
	-999.00	4,281.00	20%	6	3%		
	$1,000.00	2,600.00	12%	1	1%		
		$21,285.70	100%	199	100%		
						Avg Item Price	**$106.96**
			(Based on keystone pricing)			Avg Item Profit	**$53.48**

Proposal for Limited Partnership

Borrow $130,000.00 from private investors as limited partners as outlined:

> $130,000.00 = 45% of Marine Art of California
> $130,000.00 = 20 shares @ $6,500 each
> 1 share = 2.25% of Marine Art of California

Limited Partners will own 2.25% of the business for each $6,500 invested. The investment will be treated as a loan and paid back at 11% interest over 15 years at approximately $78 per month per shareholder.

> 1 share = $78 per month for 15 years
> 20 shares = $1,560 per month

The General Partner, Robert A. Garcia, will own 55% of the business. The Limited Partners will own 45% of the business for the duration of the partnership.

The duration of the partnership is 4 years. The General Partner will have the option of buying out the Limited Partners at the end of 4 years for $3,250 for each 2.25% interest. The buyout will not affect the outstanding loan, but the General Partner will provide collateral equal to the loan balance. The value of inventory will be used as that collateral.

Return On Investment (ROI) for each $6,500 share:

A.

Principal (15 years)		Interest (15 years)		Buy-out (4 years)		Total (15 years)
$6,500	+	$7,540	+	$3,250	=	$17,290

B. PROJECTED Annual Profits (Loss) for 1 share (2.25%):

2013	2014	2015	2016		4 Year Total
($759.53)	$833.00	$11,310.62	$19,097.78	=	$30,481.87

- ◆ Principal and Interest (15 years) $14,040.00
- ◆ Buy-Out (4 years) $ 3,250.00
- ◆ Projected Profits/loss (4 years) $30,481.87

Total Projected Return on Investment $47,771.87

or

$$\text{Net Profits} = \frac{\$41,271}{\$6,500} = \textbf{635\%}$$
$$\text{Assets}$$

Contract Highlights:

1. First Right of Refusal: Limited Partners agree to extend the First Right of Refusal to the General Partner, Robert A. Garcia, in the event the Limited Partner desires to sell, grant, or trade his/her share of the business.

2. Key Man Insurance: A life insurance policy valued at $250,000.00 shall be taken out on General Partner, Robert A. Garcia, which is approximately double the amount of the $130,000.00 loan needed. In the event of the death of Robert A Garcia, the payments of the full policy amount will be divided among the Limited Partners equal to the amount invested (e.g., 2.25% investment would equal a 1/20th layout of $12,500.00).

3. Limited Partner Purchase Program: General Partner, Robert A. Garcia, agrees to grant **at cost buying privileges** on all product line items for the purchase of 3 or more shares. For 1-2 shares, a 45% discount shall be extended. These shall be in effect for the life of the Limited Partnership contract (minimum 4 years before exercising buy-out option). For remainder of the loan contract, (2 years) a discount of 35% off retail price will be extended. At the completion of the loan repayment, a **Lifetime Discount of 20%** off retail will be extended to Limited Partners. These privileges are non-transferable.

Dayne Landscaping, Inc.
Business Plan

The Dayne Landscaping, Inc. business plan presented on the following pages is based on research for a landscaping and snow removal business in New Hampshire. It was developed by international marketing specialist, Robin Dayne, the former President of rtd Marketing International, Inc. in Nashua, New Hampshire. Robin wrote this plan specifically for you (the readers of, *Anatomy of a Business Plan* and the users of our AUTOMATE YOUR BUSINESS PLAN software). It will show you how you can follow our format and write a winning business plan for your own company.

Dayne Landscaping, Inc. Scenario

Dayne Landscaping, Inc. is a fictitious one-year old business that provides landscaping and snow removal services in Nashua, New Hampshire. The business had a successful first year (2013) and is planning to expand its customer base and purchase its present site (currently leased) for $375,000. In order to purchase the location, Dayne Landscaping, Inc. will use $100,000 of its own funds and seek a loan for the remaining $275,000 .

How is this business plan organized?

The Organizational and Marketing Plans for Dayne Landscaping, Inc. reflect the company's current status and its plans for its future expansion. It is important that the marketing plan provide convincing evidence supporting the feasibility of the loan. The lender needs to know that the company has the ability to increase its market share (and revenues) enough to insure that it can repay the loan and interest and still maintain its profitability.

Financial Documents need to reflect the company's history and project its future. This company has been in business for one year (2013) and is seeking a loan. Therefore, the financial documents need to begin with a summary of financial needs and dispersal of loan funds statement. The next section includes projections and historical financial statements for the 2013 business year (first year in business). They will show how well the company met its original projections and what its current financial status is. The third area to be covered in financial documents will address the company's projections for the future (2014-2016)—projected cash flow, three-year income projection, and projected balance sheet. The closing pages of the financial section contain a financial statement analysis of the company's history and future projections. Utilizing the financial information developed previously, ratios are computed and matched against industry standards.

Of Special Note

I found two things of particular interest is Robin's Dayne Landscaping, Inc. Plan. The Organizational Plan, very effectively addressed Personnel in terms of who they are, training, duties, profile, and salaries/benefits. In the Marketing Plan, Robin did not address the full gamut of marketing considerations. However, I liked her treatment of the target market and her example of the marketing promotion of target market #1.

As you proceed with the writing of your own plan, it may help you to look at Dayne Landscaping, Inc.'s business plan to see how Robin handled each of the corresponding sections. Some of the research material has been condensed and we have not included all of the necessary supporting documents. We have also chosen to omit any business or personal financial history that the writer or lender may wish to include in copies of the business plan.

> ***Warning!*** *This plan is to be examined for Ms. Dayne's handling of content only. It has been used as an example in our book and software because we feel it is a fine example of business plan organization. There is no judgment inferred as to appropriateness or financial potential for lenders or investors. Do not use it as a source of research for your own company.*

We are very pleased that Robin Dayne has provided us with this excellent example of a business plan for inclusion in *Anatomy of a Business Plan* and **AUTOMATE YOUR BUSINESS PLAN**. We hope that Dayne Landscaping, Inc.'s plan will be of benefit to you. We thank Robin for being so generous and for allowing us to share her interpretation of business planning with our readers.

Robin Dayne spent ten years as an international marketing consultant specializing in creating increased revenues through Customer Base Management™. Fourteen years ago, she switched gears and is now widely known as "The Trader's Coach", teaching all levels of traders in most markets. Her website is *RobinDayne.com*

Dayne Landscaping, Inc.

22 San Carlos Dr.
Nashua, New Hampshire 03060
603-335-8200

Robin T. Dayne, President
22 San Carlos Dr.
Nashua, NH 03060
(603)-335-8200

Joe Sanborn, Vice-President
56 Gingham St.
Nashua, NH 03990
(603) 446-9870

Fred Ryan, Treasurer
98 Canon St.
Nashua, NH 06223
(603) 883-0938

Trudy St. George, Secretary
31 Mill St.
Nashua, NH 08876
(603) 595-3982

Business Plan Prepared January 2014
by the Corporate Officers

TABLE OF CONTENTS

* Note. *We have included only part of the supporting documents in this sample business plan.*

Dayne Landscaping, Inc.

Executive Summary

Dayne Landscaping, Inc. is a profitable one-year-old landscaping and snow-removal company, established in January of 2013. The company is located at 22 San Carlos Ave., Nashua, New Hampshire. The currently leased location is available for sale at $375,000. Dayne Landscaping, Inc. has $100,000 to invest and is seeking a $275,000 loan to complete the purchase. By owning the facility, the company can increase its equity for an amount equivalent to the current rental expense.

Dayne Landscaping has established its niche in the landscaping and snow removal business during 2013. Projections for 2014 indicate that it is reasonable to expect expansion of its customer base to new markets and territories. Cash Flow projections support the assumption that the company will have sufficient funds to purchase equipment and hire additional employees to support implementation of the marketing programs.

Management: Dayne Landscaping is managed by Robin Dayne. She has five prior years of experience in the landscaping business, working for a local competitor. Previously she worked in a variety of service industries selling and marketing products and services. Robin has established a strong team of very dedicated people who love to work with nature. As manager her role is to identify new business, develop and implement marketing activities, and to negotiate and close new contracts.

Current Market: Today the business services 100 residential accounts, 15 small business accounts, and currently no large corporate accounts. The services include: landscaping and design, lawn care and maintenance, snow plowing and removal, and tree maintenance and removal. The success of the company has been a direct result of our ability to provide personal service at a competitive rate, thus creating a dedicated customer base. Currently, the average cost for lawn maintenance of a residential home is $25-30 per hour, small business accounts $50-100 per hour, and large corporate accounts are negotiated on a per contract basis. Due to the seasonal changes in New Hampshire, snow removal becomes an important part of the business to maintain the company's revenues during the slower winter months of December, January, February, and March.

Projected Market: The projected growth rate for the landscaping industry, based the previous years is 28%. We will be expanding our business with new equipment, marketing, and additional employees to meet and exceed that demand. We are expecting to grow our customer base by 50% based on our first year's track record, our unique offering, and planned marketing activities.

Loan Repayment: The $275,000 in loan funds will be required for April 2008 closing. Repayment of the 15-year loan, plus interest, can begin promptly in May. Early retirement of the loan is anticipated, possibly by the end of tax year 2019. In addition to the property and facility, itself, the loan can further be secured by the owner's home equity which is currently $167,000.

1

Dayne Landscaping, Inc.

I. The Organizational Plan

Summary Description of the Business

Dayne Landscaping, Inc., established in January 2013 as a corporation, handles landscaping, lawn maintenance and snow removal, of residential homes, and small businesses in New Hampshire. It began with 20 residential accounts and 2 small business accounts. As of January 2014, the company has grown to 100 residential accounts and 15 small business accounts, totaling $750,000 in revenue, a growth of 520%.

Mission
Dayne Landscaping's mission is to be perceived as the most valued provider of landscaping and snow removal services. The company has been very successful due to the high standard of service and care provided to the customer and because of its reputation for quick response times during snowstorms.

Business Model
The company also offers a unique service of oriental garden design landscaping, the only one in the tri-state area. Today that service is offered in New Hampshire only. Twenty-five of the 115 accounts have contracted for these unique gardens. Our plan is to open markets in Connecticut and Massachusetts over the next 3 years. It is important to note that these gardens are a not only a unique service; they are also our premium high ticket service and provide a larger profit margin, directly impacting the company's bottom line.

Strategy
The company's growth strategy is to buy out smaller landscaping companies as we expand the business in to Massachusetts and Connecticut and increase our Large Corporate accounts for snow removal. Currently, with local corporations "downsizing", "out-sourcing" these services to local businesses has become prevalent.

Facility
The company currently leases a 20,000 sq. ft. area, which includes a 4,000 sq. ft. building for the main office, a large attached garage for trucks, maintenance equipment and supplies, two large lots, one fenced in for parking equipment, plows, flatbeds, and storage of trees, shrubs, and plants.

Products and Services

Dayne Landscaping offers three categories of landscaping services to three varieties of customers. The customers consist of residential homes, small businesses, and large corporations. Each group has the option of purchasing the same types of services. Lawn care includes, mowing, weeding, planting, re-sod, pest control, and tree and shrub maintenance. Customized landscape design can be purchased on a contract basis, including specialties in oriental gardens, tree sculpture, and complete landscape design. The third service offered is snow plowing and removal.

All the plantings are high quality and are purchased from a local nursery that has been in the business for over 35 years. We also have an arrangement to use the nursery as a consultant when there is a need for it.

Customer Profiles

The following are descriptions of the three types of customer and the services that are typically purchased by each.

1. **Residential homes** in mid- to high-income areas, typically purchase lawn care that consists of mowing, weeding, pest control, and tree/scrub maintenance. There are two people assigned per job: two part-time college students, over-seen by a supervisor. This job can take an average of two hours to complete. Each home receives a contract for two visits per month unless there is a special need, which is an additional cost to the basic contract. These lawn contacts run from March thru November. Additionally, 50% of the residential customers also purchase winter snow removal for their driveways, and these customers are charged a minimal flat fee and a per call fee, with an up-front deposit to insure they get priority service.

2. **Small business account or office park** is the second type of customer. They typically consist of banks, or small office buildings and require shrub and landscaping care, weed and pest control and minimal lawn mowing. The average time required to service this type of account is three to four hours with one supervisor and two or three part-time employees. All the small business accounts have a contract for snow removal. A pre-determined amount for the contract is negotiated in Oct. for the four months November thru February, with a per call fee for the month of March, which can have unpredictable snow storms. These customers require quick response times and are charged for that level of service, as they need to accommodate their own customers during business hours.

3. **Large corporate account or condo complex** are the third type of customer. They require   the same services as the small corporate account, but require many more hours, employees, and equipment. Additionally, included in their lawn maintenance is routine watering. The accounts that are being targeted will require an average of one week of maintenance per month. This is the area to be expanded over the next three years. To support the watering needed every other day during the summer months, one part-time worker is hired and dedicated to watering for every two companies. Corporate account contracts are negotiated individually, and range from 60K to 350K per year depending on the amount of square footage and specific landscaping requirements. These customers also require immediate response times, especially in winter during the snow season.

Administrative Plan

Legal Structure

Dayne Landscaping, Inc. is a corporation filed under the same name. The legal and financial advisors recommended a corporation as the most efficient structure based on the plan to purchase pre-existing small landscaping companies in the tri-state area over the next two years. There have been 300 shares of stock applied for, and 100 issued to the sole shareholder (President) at the time of incorporation. This will leave the flexibility of having additional shares on hand should we need to use them in negotiations of larger landscaping company buy-outs.

Corporate Officers:	Robin Dayne, President
	Bob Sanborn, Vice President and Accountant
(see resumes in	Fred Ryan, Treasurer
Supporting Documents)	Trudy St. George, Secretary and Legal Counsel

The officers of the company determine the direction of the corporation through its board meetings. Additionally, there is an incentive plan for board members to acquire company stock based on set profit goals.

It should be noted that the President is the only officer working in the day-to-day business. All other officers interact at the monthly board meetings as well as on an "as needed" basis. This allows the company to have access to expertise and advice at large cost savings, which has a direct impact on the bottom line and growth of the company.

Management & Personnel

Management

At present, Robin Dayne is the President and sole shareholder in Dayne Landscaping, Inc. Robin has five prior years of experience in the landscaping business, working for a local competitor. Previously she worked in a variety of service industries selling and marketing products and services.

Dayne Landscaping, Inc. has been incorporated for almost one year, realizing a 520% growth rate between January to November. The growth rate is attributed to high standards set for customer service. Many customers shifted from the prior company because of their loyalty to Robin Dayne. She has set up an incentive plan for her employees that rewards them for outstanding customer service based on year-end survey results, or when contracts are renewed or new business is closed.

Under Ms. Dayne's management, a strong team of very dedicated people who love to work with nature has been formed. As manager her role is to identify new business, develop and implement marketing activities, and to negotiate and close new contracts.

The four supervisors manage the accounts and part-time workers. They also determine staffing and equipment needed to maintain the account. There are also two design specialists, one of which is specifically trained in oriental garden design and tree topiaries.

Personnel

There are three full-time office employees - one office manager and two administrative assistants. Four supervisors and two design specialists work in the field. The remainder are part-time workers, numbering from four to twenty-five or more, depending on the time of the year and work load.

1. Owner-President: 2013 Guaranteed Salary $65,000 with yearly increases justified by profitability.
2. Design Specialists: 2 in 2014; Salaries @ $25,000 + 5% commission on new business contracts.
3. Four Supervisors: Salaries @ $15,000 + 3% bonus per contract for excellent year-end customer surveys.
4. Office Manager: Salary @ $22,000 per year
5. Administrative Assistants (1 in 2013, 2 in 2014): Salaries @ $15,000 per year.
6. Part-time workers: 5-25 @ $9 per hour (more added as volume increases).

Training

All employees receive training from the President and Supervisor in the following areas:

Given by the President

   a. Company policies and procedures regarding the customers and company standards
   b. Landscaping orientation at the time they are hired
   c. Liability and safety procedures
   d. Equipment care and theft policies

Given by the Supervisors

   a. Overview of each account assignment
   b. Equipment assignment and training - operation of mowers, tools, and supplies
   c. Chemicals precautions

Personnel Duties

1. President/Owner

   a. Sets company policies and trains all new employees
   b. Solicits, interviews and hires new employees
   c. Assigns accounts to Supervisors
   d. Negotiates new and large contracts
   e. Approves the purchases of equipment and supplies
   f. Handles customer service issues that can not be satisfied by Supervisor
   g. Reviews and signs all checks
   h. Follows up on Supervisor sales leads

2. Four Supervisors - report to President

   a. Manages on average 25 residential accounts and 4 small business accounts
   b. Will be managing 1-2 Large Corporate accounts
   c. Responsible for training part-time help on account profiles and equipment
   d. Forecasts supplies needed for each account
   e. Forecasts and manages work schedules
   f. Conducts second round of interviews of part-timers and approves
   g. Handles account problems related to service and quality issues
   h. Solicits new business leads to President.
   i. Responsibility for inventory and equipment assigned to their team

3. Office Manager - reports to president

   a. Manages account scheduling
   b. Supports Supervisors - back-up supplies misc.
   c. Takes account calls and passes to supervisors
   d. Performs yearly customer survey
   e. Answers phone
   f. Dispatches and is in "beeper" contact with supervisors
   g. Assigns and maintains equipment for supervisors

4. Administrative Assistant - reports to president

   a. Responsible for Bookkeeping functions of:
      Daily sales reconciliation
      Accounts receivable and accounts payable
      Payroll
      General Ledger

   b. Computer Typing - 60 WPM, with software knowledge - WP/Excel/D-Base
   c. 10- key adding machine
   d. Access to safe
   e. Tracks orders placed for equipment and supplies

5. Part-time Employees - report to supervisor

   a. Assigned to work specific accounts
   b. Mows, weeds, does manual labor
   c. Identifies any problems
   d. Follows instructions from supervisor
   e. Manages inventory of supplies

Employee Profile

All employees must be:
   a. Hard working and neat in appearance
   b. Like working outdoors
   c. Good communicators
   d. Team workers
   e. Educated for full-time work with a minimum HS degree, or in College
   f. Able to follow directives and be a quick learner
   g. Dedicated to doing an outstanding job
   h. Responsible, regarding safety

Accounting and Legal

Accounting

All bookkeeping is kept on computer, on a regular basis, by the Administrative Assistant on the software "QuickBooks Pro" from Intuit. At the end of the year the files are printed and passed to the accountant Bob Sanborn, CPA who has been a personal friend for many years and has 35 years experience as a CPA. His fees are reasonable and there is a high level of trust in his input to the business as he is the Vice President for the corporation as well.

The customer base and prospect database is kept on the software "ACT" from Contact Software International that allows us to keep precise timelines of our scheduling and mange our accounts accurately. "Office Professional" from Microsoft allows us to perform WP, develop customized Spreadsheets, and develop proposals and presentations to larger accounts. All the above programs are "off-the-shelf" and are easy to get support for at very reasonable prices.

Legal

All contracts and other legal matters are handled by Trudy St. George, corporate officer and board member. Trudy is the senior partner of a 20-year old law firm specializing in business contracting.

Insurance

Carrier: Primercia   **Agent:** Sam Bickford
111 Shoe St, Manchester, New Hampshire

Type of Insurance:

Business/personal	600,000
Deductible	4,000
Liability	1,000,000
Equipment	40,000
Deductible	500
Liability	2,000,000
Vehicles	150,000
Deductible	1,000
Liability	1,000,000
Annual Premium	**$8,000**
Monthly Premium	670
Workers Comp. 1.43 per/1k gross Payroll	

Security

Problems situations to be considered and protective measures to be taken:

1. Internal theft - Employee Dishonesty

   a. Shoplifting - of supplies - (4) closed circuit cameras in garage recording 24 hours
   b. Cash Theft - petty cash limit of $600. Daily receipt drop-off to bank of all receivable
   c. Falsifying signatures - all checks signed by President at the end of the day
   d. Employee orientation - to reduce theft and stress security procedures
   e. Monthly Inventory - responsibility of the Supervisors

2. External Theft

   d. Walk-in theft Cameras at each doorway exits (2)
   e. Cameras in garage and on parking area, and fenced in plant lot
   f. Break-in theft/robbery - Alarms set nightly and connected directly to local Police station

Dayne Landscaping, Inc.

II. Marketing Plan

➡ **Author Note:** *The Marketing Plan for Dayne Landscaping, Inc. focuses on three of the basic elements presented in our marketing chapter for a smaller business— Market Analysis (Target Markets and Competition), Sales Strategy, and Advertising. This marketing plan has a special strength in the target marketing area in that the company planned its strategy for each of its market segments by evaluating the target in terms of who they are, what the company will do to approach the target, when the campaign will take place, and where the campaign will be positioned. Also, the Target Market Worksheet for Target #1 at the end of this section is a great tool for analyzing and planning your own target marketing.*

*It is my suggestion that the marketing plan for your company should address the components in a way that more closely follows the marketing plan outline in Chapter 5. However, I think this marketing plan may provide you with an organized means for developing your strategy for individual market **segments.***

Target Markets with Sales Strategies

Target #1

Large Corporate Facilities and Condominiums

Who: Corporations that are "outsourcing" the landscaping maintenance of their facilities to outside vendors, and condominium complexes. There are approximately 75 accounts that are potential customers within a 50 mile radius. Our goal is to secure five in 2014.

What: Tele-market for background information, and send a direct mail with telemarketing follow-up. Describe landscaping, lawn maintenance, pest control and all other landscaping services, such as tree removal and replacement, landscaping design and care, and snow plowing and removal from their parking lots and driveways. Provide a guarantee for the services and show competitive comparison pricing from local companies.

When: Begin January to determine the bidding process and RFP schedule to determine the timing of proposals. Call each account to determine the timing and arrange for an on-site inspection, to determine the amount of work needed and special needs to develop an estimate. If possible inquire what the previous years costs were and if the customer was satisfied with the work of their current landscaper.

Where: Position joint services with local garden stores for promotions and advertising.

Target #2

Small Businesses or Office Parks

Who: All small businesses and office parks that have outdoor grounds that want to save money, or are unhappy with their present landscaping company. In the 50 mile radius there are approximately 125 accounts that are potential customers. Our goal is to add 15 new contracts in this category in 2014.

What: Tele-market for background information and send a direct mail with telemarketing follow-up. Describe all the same landscaping and snow plowing services, referencing existing satisfied customers. Provide a guarantee for services rendered, show the cost savings using Dayne Landscaping, Inc., and develop a plan for continued snow and landscape maintenance. Offer the company's quality guarantee, and comparison chart of competitive pricing.

When: Begin January to determine when existing contracts expire and provide information on the company and services. Request an on-site evaluation to determine costs and uncover any problem areas needing work.

Where: Position joint services with local garden stores for promotions and advertising. Advertise in the local papers, Yellow Pages and Business to Business Directory.

Target #3

Residential Homes

Who: Target all residential homes in the 50 mile radius that are in mid to high income areas and over 3+ acres. Contact all existing customers with satisfaction survey, and solicit at the same time for:

> a. Additional business - renew contracts for next year
> b. New customers - referrals

What: Develop and send company brochure that targets the residential homes supplying them with information on all services offered by Dayne Landscaping, Inc. with price comparisons.

When: Develop brochure in January and mail in February prior to Spring and Summer contracts. Follow-up with existing customers and potential customers in September for the snow plowing contracts.

Where: Position joint services with local garden stores for promotions and advertising

Competition

Dayne Landscaping currently has two competitors in the local area: The Garden Shop and Landscaping Plus. While they have been in the New Hampshire area for several years, they are family-owned businesses that have a limited number of clientele and the same number of accounts year after year. They also have no type of Landscaping specialty. Only the Garden Shop offers snow removal. Landscaping Plus has only three snow plows that are active during the winter months.

Methods of Distribution

Dayne Landscaping sells directly to the customer, is primarily a service business, with the exception of selling the landscaping plants and shrubs, which come from a local nursery wholesaler.

Advertising Strategy

Paid Advertising

We currently participate in several forms of advertising:

1. **Newspaper ads**: All ad copy is identical, and include information required by the newspaper:

     a. **Ad information**:
     1. Ad size: The ad is two column x 3 ins.
     2. Timing: Monthly
     3. Section: Garden section

     b. **Ad location, Contact and fees:**

Nashua Telegraph P.O. Box 1008 Nashua, NH 03061-1008	Contact: Mark Potts Circulation: 50,000 Fee: $126.00
Manchester Union Leader 100 William Loeb Drive Manchester, NH 03109	Contact: Ken Coose Circulation: 125,000 Fee: $171.99
Lowell Sun 15 Kearney Square Lowell, MA 01852-1996	Contact: Carol McCabe Circulation; 75,000 Fee: $153.00
Hartford Daily news 100 Main St. Hartford, CT 10002	Contact: Sue Betz Circulation: 150,000 Fee: 190.00

2. Phone books - Yellow pages and directories

a. NYNEX Phone Book - Yellow Pages

Ad Information:

Coverage:	So. NH area
Yearly Fee:	$650.00
Ad Size:	1/4 page
Renewal date:	February 1st
Contact:	Sam Moore

b. Business to Business Directory (NH only)

Ad Information

Coverage:	All NH
Yearly Fee:	$250.00
Ad Size:	1/4 page
Renewal Date:	January 1st
Contact:	Karl Hess

3. Local Cable Channels

a. Channel 13 - Local Nashua station reaching all of So. NH

Ad Information:

Length of ad "spot":	**60 seconds**
Development costs:	$250.00 (one time fee)
Length of campaign:	3 mos.
Runs per month:	Three times per day, everyday
Cost for 3 mos.:	$300.
Total campaign cost:	**$550.**

b. Weather Channel "tag line" - reaching 400,000 homes

Ad Information:

Length of ad "spot":	15 seconds
Development costs:	$100. (one time fee)
Length of campaign:	3 mos.
Runs per month:	20 times per day, everyday
Cost for 3 mos.:	$900.
Total campaign cost:	**$1000.**

Direct Mail

Note: There was no direct mail done in the first year of business. With the development of the Marketing plan, two direct mail pieces will need to be developed to target our three potential customer bases for 2014. (see detailed plan of this activity)

Direct mail #1

Designed for: Target market #1- large corporations and condominiums
Target market #2 - small business and office parks.

Creative Strategy: Design needs to be glossy, appropriate for corporate, professional environment.

Highlight: Customer service - testimonials
Quick response time
All services
Guarantee
Free evaluation

Direct mail #2

Designed for: Target market #3 - residential homes

Creative Strategy: Design should be a tri-fold brochure "self-mailer" (no envelope required) Direct highlights for the homeowner

Highlight: Customer service - testimonials
Quick response time
All services
Guarantee
Free evaluation

Community Involvement

Member of the Chamber of Commerce in Nashua. Board Member of the local Garden Club, involved with teaching kids about plants and nature, as well as involved with the "Beautification of Nashua" program.

> ➡ **Note:** *In this example plan, we have included the promotion for target market #1 only. All target markets would have their own separate plan using the same format.*

Worksheet for
Individual Marketing Promotion

Target Market #1: Large Corporate or Condo Landscaping   **Date:** 01/08

Program Name: Corporate Promo   **Media:** Direct Mail & Telemarketing

Program Objectives:

* Generate a minimum of 500k in additional revenue in 2014

* Increase corporate account base by 5 new accounts

* Establish Dayne Landscaping as a landscaping provider to large corporations and condominiums

Audience:

Direct Mail

Who - the 70 identified accounts consisting of condominiums and large corporations.

What - Send direct mail (company brochure) to Corporate and Condo contacts listing services and benefits of Dayne Landscaping. Position money back guarantee as an added promotion.

Where - in the New Hampshire, and Massachusetts areas (50 mile radius).

When - Drop mail in mid- January.

Telemarketing (Prior to mailing):

Who - Call all accounts to identify landscaping contact in the large corporation or in property management company of the condominium.

What - Find out the contract renewal dates and bid submission dates for each prospect.

When - Make phone calls first two weeks of January.

Where – NA

Telemarketing (Post Direct Mail):

Who - Call all contacts and confirm bid dates

What - ask if they received the direct mail and offer a free landscaping consultation.

When - Calling begins 5-8 working days after the direct mail is received.

Where – NA

List source:
The list was taken from the library in the "New Hampshire Corporate Directory", and "Massachusetts Corporate Directory" as well as the Realty listing of Condominiums.

Creative Strategy - for Direct Mail:

* Position Dayne Landscaping, Inc. as a leader in quality service
* Position Guarantee
* Leverage existing customer base with success stories
* Position against the competition
* Position "free" consulting offer
* The telemarketing call back in a week

Creative Strategy - for Telemarketing:

* Develop script with the same messages as the direct mail will have
* If possible position - Company and Promotional offer

Components of mailing: Tri-fold brochure - components

* Self-mailer, with reply card
* Address hand written on the backside

Timing:

Pre- Mailing Telemarketing

% Called	Location	Call dates
50%	New Hampshire	1/2 - 1/9
50%	Massachusetts	1/9 - 1/18

Direct Mail

% Mailed	Location	Mail date
50%	New Hampshire	Jan. 1/12
50%	Massachusetts	Jan. 1/19

Post- Mailing Telemarketing

% Called	Location	Call dates
50%	New Hampshire	1/22
50%	Massachusetts	1/29

Call to action: Reply card to be sent to office or and #800 number can be called

Lead criteria:

"Hot" leads are classified as anyone getting a proposal, evaluation, or call back from the mailing or telemarketing. They have the potential of closing in 2014.

"Warm" leads are any accounts that are interested and cannot do anything until 2015 due to their current contracts.

"Cold" leads are those accounts that are not interested at all, and have no revenue potential in the future.

Training:

Employees in the field - will be given an overview of the entire promotion to prepare them for customers asking questions, while on the job.

Office staff - will receive training and instructions on how to answer to phone and track the responses from the #800 and mailer. They will also be assisting on the pre and post telemarketing activities.

Expenses: Will not exceed $3000. for the entire promotion.

Measurement:

Revenue Goal	500k
Expenses	3K
Total # (list)	70
# or responses	TBD
# of leads	TBD
Cost/ per Response	TBD
Cost/ per Lead	TBD
Revenue/Expense ratio	TBD

*TBD = To be determined at the end of the program.

Assumptions:

* Average value per contract = 100K

* Response rate = 2.0 % on the Direct mail and 15-20% on the telemarketing or 1.5 responses on the direct mail, and 10-14 on the telemarketing.

* "Hot" lead rate = 0.5% on the direct mail and 5%- 7% on the telemarketing or 3.5 leads on the direct mail and 3.5-5 leads on the telemarketing

Lead tracking Process:

* All Direct mail responses will be tracked

* All Phone calls will be logged when responding on the # 800.

* All regular calls will be screened "are you calling regarding our direct mail promotion?"

Program review: 30 days after last tell-marketing follow-up call.

Dayne Landscaping, Inc.

Part III: Financial Documents

Sources and Uses of Loan Funds

2013 Historical Financial Statements

2014-16 Financial Projections

Financial Statement Analysis

Business Plan Financial Assumptions

Summary of Financial Needs

I. Dayne Landscaping, Inc. is seeking a loan to increase its equity capital through real estate investment:

    A. By purchasing the buildings currently being leased by the company.

    B. By purchasing the parcel of land on which the buildings now stand.

II. Dayne Landscaping, Inc. has $100,000 in cash to invest. An additional amount of $275,000 in loan funds is needed to complete the purchase.

Loan Fund Dispersal Statement

1. Dispersal of Loan Funds

Dayne Landscaping, Inc. will utilize the anticipated loan in the amount of $275,000 to purchase the facility (land and buildings) that it currently leases. The full purchase price is $375,000. The present owner of the premises is John S. Strykker. The parcel and accompanying buildings, located at 22 San Carlos Drive in Nashua, New Hampshire, are currently owned by John S. Strykker.

2. Back-Up Statement

    a. The land is currently appraised at $200,000. Attached buildings appraise at $175,000. The owner, Mr. John S. Strykker is agreeable to close of escrow on or about April 15, 2014

    b. Dayne Landscaping, Inc. has appropriated $100,000 in retained earnings to be used as a capital investment in the facility. The additional $275,000 in loan funds will make up the full purchase amount of $375,000.

    c. The buildings sit on a 20,000 square foot parcel of land, centrally located in Nashua, New Hampshire. The land is currently appraised at $200,000 and the buildings at $175,000. There are two large lots. One is fenced in for parking equipment and also serves as a storage area for trees, shrubs and plants. There is a 4,000 square foot building that serves as the main office and a large attached garage to house trucks, maintenance equipment and supplies.

    d. The $275,000 in loan funds are needed by April 1 in order to proceed with escrow. Loan repayment can begin promptly on May 1st for a 15-year period. The company has a strong cash flow and a rapidly-growing market. Early payoff is anticipated.

    e. Dayne Landscaping is currently paying $2850 in monthly rental expense. Payments on the anticipated $275,000, 15-year loan @ 9% would amount to $2,789. Purchase of the land and buildings will enable Dayne Landscaping, with no additional expense, to repay the loan + interest and to divert the current rental expense into equity growth.

2013 Profit & Loss (Income) Statement
Dayne Landscaping, Inc.

For the Year: 2013	6-MONTH TOTALS	% of Total Revenues	12-MONTH TOTALS	% of Total Revenues
INCOME	AMOUNT	PERCENT	AMOUNT	PERCENT
1. Sales/Revenues	488,610	100.00%	777,864	100.00%
Landscaping - Residential	138,000	28.24%	216,000	27.77%
Landscaping - Small Business	104,000	21.28%	160,700	20.66%
Landscaping - Customized	130,250	26.66%	199,374	25.63%
Snow Removal - Residential	14,300	2.93%	18,250	2.35%
Snow Removal - Small Business	96,800	19.81%	167,100	21.48%
Miscellaneous Accessories	5,260	1.08%	8,500	1.09%
5% Snow Removal Contracts	0	0.00%	7,940	1.02%
2. Cost of Goods to be Sold	91,030	18.63%	101,030	12.99%
a. Beginning Inventory	0	0.00%	0	0.00%
b. Purchases	91,030	18.63%	106,030	5.79%
(1) Fertilizer	13,000	2.66%	19,000	2.44%
(2) Pesticide	8,000	1.64%	11,000	1.41%
(3) Plants/Shrubs	22,000	4.50%	23,000	2.96%
(4) Salt/Sand	3,030	0.62%	8,030	1.03%
(5) Seed	45,000	9.21%	45,000	5.79%
c. C.O.G. Available for Sale	91,030	18.63%	106,030	5.79%
d. Less Ending Inventory	0	0.00%	5,000	0.64%
3. GROSS PROFIT	397,580	81.37%	676,834	87.01%
EXPENSES				
1. Variable (Selling) Expenses				
a. Design Specialist Salary	10,000	2.05%	20,000	2.57%
b. Machinery, Hand Tools, Equip.	9,000	1.84%	11,000	1.41%
c. Marketing	3,205	0.66%	5,400	0.69%
d. Part-time Worker Salaries	72,250	14.79%	182,000	23.40%
e. Sales Bonuses	2,000	0.41%	2,000	0.26%
f. Sales Commission	6,300	1.29%	10,800	1.39%
g. Supervisor Salaries	30,000	6.14%	60,000	7.71%
h. Travel Expense	6,700	1.37%	10,400	1.34%
i. Miscellaneous Selling Expense	900	0.18%	1,200	0.15%
j. Depreciation (Variable Assets)	7,598	1.56%	15,200	1.95%
Total Variable Expenses	147,953	28.23%	318,000	40.88%
1. Fixed (Administrative) Expenses				
a. Admin. Fees-Legal/Acct.	2,048	0.42%	3,050	0.39%
b. Insurance (Liab,Cas,Fire,Theft)	5,802	1.19%	11,600	1.49%
c. Licenses and Permits	4,200	0.86%	4,200	0.54%
d. Machinery, Tools, Equipment	6,700	1.37%	7,700	0.99%
e. Office Salaries	21,000	4.30%	42,000	5.40%
f. Owner's Guaranteed Payment	32,502	6.65%	65,000	8.36%
g. Rent Expense + Security Dep.	22,800	4.67%	39,900	5.13%
h. Utilities	2,160	0.44%	4,320	0.56%
i. Miscellaneous Fixed Expense	400	0.08%	500	0.06%
j. Depreciation (Fixed Assets)	0	0.00%	0	0.00%
Total Fixed Expenses	97,612	19.98%	178,270	22.92%
Total Operating Expense	245,565	48.21%	496,270	63.80%
Net Income From Operations	152,015	33.16%	180,564	23.21%
Other Income (Interest)	625	0.13%	1,250	0.16%
Other Expense (Interest)	2,918	0.60%	5,535	0.71%
Net Profit (Loss) Before Taxes	149,722	32.69%	176,279	22.66%
Provision for Income Taxes				
a. Federal	41,642	8.52%	51,999	6.68%
b. State	11,230	2.30%	13,221	1.70%
NET PROFIT (LOSS) AFTER TAXES	96,850	21.87%	111,059	14.28%

Balance Sheet

Business Name:

Dayne Landscaping, Inc.   Date: December 31, 2013

ASSETS		% of Assets
Current Assets		
Cash	$ 31,178	15.83%
Savings (Land & Building)	$ 100,000	50.77%
Petty Cash	$ 0	0.00%
Accounts Receivable	$ 0	0.00%
Inventory	$ 5,000	2.54%
Long Term Investments	$ 0	0.00%
Fixed Assets		
Land (valued at cost)	$ 0	0.00%
Buildings	$ 0	0.00%
1. Cost 0		
2. Less Acc. Depr. 0		
Improvements	$ 0	0.00%
1. Cost 0		
2. Less Acc. Depr. 0		
Equipment	$ 12,800	6.50%
1. Cost 16,000		
2. Less Acc. Depr. 3,200		
Furniture	$ 0	0.00%
1. Cost 0		
2. Less Acc. Depr. 0		
Autos/Vehicles	$ 48,000	24.37%
1. Cost 60,000		
2. Less Acc. Depr. 12,000		
Other Assets		
1.	$ 0	0.00%
2.	$ 0	0.00%
TOTAL ASSETS	$ 196,978	100.00%

LIABILITIES		% of Liabilities
Current Liabilities		
Accounts Payable	$ 0	0.00%
Notes Payable	$ 16,332	26.81%
Interest Payable	$ 0	0.00%
Pre-Paid Deposits	$ 0	0.00%
Taxes Payable		
Accrued Federal Income Tax	$ 0	0.00%
Accrued State Income Tax	$ 0	0.00%
Accrued Payroll Tax	$ 0	0.00%
Accrued Sales Tax	$ 0	0.00%
Payroll Accrual	$ 0	0.00%
Long Term Liabilities		
Notes Payable to Investors	$ 0	0.00%
Notes Payable Others	$ 44,587	73.19%
TOTAL LIABILITIES	$ 60,919	100.00%

NET WORTH (EQUITY)		% of Net Worth
Corporation		
Capital Stock	$ 20,000	14.70%
Surplus Paid In	$ 5,000	3.67%
Retained Earnings, Appropriated	$ 100,000	73.50%
Retained Earnings Unappropriated	$ 11,059	8.13%
TOTAL NET WORTH	$ 136,059	100.00%

Assets - Liabilities = Net Worth
and
Liabilities + Equity = Total Assets

1. See Financial Statement Analysis for ratios and notations

2014 Pro Forma Cash Flow Statement

Page 1 (January thru June)

Dayne Landscaping, Inc.

For the Year 2014	Jan	Feb	Mar	Apr	May	Jun
BEGINNING CASH BALANCE	131,178	137,633	140,273	139,746	45,856	115,074
CASH RECEIPTS						
A. Sales/Revenues	**123,850**	**89,100**	**184,400**	**169,200**	**200,600**	**192,900**
1. Landscaping - Residential	0	0	41,000	21,000	23,000	24,000
2. Landscaping - Small Business	0	0	56,500	50,500	40,000	39,500
3. Landscaping - Large Corporations	0	0	73,500	57,200	55,100	51,000
4. Customized Landscaping	0	0	13,400	40,500	82,500	78,400
5. Snow Removal - Residential	11,050	5,700	0	0	0	0
6. Snow Removal - Small Business	66,900	53,000	0	0	0	0
7. Snow Removal - Large Corporations	45,900	30,400	0	0	0	0
8. 5% Snow Removal Contracts	0	0	0	0	0	0
B. Interest Income	108	110	109	110	109	110
C. Sale of Long-Term Assets	0	0	0	0	0	0
TOTAL CASH AVAILABLE	**255,136**	**226,843**	**324,782**	**309,056**	**246,565**	**308,084**
CASH PAYMENTS						
A. Cost of goods to be sold						
1. Fertilizer	0	0	10,700	12,800	9,800	3,100
2. Pesticide	0	0	6,250	2,400	5,500	3,500
3. Plants/Shrub	0	0	16,100	13,000	3,500	3,200
4. Salt/Sand	5,375	0	0	0	0	0
5. Seed	0	0	21,000	41,500	24,500	5,000
Total Cost of Goods	**5,375**	**0**	**54,050**	**69,700**	**43,300**	**14,800**
B. Variable Expenses						
1. Design Specialists (2 - w/taxes & benefits)	5,834	5,834	5,834	5,834	5,834	5,834
2. Machinery, Tools, Equipment	350	6,000	0	500	500	1,000
3. Marketing	3,500	6,500	6,500	3,500	3,500	5,000
4. Part-time Worker Salaries (w/ taxes)	23,500	30,000	37,600	40,000	39,000	38,033
5. Sales Bonuses	0	2,000	2,500	500		
6. Sales Commissions	0	0	1,100	5,750	2,250	1,500
7. Supervisor Salaries (w/taxes & benefits)	7,500	7,500	15,000	15,000	15,000	15,000
8. Travel Expense	550	850	1,200	1,300	1,200	860
9. Miscellaneous Selling Expense	500	500	500	500	500	500
Total Variable Expenses	**41,734**	**59,184**	**70,234**	**72,884**	**67,784**	**67,727**
C. Fixed Expenses						
1. Administration Fees - Legal/Accounting	509	508	508	2,250	508	508
2. Insurance (Liab, Casualty, Fire/Theft, W Comp)	704	714	735	739	737	736
3. Licenses and Permits	100	200	750	2,350	1,300	1,025
4. Office Equipment	1,750	8,650	1,100	900	825	525
5. Office Salaries (w/taxes & benefits)	5,250	5,250	5,250	5,250	5,250	5,250
6. Owner's Guaranteed Payment	6,833	6,833	6,833	6,833	6,833	6,833
7. Rent Expense	2,850	2,850	2,850	0	0	0
8. Utilities	480	463	360	376	247	378
9. Miscellaneous Administrative Expense	200	200	200	200	200	200
Total Fixed Expenses	**18,676**	**25,668**	**18,586**	**18,898**	**15,900**	**15,455**
D. Interest Expense (Vehicles, Equipment)	406	397	389	380	371	362
E. Interest Expense (Land & Buildings)	0	0	0	0	2,062	2,057
F. Federal Income Tax	0	0	33,249	0	0	33,249
G. State Tax	0	0	7,199	0	0	7,199
H. Capital Asset Purch, Cash (Land & Buildings)*	0	0	0	375,000	0	0
I. Capital Asset Purch, Cash (Vehicles,Equipment)**	50,000	0	0	0	0	48,000
J. Loan Repayment (Land & Buildings)	0	0	0	0	727	732
K. Loan Repayment (Vehicles, Equipment)	1,312	1,321	1,329	1,338	1,347	1,356
TOTAL CASH PAID OUT	**117,503**	**86,570**	**185,036**	**538,200**	**131,491**	**190,937**
CASH BALANCE/DEFICIENCY	137,633	140,273	139,746	(229,144)	115,074	117,147
LOAN TO BE RECEIVED (Land & Buildings)	0	0	0	275,000	0	0
EQUITY DEPOSITS	0	0	0	0	0	0
ENDING CASH BALANCE	**137,633**	**140,273**	**139,746**	**45,856**	**115,074**	**117,147**

20

2014 Pro Forma Cash Flow Statement
Page 2 (July thru December + 6 & 12-month Totals)

Dayne Landscaping, Inc.

6-MONTH TOTALS	Jul	Aug	Sep	Oct	Nov	Dec	12-MONTH TOTALS
131,178	117,147	122,610	104,184	100,611	119,509	110,104	131,178
960,050	149,400	138,000	122,000	83,900	67,090	87,760	1,608,200
109,000	24,000	24,000	24,000	24,000	0	0	205,000
186,500	33,400	32,000	30,000	28,000	0	0	309,900
236,800	28,000	35,000	30,500	12,900	0	0	343,200
214,800	64,000	47,000	37,500	9,000			372,300
16,750	0	0	0	0	5,000	6,750	28,500
119,900	0	0	0	0	30,000	42,410	192,310
76,300	0	0	0	0	25,090	38,600	139,990
0	0	0	0	10,000	7,000	0	17,000
656	109	109	109	110	110	110	1,313
0	0	0	0	0	0	0	0
1,091,884	266,656	260,719	226,293	184,621	186,709	197,974	1,740,691
36,400	7,600	4,000	0	0	0	0	48,000
17,650	4,500	1,850	0	0	0	0	24,000
35,800	1,700	2,700	2,300	1,500	0	0	44,000
5,375	0	0	0	0	4,700	5,000	15,075
92,000	2,000	2,000	0	0	0	0	96,000
187,225	15,800	10,550	2,300	1,500	4,700	5,000	227,075
35,004	5,834	5,834	5,834	5,834	5,834	5,834	70,008
8,350	10,000	650	0	0	350	475	19,825
28,500	3,500	3,500	3,500	6,500	6,500	3,500	55,500
208,133	42,000	39,400	38,000	14,000	19,000	21,500	382,033
5,000					500	500	6,000
10,600	500	500	0	2,500	5,000	2,500	21,600
75,000	15,000	15,000	15,000	15,000	15,000	15,000	165,000
5,960	940	1,130	970	400	400	600	10,400
3,000	500	500	500	500	500	500	6,000
379,547	78,274	66,514	63,804	44,734	53,084	50,409	736,366
4,791	508	508	509	508	508	509	7,841
4,365	742	741	739	705	712	716	8,720
5,725	1,175	500	405	295	200	100	8,400
13,750	250	450	350	200	200	200	15,400
31,500	5,250	5,250	5,250	5,250	5,250	5,250	63,000
40,998	6,833	6,833	6,834	6,834	6,834	6,834	82,000
8,550	0	0	0	0	0	0	8,550
2,304	457	432	286	329	360	387	4,555
1,200	250	250	250	250	250	250	2,700
113,183	15,465	14,964	14,623	14,371	14,314	14,246	201,166
2,305	353	344	335	325	316	306	4,284
4,119	2,051	2,046	2,040	2,035	2,029	2,023	16,343
66,498	0	0	33,249	0	0	33,249	132,996
14,398	0	0	7,199	0	0	7,200	28,797
375,000	0	0	0	0	0	0	375,000
98,000	30,000	60,000	0	0	0	0	188,000
1,459	738	743	749	754	760	766	5,969
8,003	1,365	1,374	1,383	1,393	1,402	1,412	16,332
1,249,737	144,046	156,535	125,682	65,112	76,605	114,611	1,932,328
(157,853)	122,610	104,184	100,611	119,509	110,104	83,363	(191,637)
275,000	0	0	0	0	0	0	275,000
0	0	0	0	0	0	0	0
117,147	122,610	104,184	100,611	119,509	110,104	83,363	83,363

Three Year Income Projection
Dayne Landscaping, Inc.

Updated: December 31, 2013	YEAR 1 2014	YEAR 2 2015	YEAR 3 2016	TOTAL 3 YEARS
INCOME				
1. SALES/REVENUES	**1,608,200**	**2,010,250**	**2,311,788**	**5,930,238**
a. Landscaping - Residential	205,000	256,250	294,688	755,938
b. Landscaping - Small Business	309,900	387,375	445,481	1,142,756
c. Landscaping - Large Corporations	343,200	429,000	493,350	1,265,550
d. Customized Landscaping	372,300	465,375	535,181	1,372,856
e. Snow Removal - Residential	28,500	35,625	40,969	105,094
f. Snow Removal - Small Business	192,310	240,388	276,446	709,143
g. Snow Removal - Large Corporations	139,990	174,988	201,236	516,213
h. 5% Snow Removal Contracts	17,000	21,250	24,438	62,688
2. Cost of Goods Sold (c-d)	**222,075**	**273,844**	**323,420**	**819,339**
Cost of Goods (as a Percentage of Sales)	**13.81%**	**13.62%**	**13.99%**	**13.82%**
a. Beginning Inventory	5,000	10,000	20,000	5,000
b. Purchases	**227,075**	**283,844**	**326,420**	**837,339**
(1) Fertilizer	48,000	60,000	69,000	177,000
(2) Pesticide	24,000	30,000	34,500	88,500
(3) Plants/Shrubs	44,000	55,000	63,250	162,250
(4) Salt/Sand	15,075	18,844	21,670	55,589
(5) Seed	96,000	120,000	138,000	354,000
c. C.O.G. Avail. Sale (a+b)	232,075	293,844	346,420	842,339
d. Less Ending Iventory (12/31)	10,000	20,000	23,000	23,000
3. GROSS PROFIT ON SALES (1-2)	**1,386,125**	**1,736,406**	**1,988,367**	**5,110,898**
Gross Profit (as a Percentage of Sales)	**86.19%**	**86.38%**	**86.01%**	**86.18%**
EXPENSES				
1. VARIABLE (Selling) (a thru j)	**772,933**	**916,341**	**1,027,822**	**2,717,097**
Selling Expenses (as a Percentage of Sales)	**48.06%**	**45.58%**	**44.46%**	**45.82%**
a. Design Specialist Salaries/PayrollTaxes	70,008	77,000	84,700	231,708
b. Machinery, Tools, Equipment	19,825	15,000	17,000	51,825
c. Marketing	55,500	55,000	55,000	165,500
d. Part-time Worker Salaries/PayrollTaxes	382,033	477,541	549,172	1,408,747
e. Sales Bonuses	6,000	13,500	18,500	38,000
f. Sales Commission	21,600	24,000	27,000	72,600
g. Supervisor Salaries/Payroll Taxes	165,000	181,500	199,650	546,150
h. Travel expense	10,400	12,000	14,000	36,400
i. Miscellaneous Selling Expense	6,000	8,000	10,000	24,000
j. Depreciation (Product/Service Assets)	36,567	52,800	52,800	142,167
2. FIXED (Administrative) (a thru j)	**209,916**	**246,967**	**290,467**	**747,350**
Admin. Expenses (as a Percentage of Sales)	**13.05%**	**12.29%**	**12.56%**	**12.60%**
a. Administration Fees- Legal/Acct.	7,841	7,800	7,800	23,441
b. Insurance - Liability, Casualty, Fire/Theft,	8,720	10,500	12,000	31,220
c. Licenses and Permits	8,400	10,300	12,200	30,900
d. Office Equipment	15,400	30,800	45,200	91,400
e. Office Salaries/Payroll Taxes	63,000	77,000	91,000	231,000
f. Owner's Guaranteed Payment	82,000	90,000	100,000	272,000
g. Rent Expense	8,550	0	0	8,550
h. Utilities	4,555	5,500	6,500	16,555
i. Miscellaneous Administrative Expense	2,700	3,400	4,100	10,200
j. Depreciation (Facility, Admin. Assets)	8,750	11,667	11,667	32,084
TOTAL OPERATING EXPENSES (1+2)	**982,849**	**1,163,308**	**1,318,289**	**3,464,447**
NET INCOME OPERATIONS (G.Profit - Expenses)	**403,276**	**573,098**	**670.078**	**1,646,452**
Net Income Operations (as a Percentage of Sales)	**25.08%**	**28.51%**	**28.99%**	**27.76%**
OTHER INCOME (Interest Income)	1,313	1,378	1,447	4,138
OTHER EXPENSE (Interest Expense)	20,627	28,105	25,844	74,576
NET PROFIT (LOSS) BEFORE TAXES	**383,962**	**546,371**	**645,681**	**1,576,014**
TAXES 1. Federal, S-Employment	132,996	196,335	235,066	564,397
2. State	28,797	40,978	48,426	118,201
3. Local	0	0	0	0
NET PROFIT (LOSS) AFTER TAXES	**222,169**	**309,058**	**362.189**	**893,416**
Net Profit (Loss) (as a Percentage of Sales)	**13.81%**	**15.37%**	**15.67%**	**15.07%**

Projected Balance Sheet

Business Name:

Dayne Landscaping, Inc.   **Projected for: December 31, 2014**

ASSETS			% of Assets	LIABILITIES			% of Liabilities
Current Assets				**Current Liabilities**			
Cash	$	83,363	12.41%	Accounts Payable	$	0	0.00%
Petty Cash	$	0	0.00%	Notes Payable	$	27,337	8.72%
Accounts Receivable	$	0	0.00%	Interest Payable	$	0	0.00%
Inventory	$	10,000	1.49%	Pre-Paid Deposits	$	0	0.00%
Short Term Investments	$	0	0.00%				
				Taxes Payable			
				Accrued Federal Income Tax	$	0	0.00%
Long Term Investments	$	0	0.00%	Accrued State Income Tax	$	0	0.00%
				Accrued Payroll Tax	$	0	0.00%
				Accrued Sales Tax	$	0	0.00%
Fixed Assets							
Land (valued at cost)	$	200,000	29.77%	Payroll Accrual	$	0	0.00%
Buildings	$	163,050	24.27%	**Long Term Liabilities**			
1. Cost 175,000				Notes Payable to Investors	$	0	0.00%
2. Less Acc. Depr. 11,950				Notes Payable Others	$	286,281	91.28%
Improvements	$	0	0.00%				
1. Cost 0				**TOTAL LIABILITIES**	$	313,618	100.00%
2. Less Acc. Depr. 0							
Equipment	$	92,833	13.82%				% of Net Worth
1. Cost 104,000				**NET WORTH (EQUITY)**			
2. Less Acc. Depr. 11,167							
Furniture	$	0	0.00%	**Corporation**			
1. Cost 0							
2. Less Acc. Depr. 0				Capital Stock	$	20,000	5.58%
Autos/Vehicles	$	122,600	18.25%	Surplus Paid In	$	5,000	1.40%
1. Cost 160,000							
2. Less Acc. Depr. 37,400				Retained Earnings, Appropriated	$	333,228	93.02%
Other Assets				Retained Earnings	$	0	0.00%
1.	$	0	0.00%	Unappropriated			
2.	$	0	0.00%				
				TOTAL NET WORTH	$	358,228	100.00%
TOTAL ASSETS	$	671,846	100.00%	*Assets - Liabilities = Net Worth*			
				and			
				Liabilities + Equity = Total Assets			

1. See Financial Statement Analysis for ratios and notations

FINANCIAL STATEMENT ANALYSIS SUMMARY

This page is a summary of Dayne Landscaping, Inc.'s 2013 and 2014 financial statemant analysis as calculated on the Ratio Table on the next page and measured against current industry standards.

*Author notation:
Writer must research industry standards.

	2013 HISTORICAL	2014 PROJECTED	INDUSTRY STANDARD
1. Net Working Capital	$119,846	$66,026	$80,000 + or -
2. Current Ratio	8.34	3.42	2.0 +
3. Quick Ratio	8.03	3.05	1.0 + or -
4. Gross Profit Margin	87.01%	86.19%	85.0%
5. Operating Profit Margin	23.21%	25.08%	25.0%
6. Net Profit Margin	14.28%	13.81%	14%
7. Debt to Assets	30.93%	46.68%	33.0% -
8. Debt to Equity	44.77%	87.55%	100% -
9. ROI (Return on Investment	56.38%	33.07%	24% +
10. Vertical Income Statement Analysis *			
Sales/Revenues	100.00%	100.0%	
Cost of Goods	12.99%	13.81%	15.0% + or -
Gross Profit	87.01%	86.19%	85.0%
Operating Expense	63.80%	61.11%	62.0% + or -
Net Income Operations	23.21%	25.08%	23.0% + or -
Interest Income	0.16%	0.08%	N/A Variable
Interest Expense	0.71%	1.28%	4.0% Variable
Net Profit (Pre-Tax)	22.66%	23.88%	19.0% + or -
* All items stated as % of Total Revenues			
11. Vertical Balance Sheet Analysis			
Current Assets	69.14%	13.90%	18.0% +
Inventory	2.54%	1.49%	2.0%
Total Assets	100.0%	100.00%	
Current Liabilities	8.29%	4.07%	15.0% -
Total Liabilities	30.93%	46.68%	50.0% -
Net Worth	69.07%	53.32%	50.0% +
Total Liabilities + Net	100.0%	100.00%	

* All Asset items stated as % of Total Assets;
Liability & Net Worth items stated as % of Total Liabilities + Net Worth

Notes:

Dayne Landscaping, Inc. has taken advantage of a rapidly-increasing marketplace, and has also neatly incorporated snow removal services to increase revenues significantly during winter months. The company earned an unusually high 2013 net profit for a start-up service business ($111,059). Debt Ratios (Debt:Assets, 30.93% and Debt:Equity, 44.77%) are better than industry average. A 2014 beginning cash balance of $131,178, with no current liabilities other than $16,332 of notes payable on a previous loan, give the company sufficient marketing funds to expand services into the corporate landscaping and design areas. The purchase of their present facility, currently under a lease agreement (using $100,000 cash + $275,000 loan funds) will not raise the Debt to Equity Ratio (projected at 87.55%) beyond a safe limit. Projections indicate high sales growth with the acquisition of new personnel, vehicles, and equipment to service the increased customer base. The company is experiencing rapid, but controlled growth. Financial projections indicate that the company will be more than able to fulfill its obligations to repay the $275,000 loan with interest and still maintain good cash flow and increased profitability.

Financial Statement Analysis
Ratio Table
Dayne Landscaping, Inc.

Type of Analysis	Formula	Historical: 2013	Projected: 2014
1. Liquidity Analysis a. Net Working Capital	**Balance Sheet** Current Assets — Current Liabilities	Current Assets 136,178 Current Liabilities 16,332 **Net Working Capital $119,846**	Current Assets 93,363 Current Liabilities 27,337 **$66,026**
b. Current Ratio	**Balance Sheet** Current Assets Current Liabilities	Current Assets 136,178 Current Liabilities 16,332 **Current Ratio 8.34**	Current Assets 93,363 Current Liabilities 27,337 **Current Ratio 3.42**
c. Quick Ratio	**Balance Sheet** Current Assets minus Inventory Current Liabilities	Current Assets 136,178 Inventory 5,000 Current Liabilities 16,332 **Quick Ratio 8.03**	Current Assets 93,363 Inventory 10,000 Current Liabilities 27,337 **Quick Ratio 3.05**
2. Profitability Analysis a. Gross Profit Margin	**Income Statement** Gross Profits Sales	Gross Profits 676,834 Sales 777,864 **Gross Profit Margin 87.01%**	Gross Profits 1,386,125 Sales 1,608,200 **Gross Profit Margin 86.19%**
b. Operating Profit Margin	Income From Operations Sales	Income From Ops. 180,564 Sales 777,864 **23.21%**	Income From Ops. 403,276 Sales 1,608,200 **Op. Profit Margin 25.08%**
c. Net Profit Margin	Net Profits Sales	Net Profits 111,059 Sales 777,864 **14.28%**	Net Profits 222,169 Sales 1,608,200 **13.81%**
4. Debt Ratios a. Debt to Assets	**Balance Sheet** Total Liabilities Total Assets	Total Liabilities 60,919 Total Assets 196,978 **Debt to Assets Ratio 30.93%**	Total Liabilities 313,618 Total Assets 671,846 **Debt to Assets Ratio 46.68%**
b. Debt to Equity	Total Liabilities Total Owners' Equity	Total Liabilities 60,919 Total Owners' Equity 136,059 **Debt to Equity Ratio 44.77%**	Total Liabilities 313,618 Total Owners' Equity 358,228 **Debt to Equity Ratio 33.07%**
4. Investment Measures a. ROI *(Return on Investment)*	**Balance Sheet** Net Profits Total Assets	Net Profits 111,059 Total Assets 196,978 **ROI (Ret. on Invest.) 56.38%**	Net Profits 222,169 Total Assets 671,846 **ROI (Ret. on Invest.) 33.07%**
5. Vertical Financial Statement Analysis	**Balance Sheet** 1. Each asset % of Total Assets 2. Liability & Equity % Total L&E **Income Statement** 3. All items % of Total Revenues	**NOTE:** **See Attached** **Balance Analysis - page 31** **Income Analysis – page 30**	**NOTE:** *See* **Projected Balance Sheet - 27** **3-Year Income Statement - 26**
6. Horizontal Financial Statement Analysis	**Balance Sheet** 1. Assets, Liab & Equity measured against 2nd year. Increases and decreases stated as amount & % **Income Statement** 2. Revenues & Expenses measured against 2nd year. Increases and decreases stated as amount & %	**NOTE:** **Horizontal Analysis** **Not Applicable** Only one year in business	**NOTE:** **Horizontal Analysis** **Not Applicable** Only one year in business

Financial Assumptions
Dayne Landscaping, Inc. Business Plan

Seeking Bank Loan

- **Purpose:** To purchase land and facilities currently leased by Dayne Landscaping, Inc.

- **Projected Terms:** $275,000 for 15 Years @ 9%; need funding by April 1, 2014, repayments can begin on May 1, 2008 (see amortization schedule C)

Financial Assumptions

- $25,000 initial capital contribution by owner in corporation (not a loan).

- 5% required up front fees for all snow contracts.

- 5% Sales Commission to be paid to sales representatives..

- Bonuses of $500 each to be paid for landing new corporate accounts.

- Salaries for (4) Supervisors @ $15,000, totaling $60,000. (+ benefits and payroll taxes)

- Salary for the President to be guaranteed @ $65,000 for 2013; projected raise to $82,000 for 2014.

- Salary for the Office Manager @ $22,000 (+ benefits and payroll taxes).

- Salary for Administration Assistants (1 in 2013, 2 in 2014) @ $15000 (+ payroll taxes and benefits).

- Salary for part time people at $9.00 per hour. Hired as needed to meet volume

- Licensing permit fees with City and State during the year.

- Rent deposit at $5,700 for first and last month.

- Heat and Electricity at $60 per sq. ft, totaling $360 per month, and $4.320 per year.

- Fire and Liability Insurance at $50 per sq. ft, totaling $300 per month, and $3,600 per year.

- All insurance at $8,000 per year. The total cost of insurance at $11,600.

- 2 Trucks purchased with 2013 loan: $60,000 @ 8%; interest 5-year period = $12,995.05 (see amortizing schedule A)

- 4 Large Mowers purchased with 2013 loan: $16,000 @ 8%; interest 3-year period = $2049.79 (see amortizing schedule B)

- State Income Taxes charges at 7.5% of net profits.

- Federal Income Taxes based on Federal Corporation Tax Schedule (15%-25%-34%-39% of net profits)

- Estimated Taxes paid on schedule quarterly, based on actual and projected net profits for 2013 and 2014.

- Ending inventory: 2013 = $5,000; 2014 projected at $10,000

Dayne Landscaping, Inc.

Part IV – Supporting Documents *

✓ **Competition Comparison**

✓ **Owner's Resume**

✓ **Letter of Reference**

* Note: *For purposes of brevity, we have chosen to include only a portion of the supporting documents that would be found in Dayne Landscaping, Inc's business plan.*

Competition Comparison

Vendor	Garden Shop	Landscaping Plus	Dayne Landscaping
Landscaping			
Design	Yes	Yes	Yes
Oriental design	No	No	Yes
Maintenance	Yes	Yes	Yes
Pest control	No	No	Yes
Snow Services			
Plowing	Yes	Yes	Yes
Removal	No	No	No
Response time	Whenever	Whenever	Designated
Guarantee	No	No	Yes
Servicing	NH only	NH, MA	NH, MA, CT
Price per hour	$25-30	$30-35	$20- 30

Robin T. Dayne

181 Thoreaus Landing
Nashua, NH 03060
603-888-2020 (W)   603-889-2293 (H)

Summary

Five years' experience in the Landscaping Industry. Skilled in sales, support and operations of new accounts for an established landscaping company. Managed office of 10 employees related to customer service. Proficient in management and workings of the landscaping service industry. Knowledgeable in landscaping design, and planning.

Experience

Landscaping Plus, Nashua, NH   **2007 – 2012**

Office Manager, Jan. 2011-December 2012

Managed 10 employees that sold and serviced customer accounts. Responsible for planning scheduling, and managing inventory (equipment and tools) for the ten employees. Implemented the first "customer satisfaction survey" over the phone, to the entire base of customer's.

- Developed a tool "check-in" process saving the company $10,000 a year in lost inventory.

- Organized the telemarketing necessary for the customer survey resulting in additional sales revenue of $25,000

- Implemented and managed service issue "hot line" for dissatisfied customers.

- Responsible for all major accounts and employees that worked at the sites

Account Supervisor, Dec. 2009 – Dec. 2010

Managed 20 assigned accounts for landscaping and snow maintenance. Responsible for reporting to the President all account updates and potential revenue opportunities.

- Maintained the 20 accounts by scheduling all part-time workers

- Trained part-time employees in proper lawn care maintenance

- Managed the inventory, equipment and supplies of each worker

- Managed all customer service issues and received excellence award for all accounts at the end of the year.

- Scheduled all snow removal and coordinated snow emergencies

Account Landscaping Specialist, June 2007 – Nov. 2009

- Worked the landscaping contract of a large corporate account
- Recommended landscaping design changes and secured additional contract with company
- Provide snow removal during storm and emergencies
- Learned the operation of all landscaping equipment, tools and vehicles

Equipment Rental, Inc., Nashua, NH   **Jan. 2004 – May 2007**

Service Desk Manager

- Responsible for handling any service issues related to the renting of the company's equipment or machinery
- Managed all bill disputes to resolution
- Interfaced with office manager on large account problems
- Recommended improvements in the problem solving process that resulted in speedy results for the customers

Personal Strengths

Excellent organizational and communication skills
Dedicated to customer service excellence
Strong management training and experience
Strong knowledge of landscaping industry

Education

Completed Bachelors Degree in Horticulture at the University of New Hampshire. Independent studies at the Institute for Higher Learning majoring in Environmental Protection.

Affiliations and Interests

Board member of the Nashua Chamber of Commerce
Committee member of the City's "Beautification Program"
Volunteer at Community Services of Nashua

rtd Marketing International, Inc.
81 Walden Pond Ave., Nashua, NH 03060

November 22, 2013

Dear Prospective Investor,

I am delighted to have the opportunity to write this letter of recommendation for Robin T. Dayne.

We have had a contract with Dayne Landscaping, Inc. since February. We came to them initially for snow removal because the company we were using could not guarantee our facility would be plowed by 7:00 am, which we needed in order for our employees to park for work. Dayne Landscaping was able to provide us that guarantee and did an excellent job of fulfilling their commitment, during some very tough storms.

We have since contacted with them for landscaping maintenance and have found the same quality of service. They recommended changes that would save us money and our property hasn't looked this good in years.

Recently we secured their services to install an Oriental garden, which is unique and attractive. Our international clientele has even commented on our unique landscaping and in our business, first impressions can mean everything.

I would recommend them highly, based on their level of service, quality of work and commitment as well they should be considered for the funding they seek.

If you have further questions, feel free to contact me. I can be reached on my private number 603-882-2221, during business hours.

Cordially,

Heather Pope

Heather Pope
President

Wholesale Mobile Homes.com, Inc.
Business Plan

The business plan presented in Appendix III is an actual business plan developed for *Wholesale Mobile Homes.com, Inc.* using *Anatomy of a Business Plan* and its software companion, **AUTOMATE YOUR BUSINESS PLAN**. Mr. Paul Jarolimek II, President and CEO of the company has generously allowed us to publish the plan in the new edition of our book and the new revision of our software. *Wmhinc.com* is modeled as an Internet Portal with primary focus on the housing industry. Their web site provides consumers the opportunity to design and purchase a home online. *Wmhinc.com's* vision as an innovative, dynamic start up company is to provide services that will establish the Company as the premier online provider of manufactured housing, industry information, and associated services.

The Company was in the process of development and the business plan was written for the purpose of raising venture capital. The Company expected to raise the needed capital by the end of 2008 and begin operations in January 2009. They have since, renamed their company and expanded their focus.

Working with a business plan consultant

Wmhinc.com's business plan was developed by the owners of the business with professional assistance from a very reputable business plan consultant, Mr. Ndaba Mdhlongwa of Dallas, Texas (businessplansolutions.net -or- 469-223-4474). I also owe Mr. Mdhlongwa a debt of gratitude because he has put in many extra hours of volunteer time to work with me in preparing the business plan for presentation to my readers and software users. Many times, the owners of the business either feel too pressed for time to write their plans—or sometime they just feel that they would have more confidence in the result—if they could engage the services of a business plan professional. In this case, they found the right person to work with. Before you hire someone yourself, be sure that you know what you are getting into. Hiring the wrong person can be very costly both in terms of money and the quality of your business plan. Hiring the right person can be very beneficial.

This plan is for a more aggressive business

Wmhinc.com is seeking venture capital in the amount of $10 million. As you learned in Chapter 1, investors become equity partners in your company. Because of the risks involved in venturing with a company, they are looking for rapid growth/profitability projections backed by reason. Therefore, you will notice that they have written their business plan with a heavy focus on the Summary Description of the Business, Marketing Plan, Sources and Uses of Financing, and Executive Summary.

- ### *The* Wmhinc.com *marketing plan*
  In Chapter 5, Part II, The Marketing Plan, you were presented with a very comprehensive list of marketing plan components, representing a full spectrum of marketing possibilities. Mr. Jarolimek, with the assistance of Mr. Mdhlongwa has addressed all of these components in the *Wmhinc.com* marketing plan. It is a good example of a very fine market planning effort.

- ### Financial documents
  This is a plan for a start up company. For this reason, you will note that all of the financial documents are pro forma, or projected, spreadsheets. Only after the company has been in business for one accounting period will it have historical financial statements.

- ### Note the Executive Summary
  Venture capitalists like to see an exciting Executive Summary. The one in this plan is an example of a more comprehensive one, addressing important highlights of the company and an Income Statement Summary for their Four-Phases of Development.

Thank you again to Mr. Paul Jarolimek and to Mr. Ndaba Mdhlongwa for allowing me to share this interpretation of business planning with our readers and software users. I know that it will be a great help to them as they write their plans.

> **Warning!** *The plan is to be examined for Wmhinc.com's handling of content only. There is no judgement inferred as to appropriateness or financial potential for lenders or investors. Do not use this plan as a source of research for your own company.*
>
> *Please do not contact the company. Mr. Jarolimek has been generous in sharing his plan and I would not want to be responsible for taking up more of his valuable time. Also, remember that his name and other things have changed with his company. Names, links, addresses, or phone numbers in this document may no longer be valid.*

Wholesale Mobile Homes.com, Inc.

5300 W Sahara suite 101
PO Box 27740
Las Vegas, NV 89146

Telephone: 509-663-3876
URL: www.Wmhinc.com

Paul Jarolimek II: President and CEO

Mary Lou Jarolimek: CFO

Suzanne Jarolimek: Director of Customer Relations

Mike Gage: CTO

Kerry Lease: Executive VP of Marketing

Plan prepared November 2008
by the Corporate Officers

TABLE OF CONTENTS

Note. *For brevity, only one of Wmhinc.com's Supporting Documents has been included in this plan.*

EXECUTIVE SUMMARY

Wmhinc.com is an innovative, dynamic start-up company providing services that will establish the Company as the premiere online provider of manufactured housing, industry information, and associated services. The web site provides consumers the opportunity to design and purchase a home online. Additionally, it provides comprehensive industry information, nationwide Associated Services Yellow Pages, and industry and government links.

The Company plans to establish itself as the "next generation provider" of manufactured homes, products, and related services and capture a sizable portion of this market in the next decade. Furthermore, *Wmhinc.com* is modeled as an Internet Portal, constructed and designed after well-known portals such as C/Net (information technology), CNNfn (finance), Showbiz (entertainment), WebMD (health and fitness), and Thrive Online (health and fitness) with primary focus on the housing industry.

HIGHLIGHTS of *Wmhinc.com*

- **Management Experience.** The Management team is highly qualified and capable in the areas of eCommerce, marketing, manufactured home, and housing related services.

- **Industry knowledge.** *Wmhinc.com* will leverage its knowledge of the industry to establish a dominating presence in its delivery of homes and related services to consumers.

- **Web site.** With its *three-click* ease of navigation, the consumer will be smoothly transported from the front page to a 'state specific' choice page. This second page will have multiple directions in which the customer may travel.

- **Diverse Sources of Revenues.** Unlike a number of other transaction-based businesses operating on the Internet, *Wmhinc.com's* business model is not based on 'click through' advertising revenue nor is it based on subscription, membership dues, or user fees.

- **Aggressive Marketing.** Management is positioning *Wmhinc.com* to grow aggressively through strategic alliances, innovative marketing and branding programs, and first mover initiatives.

- **Growing Market Segment.** Today manufactured homes make up over 25% of new homes in the United States. Sales of new manufactured homes exceeded $16 billion in 2007, an increase of 400% in the last ten years. With new design elements and customizable options, manufactured homes have begun to cross over into the mainstream.

Management has developed a clear and defined path that will help establish the Company as the leading provider of manufactured housing, industry information, and associated services on the Internet. At the forefront of its model, is the establishment of departments that will handle various aspects of operations including the sale and distribution of new, factory over-run, and bank-owned homes.

While the Company fully expects competition to materialize in some form, management also believes its business model will mitigate competitive threats and capitalize on the identified opportunity gaps such as geographic specialization/expertise, superior customer service and usability.

Customers will be the focal point of the *Wmhinc.com* business model and overall strategy. All customers will be treated with respect, their housing choices made simple, and their decision making process made positive. *Wmhinc.com* will continually develop its customer network, continually striving to receive referrals from existing customers and visitors.

Wmhinc.com has established strategic relationships with several leading industry specialists in the areas of financing, decoration, and manufacturing. By the first fiscal year, the Company expects to have set up additional partnerships with major manufacturers, state and national manufactured housing associations, relevant Internet partner suppliers, and other services providers thereby making *Wmhinc.com* a hub for manufactured homes and related services. In addition, these alliances will enable the Company to draw and retain a strong customer base.

Wmhinc.com intends to derive its revenue from various business activities including:

- E-commerce revenues from the sale of new customer built homes
- E-commerce revenues from the sale of factory over-run homes through partner suppliers
- Fees and commissions paid by partner suppliers of Bank-Owned Homes
- Sales of advertising space to service providers (exclusive, proprietary Yellow Pages)
- Fees paid by regional and international Internet partner suppliers of *Wmhinc.com* for certain exclusive rights
- Fees paid by state and municipality commerce and tourism departments for placement referrals
- E-commerce revenues and fees paid by land and community developers
- Fees for design, positioning and management of "Auction Sites" for maximum speed in disposing of large inventory blocks
- Resale/income stream from company owned land and community developments

The company is seeking venture capital in the amount of $10 million for its Four-Phase Development. The company's revenue projections for 2009, 2010, and 2011 are $17 million, $77 million, and $136 million, respectively.

Income Statement Summary

	2009	2010	2011
Income	$ 17,216,075	$ 77,631,985	$ 136,623,886
Variable Expenses	5,081,104	18,072,884	34,871,019
Fixed Expenses	1,427,176	6,449,120	11,107,191
Income Taxes	5,196,029	23,262,736	40,652,953
Net Income	$ 5,511,766	$ 35,428,528	$ 51,675,986

Part I: Organizational Plan
Wholesale Mobile Homes.com, Inc

Summary Description of the Business

Wmhinc.com is an innovative, dynamic start-up company providing services that will establish the Company as the premiere online provider of manufactured housing, industry information, and associated services.

Mission

At *Wmhinc.com*, our mission is to provide the most innovative and practical web based housing solutions. *Wmhinc.com* plans are to become a dominant player in the online marketplace, providing new, factory over-run, and bank-owned homes direct to the consumer.

Business Model

Wmhinc.com is modeled as an Internet Portal, constructed and designed after well-known portals such as C/Net (information technology), CNNfn (finance), Showbiz (entertainment), and Thrive Online (health and fitness) with primary focus on the housing industry. Making the company's business model unique is the dual strategy of selling and distributing new, factory over-run, and bank-owned homes as well as selling associated products and services. *Wmhinc.com* will also serve as a resource center, providing manufactured housing information, message boards and forums for discussions concerning the purchase and installation of manufactured housing, as well as non-specific games and varied interest content.

The *Wmhinc.com* business model is based on strategic alliances with various manufacturing industry leaders. Through these alliances, the Company will showcase floor plans, option books, and color choice catalogs. The model is designed to encourage visitors to make repeated, almost daily, visits in order to gain additional information, services, and a sense of community with others in like situations. This strategy will increase page views, repeat traffic, and value to the company's advertisers. Furthermore, this portal presence will allow *Wmhinc.com* to cultivate additional advertisers from non-related industries in order to take advantage of the relationship with its customers.

Strategy

The Company's long-term goal is to dominate the Manufactured Housing Internet sector as well as create a Brick and Mortar presence in the manufacturing and retailing of homes and associated products. *Wmhinc.com* will accomplish this goal by developing a website that will become a "one-stop" destination for consumers seeking manufactured housing and presenting long-term opportunities for its partner suppliers by enabling them to increase their product deliveries and market share. Furthermore, this goal will be accomplished as a result of ongoing investments in search engine optimization, Internet advertising, and traditional advertising. Management is projecting first year traffic will place *Wmhinc.com* firmly in the *Media Metrix* top 100 web sites.

Strategic Relationships

The Company has strategic alliances with several leading housing related companies. These alliances are valuable because they provide *Wmhinc.com* with established companies and distribution channels. Establishing dominance in the Internet market for manufactured housing and further increasing and expanding market share, *Wmhinc.com* will add value to the products and services offered by its partner companies.

Cavalier Homes has agreed to partner with *Wmhinc.com* for their work with developers, the sale of the computer programs, and the promotion of a yet publicly undisclosed financing company that they are developing. The agreement with Cavalier Homes is expected to be finalized by the end of January. Additionally, an agreement is expected to be reached with Fleetwood Homes also by the end of January. Currently, *Wmhinc.com* has working agreements for 4,000 homes with several developers for an average of $2,000 to $5,000 per house.

SWOT Analysis

Wmhinc.com conducted a SWOT Analysis to examine key factors that are internal (strengths and weaknesses) and external (opportunities and threats). Following are the results:

STRENGTHS

- Strategic alliances with several leading companies that have established distribution channels
- Internet Portal with primary focus on the housing industry
- Extensive experience in eCommerce, marketing, manufactured homes, and housing related services
- Innovative web site with ease of navigation and complete "state specific" web pages
- Centralized point for FEMA to procure homes in the event of a natural disaster for replacement of destroyed property

WEAKNESSES

- Wmhinc.com has a relatively short operating history
- Security of sensitive customer information
- Brand recognition
- Limited sales force

OPPORTUNITIES

- Manufactured homes make up over 25% of new homes in the United States
- Sales of new manufactured homes exceeded $16 billion in 1999, an increase of 400% in the last ten years
- Housing and support for land and community developers
- Company owned and independent manufacturers are having extreme difficulty moving their products
- Overproduction of 'stock' homes in an already over-saturated market
- Development of personnel housing on military bases

THREATS

- Established competitors in the marketplace
- Changes in customer requirements and preferences
- Frequent new product and service introductions which embody new processes and technologies
- Evolving industry standards and practices
- Acceptance of customers to use the Internet and other online services as a medium for buying manufactured homes
- Failure of subcontractors/partners to perform services to customer's satisfaction

---

Risks

As with all companies, the opportunity is tempered with certain risks. Important risks to consider are described below according to internal and external risk categories.

Wmhinc.com Associated Risks

- **Early Stage Business** – *Wmhinc.com* was incorporated in August 2008 and has a relatively short operating history. To mitigate this risk, the company has assembled a Management Team with experience in the areas of business management, manufactured housing, e-commerce, and various types of expertise that contribute to managing startups.

- **Establishing, Building, Maintaining, and Strengthening Brand** – *Wmhinc.com*'s brand is new and this will hinder its ability to attract and retain customers. To mitigate this risk, the company will implement aggressive marketing and promotional efforts. In addition, *Wmhinc.com* will undertake various Public Relations activities and tasks aimed at increasing brand recognition.

Internet Associated Risks

- **Technology** – The market for manufactured homes is constantly undergoing change. To mitigate this risk, *Wmhinc.com*'s will rely on the strategic partners for information on industry standards and new product and service introductions so the company can remain at the top of the industry.

- **eCommerce** – *Wmhinc.com*'s future revenues and profits are substantially dependent upon broad acceptance of customers to use the Internet and other online services as a medium for buying manufactured homes. To mitigate this risk, the company will gain credibility by joining the Better Business Bureau and developing marketing campaigns aimed at educating the public.

- **Database Security** – Through its Web site, *Wmhinc.com* will maintain sensitive customer data in its database creating a risk of exposure to hackers. To protect customer records, a sophisticated security system has been incorporated into the Web site that relies on a combination of security devices and methods that make the data virtually scrambled to the point that the likelihood of a hacker has an extremely low probability of accessing customer records.

Business and Financial Risks

- **Competition** – *Wmhinc.com* operates in highly competitive markets and may not be able to compete effectively. To mitigate this risk, the company has established strategic relationships with some of the leading and well known manufacturers and distributors in the country.

- **Dependency on Effective Marketing and Sales** – *Wmhinc.com* expects that its future financial performance will depend in part on the marketing and sales of its services. Market acceptance of the company depends on the market demand for the specific functionality of such services. To mitigate this risk, the company plans to begin with an effective public relations campaign that will include cold calling and visits to trade shows.

- **Dependency on Sales Force and Distribution** – To increase its revenue, *Wmhinc.com* must increase the size of its sales force and the number of its indirect channel partners, including original equipment manufacturers, value-added resellers and systems integrators. To mitigate this risk, the company plans to attract and retain a sales force with experience in manufactured home industry sales and compensate them at levels higher than the industry standard.

- **Poor results by service providers may damage *Wmhinc's* reputation** – Wmhinc's business could be adversely affected if its subcontractors/partners fail to perform services to its customer's satisfaction. The occurrence of various situations could result in loss of or delay in revenue, loss of market share, failure to achieve market acceptance, diversion of development resources, injury to *Wmhinc.com*'s reputation, or damage to its efforts to build brand awareness, any of which could have adverse effects on its business, operating results and financial condition. To mitigate this risk, the company plans to establish relationships with service providers with a reputation for exceptional service and delivery.

Products and Services

The Company plans to establish itself as the "next generation provider" of manufactured homes, products, and related services. The Company's web site not only provides the opportunity for the consumer to design and purchase a home online, but also includes comprehensive information, a nationwide Associated Services Yellow Pages, and industry and government links. Designed to be user friendly with a simple 'three click' system and 'state specific' listings of products and services, the web site enables the consumer to find the home or information needed with ease.

Intellectual Property

Patents, copyrights, and/or trademarks

Wmhinc.com regards its copyrights, trademarks, trade secrets (including methodologies, practices, and tools) and other intellectual property rights as critical to success. To protect its rights, *Wmhinc.com* relies on a combination of trademark and copyright laws, trade secret protection, nondisclosure agreements, and other contractual agreements with its employees, affiliates, clients, strategic partners, acquisition targets, and others.

Location

The Company's principal offices are located at 5300 W Sahara, Suite 101, Las Vegas, NV 89146. Currently, the Company is paying a monthly rental fee of $1,500. The Company plans to develop a gated compound on 10–20 acres of land consisting of 2 converted Manufactured homes (total area 5000 square feet) which will serve as the office area. Also on the compound will be a housing development featuring 6 manufactured homes. In January 2002, the Company will begin its search for potential sites. Site selection is expected to be completed by the middle of February with construction beginning in March.

Legal Structure

Wholesale Mobile Homes.com, Inc. (*Wmhinc.com*) is a privately-held Nevada C Corporation. The Company was formed on August 1st, 2008 and incorporated on August 23rd, 2008. Provided below is a list of the Company's corporate officers and their compensation.

Compensation		
Paul S Jarolimek II	President/CEO	$ 52,500
Michael Gage	CTO	$ 52,500
MaryLou Jarolimek	CFO	$ 52,500
Stephen Massie	EVP Warranty/Service	$ 52,500
Jim Stephens	EVP Sales	$ 52,500
Suzanne Jarolimek	EVP Customer Service	$ 52,500
Kerry Lease	EVP Marketing	STOCK ONLY
Larry Queen	VP Technology - Graphics	$ 52,500
Leon Jarolimek	VP Customer Service/Warranty	$ 52,500
William Smith	Corporate Counsel	STOCK ONLY

Management

The Company's management philosophy is based on responsibility and mutual respect. At *Wmhinc.com*, we have an environment that encourages creativity and achievement. *Wmhinc.com* management is highly experienced and qualified. *Wmhinc.com.*'s management team provides strong leadership ability, sales and marketing expertise, and extensive knowledge in both Manufactured Housing and the Internet. See resume in Supporting Documents. Descriptions of the management team and responsibilities are as follows.

- **Paul Jarolimek II, Founder, Chairman, President and CEO** – Paul Jarolimek II, Founder, Chairman, President and CEO is a veteran in the manufactured housing industry who has proven his leadership in both independent retail enterprises and from within the corporate structure. A top salesperson for one of the leading manufactured housing companies in the nation prior to taking on management roles, he has the management experience, customer service, and people skills to facilitate his role in this company.

- **MaryLou Jarolimek, Board Member and CFO** – Mary Lou Jarolimek has nearly 30 years of business acumen. Having successfully run a number of businesses and trained in financial services, her role as CFO is most suited.

- **Suzanne Jarolimek, Board Member and Director of Customer Relations** – Suzanne Jarolimek, brings with her a pragmatic and laser focused vision of the needs of our customers.

- **Mike Gage, Board Member and CTO** – Mike Gage brings value to the Company with his many years of Internet commerce experience and deep understanding of hardware and software applications.

- **Kerry Lease, Board Member and Executive VP of Marketing** – Kerry Lease, delivers twenty-five years of highly successful business ownership in the highly competitive field of advertising and marketing.

Personnel

Management realizes that the strength of the Company's personnel is key to its success. As such, plans include filling staff positions with professionals who have proven success and records in the *dot.com* world and have an understanding of the housing industry. The Company plans to hire 5 department managers at an average salary of $40,000 per year each and 10 hourly employees at an average wage rate that totals $16,800 per year per employee.

Accounting and Legal

Accounting

Wmhinc.com will follow Generally Accepted Accounting Principles (GAAP). The Company will use the Accrual Basis for recognition of revenues and handle accounting and bookkeeping internally. The CFO is responsible for the overall financial condition of the Company and managing all financial functions in keeping *Wmhinc.com* a profitable corporation.

All bookkeeping activities will be handled internally by the Administrative Assistant using Peachtree Accounting. Peachtree Accounting has been selected over other accounting packages because of its powerful business management and Internet tools. An outside CPA firm will provide auditing services and develop financial reports for *Wmhinc.com*.

The Company will keep its customer database on ACT contact management software by Symantec. ACT allows users to create a database, fax, run reports, and do mail merge. A new feature also allows users to send and receive e-mail messages from within Act's interface.

Legal

For all legal aspects of the business, the Company has retained the services of the Maryland based Law Office of Kerwin A. Miller, LLC. Provided below is the company's contact information.

> Law Office of Kerwin A. Miller, LLC
> Principal – Kerwin Miller
> 6905 Rockledge Drive
> Suite 600
> Bethesda, MD 20817
> Off: (301) 896-9421
> Fax: (301) 941-9009

Insurance

Management has assessed insurance requirements and has concluded that the Company will need business liability coverage, industry specific liability insurance coverage, workers' compensation coverage, medical coverage, and key-man coverage. (**Note**: *see Insurance Update Form in supporting documents.*)

Security

The Company will maintain sensitive customer data in its database and from transactions on the Internet. To protect customer records, a sophisticated security system will incorporate into the Web site that relies on a combination of security devices and methods that encrypt the data leaving an extremely low probability of accessing customer records.

Part II: MARKETING PLAN
Wholesale Mobile Homes.com, Inc.

I. Overview and Goals

A. Overview of Marketing Strategy

The Marketing Plan is developed in order to support *Wmhinc.com*'s goals and strategies. It is based on strategic goals as well as from knowledge gained during analysis of the industry, competitive intelligence, and what *Wmhinc.com* knows (or assumes) about its customers and partners. Initial marketing tactics will focus on the development of the *Wmhinc.com* promotional material, an efficient public relations campaign, including a strong Internet search engine presence, cold calling, and visits to trade shows and a corporate sales force.

B. Goals of Marketing Strategy

- Creating a Well Known Brand
- Building an Strong Customer Base
- Increasing Product/Service Sales

II. Market Analysis

A. Target Market(s)

Customers will be the focal point of the *Wmhinc.com* business model and overall strategy. All customers will be treated with respect, their housing choices made simple, and their decision-making process made positive. *Wmhinc.com* will continually develop its customer network, striving to receive referrals from existing customers and visitors. *Wmhinc.com* caters to the following customer groups/target markets:

- Individuals (*Wmhinc.com's NASCAR advertising campaign that is explained below, will primarily target this market segment*)
- Government
- Developers
- Manufacturers
- Retail Sale Centers
- Advertisers

Value Propositions

Wmhinc.com offers the following value propositions for each customer group/target market.

Individuals

<u>Ease of Use</u> – Easy navigation through the web site utilizing a 'three click' process to find the right section, build and purchase homes, and find information. Prices posted, options and features from many different manufacturers allow a greater choice than can be found on a local level.

<u>Unparalleled Information sources</u> – *Wmhinc.com* has access to tens of thousands of pages of information and is developing a joint information venture with FEMA for the prevention of disasters.

Government

<u>Disaster Relief Services</u> – Centralized point for FEMA to procure homes in the event of a natural disaster for replacement of destroyed property. Also a joint venture with FEMA for disaster awareness and preventative measures that can be undertaken before or after the home is installed.

<u>VA Preferred Provider of Manufactured Housing</u> – Provide the VA department a definitive provider of housing for post-military personnel. This will be done in such a way that the VA recommends us for those in need of manufactured homes.

Developers

<u>Provide large blocks of housing and support for land and community developers</u> – This program provides a tremendous resource for the developer in availability of many choices of homes with one contact, standardized pricing, reference materials, as well as follow-up marketing opportunities.

Manufacturers

<u>Marketing their Homes</u> – Through their traditional retail outlets, both company owned and independent, manufacturers are having extreme difficulty moving their products. This is primarily due to high overhead, accelerated collapse of retailing outlets, and zero market penetration in some areas (due to extremely high startup costs for new retail centers).

<u>Immediate Payment on Sold homes</u> – One of the most innovative and attractive aspects of the *Wmhinc.com* model is the lack of 'floor planning'. This has long been a risk to manufacturers due to the guarantees required by the finance companies to secure the loans for a retailer's inventory. By eliminating this, *Wmhinc.com* will virtually eliminate any risk to the manufacturers in our partnership circle.

Retail Sale Centers and Parent Companies

<u>Technology</u> – The technology of the Company's tracking program, which will be installed on the web site will give *Wmhinc.com* the ability to track virtually every aspect of the customer's buying process. Additionally, this will enable the Company to constantly communicate with potential customers.

<u>Pre-built Garages</u> – Patentable product in development, which can be sold to industry brick & mortars on a wholesale level for eventual resale. *Wmhinc.com* has procured engineering and design, as well as manufacturing space to facilitate the production of these units.

Advertisers

<u>Copyrighted, exclusive, industry specific Yellow Pages</u> – This is designed to provide companies, both on and off the Internet, in related industries the ability to put their products directly in front of the people who need them the most. High volume specific traffic, needing the services listed, provides huge benefits to this program.

B. Competition

1.   Description of Major Competitors

<u>Chandler, Inc.</u> – Chandler's is committed to being number one in the South by offering customers "direct from the builder pricing". Chandler drop ships custom ordered homes directly from the manufacturer to the customer's lot. This amounts to thousands of dollars in savings to the customer. Chandler offers the above propositions that make it one of the best sites to purchase mobile homes:

2254 U.S. 84 West
Valdosta, Georgia 31601
Phone (912) 242-5900
Fax (912) 242-8833
http://www.chandlersmfg.com/

<u>Homestore.com, Inc.</u> – Homestore.com with its family of sites is one of the leading destinations for home and real estate-related information on the Internet. RealSelect, Inc., is the official Internet site of the National Association of Realtors® and has pioneered the use of the Internet as a channel for buying and selling homes. Each site in the Homestore.com™ family provides definitive resources for both professionals and consumers, including advanced search functions, rich editorial content, marketplaces for related products and services, and tools such as checklists and calculators.

225 West Hillcrest Drive, Suite 100
Thousand Oaks, CA 91360
Phone: (805) 557-2300
http://www.factorybuilthousing.com/

<u>MHShopper</u> – MHShopper was founded in 2000 to create a network of market leading manufactured home dealers across the country. Through this united network, MHShopper and the Manufactured Home Shopper Network is able to ensure value pricing and a variety of low-cost financing options - savings that are passed to both dealers and consumers. MHShopper completed it's first round of financing in July, 2000 through a private placement with Roth Capital Partners of Newport Beach, California.

15282 Newsboy Circle, Huntington Beach CA 92649
Phone: (714) 373-5001 (6:30am to 5pm PST)
Fax : (714) 373-5006
http://MHShopper.com

<u>Michael Holigan.com</u> – MH2Technologies makes building easier, more productive, and more profitable. Its service offerings, including MH2Build and MH2Marketing, were developed by builders for builders. MH2Build allows homebuilders and light commercial contractors to save time, reduce overhead, simplify ordering, and schedule efficiently. From any location, builders can use MH2Build for job management, scheduling, and materials ordering.

2.   Assessment of Their Strengths/Weaknesses

Competition exists within the industry but not at the level at which *Wmhinc.com* is participating. Individual retailers, information-only sites, and manufacturer sites all have a common denominator and that is none of them actually offer the home to the customer. The closest service competitors are offering is allowing the visitor to request more information which is then sent, sans prices.

While *Wmhinc.com* fully expects additional competition to materialize in some form, management also believes its business model will mitigate competitive threats and capitalize on the identified opportunity gaps such as geographic specialization and expertise, superior customer service, and usability.

C. Market Trends

1. Target Market Trends

Wmhinc.com believes that it provides a natural evolution in the Manufactured Housing market. A unique marketing channel has been developed as clearly shown in the Internet retailing of vehicles, heavy equipment, and *big ticket* items. Consumers are becoming increasingly more comfortable with making major purchases online. Internet vehicle sales alone exceeded $670 million in 2007 says analyst *James McQuivey of Forrester Research*, and by 2011, it is projected that eight million cars will be purchased with some help from the Internet. That market, and a nationwide figure of over 370,000 manufactured homes delivered in 2006, and over 320,000 delivered in 2007, has given *Wmhinc.com* a clearly defined and workable model.

Demographically *Wmhinc.com* is positioned on the cusp of a major resurgence in manufactured housing. While traditional buyers of manufactured housing have been, and continue to be, first-time homebuyers which is where *Wmhinc.com*'s primary marketing thrust will center early on, the aging 'baby boomer' section of the population will account for a dramatic increase in manufactured housing sales.

The year ending 2007 saw a downturn in the nationwide delivery in Manufactured housing, and while there are many reasons for the downturn, facts show that as the *baby boomers* enter the pre-retirement stages they will become a burgeoning market for manufactured housing. Empty nests, upscale 55 and older communities, the high quality and relative low expense not only in the purchase, but maintenance of Manufactured Housing, as well as other factors, will play a pivotal role in the purchase of Manufactured Housing by 'baby boomers'. This, coupled with the demographics of Internet usage showing adults 55 and older represent the fastest growing group of U.S. Internet users according to *International Data Corp.*, which found the number of seniors online will more than triple from 11.1 million in 2007 to 34.1 million in 2012, and will account for 20% of all new users, will provide *Wmhinc.com* a long-term source of customers.

2. Industry Trends

According to *Statistical Surveys*, the industries leading information source, there has been a precipitous drop in manufactured housing shipments over the last two plus years. In 2006 there were over 370,000 total shipments nationwide. In 2007 that figure dropped to over 320,000. Currently the shipments stand at approximately 120,000 through the month of May 2008.

While there has been much speculation concerning this, the industry is cyclical. Press releases by the major manufactured housing companies such as Oakwood Homes, American Homestar, Champion, and Fleetwood have repeatedly pointed to overproduction of 'stock' homes in an already over-saturated market, combined with higher than normal repossession rates further returning homes to the marketplace. These and other factors, while perceived as a negative by many, provide *Wmhinc.com* with a world of opportunity.

Through their traditional retail outlets, both company owned and independent manufacturers are having extreme difficulty moving products. High overhead, accelerated collapse of retailing outlets, zero market penetration in some areas (primarily due to extremely high startup costs for new retail centers) all have combined together to provide the overwhelming need for the services offered by *Wmhinc.com*

The Manufactured Home Market

The Federal Manufactured Home Construction and Safety Standards Act, is administered by the U.S. Department of Housing and Urban Development (HUD). This building code, which is also known as the HUD code, federally regulates the design and construction of manufactured homes. It also sets the standards for home durability and safety.

The implementation of the HUD code was a pivotal point in the manufactured home industry. No longer referred to as *mobile homes* or *trailers*, manufactured homes began a revolution in housing. Home construction became consistent industry wide, and manufacturers, lenders, and consumers began to recognize manufactured homes as a viable alternative to site-built homes.

Today, manufactured homes make up over 25% of new homes in the United States. Sales of new manufactured homes exceeded $16 billion in 2007, an increase of 400% in the last ten years. With new design elements and customizable options, manufactured homes have begun to cross over into the mainstream.

The improvement of construction standards and incredible sales growth in the industry has caused many national lenders to reconsider their views of manufactured homes. Manufactured home buyers now have more financing options than those buyers who are considering purchasing site-built homes.

D. Market Research - Additional Factors

Additional highlights of the manufactured home market include:

- Over 19 million people (about 8 % of the U.S. population) live full time in over 8 million manufactured homes.

- In 2007, the industry shipped 348,671 homes from 323 manufacturing facilities.

- 88% of manufactured home owners report satisfaction with the manufactured housing lifestyle.

- A majority of manufactured homes are never moved after they have been installed.

- Manufactured housing retail sales were estimated at $16.3 billion in 2006.
  In 2007, 20.7% of all new single-family housing starts were manufactured homes.

- According to the Census Bureau, 2007 figures show that 68 percent of new manufactured homes were located on private property, and 32 percent of new manufactured homes were located in communities.

- The average sales price of a manufactured home was $43,600 in 2007. Single-section homes average $31,800, while multi-section homes average $50,200.

- In 2007, the estimated economic impact from manufactured housing was $34.5 billion. The economic impact reflects the economic activity generated by the production and sale of a home - this includes salaries, goods purchased and auxiliary services.

III. Marketing Strategy

A. General Description

The overall marketing plan for *Wmhinc.com*'s service is based on the following fundamentals:

- The segment of the market(s) planned to reach.
- Distribution channels planned to be used to reach market segments: NASCAR, television, print, sales associates, telemarketing, and joint direct mail efforts with FEMA.
- Share of the market expected to capture over a fixed period of time.

Market Responsibilities

Wmhinc.com is committed to an extensive promotional campaign. This will be done aggressively and on a broad scale. To accomplish initial sales goals, the Company will require an extremely effective promotional campaign to accomplish two primary objectives:

- Attract quality sales personnel that have a desire to be successful.
- Attract customers that will constantly look to *Wmhinc.com* for their housing needs.

B. Method of Sales and Distribution

Wmhinc.com's sales plan is to seek business that will advance the Company's quest to vertically integrate and become a stronger force in the housing industry. The Company will continue to strive towards procuring sales of its services in the nation.

To accomplish *Wmhinc.com*'s endeavors, the Company will utilize internal and external sales tactics. By aggressively seeking new accounts and taking full advantage of the existing relationships the Company has with current customers and broadening its customer base, the Company will expand and compete with the leading companies in its markets.

C. Pricing

Wmhinc.com sets pricing based on market and competitive rates. Through its alliances with various manufacturers, *Wmhinc.com* is able to order the homes at discounted prices. With its business model, the Company is then able to pass on the direct cost savings to the customer while generating significant profit margins.

D. Sales Strategies

Wmhinc.com plans to use a combination of the following strategies to reach its markets.

- Direct sales
- Direct mail
- E-mail marketing
- Affiliate marketing
- Viral marketing

These channels are most appropriate because of the time to market, reduced capital requirements, and fast access to established distribution channels. The sales department will be headed by one general sales manager and one national sales manager that will be initially charged with developing the sales force to consist of several sales teams led by local sales managers.

E. Sales Incentives

As an extra incentive for customers and potential customers to remember *Wmhinc.com*'s name, the Company, through its NASCAR involvement, plans to enable the marketing of die-cast renderings of the sponsored racecar, T-shirts and other clothing, miscellaneous novelties, and other advertising specialties with the Company logo. This multi-billion dollar NASCAR sports merchandising program will produce dramatic branding of the *Wmhinc.com* name as these items will appear in virtually every K-Mart and Wal-Mart in the United States and abroad. Retail sales of NASCAR related merchandise has grown over 1400% in the last decade. This will be an ongoing program for the Company, when appropriate and where it is identified as beneficial.

F. Advertising Strategies

1. Traditional Advertising

Advertising will focus on building awareness of *Wmhinc.com*'s brand and on marketing (online) services as a better and cost effective way for purchasing manufactured homes. Advertising will be directed at bringing interested prospects to *Wmhinc.com*'s web site for additional information. Advertising programs will include the following channels:

- Television (network/cable)
- Radio
- Print

2. Web Advertising/New Media

Wmhinc.com plans to contract one or more third parties to handle its Web advertising requirements. *Wmhinc.com* will conduct Internet advertising in the form of Internet banner ads, newsletters, co-branding efforts, search engines, portals, and press releases on Web sites that have high traffic-visitors that match *Wmhinc.com*'s target demographics. Through the Web site, prospective customers can obtain detailed information on the services, request additional information, and opt-in or opt-out to future product/service announcements.

Cost of Advertising	
Nascar Winston Cup	$6,000,000
Internet (Primarily search engine placement)	$ 500,000
Print Advertising	$ 200,000

3. Long-term Sponsorships

Wmhinc.com will initiate a national advertising campaign in conjunction with the Company's sponsorship of a Winston cup Series team. The Company's national advertising accounts will receive a full-page advertisement (which could be their home page displayed within the *Wmhinc.com* web site, see: http://*Wmhinc.com*/yp or Moving.com within the *moving* section and FEMA in the 'FEMA' section of our site). Additionally, they will receive the following value-added propositions.

15

- Three associate sponsor placements on a NASCAR Winston Cup racecar, this could be in one race or over three races. Races are first come first serve, and include the Daytona 500 and the Brickyard 400 at the Indy Motor Speedway. The Company has selected Derrike Cope as its driver for the upcoming NASCAR season. Advertising will include mention on television (Fox and/or NBC) and radio. NASCAR boasts a viewership of over 4,500,000 people not including the individual race attendance. Location would be:

  > Leading edge of hood
  > Lower quarter panel front of rear wheel
  > Lower quarter panel rear of rear wheel
  > Trunk lid
  > Rear panel in area between rear lights (TV Panel)

- Permanent placement on the car/equipment hauler (rolling billboard from February to November)

- Invitation for two to the exclusive hospitality tent prior to race. Wine and dine with the crew and officials and meet Kenny Wallace and the crew chief, Barry Dobson. (per race)

- Two VIP garage passes (per race)

- Opportunity to be a uniformed crewmember during the race

- News and other TV placement as sponsor

- Prominently displayed and mentioned as a FEMA *"Project Impact"* associate during joint press conferences

- Prominently displayed within the *"Project Impact"* joint *Wmhinc.com* and FEMA web site

- Opportunity for advertiser's name to be in retail outlets including K-Mart and Wal-Mart. (Die-cast cars and t-shirts)

Wmhinc.com believes this joint marketing venture will help to increase its customer base as well as produce income from the sale of the advertising well over the amount required for its own marketing efforts. Effectively, this will result in an immediate return on the Company's marketing investment as well as the excellent exposure of the NASCAR association.

NASCAR Statistics: 2006-2007 Total US TV rating (Regular season – households)

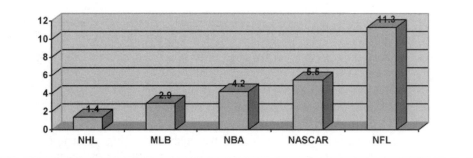

Per event average:
- In-Focus time: 9min 04sec
- Sponsor mentions: 5.4
- Value based on cost per :30 ad: $626,330

Audience brand loyalty

Audience income:		Audience age:	
>$20,000	15.9%	12 – 17	12.0%
$20 - $30,000	16.7%	18 – 24	12.8%
$30 - $50,000	30.2%	25 – 34	18.7%
$50 - $75,000	20.4%	35 – 44	22.6%
$75,000 +	16.8%	35 – 44	22.6%
		55 +	18.2%

Comparable Value

Throughout the 2007 season, there were 108 broadcasts of Winston Cup Series events, airing on ABC, CBS, ESPN, ESPN2, NBC, TBS, and TNN.

The broadcast season resulted in the collection of 344 hours, 17 minutes, and 53 seconds of exposure time, 20,507 verbal mentions and $1,438,015,450 of comparable value for 831 sponsors. The average sponsor received $1,732,550 value from their sponsorship involvement in the Winston Cup Series, which was an average of $50,960 per event. The top 25 sponsors received an even greater return averaging $21,285,245 worth of comparable value for the season or $626,330 per event.

Due to *Wmhinc.com*'s NASCAR involvement and FEMA partnership management clearly expects to drive over one million unique visitors through the web site every month within the first year. NASCAR's online site generates over 43 million page views by over 4.6 million unique users per month, each averaging 9 minutes per visit. FEMA has over 150,000,000 unique visitors per year on its web site.

G. Public Relations

As *Wmhinc.com* launches its services, it is extremely important to develop and implement a public relations campaign that creates rapid recognition by the target markets and others who can help the Company build its markets.

Wmhinc.com plans to establish and promote a favorable relationship with the public by developing communications with non-customers, including labor, public interest groups, government agencies, and press releases.

Wmhinc.com will also monitor and improve public opinion as well as developing publicity where possible. Wmhinc's public relations campaign will include the following:

- Building an Online Presence
- Communities, Chats, and Message Boards
- Events (online and offline)
- Networking (organization membership, leadership positions)
- Press releases (print, radio, television, online)
- Interviews (print, radio, television, chat rooms, online events)

H. Networking

Wmhinc.com plans to become a member of state and national manufactured housing associations, the Manufactured Housing Institute (www.manufacturedhousing.org), the National Manufactured Housing Congress (www.nmhcogress.org) and several industry publications.

IV. Customer Service

The customer service strategy is based on providing high quality service which means having sufficient staffers available to take calls without keeping a customer waiting. *Wmhinc.com* will emphasize through advertising and PR channels that clients will receive personalized service and customer service as needed. *Wmhinc.com* will use automation technology such as FAQ pages on the Web site, message and discussion boards, bulletin boards, an online help desk, and self-service help wherever possible.

Excellent customer service will enhance the Company's image, boost sales, lead to repeat business, and a high number of sales resulting from referrals.

V. Implementation of Marketing Strategy

A. In-House Responsibilities

Wmhinc.com will develop and execute its marketing strategy in-house. In addition to developing the marketing plan, the Company will set goals, objectives, and propositions.

B. Out-Sourced Functions

Wmhinc.com plans to contract one or more third parties to handle its Web advertising requirements. Additionally, the Company will outsource PR responsibilities to an established public relations company.

VI. Assessment of Marketing Effectiveness

Wmhinc.com, Inc. will evaluate the results of its marketing efforts on a monthly basis. At that time, based on the evaluation, decisions will be made and necessary changes will be implemented to increase marketing effectiveness. Participation in the evaluation process will be required for management and for key personnel in the marketing department.

Part III: Financial Documents
Wholesale Mobile Homes.com, Inc.

Sources and Uses of Loan Funds

Financial Projections

Financial Statement Analysis

Wholesale Mobile Homes.com, Inc.

Summary of Financial Needs
&
Dispersal of Investment Funds

Source of Funds

    I.   *Wmhinc.com* is seeking funding in the amount of $10 million for its Four-Phase Development.

    II. Provided below is a breakdown of the use of funds.

Use of Funds

USE OF FUNDS BASED ON $10 MILLION INVESTMENT

Phase I

	First Quarter of Operations	Projected Expense	% of Gross Proceeds
1)	Commissions Paid	$ 700,000.00	7.00%
2)	Website Development	$ 168,750.00	1.69%
3)	Rent, Lease, & Utilities	$ 81,420.00	0.81%
4)	Connectivity & Installation	$ 5,000.00	0.05%
5)	Executive & Administrative	$ 372,920.00	3.73%
6)	Professional, Legal, Advisory	$ 5,000.00	0.05%
7)	Advertising	$ 1,433,660.00	14.34%
8)	Equipment & Furniture	$ 79,000.00	0.79%
9)	Tech Support	$ 5,000.00	0.05%
10)	Networking Equipment	$ 350,000.00	3.50%
11)	Marketing	$ -	0.00%
12)	Working Capital	$ 175,000.00	1.75%
	Total	**$ 3,375,750.00**	**33.76%**

Phase II

	Third Quarter of Operations	Projected Expense	% of Gross Proceeds
1)	Commissions Paid	$ -	0.00%
2)	Website Development	$ 168,750.00	1.69%
3)	Rent, Lease, & Utilities	$ 81,420.00	0.81%
4)	Connectivity	$ 10,000.00	0.10%
5)	Executive & Administrative	$ 272,920.00	2.73%
6)	Professional, Legal Advisory	$ 20,000.00	0.20%
7)	Advertising	$ 1,433,660.00	14.34%
8)	Equipment and Furniture	$ -	0.00%
9)	Tech Support	$ 5,000.00	0.05%
10)	Networking Equipment	$ -	0.00%
11)	Marketing	$ 3,000.00	0.03%
12)	Working Capital	$ 175,000.00	1.75%
	Total	**$ 2,169,750.00**	**21.70%**

Phase III

	Third Quarter of Operations	Projected Expense	% of Gross Proceeds
1)	Commissions Paid	$ -	0.00%
2)	Website Development	$ 168,750.00	1.69%
3)	Rent, Lease & Utilities	$ 81,420.00	0.81%
4)	Connectivity	$ 15,000.00	0.15%
5)	Executive & Administrative	$ 272,920.00	2.73%
6)	Professional, Legal, Advisory	$ 20,000.00	0.20%
7)	Advertising	$ 1,433,660.00	14.34%
8)	Equipment & Furniture	$ -	0.00%
9)	Tech Support	$ 5,000.00	0.05%
10)	Networking Equipment	$ 150,000.00	1.50%
11)	Marketing	$ 3,000.00	0.03%
12)	Working Capital	$ 125,000.00	1.25%
	Total	**$ 2,274,750.00**	**22.75%**

Phase IV

	Fourth Quarter of Operations	Projected Expense	% of Gross Proceeds
1)	Commissions Paid	$ -	0.00%
2)	Website Development	$ 168,750.00	1.69%
3)	Rent Lease, & Utilities	$ 81,420.00	0.81%
4)	Connectivity	$ 20,000.00	0.20%
5)	Executive & Administrative	$ 272,920.00	2.73%
6)	Professional, Legal, Advisory	$ 20,000.00	0.20%
7)	Advertising	$ 1,433,660.00	14.34%
8)	Equipment & Furniture	$ -	0.00%
9)	Tech Support	$ 5,000.00	0.05%
10)	Network Equipment	$ -	0.00%
11)	Marketing	$ 3,000.00	0.03%
12)	Working Capital	$ 175,000.00	1.75%
	Total	**$ 2,179,750.00**	**21.80%**
	Gross Maximum Proceeds	**$ 10,000,000.00**	**100.00%**

ASSUMPTIONS FOR FINANCIAL PROJECTIONS

A summary of the significant accounting policies applied in the preparation of the accompanying projected financial statements. Enclosed, are four-year financial projections of *Wmhinc.com*. Operations, derived from stated projections beginning January 2009.

INITIAL FUNDING

The Company is seeking funding in the amount of $10,000,000 from venture capital sources.

PRE-OPERATIONAL EXPENSES / USE OF FUNDS

- Principal Office Development $ 602,480   (Tech Hardware/Software, Communication, Support, Office Furniture, Supplies…)

- Initial Promotional Budget $6,700,000   (NASCAR, Internet Promo, Print & Outdoor)

- Working Capital $ 725,840   (Licensing, Vehicle & Equip Lease, Product Development, R&D, Insurance)

- Cost of Offering $ 200,000

- Offering Commission $1,400,000

INCOME / SALES

72% to 75% of the total revenue is generated by business-to-business monthly fee transactions (B2B technology, government, developers, advertising, garages, service, motorsports, online auctions, *Wmhinc.com* branded homes). 25% to 28% of total revenues are generated by business-to-consumer monthly transactions (new home sales, bank-owned home sales, garages, parts/services, net listings of customer home sales).

The Company currently has working agreements for approximately 4,000 homes with several developers for an average of $2,000 to $5,000 per house. Today manufactured homes make up over 25% of new homes in the United States. Sales of new manufactured homes exceeded $16 billion in 2007, an increase of 400% in the last ten years. With new design elements and customizable options, manufactured homes have begun to cross over into the mainstream.

- In 2007, the industry shipped 348,671 homes from 323 manufacturing facilities.

- The average sales price of a manufactured home was $43,600 in 2007. Single-section homes average $31,800, while multi-section homes average $50,200.

- Over 19 million people (about 8% of the U.S. population live full-time in over 8 million manufactured homes).

Wmhinc.com Financial Assumptions – page 2

Due to *Wmhinc.com*'s NASCAR involvement and FEMA partnership management clearly expects to drive over one million unique visitors through the web site every month within the first year. NASCAR's online site generates over 43 million page views by over 4.6 million unique users per month, each averaging 9 minutes per visit. FEMA has over 150,000,000 unique visitors per year on its web site.

NOTES

Four-Year Cash Flow Projections

- **Venture Capital** – The Company's principals are injecting $50,000 into business. In order to fund pre-operational expenses, the Company is seeking venture capital in the amount of $10,000,000.

- **Cash Disbursements** – Expenditures of cash will be determined by the current financial position of the Company. Marketing and Product Development will include focus groups, product & campaign development. Research & Development will consist of market analysis of viable market opportunities through its hub of web-based products and services. The company will also commit monthly investments in its corporate community programs in markets that we serve and have a strong presence.

Four-Year Income Projections

- **The annual growth rate** is justified by the Company's discipline and ability to establish a web-based hub of manufactured home resources, long-term strategic alliances, and brand equity in viable markets.

- **Expenses** – Expenses are expected to increase as the Company intensifies its marketing and advertising campaigns. Furthermore, expenses are expected to increase as the Company hires additional staff. The Company plans to hire 5 department managers at an average salary of $40,000 per year each and 10 hourly employees at an average wage rate that totals $16,800 per year. Executive salaries will be as follows:

Paul S Jarolimek II	President/CEO	$ 52,500
Michael Gage	CTO	$ 52,500
MaryLou Jarolimek	CFO	$ 52,500
Stephen Massie	EVP Warranty/Service	$ 52,500
Jim Stephens	EVP Sales	$ 52,500
Suzanne Jarolimek	EVP Customer Service	$ 52,500
Larry Queen	VP Technology - Graphics	$ 52,500
Leon Jarolimek	VP Customer Service/Warranty	$ 52,500

- **Income Tax Rate** – 19% estimated federal tax; 9% estimated state tax, and 3% estimated local tax.

Pro Forma Cash Flow Statement
Page 1 (January thru June)

Wholesale Mobile Homes.com, Inc.

For the Year 2009

	Jan	Feb	Mar	Apr	May	Jun
BEGINNING CASH BALANCE	422,040	386,590	584,289	777,245	1,898,144	2,373,465
CASH RECEIPTS						
A. Sales/Revenues B2B	**604,681**	**662,229**	**691,834**	**740,481**	**772,063**	**875,799**
1. B2B Technology	80,624	88,297	92,245	98,731	102,942	116,773
2. B2B Government	65,306	71,521	74,718	79,972	83,383	94,586
3. B2B Developers	177,373	194,254	202,938	217,208	226,472	256,901
4. B2B Advertisers	161,248	176,594	184,489	197,462	205,883	233,546
5. B2B Garages	24,187	26,489	27,673	29,619	30,883	35,032
6. B2B Service	6,450	7,064	7,380	7,898	8,235	9,342
7. B2B Motorsports	9,675	10,596	11,069	11,848	12,353	14,013
8. B2B Online Auctions	16,125	17,659	18,449	19,746	20,588	23,355
9. B2B Man. *Wmhinc.com*	63,693	69,755	72,873	77,997	81,324	92,251
B. Sales/Revenues B2C	**201,561**	**220,743**	**230,611**	**246,827**	**257,356**	**291,933**
1. B2C New Home	72,562	79,467	83,020	88,858	92,648	105,096
2. B2C Bank Owned Home Sale	88,687	97,127	101,469	108,604	113,236	128,450
3. B2C Garages	24,187	26,489	27,673	29,619	30,883	35,032
4. B2C Parts/Service	7,256	7,947	8,302	8,886	9,265	10,510
5. B2C "Net Listings"	8,869	9,713	10,147	10,860	11,324	12,845
TOTAL CASH AVAILABLE	**1,228,282**	**1,490,305**	**1,737,345**	**2,011,380**	**3,184,919**	**3,833,130**
CASH PAYMENTS						
A. Cost of goods to be sold						
1. (Currently no COG)	0	0	0	0	0	0
Total Cost of Goods	**0**	**0**	**0**	**0**	**0**	**0**
B. Variable (Selling) Expenses						
1. Marketing and Advertising	102,847	113,594	119,143	128,359	134,118	143,482
2. Communications Support	4,200	4,500	4,500	4,750	4,750	4,500
3. Community Reinvestments	41,925	45,914	47,967	51,340	53,530	60,722
4. Research and Development	11,265	16,093	22,990	32,843	46,918	67,026
5. Technical Support	14,000	14,200	14,250	14,250	14,562	14,500
6. Travel and Entertainment	28,000	28,000	29,500	30,000	30,000	30,000
7. Vehicle/Equipment Leases	2,000	2,250	1,875	2,100	1,975	2,000
Total Variable Expenses	**204,237**	**224,551**	**240,225**	**263,642**	**285,853**	**322,230**
C. Fixed (Administrative) Expenses						
1. Company Benefits/Insurance	8,500	8,500	9,000	9,000	9,000	10,500
2. Executive Salaries	72,083	72,083	72,083	72,083	72,083	72,083
3. Facility Expense	3,640	3,640	3,640	3,640	3,640	3,640
4. General Office Expenses	2,000	2,050	2,350	2,010	1,989	2,100
5. Insurance and Licensing	2,000	2,000	2,000	2,000	2,000	2,000
6. Labor/Wages	14,056	14,056	14,056	14,056	14,056	14,056
7. Legal	1,000	0	0	0	0	256
8. Maintenance/Repairs	500	500	530	600	520	550
9. Memberships & Subscriptions	200	200	200	200	200	200
10. Non-Income Taxes	9,768	10,012	10,364	10,779	11,085	11,201
11. Utilities	900	900	900	900	1,200	1,200
12. Misc. Fixed Expense	1,250	1,250	1,250	1,250	1,250	1,250
Total Fixed Expenses	**115,897**	**115,191**	**116,373**	**116,518**	**117,023**	**119,036**
D. Interest Expense	0	0	0	0	0	0
E. Federal Income Tax	188,648	197,553	210,945	225,379	237,658	249,985
F. State and Other Taxes	82,975	95,000	106,599	119,251	137,654	158,954
G. Long-term asset payments	0	0	0	0	0	0
H. Marketable Investments	161,248	176,594	184,489	197,462	205,883	233,546
I. Notes Payable to Investors	88,687	97,127	101,469	108,604	113,236	128,450
TOTAL CASH PAID OUT	**841,692**	**906,016**	**960,100**	**1,030,856**	**811,454**	**1,212,201**
CASH BALANCE/DEFICIENCY	386,590	584,289	777,245	1,898,144	2,373,465	2,620,929
LOANS TO BE RECEIVED	0	0	0	0	0	0
EQUITY DEPOSITS	0	0	0	0	0	0
ENDING CASH BALANCE	**386,590**	**584,289**	**777,245**	**1,898,144**	**2,373,465**	**2,620,929**

Note:				
Beginning Cash Balance	50,000	**Pre-operational Expenses**	
Venture Capital	10,000,000	Principal Office Development	602,480
Total Cash Available	**$10,050,000**	Initial Promotional Budget	6,700,000
		Working Capital	725,480
Less Pre-operational Expenses (right)	9,627,960	Cost of Offering	200,000
		Offering Commission	1,400,000
Gross Cash Balance	**$422,040**	**Total Pre-operational Expenses**	**$9,627,96**

Pro Forma Cash Flow Statement
Page 2 (July thru December + 6 & 12-month Totals)

6-MONTH TOTALS	Jul	Aug	Sep	Oct	Nov	Dec	12-MONTH TOTALS
422,040	2,620,929	2,937,063	3,335,980	3,755,714	4,406,160	5,825,008	422,040
4,347,087	976,577	1,133,671	1,239,890	1,598,372	1,688,166	1,806,350	12,790,113
579,612	130,128	151,147	165,319	213,116	225,089	240,847	1,705,258
469,486	105,403	122,429	133,908	172,624	182,322	195,086	1,381,258
1,275,146	286,901	332,523	363,701	468,856	495,195	529,863	3,752,185
1,159,222	260,255	302,293	330,637	426,233	450,177	481,693	3,410,510
173,883	39,038	45,344	49,596	63,935	67,527	72,254	511,577
46,369	10,410	12,092	13,225	17,049	18,007	19,268	136,420
69,554	15,615	18,138	19,838	25,574	27,011	28,902	204,632
115,922	26,026	30,299	33,064	42,623	45,018	48,169	341,121
457,893	102,801	119,406	130,602	168,362	177,820	190,268	1,347,152
1,449,031	325,318	377,866	413,298	532,791	564,456	763,202	4,425,962
521,651	117,115	136,032	148,787	191,805	202,580	216,762	1,534,732
637,573	143,140	166,261	181,851	234,428	247,598	264,931	1,875,782
173,883	39,038	45,344	49,596	63,935	67,527	72,254	511,577
52,166	11,711	13,603	14,879	19,180	20,258	21,676	153,473
63,758	14,314	16,626	18,185	23,443	26,493	187,579	350,398
6,218,158	4,248,142	4,826,466	5,402,466	6,419,668	7,223,238	9,157,762	17,638,115
0	0	0	0	0	0	0	0
0	0	0	0	0	0	0	0
741,543	142,178	159,605	167,446	252,396	285,949	297,191	2,046,308
27,200	4,396	4,350	4,350	4,200	4,300	4,500	53,296
301,398	67,666	78,596	85,966	110,821	117,046	125,240	886,733
197,135	95,751	136,787	195,410	279,157	310,175	344,639	1,559,054
85,762	14,000	13,500	13,500	13,500	15,000	14,500	169,762
175,500	24,551	25,000	25,000	25,000	26,000	40,000	341,051
12,200	2,400	2,500	1,500	1,700	2,100	2,500	24,900
1,540,738	350,942	420,338	493,172	686,774	760,570	828,570	5,081,104
54,500	10,500	10,000	9,400	8,000	9,000	9,000	110,400
432,498	72,083	72,083	72,083	72,083	72,083	72,083	864,996
21,840	3,640	3,640	3,640	3,640	3,640	3,640	43,680
12,499	2,700	2,500	1,830	2,310	2,000	2,100	25,939
12,000	2,000	2,000	2,000	2,000	2,000	2,000	24,000
84,336	14,056	14,056	14,056	14,056	14,056	14,056	168,672
1,256	1,000	0	0	0	0	2,000	4,256
3,200	600	600	627	675	600	600	6,902
1,200	264	263	263	263	263	263	2,779
63,209	11,329	11,435	11,754	12,066	12,261	12,322	134,376
6,000	1,200	1,200	971	900	900	900	12,071
7,500	1,257	1,257	1,267	1,267	1,267	1,267	15,082
700,038	120,629	119,034	117,891	117,260	118,070	120,231	1,413,153
0	0	0	0	0	0	0	0
1,310,168	265,481	296,862	324,644	341,552	357,708	272,501	3,168,916
700,433	170,632	185,698	198,557	207,261	224,677	239,855	1,927,113
0	0	0	0	0	0	0	0
1,159,222	260,255	302,293	330,637	426,233	450,177	481,693	3,410,510
637,573	143,140	166,261	181,851	234,428	247,598	264,931	1,875,782
6,048,172	1,311,079	1,490,486	1,646,752	2,013,508	1,398,230	2,207,781	16,876,578
169,986	2,937,063	3,335,980	3,755,714	4,406,160	5,825,008	6,949,981	761,537
0	0	0	0	0	0	0	0
0	0	0	0	0	0	0	0
169,986	2,937,063	3,335,980	3,755,714	4,406,160	5,825,008	6,949,981	761,537

Three-Year Income Projection

Wholesale Mobile Homes.com, Inc.

Percentages = % of Sales/Revenues

Updated: Nov. 2008

	Year 1: 2009		Year 2: 2010		Year 3: 3011		Total: 3 Years	
	AMOUNT	%	AMOUNT	%	AMOUNT	%	AMOUNT	%
INCOME								
1. SALES/REVENUES (Total)	17,216,075	100.00%	77,631,985	100.00%	136,623,886	100.00%	231,471,946	100.00%
a. B2B Technology	1,705,258	9.91%	7,842,148	10.10%	13,673,847	10.01%	23,221,253	10.03%
b. B2B Government	1,381,258	8.02%	6,330,184	8.15%	11,070,952	8.10%	18,782,394	8.11%
c. B2B Developers	3,752,185	21.79%	17,143,833	22.08%	28,695,395	21.00%	49,591,413	21.42%
d. B2B Advertisers	3,410,510	19.81%	15,551,942	20.03%	27,325,714	20.00%	46,288,166	20.00%
e. B2B Garages	511,577	2.97%	2,330,164	3.00%	4,098,726	3.00%	6,940,467	3.00%
f. B2B Service	136,420	0.79%	621,149	0.80%	1,092,991	0.80%	1,850,560	0.80%
g. B2B Motorsports	204,632	1.19%	931,623	1.20%	1,639,487	1.20%	2,775,742	1.20%
h. B2B Online Auctions	341,121	1.98%	1,552,657	2.00%	2,732,478	2.00%	4,626,256	2.00%
i. B2B Man. *Wmhinc.com* Homes	1,347,152	7.82%	5,532,123	7.13%	9,725,243	7.12%	16,604,518	7.17%
Total B2B Sales	12,790,113	74.29%	57,835,823	74.50%	100,054,833	73.23%	170,680,769	73.74%
j. B2C New Home	1,534,732	8.91%	7,375,043	9.50%	13,088,218	9.58%	21,997,993	9.50%
k. B2C Bank Owned Home Sale	1,875,782	10.90%	8,539,519	11.00%	15,805,450	11.57%	26,220,751	11.33%
l. B2C Garages	511,577	2.97%	2,328,960	3.00%	4,800,686	3.51%	7,641,223	3.30%
m. B2C Parts/Service	153,473	0.89%	698,688	0.90%	1,301,162	0.95%	2,153,323	0.93%
n. B2C "Net Listings"	350,398	2.04%	853,952	1.10%	1,573,537	1.15%	2,777,887	1.20%
Total B2C Sales	4,425,962	25.71%	19,796,162	25.50%	36,569,053	26.77%	60,791,177	26.26%
2. COST OF GOODS SOLD	0	0.00%	0	0.00%	0	0.00%	0	0.00%
3. GROSS PROFIT ON SALES (1-2)	17,216,075	100.00%	77,631,985	100.00%	136,623,886	100.00%	231,471,946	100.00%
EXPENSES								
1. VARIABLE (Selling) (a thru g)	5,081,104	29.51%	18,072,884	23.28%	34,871,019	25.52%	58,025,007	25.07%
a. Marketing and Advertising	2,046,308	11.89%	12,456,948	16.05%	23,845,694	17.45%	38,348,950	16.57%
b. Communications Support	53,296	0.31%	264,894	0.34%	275,946	0.20%	594,136	0.26%
c. Community Reinvestments	886,733	5.15%	1,250,000	1.61%	2,000,000	1.46%	4,136,733	1.79%
d. Research and Development	1,559,054	9.06%	2,398,512	3.09%	5,200,000	3.81%	9,157,566	3.96%
e. Technical Support	169,762	0.99%	473,955	0.61%	521,658	0.38%	1,165,375	0.50%
f. Travel and Entertainment	341,051	1.98%	492,753	0.63%	1,732,856	1.27%	2,566,660	1.11%
g. Vehicle/Equipment Leases	24,900	0.14%	735,822	0.95%	1,294,865	0.95%	2,055,587	0.89%
2. FIXED (Administrative) (a thru m)	1,427,176	8.29%	6,449,120	8.31%	11,107,191	8.13%	18,983,487	8.20%
a. Company Benefits/Insurance	110,400	0.64%	834,426	1.07%	1,859,465	1.36%	2,804,291	1.21%
b. Executive Salaries	864,996	5.02%	1,648,651	2.12%	2,354,986	1.72%	4,868,633	2.10%
c. Facility Expense	43,680	0.25%	1,469,512	1.89%	3,654,895	2.68%	5,168,087	2.23%
d. General Office Expenses	25,939	0.15%	192,645	0.25%	272,698	0.20%	491,282	0.21%
e. Insurance and Licensing	24,000	0.14%	359,485	0.46%	426,595	0.31%	810,080	0.35%
f. Labor/Wages	168,672	0.98%	495,365	0.64%	921,589	0.67%	1,585,626	0.69%
g. Legal	4,256	0.02%	50,000	0.06%	70,000	0.05%	124,256	0.05%
h. Maintenance/Repairs	6,902	0.04%	64,974	0.08%	75,913	0.06%	147,789	0.06%
i. Memberships & Subscriptions	2,779	0.02%	5,139	0.01%	7,968	0.01%	15,886	0.01%
j. Non-Income Taxes	134,376	0.78%	578,624	0.75%	716,945	0.52%	1,429,945	0.62%
k. Utilities	12,071	0.07%	122,698	0.16%	254,658	0.19%	389,427	0.17%
l. Depreciation	14,023	0.08%	42,978	0.06%	64,895	0.05%	121,896	0.05%
m. Misc. Fixed Expense	15,082	0.09%	584,623	0.75%	426,584	0.31%	1,026,289	0.44%
TOTAL OPERATING EXPENSE (1+2)	6,508,280	37.80%	19,500,060	25.12%	45,978,210	33.65%	77,008,494	33.27%
NET INCOME OPERATIONS (GP-Exp)	10,707,795	62.20%	58,131,925	74.88%	90,645,676	66.35%	154,463,452	66.73%
OTHER INCOME (Interest Income)	0	0.00%	0	0.00%	0	0.00%	0	0.00%
OTHER EXPENSE (Interest Expense)	0	0.00%	0	0.00%	0	0.00%	0	0.00%
NET PROFIT (LOSS) BEFORE TAXES	10,707,795	62.20%	58,131,925	74.88%	90,645,676	66.35%	154,463,452	66.73%
TAXES 1. Federal, S-Employment	3,268,916	18.99%	16,895,236	21.76%	28,694,855	21.00%	48,859,007	21.11%
2. State	1,456,855	8.46%	4,956,265	6.38%	8,956,212	6.56%	15,369,332	6.64%
3. Local	470,258	2.73%	851,896	1.10%	1,318,623	0.97%	2,640,777	1.14%
NET PROFIT (LOSS) AFTER TAXES	5,511,766	32.02%	35,428,528	45.64%	51,675,986	37.82%	87,594,336	37.84%

26

Projected Balance Sheet

Business Name:

Wholesale Mobile Homes.com, Inc.

Date of Projection: November 2008

Date Projected for: December 31, 2009

ASSETS

		% of Assets
Current Assets		
Cash	$ 6,949,981	35.40%
Petty Cash	$ 0	0.00%
Accounts Receivable	$ 7,054,432	35.93%
Inventory	$ 0	0.00%
Marketable Investments	$ 1,875,578	9.55%
Long Term Investments	$ 0	0.00%
Fixed Assets		
Land (valued at cost)	$ 0	0.00%
Buildings	$ 0	0.00%
1. Cost 0		
2. Less Acc. 0		
Improvements	$ 0	0.00%
1. Cost 0		
2. Less Acc. 0		
Equipment	$ 485,977	2.48%
1. Cost 500,000		
2. Less Acc. 14,023		
Furniture	$ 0	0.00%
1. Cost 0		
2. Less Acc. 0		
Autos/Vehicles	$ 0	0.00%
1. Cost 0		
2. Less Acc. 0		
Other Assets		
1. Non-Depreciable Assets	$ 3,265,874	16.64%
2.	$ 0	0.00%
TOTAL ASSETS	**$ 19,631,842**	**100.00%**

LIABILITIES

		% of Liabilities
Current Liabilities		
Accounts Payable	$ 1,166,475	14.16%
Notes Payable	$ 0	0.00%
Interest Payable	$ 0	0.00%
Tax Accruals		
Federal Income Tax	$ 3,268,916	39.68%
State Income Tax	$ 1,456,855	17.68%
Local Income Tax	$ 470,258	5.71%
Sales Tax Accrual	$ 0	0.00%
Property Tax	$ 0	0.00%
Payroll Accrual	$ 0	0.00%
Long Term Liabilities		
Notes Payable to Investors	$ 1,875,782	22.77%
Notes Payable, Others	$ 0	0.00%
TOTAL LIABILITIES	**$ 8,238,286**	**100.00%**

NET WORTH

		% of Net Worth
Corporation		
Capital Stock	$ 10,500,000	92.16%
Surplus Paid In	$ 0	0.00%
Retained Earnings	$ 893,556	7.84%
TOTAL NET WORTH	**$ 11,393,556**	**100.00%**

Assets + Liabilities = Net Worth
and
Liabilities + Equity = Total Assets

Break-Even Analysis

Wholesale Mobile Homes.com, Inc.

Date of Analysis: November 2008

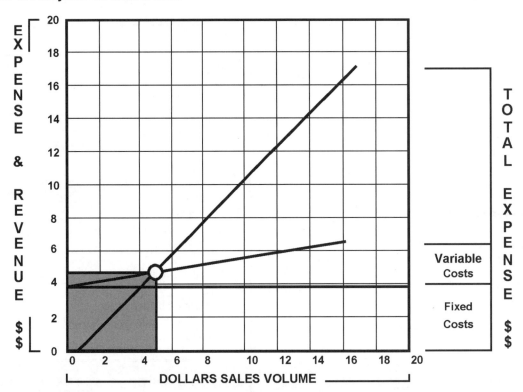

NOTE: *Figures shown in one (1) millions of dollars (Ex: 2 = $ 2,000,000)*

B-E POINT (SALES) = Fixed costs + [(Variable Costs/Est. Revenues) X Sales]

B-E Point (Sales) = $ 3,872,963 + [($ 2,635,317 / $ 17,052,654) X Sales]

Wholesale Mobile Homes.com, Inc.
Break-Even Point Calculation

FC (Fixed Costs) = (Administrative Expenses + Interest)	$	**3,872,963**
VC (Variable Costs) = (Cost of Goods + Selling Expenses)	$	**2,635,317**
R (Est. Revenues) = (Income from sale of products and services)	$	**17,052,564**
Break-Even Point =	$	**4,580,899**

Financial Statement Analysis Summary

This page is a summary of 2009 projected financial statement analysis information as determined by ratio table calculations (supporting docs) and measured against current industry standards.

		2009 PROJECTED	**INDUSTRY STANDARD**
1.	Net Working Capital	$9,517,487	$0 + or -
2.	Current Ratio	2.50	1.60 + or -
3.	Quick Ratio	2.5	0.4 + or -
4.	Gross Profit Margin*	100.00%	22.70%
5.	Operating Profit Margin*	62.20%	2.60%
	* See explanation below (Notes)		
6.	Net Profit Margin	32.00%	0.0%
7.	Debt to Assets	41.96%	0.0%
8.	Debt to Equity	72.31%	12.5:1 +
9.	ROI (Return on Investment)	28.08%	0.0% +

10. Vertical Income Statement Analysis *

	2009 PROJECTED	**INDUSTRY STANDARD**
Sales/Revenues	100.00%	
Cost of Goods	0.0%	0.0% + or -
Gross Profit	100.00%	22.70% + or -
Operating Expense	37.80%	20.30% + or -
Net Income Operations	62.20%	2.40% + or -
Interest Income	0.0%	N/A
Interest Expense	0.00%	Variable
Net Profit (Pre-Tax)	62.20%	2.60% + or -

* All items stated as % of Total Revenues

11. Vertical Balance Sheet Analysis *

	2009 PROJECTED	**INDUSTRY STANDARD**
Current Assets	80.90%	77.40%
Inventory	0.0%	61.50%
Total Assets	100.00%	100.00%
Current Liabilities	32.40%	62.30% + or -
Total Liabilities	42.00%	
Net Worth	58.00%	26.50% + or -
Total Liabilities + Net Worth	100.0%	

* All Asset items stated as % of Total Assets;
Liability & Net Worth items stated as % of Total Liabilities + Net Worth

Notes:

Wholesale Mobile Homes.com, Inc. is entering a rapidly growing marketplace and has developed a business model that will keep operating expenses at a minimum. By outsourcing activities related to the development of mobile homes, the Company will initially have zero cost of goods sold. Due to the nature of business activities, Management does not anticipate carrying inventory. The operating expenses are higher than industry standards in year 1 because of the high costs associated with entry into the marketplace. With zero cost of goods sold, *Wmhinc.com* has higher profit margins than RMA figures. Financial projections show that, based on an investment of $10 million, *Wmhinc.com* will maintain good cash flow, increase profitability, and provide a timely and healthy return for investors.

SUPPORTING DOCUMENTS

✓ Insurance Update Form

* Note: *For purposes of brevity, we have chosen to include only one of the supporting documents from Wholesale Mobile Homes.com, Inc.'s business plan.*

Insurance Update Form
Wholesale Mobile Homes.com, Inc.

Updated as of November 2008

Company	Contact Person	Coverage	Cost Per Year
1. HealthWest Insurance 2526 St. John's Street Las Vegas, NV 89247	James Boyd (509) 523-9568	Medical and Other Benefits	$ 110,400
2. The Insurance Agency 16432 Midway Street Las Vegas, NV 89147	Michael Smith (509) 795-7556	Business Liability	$ 4,800
3. The Insurance Agency (Address: see above)	Michael Smith (509) 795-7556	Industry Specific Liability	$ 8,100
4. The Insurance Agency (Address: see above)	Michael Smith (509) 795-7556	Workers Compensation	$ 6,100
5. The Insurance Agency (Address: see above)	Michael Smith (509) 795-7556	Key-man Coverage	$ 3,000
6. Auto Insurance Brokers 4589 Marsh Lane Las Vegas, NV 89146	Gene Hastings (509) 465-1235	Auto - Vehicle 1	$ 1,000
7. Auto Insurance Brokers (Address: see above)	Gene Hastings (509) 465-1235	Auto - Vehicle 2	$ 1,000
	1. Total Annual Insurance Cost		$ 134,400
	2. Average Monthly Insurance Cost		$ 11,200

KARMA JAZZ CAFÉ

Business Plan

The business plan presented in Appendix IV is an actual business plan developed for Karma Jazz Café using *Anatomy of a Business Plan* and its software companion, **AUTOMATE YOUR BUSINESS PLAN**.

KARMA JAZZ CAFÉ Scenario

This business was established by DeShea Cook, a veteran of the restaurant industry with over 12 years experience. She developed the concept for Karma Jazz Café in response to emerging trends and the need for unique dining concepts with an ethnic flavor. DeShea moved forward by opening a location in Atlanta, GA. Based on the success of that location, she then set out on a mission to open up a second location in Fort Worth, TX. This business plan was developed for the setup of the new location.

Finally, a Business Plan for a Restaurant

I have been asked many times whether or not we have a business plan for a restaurant. Because of DeShea, we now have this fine example. Although restaurant businesses vary greatly regarding their business visions, the types of food and beverages they specialize in, the services they offer, the customers they cater to, and the business procedures they follow, this plan should help to give you a jump start when it comes to planning for your own business.

A special thank you to DeShea Cook for her generosity and her willingness to share her business plan with our readers and software users. Business plans take lots of time to develop and they are considered to be extremely personal and proprietary. It is not often that I find business owners who are willing to put their companies' business plans in print for the benefit of other people who are looking for information and guidance during the writing process. DeShea's sharing of her Karma Jazz Café business plan with my readers is a great example of entrepreneurs helping each other.

I would also like to note that Ndaba Mdhlongwa, the same business plan specialist that wrote the *Wholesale Mobile Home, Inc.* business plan (Appendix III), was instrumental in working with DeShea Cook on the development of the plan for the Atlanta location and on the translation of that plan into a new plan for the Fort Worth location. It is most important that business owners actively participate in the writing of their business plans. However, it is not uncommon to hire the services of a professional to work with them at various stages in the process to look for strengths and weaknesses and to help them through portions of the plans in which they need to work out problems. The combined effort can prove to be very effective.

Of Special Note in This Plan

Although this is a business plan for a second Karma Jazz Café based on the same concept as the first one in Atlanta, this plan is treated as one for a start-up business. Many things would be the same. However, since the two locations are different, it was especially important to conduct adequate research on the demographics and psychographics for the Fort Worth, Texas target market. It also follows that a current competitive analysis was needed for the new area. Although the two restaurants are branded the same and have the same owner, each has its own identifying factors.

I would also like to note, that the financial projections in the current plan have been scaled down to reflect a more conservative scenario. One of the most common errors in making financial projections is the overstating of revenues and the understating of expenses. In this case, historical financial statement analysis from the initial location has helped the owner to make more realistic projections for the new location.

When you develop and write your own plan, it will help you to see how each of the corresponding sections was handled in the Karma Jazz Café business plan. However, remember that your own company will be unique. The business planning process is the same, but your plan will have to match your vision and your financial and marketing plans will have to be based on your own area and target market.

> *Warning!* *This plan is to be examined for the handling of content only. It has been included in Anatomy of a Business Plan because it is a sound business plan for a restaurant that was launched and successfully operating in Atlanta, Georgia. There is no judgment inferred as to appropriateness or financial potential for lenders or investors. Do not use it as a source of research for your own company.*

 Important. *Do not try to contact DeShea Cook or any of the other people mentioned in this business plan. It would not be appropriate.*

Karma Jazz Café

"Jazz is Alive and Well"

224 Goldeneye Lane

Fort Worth, TX76120

817-939-9152

Website: www.karmajazzcafe.com

Email: writedeshea@hotmail.com

Contact: DeShea Cook

Prepared January 2014

Table of Contents

Executive Summary

Karma Jazz Café was established by DeShea Cook, a veteran of the restaurant industry with over 12 years experience. She has also assembled a highly capable management team along with an advisory board consisting of individuals with over 25 years experience in restaurant and nightclub ownership.

DeShea Cook established the concept for Karma Jazz Café in 2012, this in response to emerging trends and the need for unique dining concepts with an ethnic flavor. In 2013, she moved forward by opening a location in Atlanta, GA. Based on the success of that location, DeShea Cook is on a mission to open up a second location in Fort Worth, TX. This business plan has been developed for the setup of the new location.

Located in Sundance Square, in the heart of downtown Fort Worth, TX, Karma Jazz Café will be an enchanting full-service restaurant offering the finest Creole style cuisine. Karma Jazz Café will also provide customers with a unique dining experience, featuring live smooth jazz on Thursday, Friday, Saturday, and Sunday. Karma Jazz Café will be the only live jazz venue in the very lucrative tourist district of Fort Worth.

The 200 capacity Karma Jazz Café will have cozy lounge areas and intimate table settings with direct view of the stage area. Patio dining will allow guests to dine with enjoying the elements. The menu will be a collaborative effort between the company owner and the Head Chef. This approach will be necessary in order to combine the owners' many years of experience in Creole cuisine with new and creative culinary techniques. The result will be a selection of dishes that will appeal to the sophisticated consumer while maintaining exceptional dining value.

Market Opportunity

According to the National Restaurant Association, the U.S. restaurant industry with 945,000 restaurant locations is expected to generate $558 billion in 2014. In Texas, the National Restaurant Association estimates that the restaurant industry hit sales of $32 billion in 2013.

Restaurant operators are increasingly optimistic about the direction of the restaurant industry and the overall economy, according to the latest results of the National Restaurant Association's Restaurant Performance Index. During the next several months, restaurant operators are expecting positive trends in terms of sales, staffing levels, capital expenditures, as well as the overall economy[1]. Karma Jazz Café will develop a captivating, friendly atmosphere, provide outstanding service and offer an extensive selection of quality Creole food. These key elements will add up to a highly successful venture that will yield high returns.

---

[1] National Restaurant Association

Restaurant operators remain solidly optimistic about sales growth in their establishments. Sixty-one percent of restaurant operators expect to have higher sales in six months (compared to the same period in the previous year), while only 6 percent of operators expect their sales volume in six months to be lower than it was during the same period in the previous year. Restaurant operators are also more confident in the direction of the overall economy. Fifty-five percent of restaurant operators expect economic conditions in six months to be better than they are now – up from 52 percent last month and the strongest outlook in eight months[2]. Karma Jazz Café will take advantage of the positive outlook being portrayed by existing restaurant operators to develop a dynamic restaurant that will grow to become the establishment of choice for fine dining and live jazz experiences. To accomplish this goal, the company will leverage the experience of its highly experienced management team and the support of its advisory board.

Management

DeShea Cook brings several years of experience in various entertainment avenues and over five years of finance management along with over a decade of exceptional customer service training. She is no stranger to business ownership. For the past three years, she has owned and operated a successful entertainment company that promotes local events with entertainers. DeShea Cook worked in various positions in restaurants and nightclubs that her stepfather has owned and/or managed. These positions included, but are not limited to; waitstaff, hostess, inventory control, booking acts for events, etc. DeShea Cook currently serves as Consumer Finance Manager for New Beginnings, a company that takes care of mentally challenged adults and children.

DeShea Cook attended Collin County Community College where she studied Telecommunication Management and Fine Art. After a move to Atlanta, she studied real estate and worked for Harry Norman Realtors and Coldwell Banker Residential under their top Sales Representative. While at Harry Norman Realtors, she worked on several major condominium projects and grossed over $2 million in sales. During that time, she continued to work in the entertainment industry under her stepfather's guidance and assisted with celebrity parties and events.

Raymond Jones is an expert in restaurant and bar industry management. With over 20 years of experience in the restaurant and bar industry, as an owner and professional consultant, Mr. Jones has handled all areas of operations including proper food handling and preparation, safety procedures, cleanliness, temperature control, equipment controls and maintenance. He has consulted for major hotel and restaurant chains on management, health, and safety issues. Raymond Jones has also prepared training manuals and instructed staff on comprehensive restaurant policies and procedures. In his public entity consulting work, Raymond Jones was contracted to train restaurant personnel on behalf of the City of Dallas, regarding food preparation, safety procedures, hygiene, equipment use, and maintenance issues. In private entity work, he has provided consulting services and had direct employment in restaurant management positions for various corporations at numerous facilities nationwide.

---

[2] National Restaurant Association

Advisor

Steve Cook, Jr. Steve Cook is a highly respected business professional. In 2011, he retired from TXU Energy after 36 years of service. By the time he retired, he had risen to the rank of Regional Manager. In his position as Regional Manager, he was responsible for planning, executing and directing the daily functions and operations of the Waco, Texas facility. Upon his retirement, he became President of CO-GILL Financial Services, LLC dba Home Purchase Center. The Home Purchase Center is committed to helping its clients find the right home mortgage product for their needs. Steve Cook is a former Board Member for CareLinc in Waco, TX. He is affiliated with several business organizations including the Irving Black Arts Council (Irving, TX), H.O.T. Minority Business Alliance (Waco, TX), Greater Waco Chamber of Commerce, Waco Hispanic Chamber of Commerce, and Waco Cultural Arts Fest.

Competitors

The Sundance Square is home to a host of restaurants. It has been noted that one can dine there every day of the week and never eat at the same restaurant twice. While other restaurant establishments exist, their focus is not on Creole cuisine. The only establishment that offers Creole food, Razzoo's, is more of a low end restaurant. They also offer a mix of American food. None of the restaurants in the Sundance Square currently offers live jazz music.

Karma Jazz Café's Competitive Advantages

Karma Jazz Café will provide the perfect mix of premium quality food and exciting jazz entertainment. It will be the only restaurant offering live jazz music. Only one other restaurant in Sundance Square, Razzoo's, offers Creole style dishes. However, Karma Jazz Café will include many more modern dining elements than Razzoo's and the other restaurants in the area as well as superior customer service.

Management experience is a key competitive advantage for Karma Jazz Café. The owner, DeShea Cook, has been working in the restaurant industry for over 12 years in various positions. Three of the Company's principal investors have successfully started and operated their own businesses for over 30 years. A member of the advisory team have established and operated several successful restaurants and night clubs for over 25 years.

A key competitive advantage will be location. Karma Jazz Café will be located in the Tower Building in the Sundance Square. While this tourist district receives heavy traffic during the day, traffic is especially heavier on weekends. Evenings and weekends, Sundance Square takes on a whole new flavor. The area has a very large concentration of daytime workers that will not travel very far for lunch. Karma Jazz Café also has a strong opportunity to capture these guests for happy hour activities after work.

Capital Requirements

Karma Jazz Café has secured owner and investor funding in the amount of $200,000 for the development of its Fort Worth restaurant location.

Sources of Funds

- Owners $100,000
- Investors $100,000
  Total Funding   **$200,000**

Breakdown of Use of Funds

Pre-Operational Expenditures

- Improvements/Renovations $50,000
- Equipment $30,000
- Furniture & Fixtures $40,000
- Restaurant/Business Supplies $10,000
- Inventory $15,000
- Marketing & Advertising $20,000
  Total (Pre-Operational Use of Funds)   **$165,000**

Operational Funds

- Working capital   **$35,000**

  Note. *The working capital will be the beginning cash balance when the restaurant begins operations.*

Total Funding Use   **$200,000**

Financial Projections

Projected Three-Year Income Statement Summary			
	Year 1: 2014	Year 2: 2015	Year 3: 2016
Revenues	1,312,395	1,447,959	1,631,096
Operating Expenses	1,224,158	1,354,411	1,469,574
Net Income Operations	60,439	61,319	105,169

Part I: Organizational Plan
Karma Jazz Café

Summary of the Business

The Karma Jazz Café concept was established by DeShea Cook in 2012. In 2013, she moved forward by opening a location in Atlanta, GA. Based on the success of that location, DeShea Cook is on a mission to open up a second location in Fort Worth, TX. This business plan has been developed for the setup of the new location.

Karma Jazz Café is a full-service restaurant with particular focus on Creole cuisine. The Company's proprietary recipes will be combined with modern culinary techniques and a more sophisticated atmosphere that will position the Karma Jazz Café brand in the marketplace and allow for future growth. The menu will have something for everyone and focus on flavors that consumers readily identify and associate with Creole cuisine. Showcase dishes include: Seafood Gumbo, Jumbo Grilled Shrimp, Crawfish Etouffee, Mahi Mahi, and Snapper. The menu is rounded out by a selection on salads, po-boys, and a premium line of specialty Creole toppings.

Karma Jazz Café will be the premier, cozy, live jazz venue in the Dallas Fort Worth Metroplex. The Company's goal is to remain a step ahead of its competition through an exemplary service provision. Karma Jazz Café expects its guests to have a relaxed and refreshing experience. Live jazz music, which is currently not being offered anywhere within Sundance Square, will be provided four days a week (Thursday, Friday, Saturday, and Sunday) at Karma Jazz Café. On other days and during lunch hours jazz music will be played in the background.

Located on the main level of a new hi-rise development that is 98% occupied, Karma Jazz Café will have a simple, yet unique menu and atmosphere that will create a sense of romance and "belonging" for locals and tourists alike. Karma Jazz Café will also target local business professionals during lunch and happy hour. The hours of operation for Karma Jazz Café will be as follows:

Hours of Operation	
Day	**Hours**
Wednesday through Thursday	4:00 pm to 11:00 pm
Friday	4:00 pm to 2:00 am
Saturday	6:00 pm to 2:00 am

Note. Karma Jazz Café will be closed on Thanksgiving Day, Christmas Day, and New Year's Day.

Mission

The mission of Karma Jazz Café is to develop an elegant establishment and offer a variety of unique Creole foods along with an exquisite mix of live jazz entertainment.

Goals and Objectives

The following goals and objectives have been established for Karma Jazz Café:

- Create awareness of the Company's existence
- Capitalize on the excellent location opportunity within Sundance Square
- Become the venue of choice for fine dining
- Launch operations at the Sundance Square venue with a highly publicized grand opening event on or around May 1, 2014
- Closely monitor and maintain tight control of financial matters
- Exceed $1,200,000 in annual sales by the third year of plan implementation

Strategy

Karma Jazz Café will accomplish its goals and objectives by developing and implementing marketing campaigns that reach out and appeal to a broad consumer base. The restaurant will also benefit significantly from a major marketing campaign that is being done for the Sundance Square District. The live jazz entertainment will be the attraction that draws people to the restaurant for their dining needs. Adding to the appeal will be the restaurant's combination of modern kitchen procedures and an extensive product mix with consistent quality. All this will be combined with exceptional customer service.

On the operations side, Karma Jazz Café will install detailed operating procedures, standards, controls, and cooking methods and processes. To meet its goal of maintaining tight control on financials, Karma Jazz Café will use a point-of-sale (POS) cash register system that will provide management with hourly, daily, and weekly information regarding sales, inventory, food and beverage costs, labor costs, and other critical data that will assist in controlling operating expenses.

Karma Jazz Café will capitalize on its location at the Sundance Square by developing strategies aimed at attracting the general population, workers in the area, as well as people attending various festivals such as Mayfest. For the holiday season, Karma Jazz Café plans to aggressively market a corporate catering program so businesses that wish to host holiday gatherings for customers or employees can select from a special menu designed for larger parties.

SWOT Analysis	
Strengths	**Weaknesses**
Management team and advisory board with extensive restaurant industry experience	Start up restaurant
Sophisticated and inviting atmosphere with outdoor seating	No brand recognition
Authentic Cajun food	
Extensive food selection	
Live jazz music	
Marketing campaign that is being done to promote Sundance Square District	

Opportunities	Threats
Location (Sundance Square District) allows Karma to reach workers, tourists, and residents	Strong competition from established restaurants in the area
Location will allow Karma to host corporate events and gatherings	Emergence of restaurants that claim to offer Creole cuisine
Expanding the brand to other major metropolitan areas	Health and safety standards are always a potential liability in the restaurant industry
Numerous festivals are held in the area attracting large crowds	

Products and Services

Karma Jazz Café will be a classy full-service restaurant serving Cajun cuisine. The restaurant will feature a simple menu offering a variety of food that meets different tastes. Traditional "bar" appetizers will be on hand as well for people craving quesadillas, wings, calamari and an array of seafood while they drink and enjoy themselves.

Karma Jazz Café will be characterized by cozy lounge areas and intimate table settings situated in a spectator setting with views of the stage area. The restaurant will comfortably accommodate 200 guests. The area will also offer patio dining. Karma Jazz Café will feature live jazz music from local jazz artists with strong listener base and following. A satellite feed with provide smooth jazz music during breaks and off-times.

In the future, Karma Jazz Café plans to establish a catering division. The Company also has an opportunity for additional sales with the introduction of corporate and family catering programs. This revenue potential has not been considered in the projected sales as these programs are still in development.

Administrative Plan

A. Location

Karma Jazz Café will be located at 500 Throckmorton in the Sundance Square District of downtown Fort Worth, Texas. The restaurant will be situated on the street level of the Tower, an upscale hi-rise building. This positions Karma Jazz Café in an area that gets a heavy traffic flow of residents, tourists, and professionals. Karma Jazz Café plans to sign a long-term lease for approximately 6,000 square feet of space.

Karma Jazz Café will as well as the availability of parking. There are several parking lots and parking garages on all four sides of the building. These parking areas are all free to the public after 5:00 pm Monday through Friday and all day Saturday and Sunday. Karma Jazz Café will also validate parking for my restaurant patrons.

B. Legal Structure

Karma Jazz Café is registered as a Limited Liability Company (LLC) under the laws of the State of Texas.

C. Management, Personnel, and Advisor

Karma Jazz Café has a capable management team with direct knowledge of the industry and the expertise to successfully manage a restaurant business. The management team currently includes DeShea Cook and Raymond Jones.

Management

DeShea Cook is pursuing a life-long ambition of restaurant ownership. She brings several years of experience in various entertainment avenues and over five years of finance management along with over a decade of exceptional customer service training. This experience will enable DeShea Cook to make the customer feel important while maintaining the bottom line for the Karma Jazz Café. DeShea Cook is no stranger to business ownership. She also owns and operates a successful entertainment company that promotes local events with entertainers. She has had this company for over three years.

DeShea Cook worked in various positions in restaurants and nightclubs that her stepfather has owned and/or managed. These positions included, but are not limited to; waitstaff, hostess, inventory control, booking acts for events, etc. DeShea Cook has also been an apprentice under her mentor and fellow manager who has been in the business for over 25 years.

DeShea Cook currently serves as Consumer Finance Manager for New Beginnings, a company that takes care of mentally challenged adults and children. She is responsible for all accounts payable and receivable and well as the liaison between the company and the Social Security Administration. She has held this position for three years and is regularly monitored and surveyed by the State of Texas.

DeShea Cook attended Collin County Community College where she studied Telecommunication Management and Fine Art. After a move to Atlanta, she studied real estate and worked for Harry Norman Realtors and Coldwell Banker Residential under their top Sales Representative. While at Harry Norman Realtors, she worked on several major condominium projects and grossed over $2 million in sales. During that time, she continued to work in the entertainment industry under her stepfather's guidance and assisted with celebrity parties and events.

Raymond Jones is an expert in restaurant and bar industry management. With over 20 years of experience in the restaurant and bar industry, as an owner and professional consultant, Raymond Jones has handled all areas of operations including proper food handling and preparation, safety procedures, cleanliness, temperature control, equipment controls and maintenance. He has consulted for major hotel and restaurant chains on management, health, and safety issues. What's more, he has interfaced with health inspectors nationally on behalf of various clients. Raymond Jones has also prepared training manuals and instructed staff on comprehensive restaurant policies and procedures.

In his public entity consulting work, Raymond Jones was contracted to train restaurant personnel on behalf of the City of Dallas, regarding food preparation, safety procedures, hygiene, equipment use, and maintenance issues. In private entity work, he has provided consulting services and had direct employment in restaurant management positions for various corporations at numerous facilities nationwide.

Personnel

Karma Jazz Café places an extremely high value on the importance of its workforce (human capital). All employees will be treated with respect, compensated sufficiently, and provided with a professional work environment. The Company will implement various bonus programs aimed at retaining its workforce and minimizing turnover. These incentive programs will ensure that employees remain at the Karma Jazz Café. The Company will also benefit from repeat business as customers establish relationships with Karma Jazz Café employees. Karma Jazz Café will create an exceptional work environment, designed to attract and keep the best employees in the industry. This will ensure consistency in the Company's operations and provide Karma Jazz Café with a cost effective and less expensive way of operating. The Company will also organize various group events for employees aimed at promoting morale and employee relations. Karma Jazz Café plans to retain highly qualified individuals for the following key positions:

Personnel Breakdown	
Individual/Position	**Salary**
Busboys (3)	$7.50 per hour
Waitstaff (6)	$2.75 per hour
Bartenders (6)	$3.00 hour
Head Bartender (2)	$3.75 hour
Hostess	$10.00 hour
Security (4)	$12.00 hour
Janitorial service	$500 per week

Advisor

Steve Cook, Jr. is a highly respected business professional. In 2011, he retired from TXU Energy after 36 years of service. By the time he retired, he had risen to the rank of Regional Manager. In his position as Regional Manager, he was responsible for planning, executing and directing the daily functions and operations of the Waco, Texas facility. Upon his retirement, he became President of CO-GILL Financial Services, LLC dba Home Purchase Center. The Home Purchase Center is committed to helping its clients find the right home mortgage product for their needs. Steve Cook is a former Board Member for CareLinc in Waco, TX. He is affiliated with several business organizations including the Irving Black Arts Council (Irving, TX), H.O.T. Minority Business Alliance (Waco, TX), Greater Waco Chamber of Commerce, Waco Hispanic Chamber of Commerce, and Waco Cultural Arts Fest.

D. Accounting and Legal

Accounting

Day-to-day bookkeeping will be done in-house. For added accounting and financial functions, Karma Jazz Café has retained the services of Accounting Systems, Inc., 1220 N. Freeway Drive, Fort Worth, TX 76210.

Legal

For all legal aspects relating the business, Karma Jazz Café has retained the services of Parker & Parker, LLP, 6589 Williams Avenue, Fort Worth, TX 76210.

E. Insurance

The following insurance policies will be obtained for Karma Jazz Café:

- Property
- General liability
- Umbrella/Excess Liability
- Workers compensation

For all its insurance needs, Karma Jazz Café has retained the services of Texas Insurance Group, 3000 West Jordan Street, Fort Worth, TX 76210.

F. Security

Karma Jazz Café plans to procure a sophisticated point of sale system that will be the foundation of accounting controls for the restaurant. The Micros 3700 POS system will provide staff members with the means to enter all customer orders, time & attendance, and payments. This will provide the management team with detailed reports on food, beverage, and liquor usage. This information will then be utilized to conduct weekly inventory accounting for all items in the restaurant and then compared to purchases. Any variances will be analyzed and resolved weekly. The Company's inventory accounting system is the heart of operational processes; this will determine in near real time the state of the restaurant at any given time so the management team can make effective decisions.

Credit card payments will also run through the POS system and processed via an encrypted broadband connection to the company's credit card processor. This will not only help for the timeliness of each transaction, but will also eliminate the need for employees to manually record customer information as it's all done electronically. Additionally, any customer information that is retained for marketing purposes will be housed on the Company's servers with only the Restaurant Manager and owner having access.

Physical security will be controlled via an in-house closed circuit camera system. The Company will have cameras mounted at key points throughout the restaurant including; front & back entrances, bar area, kitchen line, and stock room. A monitor will be housed in the manager's office for viewing. Additionally, access to the restaurant's cameras will available to the Company owner via an encrypted connection to the Internet. A password protected VPN client on the owner's workstation off premises will provide the ability to monitor activities whenever necessary.

Cash will be housed in the office safe that only the Restaurant Manager and owner have access to. Karma Jazz Café will have a no tolerance policy that the office be locked at all times. Bank deposits will also be conducted twice daily (after lunch and store closing) so as to reduce the cash that is left on premises. All transactions will be tracked for constant auditing.

Part II: Marketing Plan
KARMA JAZZ CAFÉ

Marketing Strategy Overview and Goals
(Marketing Plan: Section I)

Overview

Karma Jazz Café will compete on the basis of taste, quality, dining value, live jazz music, and customer service to name a few. Management believes that the Karma Jazz Café concept will differentiate it from competitors. It is the only restaurant that offers high-end Creole cuisine as well as live jazz music. The Karma Jazz Café marketing strategy is to bring awareness of its existence in order to attract and acquire customers that will look to it for ongoing dining needs. This will be accomplished by using various forms of media including radio, television, and print advertising.

Goals

- **Goal #1 –** Establish Karma Jazz Café as an authentic Creole restaurant.

- **Goal #2 –** Promote Karma Jazz Café as the only restaurant that provides live jazz music.

- **Goal #3 –** Build strong brand recognition leading to the opening of additional restaurants in other metropolitan areas.

- **Goal #4 –** Establish Karma Jazz Café as the location of choice for corporate events.

- **Goal #5 –** Attract a clientele for all occasions including lunch, dinner, and happy hour.

Market Analysis
(Marketing Plan: Section II)

A. Target Market(s)

Karma Jazz Café is targeting tenants of the Tower building, professionals that work in the Sundance Square District, residents of the Dallas Fort Worth Metroplex as well as tourists. Located in the heart of one of the hottest areas in the Dallas Fort Worth Metroplex, Karma Jazz Café will benefit from an embedded clientele.

Daytime Statistics - Sundance Square District		
Radius	**Daytime Population**	**Median Age**
0.5 mile of Karma Jazz Café	36,165	32.3
1 mile of Karma Jazz Café	47,816	33.3
2 miles of Karma Jazz Café	92,698	32.8

Note. Based on 2013 day time estimates

There are several major corporations with offices in downtown Fort Worth to attract a steady lunch and happy hour crowd. The Company will benefit from easy access to the restaurant. In addition to the easy access for drivers coming from all areas of the Dallas Fort Worth Metroplex, there is a public transportation system that runs through downtown and right by the restaurant.

Target Markets	Demographics	Psychographics	Niche Market
Workers	Age 24 - 40 Average income starting at $40,000 and up	Enjoy fine dining Hold professional or managerial positions Dine out frequently Attend happy hour events frequently Enjoy music experience along with dining	Corporate clients that reserve space for happy hour or company gatherings
Tourists/ Visitors	Age 18 - 60	Out of town travelers Looking specifically for Creole cuisine Motivated to try different food types	Residents of Louisiana
Residents	Age 18 - 60	Couples looking for elegant restaurant to dine out Individuals with a taste for ethnic foods Jazz music lovers	Individuals and families that moved to the area from Louisiana due to the hurricanes (Katrina and Rita)

B. Competition

Major Competitors

The Sundance Square is home to a host of restaurants. It has been noted that one can dine there every day of the week and never eat at the same restaurant twice. While other restaurant establishments exist, their focus is not on Creole cuisine. The only establishment that offers Creole food, Razzoos, is more of a low end restaurant. They also offer a mix of American food. None of the restaurants in the Sundance Square currently offers live jazz music.

Restaurants at the Sundance Square	
Restaurant	**Cuisine Type**
Razzoo's	**American/Creole**
Taverna Pizzeria and Risotteria	Authentic Italian
8.0 Restaurant And Bar	Diverse selection including: Southwestern cuisine, steaks, seafood and pastas
Bella Vista	Authentic Italian Pizza, pasta, hot & cold subs, lasagna & daily specials
Billy Miner's Saloon	Burgers, Hotdogs, chicken & seafood options
Cabo Grande	Tex Mex
Chili's	Burgers, salads, fajitas and southwest favorites
Chop House	Steaks, Poultry & Seafood Specialties
City Club of Fort Worth	Fine dining and athletic club
Daddy Jack's Seafood	New England Seafood
Ferre Ristorante e Bar	Italian/Tuscan
La Madeleine Bakery And Cafe	French Country
Mi Cocina	Tex Mex
P.F. Chang's China Bistro	Chinese Cuisine
Piranha Killer Sushi	Japanese/Sushi
Reata at Sundance Square	Legendary Western Cuisine
Riscky's Barbecue	BBQ Ribs, Steaks, Catfish & Chicken
Uno Chicago Grill	Pizza, pasta, specialty dishes, sandwiches, salads, desserts and full bar

Karma Jazz Café's Competitive Advantages

Karma Jazz Café will be successful because there is a need for the type of restaurant the Company is bringing to the Sundance Square District. Only one other restaurant, Razzoo's, offers Creole style dishes. Karma Jazz Café will include many more modern dining elements than Razzoo's and the other restaurants in the area. Additionally, The Company's customer service approach will be superior. Karma Jazz Café will provide the perfect mix of premium quality food and exciting jazz entertainment.

Karma Jazz Café will be the only restaurant offering live jazz music. There is an abundance of talented jazz artists in the area with the closest venue to play being over 40 miles away in Dallas, Texas. Karma Jazz Café will attract the most talented jazz artists in the area. To date, the Company has secured commitments from several leading jazz artists with large followings.

Management experience is a key competitive advantage for the Karma Jazz Café. The owner, DeShea Cook, has been working in the restaurant industry for over 12 years in various positions. What's more, jazz music has always played an important role in her life and the idea of Karma Jazz Café has been a life long dream.

Karma Jazz Café will also be successful because of the team of advisors that are backing the venture. Three of the Company's principal investors have successfully started and operated their own businesses for over 30 years.

Some members of the management/advisory team have established and operated several successful restaurants and night clubs for over 25 years. This experience makes them very knowledgeable of the pitfalls and avenues for success in restaurant operations.

A key competitive advantage will be location. Karma Jazz Café will be located in the Tower Building in the Sundance Square. This location is in a vibrant downtown marketplace. Sundance Square is 20 fabulous blocks of downtown Ft. Worth where people work, live, shop, and dine. By day, tourists, office workers and residents stroll brick-paved, flower-lined sidewalks, sightsee charming, historical buildings, shop in unique stores, and visit art galleries and museums.

While this tourist district receives heavy traffic during the day, traffic is especially heavier on weekends. Evenings and weekends, Sundance Square takes on a whole new flavor. Exciting night life includes dancing to the hottest music, socializing in sleek bistros, lively outdoor concerts, laugh-out-loud comedy clubs, innovative theatre productions and 20 screens of box-office hits.

The Karma Jazz Café's dining value will also separate it from the others. Karma Jazz Café is known for generous portions at moderate prices. Karma Jazz Café will have a lunch menu specially developed for the large audience of the Sundance Square and downtown Fort Worth. The lunch menu will feature items that are similar to the dinner menu but with smaller portions and can be produced at a much faster pace meeting the limited time available for lunch. The area has a very large concentration of daytime workers that will not travel very far for lunch. Karma Jazz Café also has a strong opportunity to capture these guests for happy hour after work.

C. Market Trends

Industry Trends

Restaurants are the cornerstones of the economy, career-and-employment opportunities for millions of Americans, and local communities. Nationally, with 980,000 restaurant locations, the restaurant industry is expected to generate $660 billion in 2013. Restaurant-industry sales on a typical day in 2013 were $1.8 billion. Including the impact restaurants have on sales in related industries, the industry's overall impact on the U.S. economy is $1.3 trillion a year—about 10 percent of the U.S. gross domestic product. The restaurant industry is the nation's largest private sector employer. Restaurants employ 13.1 million people today, and are expected to add 1.9 million new jobs between 2006 and 2016[3].

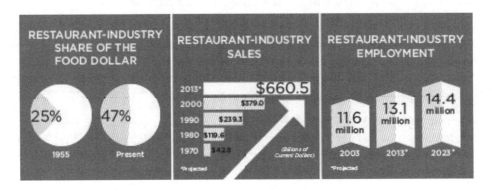

Note. Figures are in billions of current dollars. 2013 figures are projections.

---

[3] National Restaurant Association

Target Market Trends

Texas's restaurants provide appetizing, healthful and nourishing food, convenience, value, entertainment, and social occasions where people can enjoy friends and family away from the stresses of daily life.

Restaurants in Texas also are an engine of economic growth, generating tremendous sales and tax revenues for the state. They provide career-and-employment opportunities for individuals of every age, background, and skill and experience level. Restaurants are an important part of their communities and neighborhoods, enthusiastically and generously giving their time and resources to support a variety of causes[4].

Restaurant Statistics - Texas	
Category	**Number**
Number of eating and drinking places in Texas in 2011	39,296
Estimated restaurant sales in Texas in 2013	$40.8 billion
Estimated restaurant and foodservice employment in Texas in 2013	1,074,200
Projected 2023 restaurant and foodservice employment in Texas	1,245,000

Marketing Strategy
(Marketing Plan: Section III)

A. General Description

Allocation of Marketing Efforts: In order to fund the marketing efforts, the Company has allocated 5% and 3% of restaurant sales for the first and second year respectively. Management understands that a greater effort will be necessary to promote the restaurant in the first years of business until the Company reached its level run rate. Management anticipates reducing the advertising budget to 2% of restaurant sales once the Company is more established in the area. Community involvement will continue post restaurant opening and will serve as a free form of advertising in local newspapers and bulletins. Karma Jazz Café will also continue to find new and creative ways to communicate its brand to the community and adjust its advertising budget based on its effectiveness and tangible results.

B. Method of Sales and Distribution

- **Stores, offices, kiosks.** Karma Jazz Café will operate from a facility of approximately 6,000 square feet of space.

- **Catalogs, direct mail.** Karma Jazz Café plans to plans to use direct mail to reach out to businesses in the Sundance Square area. Mailers will be sending promoting the restaurant and offering coupons and specials. Mailers will also be sent to local area residents.

---

[4] National Restaurant Association

- **Web Site.** The Karma Jazz Café will be used to promote the restaurant. Additionally, patrons will be able to view the menu and information about the restaurant, artists performing, and specials.

C. Packaging

Company Image. Karma Jazz Café will establish itself as a cozy venue that features live jazz music.

D. Pricing

- **Price strategy.** The Karma Jazz Café pricing strategy was based on competitor pricing. After an analysis of the fine dining restaurants in the Sundance Square, Karma Jazz Café set its prices at an even level.

- **Competitive position.** The only direct competitor is Razzoo's. Karma Jazz Café's prices are higher than those of Razzoo's. They are higher because Karma Jazz Café is a fine dining restaurant while Razzoo's is a casual restaurant.

E. Branding

Karma Jazz Café will be an authentic Creole restaurant, featuring fine dining and live jazz music. The restaurant will blend the taste, sights, and sounds of Louisiana to create the dining destination of choice in Dallas Fort Worth.

F. Sales Strategies

- **Direct Mail -** Direct mail will be sent to all local area businesses and residents. These will be aimed, initially, at generating awareness of the existence of Karma Jazz Café. In the future, the mailings will offer coupons and promote various artists performing at the restaurant.

- **Email Marketing -** Patrons will have the option to complete a guest card. On the guest card, they will have the option to provide an email address. Karma Jazz Café will use the email addresses to send out notices of events taking place at the restaurant as well as specials and new product offerings. On their birthday, each patron will receive a "Happy Birthday" message and a coupon for a free meal during the month of their birthday.

- **Reciprocal Marketing -** Karma Jazz Café will make special arrangements with local area businesses to leave coupon at their location. Guests that bring the coupon will receive the designated discount.

- **Viral Marketing -** Word-of-mouth will be a major marketing channel for Karma Jazz Café as satisfied patrons spread the word about the great food, excellent service, and fine dining with a jazzy musical experience.

G. Sales Incentives/Promotions

- **Free Samples -** Karma Jazz Café will give away free samples at various events including Summer Fest.

- **Coupons -** Karma Jazz Café will include coupons in its direct mail packages.

- **Other -** From time to time, Karma Jazz Café will run promotions aimed at generating continued awareness and increasing sales.

H. Advertising Strategies

- **Traditional Advertising -** Word of mouth will be the primary method of attracting and retaining restaurant guests. Karma Jazz Café will also undertake aggressive advertising campaigns in the form of local newspaper and magazine advertisements, radio, and direct mail to surrounding homes and businesses.

- **Web Advertising/New Media -** Karma Jazz Café will use search engine optimization to get its web site at the top of search engines when someone conducts a search for restaurants in the Dallas Fort Worth area.

- **Long-term Sponsorships -** The marketing techniques that will employed for the restaurant's opening will include a charitable fund raising event with invitations to local business leaders and media personalities. Additionally, the Company will donate a portion of the day's food sales to local worthwhile charities.

I. Public Relations

- **Events -** Karma Jazz Café also plans to host concierge gatherings for hotels in the surrounding area so that hotel managers and key employees become acclimated with Karma Jazz Café facility and offerings. These gatherings will be conducted on an annual basis or when new programs are introduced. Karma Jazz Café will utilize a variety of printed material including restaurant brochures, hotel concierge cards, take-out menus, and electronic mailings as another form of advertising.

- **Press releases -** Karma Jazz Café will use press releases to announce special events taking place at its restaurant. This will begin with the "Grand Opening" announcement press release that will run in newspapers in Dallas and Fort Worth as well as local radio stations.

J. Networking

- **Business Community -** The Company's efforts to become more integrated into the Sundance Square community will be evidenced by participation in the many events that are hosted in and around the downtown district. This will include either donating products to the hosting organization or becoming a sponsor for various events. Karma Jazz Café will also benefit significantly from a major marketing campaign that is being done for the Sundance Square District by City officials.

- **World at-Large -** Karma Jazz Café plans to participate in various local events including the annual Summer Fest in Fort Worth. During the festival, the restaurant will create a special menu and run various promotions.

Customer Service
(Marketing Plan: Section IV)

Description of Customer Service Activities

Karma Jazz Café will implement the following in order to improve the dining experience for its patrons:

- Interaction between owner and patrons
- Interaction between head chef and patrons
- Offer complimentary samples during longer than normal waits
- Happy birthday tune played by live band
- Jazz recordings during time band is not playing

Expected Outcomes of Achieving Excellence

- Repeat business
- Businesses looking at Karma Jazz Café to host their corporate events
- Individuals and families coming to Karma Jazz Café for birthday and other family events
- Establishing and growing catering division

Implementation of Marketing Strategy
(Marketing Plan: Section V)

In-House Responsibilities

- Networking
- Concierge events

Out-Sourced Functions

- Advertising
- Public relations
- Search engine optimization
- Web site updates
- Direct mailing

Part III: Financial Documents

This financial statement is for illustrative purposes only and the figures in no way represent an actual Profit & Loss (Income) Statement for Karma Jazz Café. Furthermore, the figures are not for a complete year. They are based on three months of operations (October to December).

2013 Profit & Loss (Income) Statement
Karma Jazz Café - Atlanta Location

Beginning: October 1, 2013   **Ending: December 31, 2013**

			% Total Revenues
INCOME			
Sales Revenues		$ 323,488	100.00%
1. Meals	164,589		50.88%
2. Beer and Liquor	143,648		44.41%
3. Corporate Events	15,251		4.71%
Cost of Goods Sold (c-d)		131,294	40.59%
A. Beginning Inventory	15,000		4.64%
B. Purchases	129,395		40.00%
1. Meals	65,836		20.35%
2. Beer and Liquor	57,459		17.76%
3. Corporate Events	6,100		1.89%
C. C.O.G. Avail. Sale (a+b)	144,395		44.64%
D. Less Ending Inventory (12/31)	13,101		4.05%
Gross Profit on Sales (1-2)		$ 192,194	59.41%
EXPENSES			
A. Variable (Selling)		30,465	9.42%
1. Entertainment	15,279		4.72%
2. Laundry	628		0.19%
3. Marketing & Advertising	14,558		4.50%
4. Misc. Variable Expense	0		0.00%
5. Depreciation (Variable Assets)	0		0.00%
B. Fixed (Administrative)		141,499	43.74%
1. Dues & Subscriptions	300		0.09%
2. Insurance	1,500		0.46%
3. Licenses & Permits	125		0.04%
4. Professional Fees	8,000		2.47%
5. Rent	8,100		2.50%
6. Repairs & Maintenance	14,283		4.42%
7. Salaries & Wages	94,149		29.10%
8. Supplies (General)	3,786		1.17%
9. Telephone	987		0.31%
10. Utilities	4,269		1.32%
11. Misc. Fixed Expense	0		0.00%
12. Depreciation (Fixed Assets)	6,000		1.85%
Total Operating Expenses (1+2)		171,964	53.16%
Net Income from Operations (GP-Exp)		$ 20,230	6.25%
Other Income (Interest Income)	0		0.00%
Other Expense (Interest Expense)	0		0.00%
Net Profit (Loss) Before Taxes		$ 20,230	6.25%
Taxes			
1. Federal	5,664		1.75%
2. State	0	5,664	0.00%
3. Local	0		0.00%
NET PROFIT (LOSS) AFTER TAXES		$ 14,565	4.50%

Note about taxes: Depending on the state, county, and city your business is located, you will be responsible for state and local taxes. You will also be responsible for sales tax, property tax, and alcohol tax. Contact your county office and state department of revenue for more information.

This financial statement is for illustrative purposes only. The figures do not represent an actual Balance Sheet for Karma Jazz Café. The example below represents a "possible scenario" for the asset, liability, and net worth positions of Karma Jazz Café at the end of its first quarter.

2013 Balance Sheet
Karma Jazz Café - Atlanta Location

Business Name:

Karma Jazz Café   **Date: December 31, 2013**

ASSETS

			% of Assets
Current Assets			
Cash	$	29,873	17.24%
Petty Cash	$	0	0.00%
Accounts Receivable	$	3,928	2.27%
Inventory	$	13,101	7.56%
Short-Term Investments	$	0	0.00%
Prepaid Expenses	$	1,860	1.07%
Long-Term Investments	$	0	0.00%
Fixed Assets			
Land (valued at cost)	$	0	0.00%
Buildings	$	0	0.00%
1. Cost 0			
2. Less Acc. Depr. 0			
Improvements	$	47,500	27.40%
1. Cost 50,000			
2. Less Acc. Depr. 2,500			
Equipment	$	28,500	16.44%
1. Cost 30,000			
2. Less Acc. Depr. 1,500			
Furniture	$	38,000	21.92%
1. Cost 40,000			
2. Less Acc. Depr. 2,000			
Autos/Vehicles	$	0	0.00%
1. Cost 0			
2. Less Acc. Depr. 0			
Other Assets			
1. Intellectual Property	$	10,565	6.10%
2.	$	0	0.00%
TOTAL ASSETS	$	173,327	100.00%

LIABILITIES

			% of Liabilities
Current Liabilities			
Accounts Payable	$	6,892	11.73%
Notes Payable	$	0	0.00%
Interest Payable*	$	0	0.00%
Taxes Payable			
Taxes	$	0	0.00%
Sales Tax Accrual	$	1,462	2.49%
Property Tax	$	408	0.69%
Payroll Accrual	$	0	0.00%
Long-Term Liabilities			
Notes Payable to Investors	$	50,000	85.09%

*No note or interest payment due in the first six months

TOTAL LIABILITIES	$	58,762	100.00%

NET WORTH (EQUITY)

			% of Net Worth
Corporation			
Capital Stock	$	100,000	87.29%
Surplus Paid In	$	0	0.00%
Retained Earnings	$	14,565	12.71%
TOTAL NET WORTH	$	114,565	100.00%

Assets - Liabilities = Net Worth
and
Liabilities + Equity = Total Assets

Sources and Uses of Funds

KARMA JAZZ CAFÉ

Fort Worth, Texas Location

1. Statement of Financial Needs

Karma Jazz Café is seeking funding in the amount of $200,000 for the development of its Fort Worth restaurant location.

2. Sources of Funds

• Owners	$100,000
• Investors	$100,000
Total	**$200,000**

3. Dispersal of Loan Funds

• Improvements/Renovations	$50,000
• Equipment	$30,000
• Furniture & Fixtures	$40,000
• Restaurant/Business Supplies	$10,000
• Inventory	$15,000
• Marketing & Advertising	$20,000
• Working capital	$35,000
Total	**$200,000**

Assumptions for Financial Projections

Karma Jazz Café will have a capacity of 200 patrons. The financial projections are based on the actual results derived from the Atlanta operation. Provided below are the key assumptions used to develop the Company's financial projections.

Average Sale by Customer Type

Average Sale by Category	
Customer Purchase	Average Spent
Meals (Including soft drinks)	$15
Beer and Liquor	$8
Corporate Events	$500

Meals - Income from meals is expected to be steady throughout the year with heavy growth in the summer months when the City of Fort Worth is hosting various events. The Company expects to average approximately $21,000 per week. These numbers are based on the performances of other restaurants in the area, Billy Miner's and The Pour House. Billy Miner's is averaging approximately $28,412 per week. The Pour House is averaging approximately $32,000 per week. Karma Jazz Café was very conservative in its projections.

Beer and Liquor - As with meals, beer and liquor sales will be heaviest in the summer months due to a heavy influx of visitors to the Fort Worth area. Happy hour events will help to maintain steady revenue growth for Karma Jazz Café. Liquor sales are based on the actual 2013 liquor sales for five establishments in Downtown Fort Worth. Average annual sales were as follows: Pourhouse - $1,468,648, The Reata – 1,635,218, Razzoos - $862,356. Karma Jazz Café was very conservative in its projections.

Corporate Events - Karma Jazz Café will highly publicize its facility as the establishment of choice for hosting corporate events. By the end of the year, the number of event hosted at Karma Jazz Café will increase due to year end corporate parties.

Other Notes

Cost of Goods Sold - Food and beverage purchases have been based on industry averages. The rate of 40% has been applied to the gross food sales figure to derive the cost of goods sold amount. Liquor purchases are calculated based upon industry averages for similar full service restaurants. The rate of 40% has been applied to the total gross liquor sales.

Payroll - Salaries are only for support staff. Members of the management team will not draw a salary. They will rely on their savings for living expenses and take owner draws as cash flow allows.

Loan Payments - Loan payments will be made over a five year period at an interest rate of 8%. No payments will be due during the first six months.

Pro Forma Cash Flow Statement
Karma Jazz Café

For the Year 2014

	Jan 08	Feb 08	Mar 08	Apr 08	May 08	Jun 08	6-MONTH TOTALS	Jul 08	Aug 08	Sep 08	Oct 08	Nov 08	Dec 08	12-MONTH TOTALS
BEGINNING CASH BALANCE	35,000	37,646	43,952	46,368	52,335	58,434	35,000	60,369	64,827	78,759	83,249	93,140	106,771	35,000
CASH RECEIPTS														
A. Sales/Revenues	98,906	99,895	100,894	110,846	99,931	100,993	611,465	111,010	122,025	110,094	111,365	122,502	123,934	1,312,395
1. Meals	48,750	49,238	49,730	54,703	49,233	49,725	301,378	54,697	60,167	54,150	54,692	60,161	60,763	646,008
2. Beer and Liquor	48,656	49,143	49,634	54,597	49,138	49,629	300,797	54,592	60,051	54,586	54,046	60,045	60,646	644,763
3. Corporate Events	1,500	1,515	1,530	1,545	1,561	1,639	9,290	1,721	1,807	1,897	2,087	2,296	2,525	21,624
B. Interest Income	0	0	0	0	0	0	0	0	0	0	0	0	0	0
C. Sale of Long-Term Assets	0	0	0	0	0	0	0	0	0	0	0	0	0	0
TOTAL CASH AVAILABLE	133,906	137,542	144,846	157,214	152,266	159,427	646,465	171,379	186,852	188,853	194,614	215,642	230,705	1,347,395
CASH PAYMENTS														
A. Cost of goods to be sold														
1. Meals	19,500	19,695	19,892	21,881	19,693	19,890	120,551	21,879	24,067	21,660	21,877	24,064	24,305	258,403
2. Beer and Liquor	19,462	19,657	19,854	21,839	19,655	19,852	120,319	21,837	24,020	21,618	21,835	24,018	24,258	257,905
3. Corporate Events	600	606	612	618	624	656	3,716	688	723	759	835	918	1,010	8,649
Total Cost of Goods	39,562	39,958	40,358	44,338	39,972	40,397	244,586	44,404	48,810	44,037	44,546	49,001	49,573	524,958
B. Variable Expenses														
1. Entertainment	5,000	5,000	5,000	6,000	5,000	5,000	31,000	7,200	7,200	6,000	6,000	7,200	7,500	72,100
2. Laundry	600	600	600	800	600	600	3,800	900	900	800	800	900	1,000	9,100
3. Marketing & Advertising	4,850	4,850	4,850	5,500	5,000	5,000	30,050	6,000	6,000	5,000	5,000	6,500	7,000	65,550
4. Misc. Variable Expense	0	0	0	0	0	0	0	0	0	0	0	0	0	0
Total Variable Expenses	10,450	10,450	10,450	12,300	10,600	10,600	64,850	14,100	14,100	11,800	11,800	14,600	15,500	146,750
C. Fixed Expenses														
1. Dues & Subscriptions	150	150	150	150	150	150	900	150	150	150	150	150	150	1,800
2. Insurance	1,860	0	0	0	0	0	1,860	1,860	0	0	0	0	0	3,720
3. Licenses & Permits	625	0	0	0	0	0	625	625	0	0	0	0	0	1,250
4. Professional Fees	2,450	2,450	2,450	2,450	2,450	2,450	14,700	2,450	2,450	2,450	2,450	2,450	2,450	29,400
5. Rent	2,700	2,700	2,700	2,700	2,700	2,700	16,200	2,700	2,700	2,700	2,700	2,700	2,700	32,400
6. Repairs & Maintenance	600	0	0	0	0	0	600	600	0	0	0	0	0	1,200
7. Salaries & Wages	34,132	34,132	34,132	34,132	34,132	34,132	204,792	34,132	34,132	34,132	34,132	34,132	34,132	409,584
8. Supplies (General)	1,978	1,998	2,018	2,217	1,999	2,020	12,229	2,220	2,441	2,202	2,227	2,450	2,479	26,248
9. Telephone	329	329	329	329	329	329	1,974	329	329	329	329	329	329	3,948
10. Utilities	1,423	1,423	1,423	1,581	1,500	1,600	8,950	1,423	1,423	1,423	1,581	1,500	1,600	17,900
11. Misc. Fixed Expense	0	0	0	0	0	0	0	0	0	0	0	0	0	0
Total Fixed Expenses	46,247	43,182	43,202	43,559	43,260	43,381	262,830	46,489	43,625	43,386	43,569	43,711	43,840	527,450
D. Interest Expense	0	0	0	0	0	0	0	667	661	655	649	643	637	3,910
E. Taxes	0	0	4,468	4,682	0	4,680	13,830	0	0	4,822	0	0	5,236	23,888
F. Other uses	0	0	0	0	0	0	0	0	0	0	0	0	0	0
G. Long-term asset payments	0	0	0	0	0	0	0	0	0	0	0	0	0	0
H. Investor Payments	0	0	0	0	0	0	0	892	898	904	910	916	922	5,442
I. Equity Withdrawals	0	0	0	0	0	0	0	0	0	0	0	0	0	0
TOTAL CASH PAID OUT	96,260	93,590	98,477	104,879	93,832	99,058	586,096	106,552	108,093	105,604	101,474	108,870	115,708	1,232,398
CASH BALANCE/DEFICIENCY	37,646	43,952	46,368	52,335	58,434	60,369	60,369	64,827	78,759	83,249	93,140	106,771	114,997	114,997
LOANS TO BE RECEIVED	0	0	0	0	0	0	0	0	0	0	0	0	0	0
EQUITY DEPOSITS	0	0	0	0	0	0	0	0	0	0	0	0	0	0
ENDING CASH BALANCE	37,646	43,952	46,368	52,335	58,434	60,369	60,369	64,827	78,759	83,249	93,140	106,771	114,997	114,997

Note 1: Beginning Cash Balance comes from the working capital portion of initial investment of $200,000 (See Sources & Uses of Funds - Pg 22)

Note 2: No investor principal or investor payments due during the first six months (See Assumptions for Financial Projections - Pg 23)

Three-Year Income Projection
Karma Jazz Café

Percentages = % of Sales/Revenues

Updated: January 22, 2014	Year 1: 2014		Year 2: 2015		Year 3: 2016		Total: 3 Years	
	AMOUNT	%	AMOUNT	%	AMOUNT	%	AMOUNT	%
INCOME								
SALES/REVENUES	**1,312,395**	**100.00%**	**1,447,959**	**100.00%**	**1,631,096**	**100.00%**	**4,391,450**	**100.00%**
1. Meals	646,008	49.22%	710,609	49.08%	817,201	50.10%	2,173,818	49.50%
2. Beer and Liquor	644,763	49.13%	709,239	48.98%	780,163	47.83%	2,134,165	48.60%
3. Corporate Events	21,624	1.65%	28,111	1.94%	33,733	2.07%	83,467	1.90%
Cost of Goods Sold (c-d)	**525,958**	**40.08%**	**583,184**	**40.28%**	**654,439**	**40.12%**	**1,763,580**	**40.16%**
A. Beginning Inventory	15,000	1.14%	14,000	0.97%	10,000	0.61%	15,000	0.34%
B. Purchases	**524,958**	**40.00%**	**579,184**	**40.00%**	**652,439**	**40.00%**	**1,756,580**	**40.00%**
1. Meals	258,403	19.69%	284,244	19.63%	326,880	20.04%	869,527	19.80%
2. Beer and Liquor	257,905	19.65%	283,696	19.59%	312,065	19.13%	853,666	19.44%
3. Corporate Events	8,649	0.66%	11,244	0.78%	13,493	0.83%	33,387	0.76%
C. C.O.G. Avail. Sale (a+b)	539,958	41.14%	593,184	40.97%	662,439	40.61%	1,771,580	40.34%
D. Less Ending Inventory (12/31)	14,000	1.07%	10,000	0.69%	8,000	0.49%	8,000	0.18%
GROSS PROFIT ON SALES (1-2)	**786,437**	**59.92%**	**864,775**	**59.72%**	**976,658**	**59.88%**	**2,627,870**	**59.84%**
EXPENSES								
A. VARIABLE (Selling)	**146,750**	**11.18%**	**154,543**	**10.67%**	**168,983**	**10.36%**	**470,276**	**10.71%**
1. Entertainment	72,100	5.49%	75,705	5.23%	81,761	5.01%	229,566	5.23%
2. Laundry	9,100	0.69%	10,010	0.69%	11,512	0.71%	30,622	0.70%
3. Marketing & Advertising	65,550	4.99%	68,828	4.75%	75,710	4.64%	210,088	4.78%
4. Misc. Variable Expense	0	0.00%	0	0.00%	0	0.00%	0	0.00%
5. Depreciation (Variable Assets)	0	0.00%	0	0.00%	0	0.00%	0	0.00%
B. FIXED (Administrative)	**551,450**	**42.02%**	**616,685**	**42.59%**	**646,153**	**39.61%**	**1,814,287**	**41.31%**
1. Dues & Subscriptions	1,800	0.14%	1,800	0.12%	1,800	0.11%	5,400	0.12%
2. Insurance	3,720	0.28%	3,720	0.26%	3,906	0.24%	11,346	0.26%
3. Licenses & Permits	1,250	0.10%	1,250	0.09%	1,313	0.08%	3,813	0.09%
4. Professional Fees	29,400	2.24%	30,870	2.13%	33,957	2.08%	94,227	2.15%
5. Rent	32,400	2.47%	32,400	2.24%	32,400	1.99%	97,200	2.21%
6. Repairs & Maintenance	1,200	0.09%	1,320	0.09%	1,386	0.08%	3,906	0.09%
7. Salaries & Wages	409,584	31.21%	471,022	32.53%	494,573	30.32%	1,375,178	31.31%
8. Supplies (General)	26,248	2.00%	27,560	1.90%	28,938	1.77%	82,746	1.88%
9. Telephone	3,948	0.30%	3,948	0.27%	4,145	0.25%	12,041	0.27%
10. Utilities	17,900	1.36%	18,795	1.30%	19,735	1.21%	56,430	1.28%
11. Misc. Fixed Expense	0	0.00%	0	0.00%	0	0.00%	0	0.00%
12. Depreciation (Fixed Assets)	24,000	1.83%	24,000	1.66%	24,000	1.47%	72,000	1.64%
TOTAL OPERATING EXPENSES (1+2)	**698,200**	**53.20%**	**771,227**	**53.26%**	**815,136**	**49.97%**	**2,284,563**	**52.02%**
NET INCOME OPERATIONS (GPr - Exp)	**88,237**	**6.72%**	**93,548**	**6.46%**	**161,522**	**9.90%**	**343,307**	**7.82%**
OTHER INCOME (Interest Income)	0	0.00%	0	0.00%	0	0.00%	0	0.00%
OTHER EXPENSE (Interest Expense)	3,910	0.30%	7,147	0.49%	6,188	0.38%	17,245	0.39%
NET PROFIT (LOSS) BEFORE TAXES	**84,327**	**6.43%**	**86,401**	**5.97%**	**155,334**	**9.52%**	**326,062**	**7.42%**
TAXES	23,888	1.82%	25,082	1.73%	50,165	3.08%	99,135	2.26%
NET PROFIT (LOSS) AFTER TAXES	**60,439**	**4.61%**	**61,319**	**4.23%**	**105,169**	**6.45%**	**226,927**	**5.17%**

Note about taxes: Depending on the state, county, and city your business is located, you will be responsible for state and local taxes. You will also be responsible for sales tax, property tax, and alcohol tax. Contact your county office and state department of revenue for more information.

Projected Balance Sheet

Business Name:

Karma Jazz Café

Date of Projection: January 22, 2014

Date Projected for: December 31, 2014

ASSETS			% of Assets
Current Assets			
Cash	$	114,997	31.32%
Petty Cash	$	0	0.00%
Accounts Receivable	$	7,621	2.08%
Inventory	$	14,000	3.81%
Short-Term Investments	$	0	0.00%
Prepaid Expenses	$	3,000	0.82%
Total Current Assets	*$*	*139,618*	*38.02%*
Long-Term Investments	$	0	0.00%
Fixed Assets			
Land (valued at cost)	$	0	0.00%
Buildings	$	0	0.00%
1. Cost	0		
2. Less Acc. Depr.	0		
Improvements	$	40,000	10.89%
1. Cost	50,000		
2. Less Acc. Depr.	10,000		
Equipment	$	24,000	6.54%
1. Cost	30,000		
2. Less Acc. Depr.	6,000		
Furniture	$	32,000	8.71%
1. Cost	40,000		
2. Less Acc. Depr.	8,000		
Autos/Vehicles	$	0	*0.00%*
1. Cost	0		
2. Less Acc. Depr.	0		
Total Fixed Assets	*$*	*96000*	*26.14%*
Other Assets			
1. Intellectual Property	$	11,565	3.15%
2. Other Nondepreciable Assets	$	120,008	32.68%
TOTAL ASSETS	**$**	**367,191**	**100.00%**

LIABILITIES			% of Liabilities
Current Liabilities			
Accounts Payable	$	7,146	6.69%
Notes Payable	$	928	0.87%
Interest Payable	$	630	0.59%
Taxes Payable			
Taxes	$	0	0.00%
Sales Tax Accrual	$	2,866	2.68%
Property Tax	$	624	0.58%
Payroll Accrual	$	0	0.00%
Total Current Liabilities	*$*	*12,195*	*11.42%*
Long-Term Liabilities			
Notes Payable to Investors	$	94,558	88.58%
Notes Payable to Others	$	0	0.00%
Total Long-Term Liabilities	*$*	*94,558*	*88.58%*
TOTAL LIABILITIES	$	106,753	100.00%

NET WORTH (EQUITY)			% of Net Worth
Corporation			
Capital Stock	$	200,000	76.79%
Surplus Paid In	$	0	0.00%
Retained Earnings	$	60,439	23.21%

TOTAL NET WORTH　　$　260,439　　100.00%

Assets - Liabilities = Net Worth
and
Liabilities + Equity = Total Assets

Break-Even Analysis
Karma Jazz Café

Date of Projection: January 22, 2014

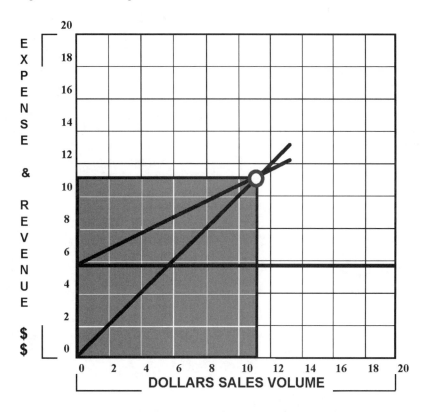

NOTE: Figures shown in hundreds of thousands of dollars (Ex: 2 = $ 200,000)

BREAK-EVEN POINT CALCULATION

FC (Fixed Costs) =	(Administrative Expenses + Interest)	$	555,360
VC (Variable Costs) =	(Cost of Goods + Selling Expenses)	$	672,708
R (Est. Revenues) =	(Income from sale of products and services)	$	1,312,395
BREAK-EVEN POINT =		**$ 1,139,388**	

Note: Company breaks even in Year 1

Financial Statement Analysis Summary

This page is a summary of the company's financial statement analysis ratios projected for the Year 2014 as compared to current industry standards.

Karma Jazz Café

		2014 Projected	Industry Standard
1.	Net Working Capital	$127,424	N/A
2.	Current Ratio	11.45	1.9 + or -
3.	Quick Ratio	10.30	1.3 + or -
4.	Gross Profit Margin	59.92%	59.70%
5.	Operating Profit Margin	6.72%	4.10%
6.	Net Profit Margin	4.61%	N/A
7.	Debt to Assets	29.07%	N/A
8.	Debt to Equity	40.99%	5.30% + or -
9.	ROI (Return on Investment)	16.46%	N/A
10.	Vertical Income Statement Analysis *		
	Sales/Revenues	100.00%	
	Cost of Goods	40.08%	40.30% + or -
	Gross Profit	59.92%	59.70% + or -
	Operating Expense	53.20%	55.70% + or -
	Net Income Operations	6.72%	4.10% + or -
	Interest Income	0.00%	N/A
	Interest Expense	0.30%	Variable
	Net Profit (Pre-Tax)	6.43%	3.30% + or -

* All items stated as % of Total Revenues

11.	Vertical Balance Sheet Analysis *		
	Current Assets	38.02%	33.50%
	Inventory	3.81%	8.80%
	Total Assets	100.00%	
	Current Liabilities	3.32%	51.30% + or -
	Total Liabilities	29.07%	
	Net Worth	70.93%	5.10% + or -
	Total Liabilities + Net Worth	100.0%	

* All Asset items stated as % of Total Assets;

Liability & Net Worth items stated as % of Total Liabilities + Net Worth

Notes:

The financial statement analysis shows that in most categories, Karma Jazz Café is operating within industry standards. The current, quick, and debt to equity ratios are unusually high because of the high ending cash balance. The owners of Karma Jazz Café chose to always maintain a high cash balance in order to be prepared for unforseen events and to avoid seeking another round of financing. These ratios are also high because no interest or loan payments will be made to investors during the first six months. Karma Jazz Café will also maintain a lower than normal inventory in an effort to always have fresh products to serve to its customers. This will not be a problem due to the ready availability of food supplies from nearby vendors.

Part IV: Supporting Documents

Note. For purposes of brevity, we have chosen to include only two of the supporting documents that would be found in the Karma Jazz Café business plan – a timeline chart for launch goals and six financial projection charts & graphs.

Timeline (Milestones)

Timeline (Milestones) - Karma Jazz Café Launch			
Activity	**Start Date**	**End Date**	**Responsible Individual**
Research potential locations	June 2013	July 2013	DeShea Cook
Conduct competitive analysis	June 2013	July 2013	DeShea Cook
Research insurance options	August 2013		DeShea Cook
Research security systems	August 2013		Raymond Jones
Research legal structure	August 2013		Raymond Jones
Retain accountant and attorney	September 2013		DeShea Cook
Determine funding needs	September 2013		Raymond Jones
Develop business plan	September 2013	October 2013	DeShea Cook
Acquire funding	October 2013	November 2013	Raymond Jones
Building Upgrades	November 2013	December 2013	Steve Cook
Equipment Upgrades	November 2013	December 2013	Steve Cook
Menu Development	November 2013	December 2013	DeShea Cook
Hire staff	November 2013	December 2013	Raymond Jones
Train staff	December 2013		Raymond Jones
Initial marketing activities	December 2013		DeShea Cook
Order initial inventory	December 2013		Steve Cook
Begin operations	January 2014		

Financial Projection Charts and Graphs

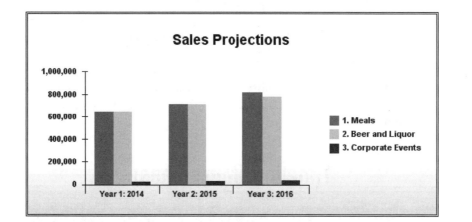

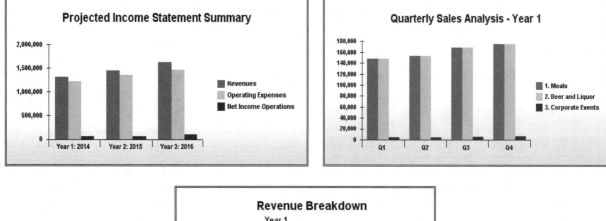

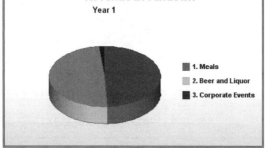

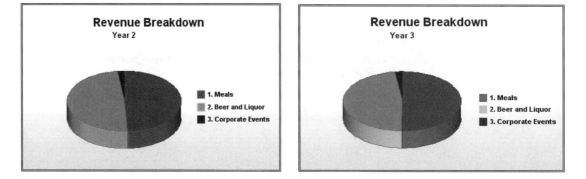

Road Runners, Inc.
Business Plan

The business plan presented in Appendix V is an actual business plan developed for Road Runners, Inc. using *Anatomy of a Business Plan* and its software companion, **AUTOMATE YOUR BUSINESS PLAN**.

Road Runners, Inc. Scenario

Jeffrey Washington established Road Runners, Inc. in 2012 with the meaningful objective of equipping underprivileged youth with important life skills as well as enhancing their academic standards. With a summer track club as its foundation, Road Runners, Inc. has evolved into a dynamic organization offering year round programs that focus on preventing violence and drug use, role model and peer mentoring, and academic enhancement tutoring. Jeffrey Washington has since handed the reins of the organization to Kathey Early and Marvin Early, who continue to aggressively champion the cause and mission. The purpose of this business plan is to develop a concise roadmap for Road Runners, Inc. as they move forward. The plan should also help them to raise more funding and attract the right board members.

A Business Plan for a Non Profit

In response to many inquiries about business planning for nonprofit organizations, we wrote Chapter 9 to illustrate the differences in a business plan for nonprofit. Readers followed up by asking if we had an actual business plan for a nonprofit organization. Thanks to Road Runners, Inc. we are proud to share this example. This business plan has addressed key areas and elements in business planning that a nonprofit organization needs to feature.

This business plan was developed by Ndaba Mdhlongwa, working in conjunction with Jeffrey Washington and Kathey Early. He also received contributions from Kay Odrosky, CPA, MBA (Kodrosky@JFSDallas.org), Chris McKee (chris@venturity.net), and Jorge Joison. I would like to extend a special thank you to all of them, especially Kathey Early for allowing me to share her business plan with my readers and software users. Each nonprofit organization will be different in its mission, program services, target audience and other elements. This plan is meant to serve an example that can guide you as you formulate a business plan for your organization.

Of Special Note in This Plan

As described in Chapter 9, there are sections in a business plan that need to have specific elements for a non profit organization. A concerted effort was placed in ensuring that all relevant sections contained the necessary elements. Below is a look at some of these sections and the approach Road Runners, Inc. took in their business plan.

- **Executive Summary**

    Road Runners, Inc. created a table showcasing their service program offerings. For each service program, they provided key highlights and accomplishments.

- **Strategy**

    Road Runners, Inc. determined that there were four organizational areas it needed to address in order to become more efficient in its operations and to grow. For each area, the current situation is described and specific goals and objectives are laid out. They followed by detailing the specific activities (action items) they will execute to in order to accomplish each of their goals and objectives.

- **Program Services**

    Road Runners, Inc. provided a description of their program services. What is unique is that, for each service program, they created a table showing the staff members needed and their responsibilities (i.e., who will deliver the service). They also have a Program Service Delivery section that shows when and how the service will be delivered.

- **Target Market**

    Road Runners, Inc. has identified and described the communities they serve (Orleans Parish and Jefferson Parish). In addition to providing a profile of their target audience, they have shown the demographics. They have also identified various funding sources they plan to target. These organizations were selected because their mission aligns with that of Road Runners, Inc.

- **Public Relations**

    Road Runners, Inc. has provided the specifics of their public relations plan including which service providers they will use in some areas such as news releases and newsletter. For each program, they have provided goals and objectives as well as specific activities that will be implemented.

- **Supporting documents**

    Road Runners, Inc. has developed a Timeline/Milestones table that shows the activities they need to accomplish, start and end dates, and the person responsible for completing each activity.

Thank you again to Ndaba Mdhlongwa, Jeffrey Washington, and Kathey Early for allowing me to share this interpretation of business planning with our readers and software users. I know that it will be a great help to them as they write their plans.

> ***Warning!*** *This business plan is to be examined for Road Runners, Inc.'s handling of content only. There is no judgment inferred as to appropriateness new or existing nonprofit organizations. Do not use this plan as a source of research for your own company.*

 Important. *Please do not contact the company, Kathey Early or any other people mentioned in the business plan. Kathey Early has been generous in sharing her business plan and I would not want to be responsible for taking up more of her valuable time.*

Road Runners, Inc.
"Keeping Our Youth on Track"

P.O. Box 1160
Gretna, Louisiana 70054
Email: lkearly@bellsouth.net
504-481-1849 (Kathey Early) • 504-251-9526 (Marvin Early)
www.roadrunnerstc.org

Plan prepared August 2013

by the Corporate Officers

Table of Contents

Executive Summary
Road Runners, Inc.

Road Runners, Inc. (RRI) focuses on promoting the success of disadvantaged youth in New Orleans by creating service programs designed to improve their education levels and open up opportunities for them to attend college. RRI has and will continue to bring a positive change to disadvantaged youth, by making them responsible citizens in life and encouraging them to always look forward to a successful future. The organization primarily focuses on male and female children between the ages of 8 and 18 from Orleans Parish and Jefferson Parish.

Service Program Highlights

- **The Road to Higher Education.** RRI is built upon a foundation of best practices in youth educational development. It offers several structured activities including homework assistance, tutoring, and preparation for standardized tests such as LEAP, ACT and SAT. In order to stimulate learning, RRI engages children in innovative learning activities that build upon, but are different from, regular school studies.

- **Preventing Violence and Drug Use.** RRI's goal is to prevent violence and drug use in youth by building their interest in school and their own future. This is also accomplished by focusing on their attitude, beliefs, expectations and desires related to violence and drug use. That is then channeled into a conscious effort to rebuild social ties, self-control and develop social skills.

- **Role Model and Peer Mentoring.** Under the mentorship program, RRI nurtures and empowers youth, by providing them with a positive influence, personal and professional development, and post-secondary opportunities for the future. RRI's innovative program recruits volunteers from colleges and universities as well as the local business community.

- **Summer Track Club.** Athletics plays an integral part in youth development. RRI has established itself as one of the preeminent summer track clubs in New Orleans. In 2013, 33 athletes qualified for the district track meet. 13 of them went on to the Regional Championships with 9 going even further to the National Junior Olympic Championships.

While competitive threats exist in some shape or form, RRI believes its business model will mitigate these threats. RRI offers a wide array of programs that incorporate educational, social, athletic and civic opportunities that prepare young people to meet the challenges of adolescence and adulthood. At the helm of RRI is Kathey Early, a highly respected elementary education teacher with over 20 years of experience in education and working with children.

Projected Statement of Activities Summary			
	Year 1: 2014	Year 2: 2015	Year 3: 2016
Revenues/Support	$100,900	$249,740	$380,266
Expenses	$99,818	$244,073	$371,225
Revenues in Excess of Expenses	$1,082	$5,667	$9,041

Part I: Organizational Plan
Road Runners, Inc.

Summary of the Business

Low high school graduation rates and lack of guidance continue to plague disadvantaged youth throughout the country. This has resulted in a high number of youth becoming premature parents and raising their own children in poverty. Jeffrey Washington had the vision that underprivileged children in New Orleans, Louisiana should have the opportunity to go to college by getting the necessary help to improve their academic skills. He recognized that children, particularly from Orleans Parish and Jefferson Parish, did not have the same opportunity to make it to college as children in other parishes. Many of these children aspired to be better students, but unfortunately did not have the best environment in which to learn fundamental academic skills, be safe, and learn life lessons they can apply in their everyday lives.

With that, Jeffrey Washington created a purpose for an organization that would set out to build and uplift youth in Orleans Parish and Jefferson Parish. Road Runners, Inc. (RRI) was established in May 2012 with the unique meaningful purpose of "Keeping our Youth on Track." RRI has given participants the opportunity to learn academics, life skills and participate in competitive track and field. The organization's inspiring program balances academics and athletics, stressing the importance of both as a means to ensure youth have a purposefully designed path to future success.

In its initial year, the program attracted 50 participants (male and female) between the ages of 8 and 18. These participants came primarily from home environments where there was a single female head of household, and most live at or below the poverty level struggling to rebuild their lives Post-Katrina. After a successful year, in which the RRI saw many students improve their basic academic skills, Jeffery Washington handed down the reins of the organization to Kathey Early and Marvin Early. Today, they passionately drive RRI forward with the goal of equipping disadvantaged youth with the necessary tools to compete, contend and vie for collegiate and professional excellence.

The purpose of this business plan is to lay out a growth plan that will allow RRI to raise funding, attract board members and assemble a management team that will run the organization efficiently. It will also put systems and procedures in place that will enable it to serve more children, with the goal of 200 in 2014, 500 in 2015, and 1,000 in 2016. In its inaugural year, RRI became recognized as an elite summer track program, with exceptional training and athlete development programs.

However, RRI is more than just a summer track program. Through its innovative Reach and Teach Program, the organization has a curriculum designed to improve proficiency levels in math, science, English, reading, vocabulary, and writing. Its Road to Preventing Violence program is designed to help youth manage anger and provide alternatives to violence in a city filled with crime. The organization has a Road to Preventing Drug Use program that has been hailed as a game changer in a city where drug use is prevalent and many underprivileged kids are lost to drug and alcohol abuse. Its Mentoring program will help to mold model youth that have gone on to become solid contributors to the community and make significant contributions to society. As if that's not all, the organization's pride and joy is its Road to Higher Education program that will help send underprivileged children to college, against all odds.

- **Mission**

  The mission of RRI is to promote athletic and academic excellence, leadership attributes and to stress the importance of teamwork and commitment in underprivileged youth in New Orleans as they strive to earn a path to college and become productive members of the community.

- **Business Model**

  The business model is based on 4 key areas of principle that have an impact on children.

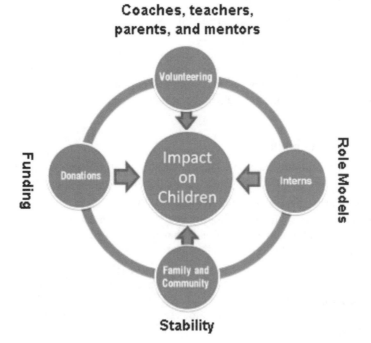

RRI will be powered by a 100% volunteer staff of coaches, teachers, parents, and mentors. The organization will rely on support from individual donors, fundraisers and in-kind support from local businesses. This year the organization has identified several local foundations to which it will apply for additional funding.

RRI will have a high presence of interns who have overcome their disadvantaged background and made it to college. The use of interns is designed to inspire participants and show them that they too can make it to college. Interns will be available 3 days per week to assist in various programs.

The family and community component of RRI plays a major role in the overall success and triumph of the youth in Orleans Parish and Jefferson Parish. A stable and unyielding family and community are paramount to raising children in New Orleans. RRI will foster and build viable relationships with families in the community in order to assist them in nurturing and cultivating well-rounded youth. To accomplish this goal, RRI will organize community picnics, socials, and other forums of esprit de corps.

The business model is unique in that the preceding four elements funnel into the most important component, impact on children. RRI will contribute to the quality of life of the youth of Orleans Parish and Jefferson Parish, by keeping them heavily active in the community, and giving them a feeling of self-worth and instilling confidence in them.

3

- **Strategy**

  Management has established key goals and objectives for the organization as well as a well thought out schedule of activities to drive the organization towards its goals. A table (Timeline/Milestones) has been developed in the Supporting Documents section, highlighting the objectives and activities as well as the project manager assigned to each task.

  Number of Children Served:
  - **Current Situation:** RRI currently serves 50 students
  - **Goal:** Increase student capacity
  - **Objective:** Increase the number of children served to 200, 500 and 1,000 in 2014, 2015 and 2016, respectively
  - **Activities:** RRI plans to build the infrastructure that will allow it to increase its capacity. This includes organizing reliable transportation for children by securing the services of a bus company and volunteer parents for car pooling. RRI will also secure a bigger facility for tutoring, and have a team of volunteers on an ongoing fixed schedule.

  Organization Management:
  - **Current Situation:** Executive Director, Kathey Early currently serves in multiple roles within the organization leaving little time to manage the organization
  - **Goal:** Improve the management of the program
  - **Objective:** Hire a full-time administrative assistant in 2014 to help Kathey Early. Assemble a full complement of staff that includes a paid Executive Director and other key personnel in 2015
  - **Activities:** RRI will seek out an administrative assistant that will provide hands-on support including office management, travel scheduling, hotel booking and coordinating parent car pool activities. RRI will place ads on job boards and reach out to local civic groups such as the New Orleans Urban League to find suitable candidates for this position.

  Implementation of Program Services:
  - **Current Situation:** With the exception of the track club (May to July), other services are offered at various times as volunteers become available
  - **Goal:** Improve the implementation of all program services
  - **Objective:** Develop a fixed schedule of when each program service will be provided, who will provide it, how it will be provided, and where it will be provided
  - **Activities:** RRI plans to assemble a team of volunteers that will serve as Program Leaders for each Program Service. The Program Leaders will be expected to commit to a full year of service. Working with the Program Leaders, RRI will develop a delivery schedule and retain volunteers from local colleges & universities and businesses to provide the service.

  Funding:
  - **Current Situation:** RRI relies on athlete participations fees ($200 per athlete), donations, and other internally driven fundraising activities
  - **Goal:** Secure funding from a professional organization and sponsorships from local businesses in New Orleans
  - **Objective:** Raise $40,000 for 2014 operations
  - **Activities:** RRI has assembled a list of organizations that offer funding to nonprofits (see Funding Sources). RRI will complete the necessary paperwork to receive funding from these sources. RRI will also seek sponsorships and donations from local businesses.

- **Strategic Relationships**

  RRI is a member of USA Track and Field (USATF) Southern Association. The USATF Southern Association is dedicated to the promotion of Track & Field in the southern region of Louisiana and Mississippi. Summer track programs, along with the other sport programs, are sponsored by USATF and comprise the backbone of youth activities designed to keep kids occupied and productive during the summer.

  The National office of USATF in collaboration with Essence Magazine and Coca Cola sponsored a 3K walk run at the 2013 Essence Festival. Jackie Joyner Kersee was the featured speaker. RRI was asked to be the host team and provide volunteers. This event was a first for USATF and RRI, providing a once in a lifetime opportunity for the organization's members and alumni to meet Jackie Joyner. The event was a complete success and RRI was recognized nationally.

  Through partnerships with various companies and organizations in New Orleans, RRI will work to develop internship opportunities. The program will have a direct impact on the students as they transition from high school into the working world. The internship program is designed to provide practical and invaluable work experience to youth by exposing them to the business world.

- **SWOT Analysis**

SWOT Analysis	
Strengths:	**Weaknesses:**
1. Strong educational component	1. Lack of funding
2. Year round program with consistent monitoring of education progress	2. Transportation for children
3. Strong relationship with local community and city leaders	3. No board of directors
4. Track and field team with members that have participated in Junior Olympics (9 in 2013)	4. Program relies heavily on two key members of the management team
5. Experience in managing track and field programs	5. Children participating with no membership fees with organization absorbing costs
6. Good coordination and monitoring	6. Lack of a treasurer
7. Host team for National USATF event in conjunction with Essence Magazine and Coca Cola at 2013 Essence Festival	7. Use of personal funds to offset cost of running organization
8. Family centric organization	**Note**: This business plan has identified key weaknesses within the organization and developed strategies and plans to overcome them.
9. Use of social media to connect with alumni	
Opportunities:	**Threats:**
1. Access to local colleges and universities for volunteers and mentors including tutors	1. Worsening economic conditions
2. Hosting events similar to Essence Festival due to success of 2013 event	2. Security problems for children
	3. Increasing number of summer track programs
3. Added exposure to RRI due to participants in Junior Olympics	4. Increased competition in other service areas
4. Funding for nonprofit organizations	5. Other programs offering monetary benefits and other perks to athletes to join them

Program Services

The Road to Higher Education: Reach and Teach

RRI's educational program is designed to help participants improve their academic proficiency and accelerate their learning. Additionally, the goal is to prepare students to pass the high stakes testing required by the state of Louisiana and college entrance exams. A high level of importance is placed on these tests and students in Orleans Parish and Jefferson Parish traditionally score below acceptable levels. RRI will raise the standards level on these tests by using a proactive hands-on approach to ensure that all components are in place for it to succeed in its mission of being able to get children to a level that will enable them to successfully apply for college entrance.

The Road to Higher Education	
Staff	**Responsibility/Service Areas**
Program Leader	1. Develop master schedule for the month 2. Schedule tutors 3. Provide tutoring
Tutors	Tutor will be available for the following areas: 1. Math (Basic, Algebra, Geometry, Calculus) 2. Science (Basic, Physics, Chemistry, Biology) 3. Social Sciences (Computer Skills, Foreign Languages, Sociology, Psychology) 4. Reading (Phonics, Comprehension, Literature) 5. English (Spelling, Grammar, Composition)
Test Preparers and Proctors	Test preparers will provide study skills and test-taking strategies for college entrance exams, including IOWA, LEAP, ACT, and the SAT. Certified teachers, parents, and coaches will serve as proctors during test sessions.
Program Service Delivery: Tutoring will be available throughout the entire year. During the school year, it will be provided in the evenings (during the week), from 6 pm to 8 pm. A tutoring session will also be available on Saturday between 10 am and 2 pm. During the summer, tutoring services will be available during the week between 10 am and 2 pm. Each session is expected to have 10 to 15 students.	

The following goals and objectives have been established for the program. Activities have also been developed to accomplish the goals and objectives.

Tutoring:
- **Goal:** Offer academic enhancement tutoring.
- **Objective:** By mid-year, at least 70% of Reach and Teach participants will engage in one to three hours of academic enhancement tutoring on a weekly basis.
- **Target Outcome:** By year end, at least 85% of Reach and Teach participants will engage in one to three hours of academic enhancement tutoring on a weekly basis.
- **Activities:** RRI will keep attendance rolls and reports of improvement for each. Reports of assignments and homework will also be kept on file to track progress. Students from various colleges and universities in New Orleans will be retained on a volunteer basis to provide tutoring services.

Grade Point Average:

- **Goal:** Improve cumulative grade point average (GPA)
- **Objective:** By mid-year, 65% of participants must achieve and maintain at minimum a 2.0 GPA
- **Target Outcome:** By year end, 90% of participants must achieve and maintain at minimum a 2.0 GPA
- **Activities:** RRI will review its participants GPA on a quarterly basis. RRI will also conduct achievement tests to assess academic strengths and weaknesses. This will help to reveal the areas of attention each individual needs. That will be followed by extended tutoring in those areas.

The Road to Success: Preventing Violence and Drug Use

The violence prevention program is designed to increase youths' awareness of the cause and effects of violence, to assist them in learning how to manage anger, and to teach that anger is a normal part of life which can be expressed and channeled in healthy and constructive ways. The substance prevention program will focus on non-use of alcohol, tobacco, and illegal substances, as well as promoting the benefits of a drug free life style. Strategies for implementing the both programs will consist of a holistic approach using an array of resources.

Preventing Violence and Drug Use		
Staff	**Responsibility/Service Areas**	
Program Leader	1. Develop master schedule for the month 2. Schedule counselors 3. Provide counseling	
Counselors	Violence prevention counselors will use the following tools: 1. Educational Materials 2. Videos 3. Role-Play 4. Educational Debates 5. Group Discussions 6. Guest Speakers	Substance prevention counselors will use the following tools: 1. Books 2. Videos 3. Role-Play 4. Group Discussions 5. Guest Speakers
Program Service Delivery: The preventing violence and drug use program will be an ongoing process that will target children during the summer and over the entire school year.		

The following goals and objectives have been established for the program. Activities have also been developed to accomplish the goals and objectives.

Life Skills:

- **Goal:** Provide life skills training and workshops with focus on substance abuse prevention, violence prevention, abstinence, and key life and job skills.
- **Objective:** By mid-year, all participants will have attended at least 70% of the life skills workshops.
- **Target Outcome:** By year end, all participants will have attended all workshops.
- **Activities:** RRI will provide a program designed to guide youth away from substance abuse and violence as well as the influence from peers. RRI will provide positive training by modeling, teaching, and reinforcing positive behavior.

The Road to Becoming Future Leaders: Role Model and Peer Mentoring

The Role Model and Peer Mentoring program is designed to empower youth and to bring awareness to the various career paths and options they may choose. To begin with, they will be introduced to and explore different professions by using the Occupational Outlook Hand Book (http://www.bls.gov/ooh). RRI will follow that up by inviting guest speakers to share their experiences and insights on different occupations. This will give participants the opportunity to hear and ask questions first hand.

As the members of RRI graduate to the next level of the program, they will be teamed up with younger members in order to demonstrate and model leadership as well as provide guidance. In order to graduate to the next level, participants will have to demonstrate effective leadership skills and commitment to helping others. Additionally, they must successfully complete peer mediation/mentoring training. This will equip them with the needed skills to become an effective leader and role model for the future. They will also be taught how to be accountable and take responsibility by setting goals and working to achieve those goals.

Role Model and Peer Mentoring	
Staff	**Responsibility/Service Areas**
Program Leader	1. Implement plans for mentoring program 2. Pair up children with mentors 3. Provide mentoring
Mentors	Mentors will provide: 1. Personalized guidance about life 2. An insight to their experience and knowledge as a professional 3. Introduction to various career options and opportunities 4. Information about academics and keys to success 5. Introductions to local community resources
Program Service Delivery: Role model and peer mentoring will be a year round program.	

The following goal and objectives have been established for the program. Activities have also been developed to accomplish the goals and objectives.

Counseling:
- **Goal:** Provide personal comprehensive counseling.
- **Objective:** By mid-year, at least 50% of participants will be offered comprehensive personal counseling to determine career paths, academic performance, needs for tutoring, and additional needed counseling.
- **Target Outcome:** By year end, 100% of participants will have received comprehensive personal counseling and will have the necessary tools to mold them into becoming future leaders.
- **Activities:** RRI will provide hands-on activities including office tours, videos and field trips, from accomplished mentors who can expose participants to a wide variety of skills and specialties. Mentors will help participants to cope with real life situations and turn negative experiences into positive building blocks. They will also provide participants with the wisdom and knowledge to become successful and to make positive contributions to the community. Through this program, RRI will set up eligible students with internship opportunities.

The Road to Athletics: Summer Track Club

The athletic component is pertinent to the success of RRI. Through athletics, RRI provides a framework of basic, fundamental quality of life issues for the youth. While sports will train the children in discipline, order, and self-control, it is the creation of a viable child and parent network that provides a basis for educational endeavors.

The track program serves as a gateway to introduce youth to college campuses, to assist them in garnering college scholarships, and to guide them into future productive endeavors. Athletes work towards developing their skills in both the running and field events. Coaches help the athletes focus their time and energy by evaluating each athlete and suggesting specific events for them to consider. Overall, the club's summer programs are designed to teach young people camaraderie and good sportsmanship in the highly competitive sport of track and field. In addition to the training, members of the track club get to participate in competitions throughout the summer, culminating in the USA Track and Field Junior Olympics (See table below for schedule).

Athletes, male and female, are required to pay a participation fee of $200 per summer. In addition to this money supporting the overall program, part of it goes towards the purchase of Gatorade, water, fruit, and uniforms (including warm ups, t-shirts, and backpack). For students whose parents cannot afford to pay the participation fee, RRI has currently been using the funds from its general pool. The new plan is to develop a sponsorship program. RRI will go out to local businesses and seek sponsorships for individual children. The organization will also develop a scholarship program that will pay the participation fee for qualifying students.

Track Meet Schedule – Summer 2013		
Date	**Event**	**Location**
May 18, 2013	Feliciana Classic – Faith Track Club	East Feliciana HS (Jackson, LA)
May 25, 2013	NIYTC Invitation	New Iberia, LA
June 1, 2013	Southern Association Championship	W. Harrison HS (Gulf Port, MS)
June 15, 2013	Greater King David Invitation	Baton Rouge, LA
June 22-23, 2013	USATF Association JU Championships	LSU (Baton Rouge, LA)
June 29, 2013	District: Gulf Coast Striders Invitational	Pass Christian, MS
July 4-7, 2013	USATF Regional JO Outdoor Champs	Natchez, MS
July 23-28, 2013	USATF National JO Outdoor Champs	Greensboro, NC

The following goals and objectives have been established for the program. Activities have also been developed to accomplish the goals and objectives.

Track Program:

- **Goal:** Build a summer track program that will send participants to the Junior Olympics.
- **Objective:** The track club is expected to have 50 athletes in 2014. This number is will go up every year as RRI expands its student capacity, to 70 in 2015 and 100 in 2016.
- **Target Outcome:** Get 60% of athletes to qualify for the Regional Junior Olympics and 40% to qualify for the National Junior Olympics Championships.
- **Activities:** RRI will provide athletes with training in their respective events five days per week for eight weeks during the summer. Athletes will also participate in competitive events, culminating with the Junior Olympics for those that qualify.

Administrative Plan

- ## Location

  RRI operates from 163 Willowbrook Drive, Gretna, Louisiana 70054. The space was donated and no money is paid for rent. The building serves as an office as well as tutoring space.

  RRI plans to secure a larger facility that will have separate offices for each Program Service provided. The organization will seek out a facility that also has a large conference room or open space for big group activities. Rent for the new facility is expected to be $1,500 per month.

- ## Legal Structure

  Road Runners, Inc. is a registered as a 501(c)(3) non-profit organization operating in the City of New Orleans.

- ## Management and Personnel

  ### Management - Current:

  Currently, Kathey Early runs all aspects of the organization. As a full time teacher, she has minimal time during the school year to effectively run all aspects of the organization. During the summer, she is able to dedicate herself to RRI on a full time basis. Her husband, Marvin Early, assists with the running of the organization. A respected and highly accomplished oil field professional, his activity level is limited due to the requirements of his job. During the time he is available, Marvin Early is totally dedicated to the organization and its success.

  > ***Kathey Early is the current Executive Director/President.*** *A long-standing member of the New Orleans community, Kathey Early is a highly respected elementary education teacher. Her background in education and working with children for over 20 years has helped her understand the needs and challenges of youth in New Orleans. Her responsibilities at RRI include grant research and application, seeking donations, organizing fundraising events, tutoring, maintaining financial records, and coaching. Kathey Early is a USATF Certified Level 1 Coach and a USATF Certified National Official. She holds a Bachelor of Arts degree from Tulane University in New Orleans, LA.*

  ### Personnel - Current:

  RRI is powered by 100% a volunteer staff of coaches, teachers, parents, and mentors. Key members of the organization include:

  - Marvin Early (Vice President/Assistant Coach)
    - USATF Certified Level 1 Coach and USATF Certified Official
  - John Gordon (Public Relations)
  - Darius Lewis (Assistant Coach)
  - Karlton Barbarian (Alumni/Assistant Coach)

Management & Personnel - Future:

Key Additions and Hires in 2014

- Board of Directors (Unpaid)
- Administrative Assistant

One of the purposes of this business plan is to introduce RRI to potential board members and to attract and retain individuals who will play an active role in helping RRI fulfill its mission. Once a board has been elected, the organization will secure Directors and Officers (D&O) insurance. RRI also plans to hire a full time paid Administrative Assistant. In addition to the general office work, the assistant will help Kathey Early with scheduling travel to track meets, coordinating transportation, hotel booking and coordinating activities and needs for Program Leaders. The annual salary for the Administrative Assistant will be $24,000.

Key Hires in 2015

If Kathey Early continues in her full time role as a school teacher, RRI will hire a paid Executive Director to lead the organization. The annual salary for the Executive Director will be $40,000. Additional hires will include:

- Public Relations Director (Annual salary - $30,000)
- Fundraising Director (Annual salary - $30,000)

Accounting & Legal

Kathey Early currently handles all the bookkeeping activities for RRI. All bookkeeping activities will continue to be handled internally by the Administrative Assistant using QuickBooks Pro. For auditing, taxes, and financial reporting, RRI will retain an outside CPA firm. The fees associated with accounting are expected to be $500 per month. RRI is seeking a law firm that will provide volunteer legal services.

Insurance

As a member of the USA Track and Field (USATF) Southern Association, RRI is fully covered under their insurance policy with Travelers Insurance. The policy includes a provision for injuries sustained in practice and at track meets. It also covers vehicle accidents during transportation to and from practice as well as track meets. Parents are required to have adequate insurance coverage as required by the state of Louisiana.

Security

RRI goes to great lengths to protect children from any harm that may come their way. To mitigate any risk factors, RRI requires background screening for every parent. Background checks are done on all coaches and program service providers such as mentors and tutors. To safe guard female athletes at track meets and practice, Kathey Early serves as a chaperone.

Part II: Marketing Plan
Road Runners, Inc.

Marketing Plan Summary

RRI's goal is to equip at-risk and underprivileged youth with the skills, abilities, and the sense of self-worth they will need to make good life decisions about education, career, family and life. To accomplish this goal, the organization has developed public relations efforts and other marketing communications aimed at generating extensive visibility in the community in order to attract students, volunteers, as well as grant and fund donors. RRI's public relations activities will include news releases, features in local media, newsletter, and social media.

Target Market

Program Recipients:
While RRI programs are available to youth throughout the New Orleans metro area, participants come primarily from Orleans Parish and Jefferson Parish. The focus is on both male and female children between the ages of 8 and 18.

Based on participants from the previous year, the breakdown is expected to be 65% male and 35% female. Participants come from low to moderate income households, with most consisting of a single female head of household and living at or below the poverty level.

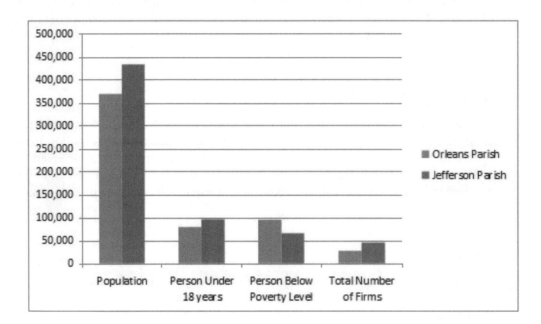

Funding Sources:

In order to provide its Program Services, RRI relies on funds from donations, grants, and funding from other sources. Below are some of the funding sources RRI plans to reach out to:

- **Peyback Foundation**

  Established by Peyton Manning in 1999, the PeyBack Foundation promotes the future success of disadvantaged youth by assisting programs that provide leadership and growth opportunities for children at risk. Each year, the PeyBack Foundation funds various programs in Indiana, Louisiana, Tennessee, and the Denver metro area. The Foundation has distributed more than $4.3 million in grants since 2002, including $500,000 in May 2012 to 88 youth based organizations. The deadline for grant applications is February 1st each year.
  http://www.peytonmanning.com/peyback-foundation/grants

- **Lloyd E. and Elisabeth H. Klein Family Foundation**

  The Lloyd E. and Elisabeth H. Klein Family Foundation was established in 1983 in Orange County, California. Its founders, Lloyd and Elisabeth Klein, envisioned a foundation that would give to organizations that support Christianity, youth, and their families, with the goal of providing safe, healthy, supportive environments that prepare children to succeed in life.
  http://kleinfamilyfoundation.org

- **MAXIMUS Foundation**

  Created in 2000, the MAXIMUS Foundation is committed to supporting organizations and programs that promote personal growth and self-sufficiency through improved health, augmented child and family development, and community development. The organization provides grants to non-profit organizations and charities that share its commitment in helping disadvantaged populations and underserved communities.
  http://www.maximus.com

- **The American Legion Child Welfare Foundation**

  Established in 1954, the American Legion Child Welfare Foundation was developed as a repository of funds from individuals who wished to contribute to the betterment of children in this country. Its foremost philanthropic priority is to provide other nonprofit organizations with the means to educate the public about the special needs of children across this nation. To date, over $11 million has been awarded to organizations to assist the children of this country.
  http://www.cwf-inc.org

- **Local Firms in New Orleans**

  The business community in New Orleans is home to over 27,000 businesses, small and large. RRI plans to reach out to the business community for:

  > Sponsorships
  >
  > Donations
  >
  > Internships
  >
  > Mentors

Competition

Primary Competitors:

There are several nonprofit organizations in New Orleans that provide a wide range of services to underprivileged youth in New Orleans. Below are profiles of the primary organizations with which RRI competes.

- **High Voltage Youth Camp**
  High Voltage Youth Camp is a non-profit organization that provides education and recreation programs for economically disadvantaged youth. The organization is dedicated to helping youth realize their potential, build character, and function effectively as contributing members of society. High Voltage also works to build community collaborations, and partnerships with organizations that serve youth.
  http://www.highvoltageyouthcamp.org

- **Rickey's Save The Youth Team**
  Rickey's Save The Youth Team is open to children between the ages of 8 and 14. The organization offers the following service programs: After school tutoring, mentor pairing, financial assistance with school uniforms/supplies, exposure and training in several trades, free haircuts, community program locating service/pairing, and informational field trips.
  http://www.rickeysyouthteam.org

- **New Era Track Club**
  Established in April 2005, the New Era Track Club serves boys and girls of the Metropolitan New Orleans area. The organization's primary goal is to provide youth athletes access to major track and field events throughout the nation at a minimum cost. The track club also focuses on positive self-esteem while exposing each member to character building experiences.
  http://neweratrackclub.org

- **Metro Track Club**
  Metro Track Club is one of the leading youth organizations in the city with a history of competitive track and field athletes. The organization operates largely in the inner city and attempts to build bridges of hope to some of the city's at-risk youth. They are involved with violence and drug prevention and work through some city officials and community groups. There is presently no academic component to their organization.

RRI Competitive Advantages:

RRI has a very strong educational component. Unlike other programs that work with students during the summer only, RRI provides tutoring and educational assistance as needed throughout the entire year. Furthermore, grades and behavior are monitored during the school year and contact is maintained with members all year. Very few teams offer this level of assistance. RRI is a family centric organization dedicated to making its members feel they are a part of a big family. Alumni return often to share their experiences and serve as role models. Using Twitter, RRI is able to remain connected with many of its alumni throughout the country. Additional competitive advantages include:

- Focus on youth from Jefferson Parish and Orleans Parish
- Year round program with consistent monitoring of education progress
- Strong relationship with local community and city leaders

Market/Industry Trends (Needs Assessment)

Underprivileged children often lead lives that lack meaning or purpose and are often left without direction. They live in environments where there is no one to buffer them from the risk factors that threaten their progression into productive adulthood i.e. violence, teen pregnancy, drug abuse, lack of positive role models, and lack of education. RRI's Program Services are aimed at helping youth overcome these challenges and rise to become strong pillars of the community. Each Program Service offering is designed to address these needs.

Teen Violence:

Teen violence is an ongoing problem nationally. News of teen violence in New Orleans has made headline news on a frequent basis. However, City officials have worked hard to find answers and alternative solutions to the wave of crime and violence that has inundated the city. Over the past few years, statistics of interrelated teen crime and violence have begun to recede and the decline is due largely to youth related programs such as RRI. These programs, and specifically the summer programs, work because they tend to occupy larger numbers of at-risk youth during the period when most teen violence is perpetrated. RRI is well positioned to provide the resources to help the city of New Orleans to continue moving in a positive direction.

Drug Abuse:

The drug abuse problem in New Orleans has always been prevalent. The fact that New Orleans hosts an international port, coupled with one of the poorest economies in the country combine to create fertile ground for the drug trade to thrive. This increases the chances of at-risk youth to be involved in substance abuse issues and increases their chances of actively participating in the lucrative drug trade. According to the Adolescent Behavioral Health report, approximately 37,000 (9.4 percent) adolescents in Louisiana used an illicit drug in the past month; 23,000 (5.8 percent) used marijuana, and 10,000 (5.9 percent) used an illicit drug other than marijuana. Additionally, 19.3 percent (76,000) of adolescents used alcohol in the past month[1]. RRI has a program in place designed to increase youths' awareness of the cause and effect of drugs and alcohol.

Mentoring Programs:

There are a number of mentoring programs in New Orleans that attempt to address the needs of the ailing youth of the community. One of the major problems with these mentoring programs is that they do not reach the youth until there are signs of trouble. Programs that start to engage the youth at younger ages through sports related programs have a better chance of success. Some of the alternative mentoring programs in the city include the Big Brother program, the Boys and Girls Club and the Boy Scouts of America. These national organizations offer youth-oriented programs in the area but don't offer the comprehensive sports component that generally attracts inner-city youth.

Education (or lack thereof for underprivileged children):

According to the Annie E. Casey Foundation's 2011 Kids Count report, 34 percent of the children in New Orleans live in poverty, compared to the national average of 20 percent[2]. The Cowen Institute at Tulane University reports that 15 percent of teenagers in Orleans parish between the ages of 16 and 19 are not in school and are not working. Youth in New Orleans are two times more likely to live in poverty and drop out of school without a high school diploma than youth elsewhere in Louisiana and four times more likely than youth living in other parts of the United States. RRI will offer after school and summer tutoring programs aimed at youth in the disadvantaged areas of New Orleans, especially Orleans Parish and Jefferson Parish.

---

[1] Inspirations Youth (http://www.inspirationsyouth.com/teen-rehab-louisiana.asp
[2] National KIDS COUNT, 2012

Promotion (Advertising & Publicity) Strategy

RRI plans to develop a strategic public relations program designed to build awareness and credibility, support fundraising efforts, and achieve organizational goals and objectives. Through its coordinated public relations efforts, RRI will cultivate a positive image that will result in more opportunities to accomplish its mission. Measuring the success of each campaign will be very important to RRI and each program will be evaluated on an ongoing basis. The RRI public relations plan is detailed below. Goals and objectives have been included for each campaign.

News Releases

News releases will be used to build awareness about RRI, especially at the beginning of each fundraising campaign. RRI will use news release sites that cater specifically to nonprofit organizations, including: PR Web (http://www.prweb.com) and 188 Press Release (http://www.1888pressrelease.com).

- **Goal:** Gain exposure for fundraising campaigns through news releases
- **Objective:** Submit press release ahead of every fundraising campaign
- **Activities:** Initially, RRI will use free local services for press releases.

Local Media

Local media outlets (newspaper, radio, and TV) are always looking for new and interesting stories to feature. RRI will take advantage of this by approaching various media outlets with stories about accomplishment such as participation in the Junior Olympics, hosting an event at the Essence Festival, and other service events that are taking place.

- **Goal:** Get featured on local media outlets
- **Objective:** Have a different story featured on various media outlets monthly
- **Activities:** Develop a list of all media outlets in New Orleans with contact info.

Newsletter

RRI plans to develop a newsletter that will be circulated on a monthly basis. It will feature key accomplishments, student of the month, and updates on past, present, and planned events the organization is involved in. For distribution of an online newsletter, RRI is planning to use the services of an email marketing company and has selected iContact (https://www.icontact.com).

- **Goal:** Develop RRI newsletter
- **Objective:** Distribute newsletter on a monthly basis via email
- **Activities:** RRI will set up an account with iContact. The monthly cost for iContact is projected to be $14 per month for 500 subscribers in 2014 and $29 per month for 2,500 subscribers in 2015 and 2016.

Social Media

Currently RRI is using Twitter to stay connected with alumni and provide updates on its activities. RRI will expand its use of social media in an effort to engage with students as well as the community at large. Additional social media outlets that will be used include: Facebook and LinkedIn.

- **Goal:** Expand RRI presence on social media
- **Objective:** Develop Facebook page, LinkedIn site, and YouTube videos
- **Activities:** RRI will work with volunteer students from local universities and colleges to develop its social media pages and sites.

Road Runners, Inc.

Part III: Financial Documents

2013 Financial Statements

2014-2016 Financial Projections (Ft. Worth Location)

2012 Statement of Activities
Road Runners, Inc.

Beginning: January 1, 2012   **Ending: December 31, 2012**

			% Total Revenues
INCOME			
Revenues/Support		$ 40,000	100.00%
1. Athlete Membership Fees	6,000		15.00%
2. Fundraising	12,000		30.00%
3. Grants	10,000		25.00%
4. In-Kind Contributions	7,000		17.50%
5. Other Income	5,000		12.50%
EXPENSES			
A. Variable (Program Related)		29,100	72.75%
1. Accommodation	4,200		10.50%
2. Athlete Food and Beverage Supplies	2,000		5.00%
3. Athlete Uniforms	7,000		17.50%
4. Background Checks	1,000		2.50%
5. Books and Supplies	4,000		10.00%
6. Educational Materials and Supplies	3,000		7.50%
7. Entry Fees	1,900		4.75%
8. Transportation	6,000		15.00%
9. Misc. Variable Expense	0		0.00%
10. Depreciation (Variable Assets)	0		0.00%
B. Fixed (Administrative)		10,500	26.25%
1. Consulting	0		0.00%
2. Directors and Officers Insurance	0		0.00%
3. Equipment Rental and Maintenance	0		0.00%
4. Marketing	0		0.00%
5. Office Supplies	600		1.50%
6. Postage and Shipping	300		0.75%
7. Professional Fees	7,500		18.75%
8. Rent and Utilities	0		0.00%
9. Salaries	0		0.00%
10. Subscription and Dues	600		1.50%
11. Telephone and Internet	1,500		3.75%
12. Misc. Fixed Expense	0		0.00%
13. Depreciation (Fixed Assets)	0		0.00%
Total Operating Expenses		39,600	99.00%
Revenues in Excess of Expenses		$ 400	1.00%
Beginning Fund Balance (Net Assets)		$ 0	0.00%
Ending Fund Balance (Net Assets)		$ 400	1.00%

Financial Assumptions (Budget)

Provided below is a summary of the key budget areas used as assumptions for the financial projections.

Revenues/Support

Sources of revenues/support include:

- Athlete Membership Dues ($200 per athlete paid in May. Athletes whose parents cannot to pay will receive a scholarship from funds that have been donated through the sponsor a child program)
    - 2014 - 50 athletes, 2015 - 70 athletes, and 2016 - 100 athletes
    - 2014 - 200 students, 2015 - 500 students, and 2016 – 1,000 students

- Fundraising (Internal fundraising programs)
    - ESPN Magazine (Sale of subscriptions – 200 subscriptions at $15 per subscriber)
    - Krispy Kreme Coupons (Sale of coupons – 500 coupon books at $5 per book)
    - Plate Lunch Sales (Hospital donations of 400 lunches for sale at $8 per plate – March, September, October, and November)
    - Shake the Can Donations (Can donations at two major events in New Orleans; Essence Festival in July - $1,500 and Jazz Festival in April - $1,500)
    - Track Meet (Annual RRI track meet in June. Sponsors donate money, equipment, and supplies to run the track. Participating teams pay entry fees. Total received - $7,000)

- Grants (Funding from professional funding source - $40,000)

- In-Kind Contributions (Non-monetary donations that are assigned a financial value)
    - Sponsor a meal (Meals for students throughout the year)
    - Athlete Food and Beverage Supplies (Water, Ice, Gatorade, Fruit during the track season)

- Other Income
    - Sponsor a Child (Donations from companies to sponsor a child)

Program Related Expenses

The following expenses are associated with each service program:

- The Road to Higher Education
    - Books and Supplies (Tutoring) - $1,000 per month

- Preventing Violence and Drug Use
    - Educational Materials and Supplies - $500 per month

- Summer Track Club
    - Accommodation (Hotel stay at regional track meet in June – 20 athletes at $100 each and national track meet in July – 15 athletes at 100 each
    - Athlete Food and Beverage Supplies (Water, Ice, Gatorade, Fruit) - $
    - Athlete Uniforms - $10,000
    - Entry Fees (Track Meet Entry Fees) – 8 track meets (May - 2, June - 4, and July 2) at $300 per meet
    - Transportation (Practice) - $300 per month in May, June and July
    - Transportation (Local Track Meets) - $400 per trip for 5 track meets
    - Transportation (Charter Bus) - $600 per trip for 2 out of state track meets in June
    - Transportation (Airplane to National Junior Olympics in July) - 15 athletes at $300

Pro Forma Cash Flow Statement

Page 1 (January thru June)

Road Runners, Inc.

For the Year 2014

	Jan 14	Feb 14	Mar 14	Apr 14	May 14	Jun 14
BEGINNING CASH BALANCE	1,000	40,065	38,629	37,394	33,558	30,073
CASH RECEIPTS						
A. Revenues/Support	45,000	4,500	4,700	2,100	13,000	10,000
1. Athlete Membership Fees	0	0	0	0	10,000	0
2. Fundraising	2,500	3,000	3,200	1,500	0	7,000
3. Grants	40,000	0	0	0	0	0
4. In-Kind Contributions	1,000	1,000	1,000	100	2,500	2,500
5. Other Income	1,500	500	500	500	500	500
B. Interest Income	0	0	0	0	0	0
C. Sale of Long-Term Assets	0	0	0	0	0	0
TOTAL CASH AVAILABLE	46,000	44,565	43,329	39,494	46,558	40,073
A. Variable Expenses						
1. Accommodation	0	0	0	0	0	2,000
2. Athlete Food and Beverage Supplies	0	0	0	0	500	500
3. Athlete Uniforms	0	0	0	0	7,000	2,000
4. Background Checks	100	100	100	100	100	100
5. Books and Supplies	1,000	1,000	1,000	1,000	1,000	1,000
6. Educational Materials and Supplies	500	500	500	500	500	500
7. Entry Fees	0	0	0	0	600	1,200
8. Transportation	0	0	0	0	2,300	1,500
9. Misc. Variable Expense	0	0	0	0	0	0
Total Variable Expenses	1,600	1,600	1,600	1,600	12,000	8,800
B. Fixed Expenses						
1. Consulting	0	0	0	0	0	0
2. Directors and Officers Insurance	200	200	200	200	200	200
3. Equipment Rental and Maintenance	0	0	0	0	0	0
4. Marketing	14	14	14	14	14	14
5. Office Supplies	100	100	100	100	250	250
6. Postage and Shipping	50	50	50	50	50	50
7. Professional Fees	500	500	500	500	500	500
8. Rent and Utilities	1,121	1,121	1,121	1,121	1,121	1,121
9. Salaries	2,000	2,000	2,000	2,000	2,000	2,000
10. Subscription and Dues	200	200	200	200	200	200
11. Telephone and Internet	150	150	150	150	150	150
12. Misc. Fixed Expense	0	0	0	0	0	0
Total Fixed Expenses	4,335	4,335	4,335	4,335	4,485	4,485
C. Interest Expense	0	0	0	0	0	0
D. Long-Term Asset Payments	0	0	0	0	0	0
E. Loan Payments	0	0	0	0	0	0
F. Mortgage Payments	0	0	0	0	0	0
TOTAL CASH PAID OUT	5,935	5,935	5,935	5,935	16,485	13,285
ENDING CASH BALANCE	40,065	38,629	37,394	33,558	30,073	26,788

Pro Forma Cash Flow Statement

Page 2 (July thru December + 6 & 12-month Totals)

Road Runners, Inc.

6-MONTH TOTALS	Jul 14	Aug 14	Sep 14	Oct 14	Nov 14	Dec 14	12-MONTH TOTALS
1,000	26,788	16,802	12,367	11,131	9,896	8,660	1,000
79,300	4,500	1,500	4,700	4,700	4,700	1,500	100,900
10,000	0	0	0	0	0	0	10,000
17,200	1,500	0	3,200	3,200	3,200	0	28,300
40,000	0	0	0	0	0	0	40,000
8,100	2,500	1,000	1,000	1,000	1,000	1,000	15,600
4,000	500	500	500	500	500	500	7,000
0	0	0	0	0	0	0	0
0	0	0	0	0	0	0	0
80,300	31,288	18,302	17,067	15,831	14,596	10,160	101,900
2,000	1,500	0	0	0	0	0	3,500
1,000	500	0	0	0	0	0	1,500
9,000	1,000	0	0	0	0	0	10,000
600	100	100	100	100	100	100	1,200
6,000	1,000	1,000	1,000	1,000	1,000	1,000	12,000
3,000	500	500	500	500	500	500	6,000
1,800	600	0	0	0	0	0	2,400
3,800	4,800	0	0	0	0	0	8,600
0	0	0	0	0	0	0	0
27,200	10,000	1,600	1,600	1,600	1,600	1,600	45,200
0	0	0	0	0	0	0	0
1,200	200	200	200	200	200	200	2,400
0	0	0	0	0	0	0	0
84	14	14	14	14	14	14	168
900	250	100	100	100	100	100	1,650
300	50	50	50	50	50	50	600
3,000	500	500	500	500	500	500	6,000
6,728	1,121	1,121	1,121	1,121	1,121	1,121	13,457
12,000	2,000	2,000	2,000	2,000	2,000	2,000	24,000
1,200	200	200	200	200	200	200	2,400
900	150	150	150	150	150	150	1,800
0	0	0	0	0	0	0	0
26,312	4,485	4,335	4,335	4,335	4,335	4,335	52,475
0	0	0	0	0	0	0	0
0	0	0	0	0	0	0	0
0	0	0	0	0	0	0	0
0	0	0	0	0	0	0	0
53,512	14,485	5,935	5,935	5,935	5,935	5,935	97,675
26,788	16,802	12,367	11,131	9,896	8,660	4,225	4,225

Projected Statement of Activities

Road Runners, Inc.

Percentages = % of Revenues/Support

Updated: August 28, 2013

	Year 1: 2014		Year 2: 2015		Year 3: 2016		Total: 3 Years	
	AMOUNT	%	AMOUNT	%	AMOUNT	%	AMOUNT	%
INCOME								
REVENUES/SUPPORT	100,900	100.00%	249,740	100.00%	380,266	100.00%	730,906	100.00%
1. Athlete Membership Fees	10,000	9.91%	14,000	5.61%	20,020	5.26%	44,020	6.02%
2. Fundraising	28,300	28.05%	79,240	31.73%	130,746	34.38%	238,286	32.60%
3. Grants	40,000	39.64%	100,000	40.04%	150,000	39.45%	290,000	39.68%
4. In-Kind Contributions	15,600	15.46%	39,000	15.62%	58,500	15.38%	113,100	15.47%
5. Other Income	7,000	6.94%	17,500	7.01%	21,000	5.52%	45,500	6.23%
GROSS PROFIT	100,900	100.00%	249,740	100.00%	380,266	100.00%	730,906	100.00%
EXPENSES								
A. VARIABLE (Program Related)	45,200	44.80%	84,400	33.80%	148,052	38.93%	277,652	37.99%
1. Accommodation	3,500	3.47%	4,900	1.96%	7,007	1.84%	15,407	2.11%
2. Athlete Food and Beverage Supplies	1,500	1.49%	2,100	0.84%	3,003	0.79%	6,603	0.90%
3. Athlete Uniforms	10,000	9.91%	14,000	5.61%	20,020	5.26%	44,020	6.02%
4. Background Checks	1,200	1.19%	3,000	1.20%	6,000	1.58%	10,200	1.40%
5. Books and Supplies	12,000	11.89%	30,000	12.01%	60,000	15.78%	102,000	13.96%
6. Educational Materials and Supplies	6,000	5.95%	15,000	6.01%	30,000	7.89%	51,000	6.98%
7. Entry Fees	2,400	2.38%	3,360	1.35%	4,805	1.26%	10,565	1.45%
8. Transportation	8,600	8.52%	12,040	4.82%	17,217	4.53%	37,857	5.18%
9. Misc. Variable Expense	0	0.00%	0	0.00%	0	0.00%	0	0.00%
10. Depreciation (Variable Assets)	0	0.00%	0	0.00%	0	0.00%	0	0.00%
B. FIXED (Administrative)	54,618	54.13%	159,673	63.94%	223,173	58.69%	437,464	59.85%
1. Consulting	0	0.00%	0	0.00%	0	0.00%	0	0.00%
2. Directors and Officers Insurance	2,400	2.38%	2,400	0.96%	2,400	0.63%	7,200	0.99%
3. Equipment Rental and Maintenance	0	0.00%	0	0.00%	0	0.00%	0	0.00%
4. Marketing	168	0.17%	348	0.14%	348	0.09%	864	0.12%
5. Office Supplies	1,650	1.64%	4,125	1.65%	8,250	2.17%	14,025	1.92%
6. Postage and Shipping	600	0.59%	1,500	0.60%	3,000	0.79%	5,100	0.70%
7. Professional Fees	6,000	5.95%	7,500	3.00%	9,375	2.47%	22,875	3.13%
8. Rent and Utilities	13,457	13.34%	13,457	5.39%	13,457	3.54%	40,371	5.52%
9. Salaries	24,000	23.79%	124,000	49.65%	180,000	47.34%	328,000	44.88%
10. Subscription and Dues	2,400	2.38%	2,400	0.96%	2,400	0.63%	7,200	0.99%
11. Telephone and Internet	1,800	1.78%	1,800	0.72%	1,800	0.47%	5,400	0.74%
12. Misc. Fixed Expense	0	0.00%	0	0.00%	0	0.00%	0	0.00%
13. Depreciation (Fixed Assets)	2,143	2.12%	2,143	0.86%	2,143	0.56%	6,429	0.88%
TOTAL OPERATING EXPENSES	99,818	98.93%	244,073	97.73%	371,225	97.62%	715,116	97.84%
REVENUES IN EXCESS OF EXPENSES	1,082	1.07%	5,667	2.27%	9,041	2.38%	15,790	2.16%
OTHER INCOME (Interest Income)	0	0.00%	0	0.00%	0	0.00%	0	0.00%
OTHER EXPENSE (Interest Expense)	0	0.00%	0	0.00%	0	0.00%	0	0.00%
BEGINNING FUND BALANCE (NET ASSETS)	1,082	1.07%	5,667	2.27%	9,041	2.38%	15,790	2.16%
ENDING FUND BALANCE (NET ASSETS)	1,082	1.07%	5,667	2.27%	9,041	2.38%	15,790	2.16%

Projected Statement of Financial Position

Business Name:	Date of Projection: August 28, 2013
Road Runners, Inc.	Date Projected For: December 31, 2014

ASSETS			% of Assets	LIABILITIES			% of Liabilities
Current Assets				**Current Liabilities**			
Cash	$	4,225	7.21%	Accounts Payable	$	5,000	100.00%
Accounts Receivable	$	1,500	2.56%	Grants Payable	$	0	0.00%
Pledges Receivable	$	40,000	68.28%	Notes Payable	$	0	0.00%
Inventory	$	0	0.00%				
Prepaid Expenses	$	0	0.00%	Interest Payable			
Short-Term Investments	$	0	0.00%	Taxes	$	0	0.00%
Total Current Assets	*$*	*45,725*	*78.05%*	Sales Tax Accrual	$	0	0.00%
				Property Tax	$	0	0.00%
Long-Term Investments	$	0	0.00%				
				Payroll Accrual	$	0	0.00%
Fixed Assets							
Land (valued at cost)	$	0	0.00%	*Total Current Liabilities*	*$*	*5,000*	*100.00%*
Buildings	$	0	0.00%	**Long-Term Liabilities**			
1. Cost	0			Notes Payable	$	0	0.00%
2. Less Acc. Depr.	0			Mortgage Payable	$	0	0.00%
				Total Long-Term Liabilities	*$*	*0*	*0.00%*
Equipment	$	4,286	7.32%				
1. Cost	5,000			**TOTAL LIABILITIES**	$	5,000	100.00%
2. Less Acc. Depr.	714						

			% of Net Assets
Furniture	$	8,571	14.63%
1. Cost	10,000		
2. Less Acc. Depr.	1,429		

NET ASSETS			
Vehicles	$	0	0.00%
1. Cost	0		
2. Less Acc. Depr.	0		
			Unrestricted	$	53,582	91.46%
			Temporarily Restricted	$	0	0.00%
Autos/Vehicles	$	0	*0.00%*	Permanently Restricted	$	0	0.00%
1. Cost	0		
2. Less Acc. Depr.	0		
Total Fixed Assets	*$*	*12,857*	*21.95%*

Other Assets				**Total Net Assets**	$	53,582	100.00%
1.	$	0	0.00%				
2.	$	0	0.00%				

TOTAL ASSETS	$	58,582	100.00%	**TOTAL LIABILITIES AND NET ASSETS**	$	58,582	100.00%

Part IV: Supporting Documents

Note. For purposes of brevity, we have chosen to include only one of the supporting documents that would be found in the Road Runners, Inc. business plan – a timeline table for specific goals.

Timeline (Milestones) – Road Runners, Inc.			
Activity	**Start Date**	**End Date**	**Responsible Individual**
Develop business plan	July 2013	August 2014	Kathey Early
Secure board members	August 2013	September 2013	Kathey Early
Acquire grant/funding from professional organization	October 2013	November 2013	Kathey Early
Hire Administrative Assistant	October 2013	November 2013	Kathey Early
Hire team of volunteer Program Leaders for each service program	November 2013	December 2013	Kathey Early
Develop curriculum, materials and schedule for each service program	November 2013	December 2013	Program Leaders
Develop list and schedule for service providers e.g. tutors, guest speakers and etc.	December 2013	January 2014	Program Leaders
Distribute first RRI newsletter	January 2014		Administrative Assistant
Develop social media presence including Facebook page, LinkedIn site, and YouTube videos	January 2014	February 2014	Administrative Assistant
Develop list of volunteer parents and car pool schedule	January 2014	February 2014	Administrative Assistant
Research potential locations for new office and service program delivery rooms	January 2014	February 2014	Administrative Assistant
Secure new location	February 2014	March 2014	Kathey Early
Secure bus company	March 2014	April 2014	Administrative Assistant
Feature on local media news outlet	April 2014	May 2014	Kathey Early
Develop summer track schedule and prepare for season	April 2014	May 2014	Marvin Early

Blank Forms
and Worksheets

T he forms and worksheets on the following pages have been provided for you to copy and use in the writing of your business plan.

Organizational and Marketing Worksheets

The first eleven pages (340-350) in this appendix are forms and worksheets that were referred to in Organizational Plan and Marketing Plan chapters. Included are: Summary of the Business Worksheet, SWOT Analysis Worksheet, Insurance Update Form, Location Analysis Worksheet, Target Market Analysis Guide, Competition Evaluation Worksheet, and four Marketing Musts Worksheets.

Financial Worksheets

The remaining pages in this Appendix (pages 351-360) are financial forms that you can fill in for your own use. The financial forms that contain "Variable Expenses" and "Fixed Expenses" have spaces for you to fill in your own categories. They should be customized to your particular business. This will require you to decide on category headings when you begin the financial section of your business plan and follow through with the same headings throughout all financial statements.

The categories you use on your financial statements are those that you determine to be the major types of expenses your business will have. Those that are frequent and sizable will have a heading of their own (i.e., advertising, rent, salaries, etc.). Those expenses that are very small and infrequent will be included under the heading "miscellaneous" in either the variable or fixed expenses sections of each of your financial statements.

If you have a difficult time developing a chart of accounts (categories) for your business, you can seek the help of a tax accounting professional.

Note: If you decide to purchase our **Automate Your Business Plan** software, all of the forms and worksheets are built into the application. Your financial spreadsheet workbook will be automatically generated and customized to your business. All of the spreadsheets are pre-formatted, pre-formulated and integrated (linked). This means that numbers input in one spreadsheet automatically flow to all related spreadsheets, saving you countless hours of your valuable time (for information, see pages ix-x).

Summary of the Business Worksheet
(SWOT Analysis – Separate Worksheet)

Mission Statement	
Concise statement (one or two sentences) projecting a sense of what your goals are regarding the company's future place within the industry and within the community.	

Business Model	
Method of doing business by which the company can generate revenue and sustain itself. Tell why it is unique to your industry.	

Strategy

Short-term objectives 1. 2 3.	How will you reach these objectives? (brief overview) 1. 2. 3.
Long-term objectives 1. 2. 3.	How will you reach these objectives? (brief overview) 1. 2. 3.

Strategic Relationships

Mutually beneficial formal contractual alliance established between two or more organizations.	Who are they? (name) 1. 2. 3.	How will they benefit your company? 1. 2. 3.

SWOT Analysis

Strengths (Internal)	**Weaknesses (Internal)**
A close look at the organization, laying out core competencies and areas in which the business has a competitive advantage.	A close look at the organization, laying out core competencies and areas in which the business has a lack of certain strengths.
1.	1.
2.	2.
3.	3.
4.	4.
Opportunities (External)	**Threats (External)**
A look at the marketplace in which the business operates that helps to identify new areas in which the business can grow and niche markets that can be pursued.	Looks at changes and trends in the marketplace that may affect the company's business operations.
1.	1.
2.	2.
3.	3.
4.	4.

Insurance Update Form

Company	Contact Person	Coverage	Cost Per Year
			$
			$
			$
			$
			$
			$

1. TOTAL ANNUAL INSURANCE COST	$
2. AVERAGE MONTHLY INSURANCE COST	$

Notes:

1.

2.

Location Analysis Worksheet

Address: _____

Property Owner: _____

Name, address, phone number of realtor/contact person: _____

_____

Lease Terms – Years: _____ Square feet: _____ Price per square foot: _____

Additional costs (utilities, insurance improvements, etc.): _____

_____

Additional conditions of lease agreement: _____

_____

History of location: _____

Location in relation to your target market: _____

Traffic patterns for customers: _____

Availability of parking (include diagram): _____

Availability for vender deliveries: _____

Crime rate for the area: _____

Quality of public services (e.g., police, fire protection): _____

Notable features of area: _____

_____

Neighboring shops and local business climate: _____

_____

Competitive businesses nearby: _____

Zoning regulations: _____

Tax rates (state, county): _____

Special assessments: _____

Target Market Analysis Guide
Information extracted from
The Product-Market Analysis (page 64)

Rule 1: Find Potential Customers Who Want Your Product or Service

If your potential customers are consumers, will they recognize that they have a need or want? If your customers are businesses, will they recognize that they have a business problem to solve or an opportunity to exploit?

Steps	Actions
1. Analysis of Customer Recognition of Needs	Determine if potential customers recognize that they have a need that can be solved by utilizing your product(s) and/or service(s)
2. Determine Broad Potential Customer Base	Identify your broad customer base and make sure they recognize their need or problem If they do not recognize their need or problem, your first action will be to educate them through an integrated marketing communications program
3. Identify Select Group of Customers	Identify a select group of potential customers who demonstrate recognition of their need or problem This group then validates your plan by becoming your target market segment
4. Understand the Customers in Your Target Market Segment	Identify key characteristics of your potential customers that are related to their need for your product(s) and/or service(s) Understanding these characteristics will help you develop marketing and selling efforts for specific customers within your target market

Rule 2: Identify Customers Who are Ready to Buy

Will the want/need/problem/opportunity cause your prospects enough pain or the prospect of enough pleasure that they will be willing to take action?

Steps	Actions
1. Refining Your Target Market Segment	Understand which of your potential customers are ready to act to fill their need or solve their problem - this group will be more likely to buy your product(s) and/or service(s) If your potential customers need or problem is not strong enough to motivate them to take action, then you will be required to expend more sales and marketing effort to convince them that they will benefit from filling the need or solving the problem Be aware that potential customers may have several needs or problems. To mitigate this challenge, you will have to show them that the one you can fill or solve is of high enough priority that they should fill it before the others
2. Determine Readiness to Buy	Determine characteristics that will tell you that potential customers are ready to buy

Target Market Analysis Guide
page 2

Rule 3: Let the Customers Know That You Can Fill Their Needs	
Will your prospects recognize that you can fulfill their need or want, or solve their business problem? If you are an existing business, do your prospects already recognize your ability to fill their need or want, or solve their business problem?	
Steps	**Actions**
1. Determine if Potential Customers Know Your Capabilities	Determine if potential customers are aware that you can fulfill their need or solve their problem
2. Demonstrate Your Capability to Meet the Customer's Need(s)	Develop marketing and sales efforts aimed at showing your capabilities to meet the need(s) of potential customers
3. Become the Resource of Choice	Make sure potential customers have come to the realization that you have the solution for their need or problem and they can come to you to buy

Rule 4: Find Customers Who Will Pay	
Will your prospects <u>pay you</u> to meet their need or solve their business problem? <u>**Note:**</u> *There are two parts to Rule #4:* *1. Will your prospect <u>pay</u>? – and – 2.Will your prospect <u>pay you</u>?*	
Steps	**Actions**
1. Ability to Pay	Determine if potential customers have funds budgeted or available to pay for your product(s) and/or service(s)
2. Identify Decision Maker	Make sure you are working with the person(s) that make the final buying decision
3. Value Demonstration	Make sure you have clearly demonstrated greater value in your product(s) and/or service(s) and instilled trust in your potential customers
4. Willingness to Pay You	Determine if potential customers are willing to pay you to meet their need or solve their problem

Competition Comparison

Competitor Profile	
COMPETITOR	Name: Location:
PRODUCTS AND/OR SERVICES	Products/Services: Pricing Comparison:
BACKGROUND & OVERVIEW OF COMPANY	Background: Current Overview:
ESTIMATED MARKET SHARE	Target Market Served: Market Share: Demographics/Psychographics of customers:
GENERAL MARKETING STRATEGY	Advertising : Promotion: Community Involvement:
STRENGTHS & WEAKNESSES	Strengths: Weaknesses:
Additional Notes:	

Marketing Musts

1. Sell Selectively

Describe your products and/or services.

What trends today have an impact on your products and services?

How can you apply information about these trends to your own marketing strategy?

"Sell Selectively" Worksheet

Marketing Musts

2. Know Your Niche

Describe your customers in detail. In addition to demographic data, consider psychographic issues:

- *hobbies*
- *disposable income*
- *leisure activities*
- *memberships*
- *vacations*
- *family status*
- *other lifestyle information*

What additional information should you obtain about your customers?

How does this information have an impact on your marketing strategy?

- *Marketing*
- *Sales*
- *Advertising*
- *Public Relations*
- *Networking*

Marketing Musts

Define precisely the attributes of your products and services.

    - Product/Service A:

    - Product/Service B:

    - Product/Service C:

How can you make your products and services come alive for your prospective customers/clients?

For one of your products or services, write a brief pitch that grabs attention. Focus on the <u>needs</u> of your customers and the product/service <u>benefits</u>.

Marketing Musts

4. Set Prices for Profits

How does your present pricing structure compare to your competitors? (Equal to, More than, or Less than)

Have you covered all of your expenses to produce this product or provide this service, considering:

- *Materials*
- *Labor*
- *Overhead expenses*
- *Shipping costs*
- *Handling costs*
- *Storage*

For services you provide, what are the advantages and disadvantages of the following pricing structures:

- *Hourly billing rates*
- *Project by project estimates*
- *Monthly retainer structure*

What is your price floor? Ceiling?

Cash to Be Paid Out Worksheet

Business Name: _____   Time Period:_____ to _____

1. **Start-Up Costs:** $ _____
    Business License   _____
    Corporation Filing   _____
    Legal Fees   _____
    Other start-up costs:
        a.   _____
        b.   _____
        c.   _____
        d.   _____

2. **Inventory Purchases**   _____
    Cash out for goods intended for resale

2. **Variable Expenses (Selling)**
        a.   _____
        b.   _____
        c.   _____
        d.   _____
        e.   _____
    Miscellaneous Variable Expense   _____
    Total Selling Expenses   _____

4. **Fixed Expenses (Administrative)**
        a.   _____
        b.   _____
        c.   _____
        d.   _____
        e.   _____
        f.   _____
    Miscellaneous Fixed Expense   _____
    Total Operating Expenses   _____

5. **Assets (Long-Term Purchases)**   _____
    Cash to be paid out in current period

6. **Liabilities**   _____
    Cash outlay for retiring debts, loans, and/or
    accounts payable

7. **Owner Equity**   _____
    Cash to be withdrawn by owner

Total Cash to Be Paid Out $ _____

Sources of Cash Worksheet

Business Name: _____

Time Period Covered: _____ to _____

---

      1. Cash On Hand $ _____

      2. Sales (Revenues)

            Sales _____

            Service Income _____

            Deposits on Sales or Services _____

            Collections on Accounts Receivable _____

      3. Miscellaneous Income

            Interest Income _____

            Payments to be Received on Loans _____

      4. Sale of Long-Term Assets _____

      5. Liabilities

            Loan Funds (Banks, Lending Inst., SBA, etc.) _____

      6. Equity

            Owner Investments (Sole Prop. or Partnership) _____

            Contributed Capital (Corporation) _____

            Venture Capital _____

                           A. Without sales = $ _____

Total Cash Available

                           B. With sales = $ _____

Pro Forma Cash Flow Statement

Business Name _____

Year: _____

	Jan	Feb	Mar	Apr	May	Jun	6-MONTH TOTALS	Jul	Aug	Sep	Oct	Nov	Dec	12-MONTH TOTALS
BEGINNING CASH BALANCE														
CASH RECEIPTS														
A. Sales/Revenues														
B. Receivables														
C. Interest Income														
D. Sale of Long-Term Assets														
TOTAL CASH AVAILABLE														
CASH PAYMENTS														
A. Cost of goods to be sold														
1. Purchases														
2. Material														
3. Labor														
Total Cost of Goods														
B. Variable (Selling) Expenses														
1.														
2.														
3.														
4.														
5.														
6.														
7. Misc. Variable Expense														
Total Variable Expenses														
C. Fixed Expenses														
1.														
2.														
3.														
4.														
5.														
6.														
7. Misc. Fixed Expense														
Total Fixed Expenses														
D. Interest Expense														
E. Federal Income Tax														
F. Other Uses														
G. Long-Term Asset Payts														
H. Loan Payments														
I. Owner Draws														
TOTAL CASH PAID OUT														
CASH BALANCE/DEFICIENCY														
LOANS TO BE RECEIVED														
EQUITY DEPOSITS														
ENDING CASH BALANCE														

Quarterly Budget Analysis

Business Name: _____   **For the Quarter Ending:** _____ ___,_____

BUDGET ITEM	THIS QUARTER			YEAR-TO-DATE		
	Budget	Actual	Variation	Budget	Actual	Variation
SALES REVENUES						
Less Cost of Goods						
GROSS PROFITS						
VARIABLE EXPENSES						
1.						
2.						
3.						
4.						
5.						
6.						
7. Miscellaneous						
FIXED EXPENSES						
1.						
2.						
3.						
4.						
5.						
6.						
7.						
NET INCOME FROM OPERATIONS						
INTEREST INCOME						
INTEREST EXPENSE						
NET PROFIT (Pretax)						
TAXES						
NET PROFIT (After Tax)						

NON-INCOME STATEMENT ITEMS

1. Long-term Asset Repayments						
2. Loan Repayments						
3. Owner Draws						

BUDGET DEVIATIONS

	This Quarter	Year-To-Date
1. Income Statement Items:		
2. Non-Income Statement Items:		
3. Total Deviation		

Three-Year Income Projection

Business Name: _____   **Updated:** _____ ___, _____

	YEAR 1 ____	YEAR 2 ____	YEAR 3 ____	TOTAL 3 YEARS
INCOME				
1. SALES REVENUES				
2. Cost of Goods Sold (c-d)				
a. Beginning Inventory				
b. Purchases				
c. C.O.G. Avail. Sale (a+b)				
d. Less Ending Inventory (12/31)				
3. GROSS PROFIT ON SALES (1-2)				
EXPENSES				
1. VARIABLE (Selling) (a thru h)				
a.				
b.				
c.				
d.				
e.				
f.				
g. Miscellaneous Selling Expense				
h. Depreciation (Prod/Serv Assets)				
2. FIXED (Administrative) (a thru h)				
a.				
b.				
c.				
d.				
e.				
f.				
g. Miscellaneous Fixed Expense				
h. Depreciation (Office Equipment)				
TOTAL OPERATING EXPENSES (1+2)				
NET INCOME OPERATIONS (GPr - Exp)				
OTHER INCOME (Interest Income) OTHER EXPENSE (Interest Expense)				
NET PROFIT (LOSS) BEFORE TAXES				
TAXES 1. Federal, S-Employment				
2. State				
3. Local				
NET PROFIT (LOSS) AFTER TAXES				

Break-Even Analysis Graph

Business Name: _____

Analysis Date: _____ ___, ____

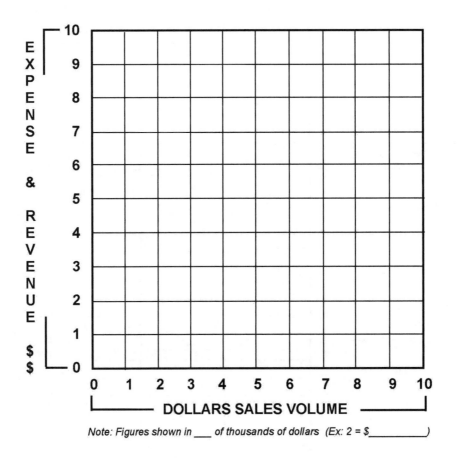

Note: Figures shown in ____ of thousands of dollars (Ex: 2 = $_____)

Break-Even Point Calculation

B-E Point (Sales) = Fixed Costs + [(Variable Costs/Estimated Revenues) x Sales]

1. B-E Point (Sales) = $_____ + [($_____ /$ _____) x Sales]
2. B-E Point (Sales) = $_____ + (_____ x Sales)
3. Sales = $_____ + _____ x Sales
4. Sales - _____ Sales = $_____
5. _____ Sales = $_____
6. Sales (S) = $_____ / _____

Break-Even Point

S = $ [   ]

Balance Sheet

Business Name: _____   **Date:** _____ ___, _____

ASSETS

Current Assets
Cash $ _____
Petty Cash $ _____
Accounts Receivable $ _____
Inventory $ _____
Short-Term Investments $ _____
Prepaid Expenses $ _____

Long-Term Investments $ _____

Fixed Assets
Land (valued at cost) $ _____

Buildings $ _____
  1. Cost   _____
  2. Less Acc. Depr.   _____

Improvements $ _____
  1. Cost   _____
  2. Less Acc. Depr.   _____

Equipment $ _____
  1. Cost   _____
  2. Less Acc. Depr.   _____

Furniture $ _____
  1. Cost   _____
  2. Less Acc. Depr.   _____

Autos/Vehicles $ _____
  1. Cost   _____
  2. Less Acc. Depr.   _____

Other Assets
1. _____ $ _____
2. _____ $ _____

TOTAL ASSETS $ _____

LIABILITIES

Current Liabilities
Accounts Payable $ _____
Notes Payable $ _____
Interest Payable $ _____

Taxes Payable
  Federal Income Tax $ _____
  Self-Employment Tax $ _____
  State Income Tax $ _____
  Sales Tax Accrual $ _____
  Property Tax $ _____

Payroll Accrual $ _____

Long-Term Liabilities
Notes Payable $ _____

TOTAL LIABILITIES $ _____

NET WORTH (EQUITY)

Proprietorship $ _____
  or
Partnership
  name_____, ___% Equity $ _____
  name_____, ___% Equity $ _____
  or
Corporation
  Capital Stock $ _____
  Surplus Paid In $ _____
  Retained Earnings $ _____

TOTAL NET WORTH $ _____

Assets - Liabilities = Net Worth
and
Liabilities + Equity = Total Assets

Profit & Loss (Income) Statement

Business Name: _____

For the Year: 2___

	Jan	Feb	Mar	Apr	May	Jun	6-MONTH TOTALS	Jul	Aug	Sep	Oct	Nov	Dec	12-MONTH TOTALS
INCOME														
1. NET SALES (Gr - R&A)														
2. Cost of Goods to be Sold														
a. Beginning Inventory														
b. Purchases														
c. C.O.G. available for sale														
d. Less Ending Inventory														
3. GROSS PROFIT														
EXPENSES														
1. Variable (Selling) Expenses														
a.														
b.														
c.														
d.														
e.														
f.														
g. Misc. Variable Expense														
h. Depreciation														
Total Variable Expenses														
1. Fixed (Admin) Expenses														
a.														
b.														
c.														
d.														
e.														
f.														
g. Misc. Fixed Expense														
h. Depreciation														
Total Fixed Expenses														
Total Operating Expense														
Net Income From Operations														
Other Income (Interest)														
Other Expense (Interest)														
Net Profit (Loss) Before Tax														
Taxes: a. Federal														
b. State														
c. Local														
NET PROFIT (LOSS) AFTER TAX														

Profit & Loss (Income) Statement
Business Name: _____

Beginning: _____ ___, _____   **Ending:** _____ ___, _____

INCOME		
1. **Sales Revenues**		$
2. **Cost of Goods Sold (c-d)**		
a. Beginning Inventory (1/01)		
b. Purchases		
c. C.O.G. Avail. Sale (a+b)		
d. Less Ending Inventory (12/31)		
3. **Gross Profit on Sales (1-2)**		$
EXPENSES		
1. **Variable (Selling) (a thru h)**		
a.		
b.		
c.		
d.		
e.		
f.		
g. Misc. Variable (Selling) Expense		
h. Depreciation (Prod/Serv Assets)		
2. **Fixed (Administrative) (a thru h)**		
a.		
b.		
c.		
d.		
e.		
f.		
g. Misc. Fixed (Administrative) Expense		
h. Depreciation (Office Equipment)		
Total Operating Expenses (1+2)		
Net Income from Operations (GP-Exp)		$
Other Income (Interest Income)		
Other Expense (Interest Expense)		
Net Profit (Loss) Before Taxes		$
Taxes		
a. Federal		
b. State		
c. Local		
NET PROFIT (LOSS) AFTER TAXES		$

Financial Statement Analysis
Ratio Table

Business Name:

Type of Analysis	Formula	Projected: 2____	Historical: 2____
1. Liquidity Analysis a. Net Working Capital	**Balance Sheet** Current Assets − Current Liabilities	Current Assets _____ Current Liabilities _____ **Net Working Capital** $ _____	Current Assets _____ Current Liabilities _____ **Net Working Capital** $ _____
b. Current Ratio	**Balance Sheet** Current Assets Current Liabilities	Current Assets _____ Current Liabilities _____ **Current Ratio** ___.___	Current Assets _____ Current Liabilities _____ **Current Ratio** ___.___
c. Quick Ratio	**Balance Sheet** Current Assets minus Inventory Current Liabilities	Current Assets _____ Inventory _____ Current Liabilities _____ **Quick Ratio** ___.___	Current Assets _____ Inventory _____ Current Liabilities _____ **Quick Ratio** ___.___
2. Profitability Analysis a. Gross Profit Margin	**Income Statement** Gross Profits Sales	Gross Profits _____ Sales _____ **Gross Profit Margin** __.__ %	Gross Profits _____ Sales _____ **Gross Profit Margin** __.__ %
b. Operating Profit Margin	Income From Operations Sales	Income From Ops. _____ Sales _____ **Op. Profit Margin** __.__ %	Income From Ops. _____ Sales _____ **Op. Profit Margin** __.__ %
c. Net Profit Margin	Net Profits Sales	Net Profits _____ Sales _____ **Net Profit Margin** __.__ %	Net Profits _____ Sales _____ **Net Profit Margin** __.__ %
4. Debt Ratios a. Debt to Assets	**Balance Sheet** Total Liabilities Total Assets	Total Liabilities _____ Total Assets _____ **Debt to Assets Ratio** __.__ %	Total Liabilities _____ Total Assets _____ **Debt to Assets Ratio** __.__ %
b. Debt to Equity	Total Liabilities Total Owners' Equity	Total Liabilities _____ Total Owners' Equity _____ **Debt to Equity Ratio** __.__ %	Total Liabilities _____ Total Owners' Equity _____ **Debt to Equity Ratio** __.__ %
4. Investment Measures a. ROI *(Return on Investment)*	**Balance Sheet** Net Profits Total Assets	Net Profits _____ Total Assets _____ **ROI (Ret. on Invest.)** __.__ %	Net Profits _____ Total Assets _____ **ROI (Ret. on Invest.)** __.__ %
5. Vertical Financial Statement Analysis	**Balance Sheet** 1. Each asset % of Total Assets 2. Liability & Equity % Total L&E **Income Statement** 3. All items % of Total Revenues	**NOTE:** *See Attached* **Projected Balance Analysis** **Projected Income Analysis**	**NOTE:** *See* **Balance Sheet &** **Income Statement**
6. Horizontal Financial Statement Analysis	**Balance Sheet** 1. Assets, Liab & Equity measured against 2nd year. Increases and decreases stated as amount & % **Income Statement** 2. Revenues & Expenses measured against 2nd year. Increases and decreases stated as amount & %	**NOTE:** *See Attached* **Balance Sheet** **&** **Income Statement (P&L)**	**NOTE:** *See Attached* **Balance Sheet** **&** **Income Statement (P&L)**

Glossary

Business and Financial Terms

The following glossary will define business and financial terms with which you may not be familiar. Use of these terms will help you to speak and write in a language that will be understood by potential lenders and investors as well as business associates with whom you may be dealing.

Account A separate record showing the increases and decreases in each asset, liability, owner's equity, revenue and expense item.

Accounting The process by which financial information about a business is recorded, classified, summarized and interpreted by a business.

Accounting professional One who is skilled at keeping business records. Generally, a highly trained professional rather than one who keeps books. An accountant can set up the books needed for a business to operate and help the owner understand them.

Accounts payable A record of what you owe to your creditors for goods or services received.

Accounts receivable A record of what is owed to your business as a result of extending credit to a customer who purchases your products or services. All of the credit accounts taken together are your "accounts receivable."

Affiliate marketing Engages the services of a virtually limitless sales force through some type of commission structure for sales, leads, or website visits. Affiliates are only paid for the actual sales, and their commission is a small percentage of the total sale.

Amortization To liquidate on an installment basis: the process of gradually paying off a liability over a period of time.

Analysis Breaking an idea or problem down into its parts: a thorough examination of the parts of anything.

Asset Anything of worth (having cash value) that is owned by your business (i.e. cash on hand, inventory, land, buildings, vehicles and equipment). Accounts receivable, notes receivable and prepaid purchases are also assets.

Articles of Incorporation A legal document filed with the state which sets forth the purposes and regulations for a corporation. Each state has different regulations.

Bad debts Money owed to you that you cannot collect.

Balance The amount of money remaining in an account.

Balance sheet An itemized statement which lists the total assets and the total liabilities of a given business to portray its net worth at a given moment in time.

Blog Short for *Weblog. A* Web site that contains an online personal journal with reflections, comments, and often hyperlinks provided by the writer. Used by businesses to gain visibility for their products and/or services.

Bookkeeping The process of recording business transactions into the accounting records.

Break-even analysis A method used to determine the point at which the business will neither make a profit nor incur a loss. That point is expressed in either the total dollars of revenue exactly offset by total expenses or in total units of production, the cost of which exactly equals the income derived by their sale.

Bottom line A business's net profit or loss after taxes for a specific accounting period.

Budget A plan expressed in financial terms. A business is then evaluated by measuring its performance in terms of these goals. The budget contains projections for cash inflow and outflow and other balance sheet items.

Business venture Taking financial risks in a commercial enterprise.

Capital Money available to invest or the total of accumulated assets available for production. See "Owner's Equity."

Capital equipment The equipment that you use to manufacture a product, provide a service, or use to sell, store, and deliver merchandise. Such equipment will not be sold in the normal course of business, but will be used and worn out or consumed in the course of business.

Capital expenditures An expenditure for a purchase of an item of property, plant or equipment that has a useful life of more than one year. (Fixed assets)

Cash Money in hand or readily available.

Cash discount A deduction that is given for prompt payment of a bill.

Cash flow The actual movement of cash within a business; cash inflow and cash outflow.

Cash receipts The money received by a business from customers.

Collateral Something of value given or held as a pledge that a debt or obligation will be fulfilled.

Contract An agreement regarding mutual responsibilities between two or more parties.

Controllable expenses Those expenses which can be controlled or restrained by the business person. Variable expenses.

Corporation A voluntary organization of persons, either actual individuals or legal entities, legally bound together to form a business enterprise; an artificial legal entity created by government grant and treated by law as an individual.

Co-signers Joint signers of a loan agreement, pledging to meet the obligations in case of default.

Cost of goods sold The cost of inventory sold during an accounting period. It is equal to the beginning inventory for the period plus the cost of purchases made during the period minus the ending inventory for the period.

Creditor A company or individual to whom a business owes money.

Current assets Cash plus any assets that will be converted into cash within one year plus any assets that you plan to use up within one year.

Current liabilities Debts that must be paid within one year.

Current ratio A dependable indication of liquidity computed by dividing current assets by current liabilities. A ratio of 2.0 is acceptable for most businesses.

Depreciable base of an asset The cost of an asset used in the computation of yearly depreciation expense.

Direct expenses Those expenses that relate directly to your product or service.

Debt capital The part of the investment capital which must be borrowed.

Debt That which is owed.

Debt measures The indication of the amount of other people's money that is being used to generate profits for a business. The more indebtedness, the greater the risk of failure.

Debt ratio The key financial ratio used by creditors in determining how indebted a business is and how able it is to service the debts. The debt ratio is calculated by dividing total liabilities by total assets. The higher the ratio, the more risk of failure. The acceptable ratio is dependent upon the policies of your creditors and bankers.

Default Failure to pay a debt or meet an obligation.

Depreciation A decrease in value through age, wear or deterioration. Depreciation is a normal expense of doing business which must be taken into account. There are laws and regulations governing the manner and time periods that can be used for depreciation.

Expenses The costs of producing revenue through the sale of goods or services.

Entrepreneur An innovator of business enterprise who recognizes opportunities to introduce a new product, a new process, or an improved organization, and who raises the necessary money, assembles the factors for production, and organizes an operation to exploit the opportunity.

Equity The monetary value of a property or business which exceeds claims and/or liens against it by others.

Financial statements The periodic reports that summarize the financial affairs of a business.

Fixed assets Items purchased for use in a business which are depreciable over a fixed period of time determined by the expected useful life of the purchase. Usually includes land, buildings, vehicles and equipment not intended for resale. Land is not depreciable, but is a fixed asset.

Fixed expenses Those costs which don't vary from one period to the next. Generally, these expenses are not affected by the volume of business.

Gross Overall total revenues before deductions.

Gross profit on sales The difference between net sales and the cost of goods sold.

Gross profit margin An indicator of the percentage of each sales dollar remaining after a business has paid for its goods. It is computed by dividing the gross profit by the sales.

Horizontal analysis A percentage analysis of the increases and decreases on the items on comparative financial statements. A horizontal financial statement analysis involves comparison of data for the current period with the same data of a company for previous periods. The percentage of increase or decrease is listed.

Income statement A financial document that shows how much money (revenue) came in and how much money (expense) was paid out (also known as a profit and loss statement)

Interest The cost of borrowing money. The price charged or paid for the use of money or credit.

Inventory The stock of goods that a business has on hand for sale to its customers.

Invest To lay out money for any purpose from which a profit is expected.

Investment measures Ratios used to measure an owner's earnings for his or her investment in the company. See "Return on investment (ROI)."

Invoice A bill for the sale of goods or services sent by the seller to the purchaser.

Lease A long term rental agreement.

Liabilities Amounts owed by a business to its creditors. The debts of a business.

Liability insurance Risk protection for actions for which a business is liable.

Limited partnership A legal partnership where some owners are allowed to assume responsibility only up to the amount invested.

Liquidate To settle a debt or to convert to cash.

Liquidity The ability of a company to meet its financial obligations. A liquidity analysis focuses on the balance sheet relationships for current assets and current liabilities.

Loan Money or other assets let out temporarily, usually for a specified amount of interest.

Long-term liabilities Liabilities that will not be due for more than a year in the future.

Management The art of conducting and supervising a business.

Marketing All the promotional activities involved in the buying and selling of a product or service.

Merchandise Goods bought and sold in a business. "Merchandise" or stock is a part of inventory.

Net income The amount by which revenue is greater than expenses. On an income statement this is usually expressed as both a pre-tax and after-tax figure.

Net loss The amount by which expenses are greater than revenue. On an income statement this figure is usually listed as both a pre-tax and after-tax figure.

Net profit margin The measure of a business's success with respect to earnings on sales. It is derived by dividing the net profit by sales. A higher margin means the firm is more profitable.

Net worth The owner's equity in a given business represented by the excess of the total assets over the total amounts owing to outside creditors (total liabilities) at a given moment in time. The net worth of an individual is determined by deducting the amount of all personal liabilities from the total of all personal assets.

Nonrecurring One time, not repeating. "Non-recurring" expenses are those involved in starting a business which only have to be paid once and will not occur again.

Note A written promise with terms for payment of a debt.

Operating expenses Normal expenses incurred in the running of a business.

Operating profit margin The ratio representing the pure operations profits, ignoring interest and taxes. It is derived by dividing the income from operations by the sales. The higher the percentage of operating profit margin the better.

Other expenses Expenses that are not directly connected with the operation of a business. The most common is interest income.

Other income Income that is earned from non-operating sources. The most common is interest income.

Owners' equity The financial interest of the owner of a business. The total of all owner equity is equal to the business's assets minus its liabilities. The owners' equity represents total investments in the business plus or minus profits or losses the business has accrued to date.

Partnership A legal business relationship of two or more people who share responsibilities, resources, profits, and liabilities.

Payable Ready to be paid. One of the standard accounts kept by a bookkeeper is "accounts payable." This is a list of those bills which are current and due to be paid.

Personal financial history A summary of personal financial information about the owner of a business. The personal financial history is often required by a potential lender or investor.

Portal A site serving as a guide or point of entry to the World Wide Web and usually including a search engine or a collection of links to other sites arranged especially by topic. Portals can be of the consumer type or enterprise type. A Portal attracts a broad (horizontal) range of users. Advertising on a portal guarantees a tremendous number of viewers at an extremely high cost.

Prepaid expenses Expense items that are paid for prior to their use. Some examples are insurance, rent, prepaid inventory purchases, etc.

Principal The amount shown on the face of a note or a bond. Unpaid principal is the amount remaining at any given time.

Pro Forma A projection or estimate of what may result in the future from actions in the present. A pro forma financial statement is one that shows how the actual operations of the business will turn out if certain assumptions are achieved.

Profit Financial gain; returns over expenditures. The sum remaining after deducting costs.

Profit margin The difference between your selling price and all of your costs.

Profit and loss statement A list of the total amount of sales (revenues) and total costs (expenses). The difference between revenues and expenses is your profit or loss. It is also known as an income statement.

Publicity Information with news value issued as a means of gaining public attention or support.

Quarterly budget analysis A method used to measure actual income and expenditures against projections for the current quarter of the financial year and for the total quarters completed. The difference is expressed as the amount and percentage over or under budget.

Quick ratio A test of liquidity subtracting inventory from current assets and dividing the result by current liabilities. A quick ratio of 1.0 or greater is usually recommended.

Ratio analysis An analysis involving the comparison of two individual items on financial statements. One item is divided by the other and the relationship is expressed as a ratio.

Receivable Ready for payment. When you sell on credit, you keep an "accounts receivable" as a record of what is owed to you and who owes it. In accounting, a "receivable" is an asset.

Reciprocal marketing Arrangements in which one company offers customers incentives to buy another company's goods.

Retail business A business that sells goods and services directly to individual consumers.

Retained earnings Earnings of a corporation that are kept in the business and not paid out in dividends. This amount represents the accumulated, undistributed profits of the corporation.

Return on investment (ROI) The rate of profit an investment will earn. The ROI is equal to the annual net income divided by total assets. The higher the ROI, the better. Business owners should set a target for the ROI and decide what they want their investments to earn.

Revenue The income that results from the sale of products or services or from the use of investments or property.

Search Engine Optomization (SEO) Insertion of search terms via coding and text in websites and social media sites in order to achieve higher ranking on search engines.

Service business A business that provides services rather than products to its customers.

Share One of the equal parts into which the ownership of a corporation is divided. A "share" represents a part ownership in a corporation.

Social Media Online platforms whose purpose is to provide interactive communications using web-based and mobile technology.

Sole proprietorship A legal structure of a business having one person as the owner.

Stock Accumulated merchandise.

Stockholders' equity The stockholders' shares of stock in a corporation plus any retained earnings.

SWOT analysis "SWOT" stands for Strengths, Weaknesses, Opportunities, and Threats. A SWOT analysis is an in-depth examination of key factors that are internal (strengths and weaknesses) and external (opportunities and threats) to a business.

Takeover The acquisition of one company by another.

Tangible personal property Machinery, equipment, furniture and fixtures not attached to the land.

Target market The specific individuals, distinguished by socio-economic, demographic, and interest characteristics, who are the most likely potential customers for the goods and services of a business.

Terms of sale The conditions concerning payment for a purchase.

Three-year projection A pro forma (projected) income statement showing anticipated revenues and expenses for a business.

Trade credit Permission to buy from suppliers on open account.

Unearned income Revenue received, but not yet earned.

Variable costs Expenses that vary in relationship to the volume of activity of a business

Vertical analysis A percentage analysis is used to show the relationship of the components in a single financial statement. In vertical analysis of an income statement, each item on the statement is expressed as a percentage of net sales.

Viral marketing Occurs when a company offers something that people find so intriguing that they spread the word on their own.

Volume An amount or quantity of business; the "volume" of a business is the total it sells over a period of time.

Vortal Sometimes called 'online communities' or ' vertical portals.' Vortals focus on a group of people with a specific passion or interest. Vortals appeal to a more narrowed (vertical) audience, offering access to niche markets on a larger scale.

Web site a group of World Wide Web pages usually containing hyperlinks to each other and made available online by an individual, company, educational institution, government, or organization.

Wholesale Selling for resale.

Wholesale business A business that sells its products to other wholesalers, retailers or volume customers at a discount.

Working capital Current assets minus current liabilities. This is a basic measure of a company's ability to pay its current obligations.

Index

Cover sheet, 18-19
    examples of, 19, 177, 211, 245, 279, 313

Credit, history and reports, 3, 121

Customer
    base, building, 45, 62
    changing needs in, 154
    rules for success with, 65-67
    service, 61-62,

D

Database analysis and marketing, 50, 52

Dayne Landscaping, Inc. business plan, 209-242

Debt measures, 116

Debt financing, 159

Demographics, 47, 122, 154

Description (Summary) of the Business, 32

Design, Gallery 194

Direct mail, 53

Direct sales, 53

Directories, 48, 60, 172

Distribution, methods of sales and, 51
    examples, 190, 222, 260, 295

Distributor, product description, 35

E

E-mail marketing, 54

E-Tailers, 16, 36

E-Tailing, steps to, 16

Employees (personnel), 40,
    Examples of, 183, 217, 253, 289, 324

Equity financing, 163-164

Event planning, 58

Executive summary, 21-30
    examples of, 27, 28, 179, 213, 247,
    281, 315

Exit strategy, 4, 7-11
    financing and choice of, 9-10
    forms of, 8-9
    legal and tax issues, 10-11

Extreme advertising, 56

F

Financial Assumptions Developing, 12-13

Financial
    goals, 3
    history, 108-11
    needs, summary of, 80-82

Financial documents, 77-118
    Dayne Landscaping, 228-238
    Karma Jazz Café, 299-308
    Marine Art of California, 196-204
    Road Runners, Inc., 331-337
    Wholesale Mobile Homes.com, 265-275

Financial statement
    business, example of, 110-11
    personal (owner), example of, 124-25

Financial statement analysis, 112-118
    horizontal analysis, 117
    ratio table, 204, 237
    summary, 203, 236, 275, 308
    vertical analysis, 236-237, 275, 308

Financing your business, 157-66
    borrowing money, 157
    costs of financing options, 164
    debt financing, 159
    equity financing, 163
    sources available, 158
    SBA guaranteed loans, 159
    SBICs, 164
    venture capitalists, 164

Focus groups, 49-50

Foreign markets, 2
    legal and tax systems in, 127
    networking in, 59

Forms, blank, 339-360

G

Glossary of business and financial terms, 361-366

Goals
    marketing, 44-46
    meeting lender's financial, 3

Guide, business plan as a, 2

H

Horizontal financial statement analysis, 117

I

In-house marketing, 62 (*See also* Marketing)

Incentives, 54

Income projection, three year, 96
        examples, 97, 200, 234, 272, 305, 336

Income statement, 79, 104-107, 114-18,
        examples, 200, 234, 272, 305, 336
        form, 106, 107
        format, 105

Industry
        organizations, networking through, 59
        trends (*See* Trends)

Insurance, 41, 109, 185, 219, 254, 290, 325

Insurance update form, 41, 276, 342

Intellectual property, 42

International organizations, 61

Internet
        marketing strategies, 16, 68, 71 (See also
                Wholesale Mobile Home.com, Inc.)
        ordering IRS information through, 134
        reaching target market through, 49
        research, 48 (See *also* Research Resources)
        sales, 36

Inventory, calculating cost of goods sold, 105

Investment measures, 116

Investors, what they look for, 2-5

IRS (Tax) information, 127-36
        Ordering forms and publications, 134
        order form, 136
        publications, 129, 135

K

Keeping the Books, accounting book, 118

Karma Jazz Café business plan, 277-310

L

Leases, copies of, 121

Legal documents, 122

Legal representation, 41, 185, 218, 253, 290

Legal structure, 38, 109, 181, 216, 252, 287, 324

Lenders, what they look for, 2-5

Letters of reference, 121, 242

Liabilities, 102, 108

Limited partnership, proposal for, 208

Liquidity ratios, 114

Loan fund dispersal statement, 80-82
        examples of, 82, 229, 266, 302

Location, 37, 193, 252, 287, 324
        analysis worksheet, 38, 343
        in organizational plan, 37
        studies, 119, 122

M

Management, 39, 182, 216, 253, 288, 324

Manufacturers of products, 34

Marine Art of California business plan, 175-208

Market
        analysis, 47-50, 64-67, 255-259, 291-295
        entry, timing of, 195
        research resources, 167-174, 189
        trends, assessing, 48-49, 258, 294

Marketing firms, hiring, 62

Marketing plan, 43-76
        assessment of effectiveness, 63, 264
        components of successful multimedia
                strategy, 68-70
        contents of, 50-61
        customer service, 61-62
        Dayne Landscaping, Inc., 220-227
        Implementation of strategy, 62
        Karma Jazz Café, 291-298
        Marine Art of California, 187-195
        Road Runners, Inc., 326-330
        outline, 75-76
        overview and goals of, 44-46
        social media, article on, 71-74
        Wholesale Mobile Homes.com, 255-264

Marketing promotion, worksheets, 344-350